FIRE ON THE WATER

FIRE ON THE WATER

China, America, and the Future of the Pacific

ROBERT HADDICK

NAVAL INSTITUTE PRESS
ANNAPOLIS, MARYLAND

Naval Institute Press
291 Wood Road
Annapolis, MD 21402

Library of Congress Cataloging-in-Publication Data
Haddick, Robert.
   Fire on water : China, America, and the future of the Pacific / Robert Haddick.
      pages cm.
   Includes bibliographical references and index.
   ISBN 978-1-61251-795-7 (hbk. : alk. paper) — ISBN 978-0-87021-060-0 (ebook)
1. Pacific Area—Strategic aspects. 2. Sea-power—Pacific Area. 3. United States—
Military policy. 4. China—Strategic aspects. 5. China—Military policy. 6. United
States—Foreign relations—Pacific Area. 7. Pacific Area—Foreign relations—
United States. 8. Security, International—Pacific Area. I. Title. II. Title: China,
America, and the future of the Pacific.
   UA830.H34 2014
   355'.03301823—dc23
                          2014020216

∞ Print editions meet the requirements of ANSI/NISO z39.48-1992 (Permanence
of Paper).
Printed in the United States of America.

22 21 20 19 18 17 16 15 14   9 8 7 6 5 4 3 2 1
First printing

Maps created by Charles Grear.

To Josh Manchester

Contents

Maps

Preface

This book grew out of a research project I conducted in 2012 and 2013 for U.S. Special Operations Command. The resulting monograph, available to the public at the website of Joint Special Operations University, examined the future role of coalition special operations forces in the context of the security competition in East Asia.[1]

As I completed that study, I concluded that the topic of East Asia's security, and America's role there, required a much broader treatment, one that included assessments and conclusions I had not read elsewhere. There are many excellent books and monographs that address various aspects of the security situation in the Asia-Pacific region, many of which are sources for this book and which are cited in the notes. I saw a need for a book that comprehensively explained the security challenges in the region, America's interests there, the shortfalls in the current U.S. strategy, and a description of needed reforms. This book thus draws on the research I performed for U.S. Special Operations Command, but goes further. That said, this book is based entirely on open-source research, freely available in the public domain. In addition, the views and conclusions of this book are mine alone and do not necessarily represent the views of any part of the U.S. government.

The growing security competition in East Asia, sparked by the rapid rise in China's economic, political, and military power, is likely to be the most consequential national security challenge the United States will face over the next two decades. Indeed, the magnitude of the challenge may exceed that which the U.S. faced during the Cold War, if only because China's economic capacity far exceeds that of the former Soviet Union and, should current economic growth trends continue, could soon eclipse that of the United States.

The goal of this book is to raise awareness inside the United States and elsewhere about the deteriorating security situation in East Asia, the consequences if the current course is not altered, and why the U.S. needs to make major changes to its military forces and policies for the region. I have written this book to introduce East Asia's emerging security problems to a general audience. I have tried to minimize the amount of military and security jargon, while keeping in mind why the technical performance of military capabilities matters in a strategic context. Many readers will find some of the conclusions in this book to be controversial. If so, a healthy debate over America's policies for Asia can only be a good thing, since the stakes for the United States are so high.

Finally, this book will have succeeded if it sparks further research on these issues and more discussion among policymakers and the public. An open discussion by policymakers and the public on America's role and strategy in the Asia-Pacific region is long overdue. It is my hope that this book will make a contribution to that conversation.

ROBERT HADDICK
Washington, D.C.
January 2014

Acknowledgments

I have received much support during the process of completing this project. I thank the staff at the U.S. Naval Institute Press for their assistance. For over a century, the Naval Institute Press has published history, analysis, and reference books that have been critical to America's security. I am honored to join that long and distinguished line. I thank Adam Kane, senior acquisitions editor, for taking on my project; Adam Nettina for improving my manuscript and managing the project; Jeanette Nakada, copyeditor, for getting the manuscript in shape; and Janis Jorgensen for assistance with the photo gallery. I also thank Claire Noble, the Press marketing manager, and Judy Heise, publicist, for their efforts promoting the final work. I thank Charles David Grear for preparing the maps. The Naval Institute Press is a remarkably efficient organization and this is due to the professionalism of these people and their colleagues. Naturally, any shortcomings in the book are my responsibility.

I have benefited from many professional relationships in recent years. In 2008 Dave Dilegge and Bill Nagle recruited me to *Small Wars Journal* and arranged for me to become a military affairs columnist at *Foreign Policy* magazine. I thank them for these opportunities. Over my years inside the defense community in Washington, D.C., I have formed many friendships and associations from which I benefit professionally every day. I have also benefited greatly from my long friendships with Dan Kingston and Capt. Robert Peters, USN (Ret.). All roads lead back to my friend Josh Manchester, who opened the first door for me, and to whom I have dedicated this book.

I must thank my family for their support. Lois, Bob, Mark, and Barbara have been great friends and supporters for decades. My wife's family has also provided friendship and support for many years.

Finally, my wife, Susan, was essential to the completion of this project. Proficient in Mandarin and a student of China for over two decades, she provided challenging questions and insights all along the way. To her and everyone, thanks.

Acronyms

ADIZ	air defense identification zone
AIP	air-independent propulsion
AMRAAM	Advanced Medium Range Air-to-Air Missile
ASBM	antiship ballistic missile
ASCM	antiship cruise missile
ASEAN	Association of Southeast Asian Nations
C4ISR	command, control, communications, computers, intelligence, surveillance, reconnaissance
CCP	Chinese Communist Party
CMC	Central Military Commission
CNOOC	China National Offshore Oil Corporation
CSBA	Center for Strategic and Budgetary Assessments
DARPA	Defense Advanced Research Projects Agency
EEZ	exclusive economic zone
EMCON	electronic emissions control
EU	European Union
EFV	Expeditionary Fighting Vehicle
GPS	Global Positioning System
IAEA	International Atomic Energy Agency
ICBM	intercontinental ballistic missile
INF	Intermediate Nuclear Forces [Treaty], INF Treaty
JASSM-ER	Joint Air-to-Surface Standoff Missile-Extended Range
JCS	Joint Chiefs of Staff

JOAC	*Joint Operational Access Concept*
JROC	Joint Requirements Oversight Council
JSOTF-P	Joint Special Operations Task Force Philippines
LADAR	laser-radar
LOCAAS	Low Cost Autonomous Attack System
MEU	Marine Expeditionary Unit
MRBM	medium-range ballistic missile
NATO	North Atlantic Treaty Organization
NSSS	National Security Space Strategy
ONA	Office of Net Assessment
PLA	People's Liberation Army
PLAAF	People's Liberation Army Air Force
PLAN	People's Liberation Army-Navy
SAM	surface-to-air missile
SLAM-ER	Standoff Land Attack Missile-Expanded Response (cruise missile)
TEL	transporter-erector-launcher
THAAD	Theater High Altitude Air Defense
TPP	Trans-Pacific Partnership
UAV	unmanned aerial vehicle
UCLASS	Unmanned Carrier Launched Surveillance and Strike (aircraft)
UNCLOS	United Nations Convention on the Law of the Sea
VBSS	visit, board, search, seizure
VLS	Vertical Launch System

INTRODUCTION

The risk of war in East Asia is rising. Nearly every week brings news of another clash over islands in the East and South China Seas, disputes over fishing and drilling rights, or accusations of armed incursions into territorial waters. In response to these growing tensions, the region is experiencing a leap in military spending, as countries scurry to defend themselves. Nationalism is ascendant, while old memories of historical grievances are fresh again.

This year is the centennial of the start of World War I, a catastrophe the magnitude of which still shocks a century later. A few experienced statesmen are openly wondering whether East Asia might be reliving that disaster.

In his book *Diplomacy,* former U.S. secretary of state Henry Kissinger said, "The relations of the principal Asian nations to each other bear most of the attributes of the European balance-of-power system of the nineteenth century. Any significant increase in the strength by one of them is almost certain to evoke an offsetting maneuver by the others."[1] In 2013 former Australian prime minister Kevin Rudd described East Asia as "a 21st-century maritime redux of the Balkans a century ago—a tinderbox on water," a comparison to the nationalist hothouse that sparked World War I.[2] Regarding the ongoing tensions between China and Japan over small islands in the East China Sea, Kurt Campbell, a former U.S. assistant secretary of state for East Asian and Pacific Affairs concluded in 2013, "there is a feeling of 1914 in the air. Just as with tensions between European armies at the turn of the last century, both Tokyo and Beijing are absolutely certain of the rightness of their positions. More importantly, both believe that with a little further pressure, the other side is on the verge of blinking and backing down."[3] In 2006 China had its own public conversation about

1

Imperial Germany and the origins of World War I when China Central Television broadcast a highly popular twelve-part series titled "Rise of the Great Powers."[4]

We can hope that the disastrous consequences of World War I, restored to memory this centennial year, will draw attention to the ominous resemblances now accumulating in East Asia. Large historical forces proved too much for statesmen a hundred years ago. Some of the same remorseless forces are now placing stress on Asia. The region and the world can avoid another tragedy. But doing so will require better strategies than those at work today.

A change in the distribution of power is the source of today's growing conflicts in Asia. Over the past three decades, China has reemerged as an economic and political great power, with rapidly expanding interests in the region and across the world. China's leaders perceive the need to protect these interests, an unsurprising result with numerous parallels in history. Unfortunately history also has recorded the many cases when a new great power appeared and war was the result. The rapid ascent of Athens before the Peloponnesian War, Germany before World War I, and Japan before World War II are a few of the many examples of wars that resulted when statesmen failed to adapt to the sudden arrival of a new great power.

In order to protect its growing overseas interests and gain control over its links to the outside, China is now pressing previously dormant claims for maritime territory in the East and South China Seas. If successful, China would not only gain security for itself over vital lines of communication to its economy, it would also gain control over vast hydrocarbon, mineral, and fishing resources. But these gains would come at the expense of its neighbors, most of whom are now resisting China's increasingly aggressive assertions.

China is also undertaking a rapid and well-designed modernization of its air, naval, missile, and military space power. The U.S. Department of Defense estimated that between 2003 and 2012, China's real, inflation-adjusted defense budget grew at an average rate of 9.7 percent per year.[5] At that rate China's real defense spending will double every 7.5 years. By next decade China's military buildup will give it the ability to dominate the air and sea lines of communication in the western Pacific. Although China's intentions remain murky, the emerging military capability is clear. Since intentions can change rapidly, statesmen are forced to focus on threatening capabilities. As a result China's neighbors are now engaged in their own arms buildups, with the military spending of China's neighbors expected to jump more than 55 percent during the middle five years of this decade compared to the previous five years.[6] An open-ended and accelerating security competition in East Asia is under way, with dangerous implications for peace and security in the region.

The stakes at risk in the region are immense. East Asia has long been the most economically dynamic region in the world. A major conflict there would cripple the global economy. For the United States, nearly a tenth of its economic output and employment is tied directly to trade with the region, with the second- and third-order effects of disruption likely as large. In sum, millions of American jobs are tied to Asia's security. From a strategic perspective, the United States has five security treaty relationships in the region, which benefit U.S. security but are also a measure of America's credibility as an ally. Finally, since its founding the United States has relied on, and has defended, the freedom of navigation and rights to the global commons. Today's disputes in the western Pacific, tied to China's territorial assertions in the region, place these principles at risk.

The U.S. government belatedly perceived the deteriorating security situation in East Asia and is now giving the region more attention.[7] But this book will show that the United States does not have an effective response to China's territorial assertions or its military modernization. Fearful of enabling a confrontation over which it could lose control, U.S. diplomats are standing aside while China increasingly bullies its small neighbors over its territorial claims. This is leading to confusion, demoralization, and an accelerating and likely destabilizing arms race in the region. America's partners in East Asia are key to a successful strategy. But the United States will need a new diplomatic approach if it is to achieve the cohesion among these partners that will be necessary to preserve stability.

Meanwhile U.S. policymakers and military planners have underestimated the military potential China is on track to achieve by next decade. Bureaucracies inside Washington resistant to change and policymakers fearful of creating controversy have hampered an effective response to the emerging political and military challenges posed by China. The United States needs a reformed military strategy for the region. These reforms are needed to convince China's leaders that military coercion won't work. In addition, the present structure of U.S. military forces in the region leaves these forces vulnerable to attack and creates a dangerous incentive for offensive escalation during a crisis. Reforming America's military force structure in the region will be difficult and expensive. But it is necessary if the region is to maintain stability as China's military power continues to expand.

Statesmen everywhere are aware of 1914's harsh lessons. Yet in spite of this forewarning, Asia now seems to be on a very similar path as then. A century ago Europe's statesmen were unable to adapt to Germany's dramatic rise and fashion a stable and mutually satisfactory balance of power. In this era the United States, acting as an outside balancer, has played the central role in East Asia's security, a responsibility that has boosted the prosperity of all. But just like Europe a century ago, it is doubtful that Asia, left on its own, could shape a stable balance of power in the face of China's dramatic rise.

America's role as outside balancer is essential for the region's stability. But this time, it is Washington—its policymakers and institutions—that has been slow to adapt to the rapidly changing security situation in Asia. Without a better American strategy for the region, the risk of conflict in East Asia will continue to grow. Indeed, the next ten years may prove to be a particularly dangerous period, as China's leaders ponder what to do with a strategic window that will open for them. Designing and implementing a new U.S. strategy won't be easy, but it is vital for America's own interests for it do so, and quickly.

This book describes a better U.S. strategy for the Asia-Pacific region. Chapters 1 and 2 discuss the sources of conflict in Asia and explain why it is in America's interest to maintain its active forward presence in the region. Chapter 3 discusses the history of America's military presence in East Asia and explains why that presence, as it is presently constituted, is increasingly vulnerable. Chapter 4 explains in detail China's military modernization program and why by next decade it will pose a grave threat to U.S. and allied interests. Chapter 5 explains why the current U.S. responses to China's military modernization are ineffective and possibly dangerous.

The remainder of the book lays out a new security strategy for the United States in East Asia. Chapter 6 discusses the principles of strategy as they apply to the problems the United States faces in the region. Chapter 7 discusses the role of America's partners in the region and how the United States should refashion its diplomacy and security relationships. Chapters 8 and 9 describe the major changes the United States needs to make to its defense programs in order to cope with China's emerging military power. Finally, Chapter 10 summarizes a new strategic approach to the region and the barriers U.S. policymakers will have to overcome to implement it.

The goal of a new American strategy in Asia is to prevent conflict while preserving an existing international order that benefits all. The strategy proposed will call for the United States and its partners to implement specific military and diplomatic reforms to balance China's rising power. The strategy displays respect for China's arrival as a great power, offers it a role in the region's security, and welcomes China's continued economic and social progress. The strategy discussed in this book is not a war plan. It is a strategy for managing a peacetime competition in a highly dynamic region. The strategy's success will be measured by the crises that never occur, the wars that are never fought, and the long continuation of the region's prosperity and development, including inside China.

The Asia-Pacific region has long been a challenge for the United States. Over the past century, America fought four wars in the region and struggled with a dangerous, four-decade competition against the Soviet Union. But with these challenges and tragedies have also come opportunity, trade, wealth, and cultural enrichment for countless millions on both sides of the Pacific Ocean. America's ties with the region have delivered millions of jobs, higher standards of living, growing investments, and cultural interactions that have enriched all.

For all of these reasons, East Asia will arguably be the most consequential region of the world for U.S. interests in the decades ahead. But it seems to only now be dawning on some policymakers in Washington what the risks—and possible rewards—are that China's rapid rise poses for U.S. interests. For a general public distracted by other conflicts and economic anxiety, the growing perils in East Asia have yet to meaningfully register.

This book explains why the region is crucial to the United States, why current policies for the region are falling short, and what changes the United States must make to ensure a peaceful and prosperous future for Asia and for America's interests. Getting on the right course will not be cheap or easy. But the rewards for doing so will be immense. The risk of war in East Asia is rising. But the United States and its partners in Asia have the power to prevent another tragedy and to shape a better future that will benefit all.

 *Chapter 1*

A THREE-DECADE DRIVE TO A COLLISION

It was inevitable that China and the United States would find their interests clashing in the Western Pacific. A clash was bound to occur once both countries simultaneously became great powers and thus acquired global and overlapping interests. A collision would have occurred much earlier than the second decade of the twenty-first century, had China's status as a world power not slid into a period of temporary eclipse two centuries earlier. By 1945, when in the wake of World War II the United States became the undisputed hegemon of the entire Pacific, China's power, devastated by Japanese aggression and civil war, was at its low ebb. Mao Tse-tung's long reign of ideological mismanagement extended China's period of weakness, during the time when the United States found itself responsible for guarding the security of the Pacific Ocean.

Deng Xiaoping's arrival as China's leader in the late 1970s was a watershed in modern Chinese history, the magnitude of which few recognized at the time. Observers of China appreciated China's long history, its former great power status, and the latent potential of its massive population. But given China's long period of political chaos and a society for the most part trapped in a life of subsistence agriculture, the economic colossus that emerged over the next three decades certainly exceeded the most optimistic forecasts made at the time Deng assumed power.

Deng's reforms, which began in Guangdong province in the early 1980s and slowly spread across the country, mobilized China's previously unproductive population and, in doing so, led to one of the largest and most strategically consequential economic booms in history. After three decades of frenetic expansion, China has transformed from a country under Mao deliberately shut off from the world, to a major power with linkages and interests in every corner of the globe. The boom has likewise provided the resources to pay for one of the most dramatic military modernizations in history.

China has thus regained much of the status it began to lose two centuries ago. But the attributes and burdens of that status now rub up against those of the incumbent great power in the Pacific, the United States. Whether the two great powers will be able to peacefully manage the resulting friction is one of the momentous questions of this decade. The challenge that China now presents is forcing policymakers in Washington to face the rising price of maintaining America's position in the region and to wonder whether there are better and cheaper alternatives available.

★ ★ ★

Leaders who find themselves coping with an ambiguous and emerging threat are compelled to evaluate the potential adversary from two perspectives. First, what capacity does the potential adversary possess to inflict harm? And second, what are the potential adversary's intentions? This book will make the case that with respect to China, U.S. policymakers will be wise to focus on China's projected military capabilities and waste little effort attempting to discern the current or future intentions of China's leaders. The reason is straightforward: intentions, and thus a country's national security policies, can change suddenly. What matters for a leader's calculations is whether the adversary has the instruments, including military capacity, to implement a revised policy.

The futility of formulating policy based on an attempt to discern a potential adversary's intentions is not limited to the difficulty of peering inside the decision-making process of an opaque authoritarian regime. Rapid and dramatic policy shifts are equally possible in ostensibly transparent democracies. The most vivid recent case was the sudden change in America's policy toward Iraq, from the Clinton administration's policy of containment to forcible regime change under the George W. Bush administration. Similarly the late Colonel Muammar al-Qaddafi of Libya was no doubt stunned by the rapid change in the policies of several Western European leaders, from a benign neglect of Qaddafi's ruling style to a sudden hostility that resulted in Qaddafi's violent end. For the departed leaders of Iraq and Libya, the adversary's military capacity was the constant and latent threat and should have been the planning factor most in their minds. That these rapid policy changes were made by transparent democratic governments, and not by opaque authoritarian leaders, should indicate the futility of relying on assumptions of an adversary's intentions while formulating security strategy.

That said, it is still essential to explain why conflict between China and the United States over clashing interests in the Pacific is plausible and perhaps even likely, absent a new strategy by the United States and its coalition partners in the region. For many observers, it is not self-evident that China's rise should increase the risk of conflict with either China's neighbors or with the United States. The expanding interactions between China's economy and those of its neighbors, the United States, and the rest of the world have greatly benefited all of these players. Presumably none would have an incentive to upset this valuable interdependence.

Likewise, until recently there was minimal friction regarding security issues. Unlike the Cold War relationship between the United States and the former Soviet Union, there are frequent interactions between Chinese officials and military leaders and their counterparts in the region and in the United States. Many observers hope that these frequent contacts will result in procedures that will avoid misunderstandings and resolve incidents without escalation. With three decades of peaceful and beneficial interaction to point to, one may wonder why such a benign trend shouldn't continue. Without a convincing explanation for why a conflict between China and the United States is plausible, there would be little point in critiquing U.S. strategy and defense programs for the region.

Preventing conflict, preserving the region's gains in freedom and prosperity, and assembling a better security architecture that benefits all players, including China, will be a heavy burden for the United States. Making the case for this obligation requires an explanation of the sources of potential conflict between China and the United States, the consequences of such conflict, and an examination of the choices available to U.S. policymakers. This chapter and the next will explore these topics.

China Rises Again—and Acquires a World of Interests

The economic reforms implemented around 1979 by Deng Xiaoping and continued by his successors unleashed one of the largest and most dramatic economic expansions in history. From the beginning of Deng's reforms to the present, China's economic output, adjusted for inflation, expanded more than tenfold, becoming the second largest economy in the world, behind the United States.[1]

In current dollars, and adjusted for purchasing power parity, China's economy grew at a compound annual rate of 13.1 percent between 1980 and 2010. In 1980 China's economy was 10 percent the size of the U.S. economy. By 2010 China's economy, adjusted for purchasing power parity, was 75 percent the size of the U.S. economy.[2] According to the U.S. Central

Intelligence Agency, China is now the world's largest exporter, is the largest producer of agricultural products, leads the world in industrial production, is second to the United States in services output, and has the largest labor force in the world.[3]

These stupendous economic achievements have, over a very brief period, raised hundreds of millions of Chinese citizens out of poverty. China's exports have provided inexpensive goods to consumers around the world, increasing their living standards. China's imports of raw materials, capital equipment, and consumer goods have provided employment to millions of workers around the world. China's emergence as an economic superpower has also displaced workers and investments that could not compete against China's cost advantages in the global marketplace. Yet there is little doubt that the nation's arrival over the past three decades has been hugely beneficial to hundreds of millions of Chinese who might otherwise be stuck in subsistence agriculture, as well as millions of consumers, workers, and investors around the world who benefit from trade with China. And while the per capita income of China's enormous population is still relatively low, China's economy now easily provides its government with the resources it needs to acquire a competitive regional military strategy against the United States and its allies in East Asia, a goal the People's Liberation Army (PLA) is rapidly pursuing.

China has acquired global interests in parallel with its rising economic power. In 2012 exports were over 24 percent of China's economic output, with China's largest export customers located in the United States, Asia, and Europe. Equally important for China's geostrategic interests, China's imports, totaling nearly 22 percent of gross domestic product in 2012, similarly flowed in from nearly every corner of the globe.[4] China's opening to the world after the Mao era vaulted the country onto the top tier of global powers. But with this rise came China's dependence on the security and stability of trade flows essential for its economy.

Of particular note is China's growing reliance on overseas crude oil. In 2013 China surpassed the United States to become the largest net importer of crude oil.[5] In 2012 China imported nearly 5.9 million barrels of oil per day, over half of its average daily oil consumption—a figure that is expected to rise to 75 percent of China's daily consumption by 2035. The country's imported oil came from South America, Africa, the Middle East, Central Asia, and Russia. China's energy sources are diversified but have also extended China's strategic interests to every continent.[6] In spite of this diversification, 85 percent of China's oil imports must transit the Strait of Malacca, making that waterway a critical Chinese interest.[7]

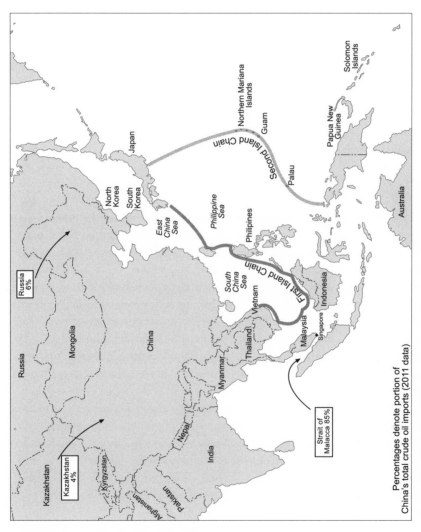

Percentages denote portion of
China's total crude oil imports (2011 data)

Map 1: Pacific Island Chains and China's Crude Oil Import Routes

China's dependence on imported oil is likely to increase in the years ahead—continued rapid growth, not to mention the expanding ownership of automobiles, will lead to an increase in demand for oil. The production of China's domestic oil fields has peaked, leading to increased attempts to find oil in both offshore waters and with foreign partners. Natural gas consumption in China amounts to only 4 percent of energy use and is unlikely to be a major component of China's energy mix in the foreseeable future.[8] By contrast, coal is the major energy source for electricity production, a fuel source that is causing ever-worsening health problems for China's immense urban populations.[9] China will thus be under increasing pressure to convert at least some of its electrical production to oil-based products from coal, adding to the quest for overseas oil supplies. As we will see, this quest is already creating friction with China's neighbors and compounding China's interests in distant corners of the globe.

China's Changing Strategic Behavior

The weight of China's new security interests, a by-product of a three-decade economic boom, is understandably causing China's leaders to revise their views of the nation's proper role in the world. In the early 1990s, when China's new growth trajectory was clear but before the country became an economic superpower in its own right, Deng Xiaoping's dictum guided China's approach to foreign policy: "observe calmly; secure our position; cope with affairs calmly; hide our capabilities and bide our time; be good at maintaining a low profile; and never claim leadership."[10] That advice was suitable for a China that was then an oil exporter, not a massive importer, and a country that still had a small economy and a negligible presence in global commodity, trade, and financial markets. Today's China is highly dependent on the global commons and many other commercial and financial connections. The leaders of the Chinese Communist Party (CCP) count on a growing economy to provide the legitimacy that leaves their rule of the country unchallenged. The global commons in the Western Pacific and Indian Oceans are patrolled by competitors such as the United States and India. At issue is the tolerance that future Chinese leaders will have for this possible vulnerability to their interests.

Over the past decade, China's leaders, compelled by the requirements of their nation's accumulating interests, began discarding Deng's dictum and have adopted a more openly assertive national security strategy. This still-emerging strategy takes greater account of China's global interests that were not so widely present in the early 1990s. China's national security strategy is undoubtedly a subject of continuing debate among China's leaders. We can see from its evolution, and from China's actions and military investments, that China's emerging strategy recognizes the vulnerabilities that economic growth have created. The evolving strategy attempts to cope with these vulnerabilities.

In 2004 Hu Jintao, then China's president and general secretary of the CCP, announced a new mission statement for the PLA. Titled "Historic Missions of the Armed Forces in the New Period of the New Century," the mission statement made note of China's global interests and expanded the PLA's responsibilities for protecting those interests. In 2007 the "new historic missions" were codified through an amendment to the CCP constitution. This amendment reaffirmed the PLA's fundamental role in protecting the party's ruling position in Chinese society, assigned the PLA a lead role in providing a security guarantee during "the period of strategic opportunity for national development," and directed the PLA to "provide a powerful strategic support for safeguarding national interests."[11]

It is notable that the "new historic missions" statement and subsequent codifications reemphasized the Chinese military's relationship to the Communist Party. The PLA is first and foremost the armed instrument of the Chinese Communist Party. Career military officers are party members and the Central Military Commission (CMC), the PLA's top decision-making body, is a department of the CCP Central Committee. The chairman of the CMC is the general secretary of the CCP and also president of China. This organization is specifically designed to keep the military under the party's command and to ensure that the PLA protects the CCP's ruling position in the country.[12]

From the perspective of the party leaders, it is not simply avarice that leads them to believe that the CCP's leadership of the country should remain beyond question. These leaders view the party as the indispensable power in China. It was the CCP that ejected foreign invaders from Chinese soil, unified the mainland, delivered political stability to a nation that has had so little during its history, and has lately engineered a three-decade economic boom. Such a record of success would logically lead CCP leaders to presume that their continued leadership is both necessary and welcome to meet present and future challenges, and they expect the PLA to protect their positions.[13]

This conception of the military's role differs from Western norms. What effect, if any, the "new historic missions" statement and China's conception of the role of the PLA might have on China's future employment of military power is uncertain. Countries employ military power for a variety of purposes including deterrence, signaling during crises, and coercion during conflict. In all of these examples, military force is used to influence the behavior of adversaries. Differing conceptions of the role of military forces in society could lead to misperceptions about adversary behavior and errant decision making during crises and conflicts. Policymakers and military planners should take account of these differences, a topic to be addressed later.

Various actors inside China are now taking actions to assert that nation's newfound status and defend its new interests, and are doing so in ways that didn't appear just a few years ago. For example, until recently, clashes between China and its neighbors in the South China Sea occurred about once every decade.[14] As we will see, that pace has accelerated over the past decade, soon after the "new historical missions" statement was promulgated to the PLA. Even as China settled land border disputes with its neighbors to the north and west, it stepped up assertions of its maritime claims to the east and south. The operations of the PLA's cyber-intelligence unit are another example of aggressive behavior recently emerging from inside the Chinese government.[15]

In his book *The Rise of China vs. the Logic of Strategy,* strategist Edward Luttwak asserted that the numerous examples of increased Chinese diplomatic and military assertiveness observed in recent years are less the manifestation of a tightly coordinated grand strategy and more the result of cultural behavior.[16] One aspect of this behavior appears within China's vast government bureaucracy, where opportunistic and entrepreneurial mid-level officials display aggressiveness as a means of increasing the resources allocated to the agencies they control.[17] Regardless of the explanation, there is no question that Chinese assertive behavior is expanding in line with the country's economy, its interests, and its military and political capacities.

China's Territorial Interests

From the Chinese perspective, China is a divided country. Although Taiwan is the most notable example of wayward territory outside Beijing's rule, the island is one of several critical territorial disputes that remain important priorities for China's leaders.

Completing the reunification of China in accordance with the borders claimed by Beijing would deliver several substantial benefits to the leaders of the CCP and to China generally. For the leaders of the CCP, establishing Beijing's dominion over the remaining territorial claims would greatly boost the prestige of the Communist Party and reinforce the justification for the party's leading role in the country. There are likely to be substantial rewards in position and prestige to those who would bring about such a success.

Equally important are the potential security gains China would accrue if it could expand the breadth of its rule without sparking a conflict by doing so. Like all powers, China has an interest in expanding its influence over areas adjacent to its periphery. Over its long history, the nation has suffered from foreign invaders who penetrated Chinese territory from nearly every direction. The history of innumerable overland invasions from the north and west extends back thousands of years. Sea battles against Japanese fleets occurred over many centuries. More recent are the harsh memories of the nineteenth century, when an expansionist Europe employed its superior sea power to establish colonies such as Hong Kong, from which it projected influence deep into China's interior. The result, in Chinese memory, was social and cultural chaos, economic decline, and a century of humiliation at the hands of foreigners.[18]

The sudden downfall of the Soviet empire in 1991 dramatically changed China's security situation, an opportunity that China's leaders soon exploited. The Soviet collapse removed the traditional threat of overland invasion from China's north and west. Beijing became free to reallocate defense resources to China's maritime approaches to its east and south. Since 1998 China settled eleven lingering land border disputes with six of its neighbors, steps that removed security friction from potential overland threats.[19] Although notable land boundary disputes remain with India, it is China's territorial claims in the East and South China Seas that are currently creating the greatest tensions in the region. Beyond China's historical claims to sovereignty over these seas, its huge reliance on maritime commerce through these waters and its memories of European maritime exploitation during the nineteenth century are combining to direct China's strategic attentions in this direction. The Soviet Union's collapse in the 1990s gave China an opportunity to focus on these waters and is likely part of the reason why clashes in these waters are becoming more frequent.

China has an additional maritime strategic interest. China is a nuclear weapons state. Its leaders acquired a strategic nuclear arsenal because they believed that these weapons were an essential deterrent against potential threats from other nuclear powers. Like the other large nuclear powers, China has an interest in establishing a fleet of long-endurance nuclear-powered submarines, armed with long-range nuclear ballistic missiles. This sea-based nuclear deterrent was a critical acquisition priority of the United States, Soviet Union, Great Britain, and France during the Cold War and is still in service with all of these countries today. Strategic planners have long considered a sea-based deterrent the most survivable and thus the most stabilizing. China wants missile-armed submarines that can hide in the oceans, ready to retaliate should the home country be attacked, thus dissuading others from attacking China.

By 2016 the Chinese navy (formally, the People's Liberation Army-Navy, or PLAN) plans to build and operate six Jin-class (Type 094) nuclear-powered ballistic missile submarines (two are already in service).[20] Each Jin-class boat will be armed with twelve JL-2 nuclear-armed ballistic missiles, with an estimated range of 7,400 kilometers. The fielding of the Jin force will give China a secure second-strike nuclear retaliatory capability, matching the retaliatory capability possessed by the Cold War–era powers mentioned above. The success of this effort, however, will depend on whether China will be able to establish secure patrol areas for these submarines, where they will be relatively protected from adversary anti-submarine warfare efforts. Finding patrol sanctuaries for the Jins will be another motivation for China to extend its maritime influence to its east and south.

China's Interests in the East and South China Seas

The dispute between Japan and China over sovereignty of the Senkaku Islands (Diaoyu Islands in Chinese) in the East China Sea has recently intensified. The five Senkaku Islands (also claimed by Taiwan) are now the site of regular flare-ups between China and Japan. One such flare-up occurred in September 2010 when a Chinese fishing boat rammed a Japanese coast guard vessel, resulting in the arrest of the Chinese captain and a two-week diplomatic crisis. In September 2012 protests in both China and Japan broke out over the disputed islands, causing disruption in trade between the two countries.[21] In February 2013 Japan alleged that a Chinese warship aimed its missile fire–control radar at a Japanese warship under way in the East China Sea.[22] According to Japan's Ministry of Defense, incursions by Chinese government ships in Japan's territorial waters around the Senkaku Islands accelerated in late 2012 and averaged about five incursions per month at the beginning of 2013.[23] In 2013 tensions in the East China Sea deepened when three Chinese state- or party-owned newspapers published articles that called for China's government to claim ownership of Okinawa, the home of 1.3 million Japanese citizens and site of bases for 27,000 U.S. troops.[24]

On November 23, 2013, China declared an air defense identification zone (ADIZ) over a portion of the East China Sea.[25] Japan, South Korea, and Taiwan declared their own ADIZs many years ago; however, China's declaration differed from international norms and thus increased tensions in the region.[26] China's declaration occurred suddenly and without coordination with its neighbors. The Chinese zone overlaps those of South Korea and Japan and thus increases the risk of accident and miscalculation. Most damaging, China's ADIZ covers the disputed Senkaku Islands, an act that

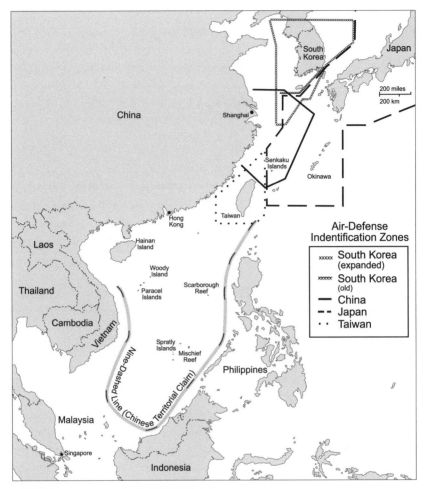

Map 2: Maritime Territorial Disputes in East Asia

heightens the sovereignty dispute with Japan and increases the risk of confrontation between Chinese and Japanese military air patrols, which will now become more frequent as a result of the declaration.

Intense nationalism, and still-fresh memories of Japan's harsh behavior in China during World War II, intensifies and complicates the Senkaku dispute. However, strategic factors are equally prevalent. Fishery resources around the islands are rich. The East China Sea is thought to contain approximately 7 trillion cubic feet of natural gas and up to 100 billion barrels of crude oil (equal to more than fifteen years of future Chinese oil consumption).[27] Sovereignty over the Senkaku Islands would affect the respective rights of China and Japan to exploit these hydrocarbon resources.

From a naval strategy perspective, Chinese control of the islands would open up a gap in the island chain between the Japanese home islands and Taiwan that would ease PLAN access to the open Pacific. Conversely, Japan could use the islands for sensor emplacement and patrol operations. Perhaps most worrisome for Japan, should China achieve legal control of the islands, that nation would be able to extend its two-hundred-mile exclusive economic zone (EEZ) right up to Japan's home waters.[28] Thus nationalism and strategic interests will combine to keep the Senkaku dispute energized.

China's territorial claims in the South China Sea have equally profound strategic implications: that claim, denoted by the "nine-dash line" that outlines virtually all of the sea, dates back to maps drawn by the former Nationalist Government in 1946.[29] This claim encompasses 2 million square kilometers, includes land features such as the Paracel Islands (also claimed by Vietnam), Scarborough Reef (claimed by the Philippines and Taiwan), and the Spratly Islands (claimed in whole or in part by Taiwan, Vietnam, the Philippines, Malaysia, and Brunei). Encounters between armed Chinese paramilitary patrol vessels and Philippine and Vietnamese commercial and patrol craft now occur regularly.

As with the Senkaku dispute, the conflicting claims in the South China Sea involve both nationalism and strategic interests. In addition to rich fishing resources, the U.S. Energy Information Administration estimates that deposits under the South China Sea may hold enough crude oil to supply China's needs for more than sixty years and enough natural gas for more than thirty years of Chinese consumption.[30] Tapping these hydrocarbon reserves immediately adjacent to China's home waters would mitigate the nation's geostrategic vulnerability to the Middle East while also improving its balance of payments position.

China has claimed the right to exclude foreign military activities in its two-hundred-mile EEZ, a legal right only a few other countries recognize.[31] In 2009 China attempted to enforce this claim when five ships from its maritime patrol forces harassed the surveillance ship USNS *Impeccable* in international waters south of Hainan Island.[32] Another such incident occurred on December 5, 2013, when a Chinese warship sailed near the bow of the guided missile cruiser USS *Cowpens,* nearly causing a collision in international waters in the South China Sea.[33] China's interpretation of EEZ rights, combined with its territorial claims in the East and South China Seas, would result in a theoretical right to exclude foreign military forces from some of the Western Pacific's most important sea-lanes.

As China Rises, So Do Its Concerns—and Its Actions

In sum, China's economic success has bolstered the prestige of the CCP and its leaders. Success has also increased China's exposure to overseas interests and vulnerabilities, over which these leaders are now striving to achieve some leverage. China's remarkable economic success has led to deep interactions with global markets of all kinds; the country's rising dependence on crude oil transiting the Indian Ocean and South China Sea is only the most notable of many such examples.

China's leaders come from an authoritarian tradition that succeeded in bringing to an end a long period of political and social chaos that had previously shattered China's position as a great power. These leaders trust the efficacy of direct control over problems. It should be no surprise if they seek to extend such methods to the overseas exposures that both fuel China's continued success but also threaten the party's continued rule, should these economic lifelines come under threat by better-positioned adversaries.

Hu Jintao's "new historic missions" assignment to the PLA recognized China's expanding global interests and the role of the armed forces in safeguarding those interests. This expansion in the PLA's role in 2004 parallels what other great powers have done throughout history. Indeed China is walking the same road the United States followed between the end of the American Civil War in 1865 and its entry into World War I in 1917. During this period the United States enjoyed rapid, albeit volatile and socially disruptive, economic growth. That growth led to expanding foreign trade and the commensurate development of U.S. strategic interests in Latin America, Europe, and Asia. Over those decades the United States acquired one of the largest and most technologically advanced navies in the world, as successive American leaders during this period perceived the need to protect the country's overseas interests.[34] After the Spanish-American War of 1898, the United States became a global power, with advanced naval bases in the Caribbean, Hawaii, and the western Pacific.

This hardly means that China will seek a nineteenth-century-style overseas empire, complete with strategically located coaling stations for its fleet. But just as with all countries in history that rose to become great powers, China will similarly seek ways to protect its wide-ranging interests. Just like those predecessors, China will use diplomacy and expanding military capacities in an attempt to secure its interests.

Even if one assumes China's intentions are wholly benign, it is inevitable that China's interests will increasingly collide with those of other powers. America's development into a global power during the end of the nineteenth century was not the result of a grand strategy by its government leaders. It

simply happened, as America's population, economy, technology, and culture expanded. But this process resulted in interests that those leaders later
took responsibility for defending. Those interests led to America's intervention in World War I, to prevent Europe's domination by a single power. Two
decades later, the collision of U.S. and Japanese interests led to war in the
Pacific. Historical processes that began without planning or ill intent led to
colliding interests and conflict. This is a pattern that has recurred throughout history and is a sober reminder as we ponder China's rise.

America's Stewardship of the Pacific

America's triumph in World War II left it with the largest and most powerful navy in history and complete domination of the Pacific. The United
States rapidly demobilized after the war, ended its colonial governance of
the Philippines, and set about administering Japan's postwar recovery. But
the collapse of Japanese power, combined with chaos inside China, left a
vacuum in Eurasia's east, which the Soviet Union soon flowed into even
before the war was over. Soviet leaders sought to protect their interests in
the Far East by supporting the CCP during China's civil war (which ended
in 1949) and by supporting China and North Korea during the Korean War
(1950–53). With fears of Soviet-supported communist movements sweep-
ing through the rest of East Asia, successive U.S. administrations maintained
a robust forward diplomatic and military presence in the region, as part of
its strategy of global containment of the Soviet Union.

The end of U.S. involvement in Vietnam in 1975 did not remove the
original reason for maintaining U.S. military power in the western Pacific.
Over the next decade Soviet naval and airpower in the Pacific continued
to expand. Soviet nuclear submarine fleets patrolled the northern Pacific
while their long-range maritime strike aircraft presented a growing threat
to U.S. Navy surface forces. Moscow developed a military relationship
with Vietnam and expanded its ties with India. The 1979 Soviet invasion of
Afghanistan created fears among some strategists that Moscow might soon
achieve the perennial Russian dream of establishing a naval base on the
Indian Ocean.

During this time Chinese military power was not a significant concern
for U.S. military planners. Indeed, for many strategists, China's military
backwardness was a problem. China had broken from Moscow in the early
1960s and was now courted by a succession of U.S. administrations, beginning with the Nixon presidency in 1969. Some policymakers favored arms
sales to China in order to bolster its role as an unofficial U.S. military ally
and balancer of Soviet military power in Asia.

During this period, and extending up to the present, the United States had two additional security objectives in the Asia-Pacific region. The first was North Korea's provocative behavior and the continuing military threat it posed to South Korea. Deterring aggression on the Korean Peninsula led U.S. military planners in the Pacific to concentrate military forces and contingency planning efforts in the northwest Pacific. The second security objective was restraining pressures and incentives that would lead to the proliferation of nuclear weapons in the region. China became a nuclear weapons state in the early 1960s, and long-running efforts to restrict North Korea's nuclear program failed to prevent that country from testing three small nuclear devices. Successive U.S. administrations have counted on the forward U.S. military presence in the region and the extension of a nuclear security guarantee covering U.S. allies, to dissuade those allies and others in the region from developing their own nuclear and ballistic missile deterrent programs.

The collapse of the Soviet Union in 1991 resulted in the crumbling of Russian military power. The George H. W. Bush and Clinton administrations responded by implementing plans that retired hundreds of warships and thousands of tactical and long-range bomber aircraft—cuts that thinned out U.S. forces in the Pacific at the same time that Russian military forces, hobbled by a broken government in Moscow and empty military maintenance and procurement accounts, largely ceased patrolling in the Pacific. In 1992 the Philippines, having deposed the authoritarian Ferdinand Marcos and still stinging from what was perceived at the time as an overbearing American presence, ejected the U.S. military from the Subic Bay Naval Base and the Clark Air Base (as it happened, Clark Air Base was simultaneously destroyed by a volcanic eruption). The collapse of the Soviet Union, and thus the end of worries about a potential Soviet presence in Vietnam across the South China Sea, made the Philippine government's decision easier.

The ongoing threat from North Korea, combined with U.S. ejection from the Philippines, resulted in an even greater concentration of the remaining U.S. military power in the northwest Pacific. In the early 1990s Chinese military power was not yet a concern. In 1996 the PLA conducted provocative missile tests into the Taiwan Strait in an attempt to dissuade the Taiwanese electorate from voting for a pro-independence candidate (he won anyway). In response the Clinton administration sailed two aircraft carrier strike groups near Taiwan, apparently without much concern about China's military capabilities.

By 2000 the steady growth of Chinese military power became noticeable, at least to analysts observing its missile forces and technology programs. Early in the decade, the U.S. Congress formed a permanent commission to study China's influence on the global economy and the security of the Asia-Pacific region and to issue annual reports on its findings.[35] The Congress also required the U.S. Defense Department to issue annual public reports on Chinese military developments.[36]

As China's neighbors now observe its growing military power with increasing concern, U.S. officials and military planners once again find themselves in the role of reassuring allies, attempting to maintain stability and acting as a diplomatic interlocutor between players—both allies and competitors—that have little trust in each other. An arms race in the region is gaining momentum, which will raise the costs for all of the players, including the United States. Those accelerating costs are sure to raise questions in Washington about what role the United States should play and what price it should be willing to pay to achieve its goals.

U.S. Interests in East and Southeast Asia

Since World War II successive U.S. presidents have articulated a surprisingly consistent view of America's foreign policy interests. The 2010 edition of the National Security Strategy of the United States, signed by President Barack Obama, states the country's enduring national security interests. These include an open international economic system; respect for universal values around the world; and a rules-based international order that promotes peace, security, and opportunity through stronger cooperation.[37] The document restates the U.S. commitment to its treaty allies and other security relationships. The strategy promotes engagement with allies and partners as an essential means of achieving the goals and interests stated in the strategy. Although the degree to which particular administrations over the past seven decades were willing to commit U.S. prestige and resources to these goals has varied, the aspirations of the Obama administration's 2010 National Security Strategy would ring true in most regards to U.S. presidents extending back to at least Harry Truman.

As the dominant power in the region since 1945, the United States has had a leading role in shaping the international order in East and Southeast Asia. During this time, virtually all the countries in the region have been remarkable successes. U.S. policymakers can point to the region's adoption, in large measure, of the principles described in the National Security Strategy as one of the main reasons for this success. The strategy discusses the goal of promoting universal values such as individual freedom, democratic choice, protection of minorities, and the rule of law.[38] East and Southeast Asia have been remarkable successes in this regard, with all but a few countries in the region having transitioned away from authoritarianism and arbitrary legal systems since World War II.

The broad acceptance across the region of another enduring interest in the strategy, an open international economic system, has led East and Southeast Asia to arguably be the most economically successful area in the world over the past seven decades, with gains in per capita income larger during this time than any other region in the world.[39] The region has been the best example to the rest of the world of how citizens' lives can improve through the application of the interests and principles in the National Security Strategy. The United States will logically have an interest in preserving what U.S. policymakers view as a triumph of U.S. values and policy.

The United States has long defended freedom of navigation in the global commons. In an essay written in November 2011 for *Foreign Policy* magazine, then–secretary of state Hillary Clinton applied the principles in the 2010 National Security Strategy to her description of U.S. interests and policy for the Asia-Pacific region.[40] Clinton made specific mention of the vital role of freedom of navigation through the global commons for the region's prosperity. For example, $5.3 trillion in trade passes through the South China Sea each year, $1.2 trillion of which passes through U.S. ports.[41] Eighty percent of the crude oil shipped to Japan, Taiwan, and South Korea passes through the sea.[42] The global trading system relies on the security the U.S. military provides in the South China Sea and elsewhere, the disruption of which would be very damaging to the global economy.

Freedom of navigation is a characteristic of an open international economic system and one of the enduring interests listed in the National Security Strategy. Trade through the global commons in the western Pacific has been an essential feature of the region's economic success and would not be possible without free navigation through the sea and open-air lines of communication. It is thus little wonder that keeping those lines of communication open is a basic mission of the U.S. military and a long-standing goal of U.S. policymakers.[43]

The United States has formal security treaty commitments with five countries in the Asia-Pacific region: Japan, South Korea, the Philippines, Thailand, and Australia.[44] In theory these treaties obligate the United States to provide military assistance to these countries in the case of overt military aggression. In addition the United States has a growing list of informal security relationships, to which Washington is committing resources and prestige. For example, in 2005 the United States entered into a strategic framework agreement with Singapore that deepened defense cooperation between the two countries.[45] In June 2012 Vietnam hosted the repair of a U.S. Navy support ship at a local ship repair facility in Cam Ranh Bay. That port visit coincided with a defense ministerial meeting in Hanoi at which the United States and Vietnam further expanded military cooperation.[46]

For decades U.S. presidents and statesmen have placed great weight in their public statements on the reliability of U.S. security commitments to allies and partners. Indeed such commitments have been expressed even when ownership of the territory the United States has obligated itself to defend is ambiguous. The dispute between Japan and China over the Senkaku Islands in the East China Sea provided one such occasion. In 2010, in response to a question about the U.S. position in the dispute, then–secretary of state Clinton stated, "With respect to the Senkaku Islands, the United States has never taken a position on sovereignty, but we have made it very clear that the islands are part of our mutual treaty obligations, and the obligation to defend Japan."[47] The United States thus has long-standing and expanding defense and diplomatic commitments in the region, which are integral to stated U.S. strategy.

U.S. economic ties to the region are substantial and bear heavily on America's standard of living. The United States exports nearly $1.3 trillion in goods and services annually to the region, equaling about 8.3 percent of U.S. economic output.[48] Sixty-one percent of all U.S. goods exports, 38 percent of U.S. private services exports, and 75 percent of U.S. agricultural exports are purchased by customers in the Asia-Pacific region.[49] With over 143 million people employed in the United States, it is safe to estimate that at least 10 million U.S. workers directly depend on trade to the Asia-Pacific region.[50] Second- and third-order effects of conflict in the region would add to the damage to the U.S. economy; the Asia-Pacific region generates 40 percent of the world's trade.[51] Any disruption of trade with this region would damage U.S. trading partners in Europe, Latin America, and elsewhere, with harmful additional consequences for the U.S. economy and its workers.

In sum, the United States has a deep commitment of interests and prestige in East Asia. Over the past seven decades, the region (with a few exceptions) has increasingly adopted the values and principles described in the National Security Strategy, a course that has improved the well-being of the countries that have done so. This success has advanced U.S. influence and has served as a positive example for other regions. U.S. policymakers have an interest in preserving this success. The United States has numerous formal and informal security commitments across the region, the preservation of which is highly important to U.S. prestige. U.S. economic interests are highly connected to the region, with much of U.S. economic output and millions of jobs tied to trade and development in the region. U.S. policymakers have consistently backed a policy of forward military deployments and engagement as the preferred means of defending U.S. interests in the region and boosting the credibility of its security commitments. The increasingly urgent question is whether China's rising interests and assertions in the region will be able to coexist with those of America.

Using Historical Analogies to Assess the Pacific's Future

When attempting to forecast the implications of China's rise with regard to security in the Asia-Pacific region, it is tempting to look to history for analogous examples of how incumbent powers dealt with a rapidly rising peer. When performed deliberately, the study of historical analogies can provide analysts and policymakers with useful guidance regarding the critical factors they should examine when attempting to resolve policy issues.[52]

Among the mostly commonly cited historical analogies to China's rise is the ascent of Imperial Germany between 1870 and 1914 and the disruption this event caused to Europe's balance of power.[53] Before its unification under Prussian leadership, Germany was fragmented, weak—a manageable strategic problem for Europe's other great powers. The German economy skyrocketed in the decades after its unification following the Franco-Prussian War of 1870–71, with dramatic strategic consequences for Europe and with striking parallels with China's recent rise.

Germany was likely Europe's biggest winner from the Industrial Revolution, at least in the decades leading up to World War I. Between 1888 and 1913, German industrial production expanded 2.8 times, a nearly 4.2 percent compound annual growth rate. During this same period, German production of steel ingots—an essential component for bridges, railroads, warships, artillery, and other military uses—expanded tenfold and by 1913 exceeded French steel output by a factor of four.[54] German unification under Prussian leadership resulted in the population, industrial output, and organization to support a very powerful army. Germany's leaders, well aware of the many occasions over past centuries when Germany had been trampled by foreign armies, didn't hesitate to build that army when they had the resources to do so.

In the century before World War I, the British navy assumed the role currently played by the U.S. Navy, that of protecting the global commons and oceanic trading networks. As Germany's economy expanded at the end of the nineteenth century, it acquired overseas interests, which went beyond its few colonial possessions in Africa and Asia. In the two decades before World War I, Germany rapidly expanded its fleet, the standard course other European powers and the United States had followed as their overseas interests grew. This brought Germany into a security competition with Great Britain.[55] Although the Royal Navy kept the global commons open for all during peacetime, the fleet could and did impose blockades on belligerents during wartime. German policymakers at the time were unwilling to live under this arrangement and sought a competitive fleet to protect Germany's interests. It should be no surprise to observe a similar calculation occurring today in Beijing.[56]

Over the span of a few decades, German military power expanded rapidly, sparking arms races and furious diplomatic hedging by Germany's neighbors. German policymakers saw no alternative to maintaining a large and highly capable army; the weak Germany prior to 1870 had been the victim too many times of aggression and proxy warfare instigated by powerful neighbors. The acquisition of a world-class fleet in the decades before World War I was viewed inside Germany as both within its rights and a prudent act to protect the nation's overseas interests. German policymakers and the public viewed these defense policies as reasonable, in light of the punishment a previously weak Germany had suffered for centuries at the hands of its great-power neighbors. The buildup of Germany's army and navy were also viewed as symbols of Germany's arrival as a great power in its own right. For Germany's neighbors, fear and an anti-German alliance consisting of France, Russia, and Great Britain was the result. Rapid changes in technology and more shifts in the balance of power led to increasing insecurity, instability, and finally war in 1914.

There are substantial differences between the culture and behavior of Imperial Germany and modern China. Yet the parallels between these two cases—Europe between 1880 and 1914 and East Asia today—are disturbing. One would hope that the very fact that today's leaders are aware of the parallels, and of the disaster that subsequently occurred in Europe, would be enough to create a different outcome in Asia.

Optimists will point to a more benign historical analogy—the peaceful passing of the baton from Great Britain to the United States that gradually occurred over the first half of the twentieth century. But Britain's slow withdrawal of its naval forces from the Western Hemisphere to protect its interests elsewhere is both a flawed analogy to the U.S. position in the western Pacific and a disturbing portent.

Britain's withdrawal of its naval forces from the Caribbean opened the way for the United States to become the hegemon in that region and for the U.S. Navy to assume responsibility for patrolling the area's maritime commons. The withdrawal of Britain as an outside balancer in the Western Hemisphere did not spark a security competition in reaction to America's assumption of hegemony because by the early twentieth century the United States did not face any other peer competitors in the region with the capacity to compete against its power. This is not the case in the Asia-Pacific region. As discussed in chapter 2, a hypothetical withdrawal of the U.S. presence in the region would almost certainly result in a scramble by India, Japan, and other smaller but potentially capable powers to arm themselves in resistance to the prospect of Chinese hegemony. The resulting arms races and hedging strategies would more likely resemble pre–World War I Europe than the Western Hemisphere's response to America's rise.

Is a China-U.S. Conflict Plausible? The View from the Ivory Tower

No one knows how the future will unfold. Policymakers, however, are responsible for preparing for the future. If China achieves the military capability to thwart American interests in the Asia-Pacific region, U.S. policymakers will need to know whether conflict with China is plausible enough to warrant the large expenditure of money and prestige required to protect American interests in the face of a potential Chinese threat.

Consciously or not, policymakers will rely on some theory of international behavior to estimate the plausibility of a future conflict with China. There is no shortage of scholarly analysis of the security situation in Asia, with conclusions ranging from dire to benign.

For John J. Mearsheimer, an international relations theorist at the University of Chicago, conflict between China and the United States is not just plausible, it is virtually inevitable. Mearsheimer believes that future U.S. policymakers will be compelled to resist China's ascension as Asia's hegemon.[57] Citing his theory of "offensive realism," Mearsheimer concludes that China will follow the strategic logic adhered to by virtually all other great powers in history (including the United States itself) and will attempt to obtain security by becoming the hegemonic power in its region. The purpose behind achieving this position is to establish a broad zone of security around the country, by either weakening potential rivals in the region or intimidating them into compliance with the regional hegemon's security requirements.

However, China's attempt to establish regional hegemony would create a conflict with America's core interests, described above. The United States will be compelled to resist China's aspirations to regional hegemony, or risk the consequences to its economic prosperity, its reliability as an ally, and its global prestige. The logic driving this resistance is the same as it was for U.S. statesmen in the twentieth century—should either end of Eurasia fall under the rule of a single power, the resulting threat to America's global interests would be too great to bear. From this perspective, Mearsheimer believes conflict between the two great powers is nearly inevitable.

Naturally there are scholars who believe that more benign outcomes are possible. For example G. John Ikenberry, a professor of politics and international affairs at Princeton University, asserts that the open and rules-based global system created mainly by the West after World War II is well designed to smoothly adapt to China's rise. At the same time, Ikenberry insists that the Western-designed global order will be difficult for China to either resist or overthrow, which in any case he believes China's leaders will conclude is not in their interests to even attempt.[58]

Ikenberry believes that, unlike previous episodes in history when a rising great power felt compelled to overthrow the incumbent, the circumstances this time are much more conducive to peaceful and self-interested power sharing among the great powers. Western-designed institutions such as the United Nations (where China already holds a great-power veto), the World Trade Organization, the International Monetary Fund, and numerous other multilateral institutions allow China to be a powerful stakeholder in the international system, obviating the need for the nation to risk the consequences of overthrowing the system from which it already benefits. Ikenberry recommends that the United States will best protect its interests by bolstering these institutions and the rules-based system it helped create, both to induce China's acceptance of them and to make it more difficult for China to challenge them.

Thomas Fingar, an academic at Stanford University, an Asia expert, and a former high-ranking official in the U.S. State Department and intelligence community, similarly believes that China has neither the incentive nor the intention of disrupting the current global system from which it has benefited so greatly. Instead, Fingar asserts that China will seek marginal adjustments to the existing rules and institutions to accommodate its growing stature and interests.[59]

The leadership in Beijing, however, may believe it does not have to choose between the acquisition of hegemony in East Asia and the continuation of the global system under which China has thus far prospered. China's policymakers can reasonably conclude that they can have both, with the burden of resisting this outcome placed on the United States and its allies in the region. Ikenberry and Fingar assume that notions of territorial security are as quaint in China as they are today in the United States and Western Europe. They assume that China has firmly forgotten the millennia of foreign conquests of its territory and the pillaging it endured within the past century at the hands of Asian and European invaders. Neither China's recent prosperity nor the existence of global institutions and a rules-based order has appeared to mollify China's security concerns or the animosities its citizens feel about their neighbors and China's recent past. Since Ikenberry's essay appeared in *Foreign Affairs* in 2008, China's territorial assertions and related incidents in the East and South China Seas have sharply accelerated, along with nationalist outbursts directed at Japan and other offenders from China's past.

This is not evidence that China wishes to overturn the existing international system. But it does suggest that China will continue to pursue its territorial claims, in order to ease its concerns about maritime security. Those claims create a serious conflict with U.S. and allied interests in the region and are evidence that China's formula for protecting its interests more closely matches Mearsheimer's equation than Ikenberry's or Fingar's. The marked increase in China's assertive behavior in the East and South China Seas and the continued growth of its naval and aerospace power support this conclusion.

Ikenberry and Fingar may be right that China does not want to overthrow the international system; but China's concerns about traditional territorial security, driven as much by China's culture and history as by its current perceptions of the balance of power, make conflict in the region plausible and therefore an event for which the United States and its allies must prudently prepare. Once that threshold question of plausibility has been answered, U.S. policymakers and military planners will then need to fashion a sustainable strategy that will reliably prevent conflict and protect the interests of the United States and its allies.

Peaceful Development or a Security Competition?

China's leaders regularly assert that their focus is on internal development and on managing that nation's difficult transition to a middle-income country. There are numerous reasons to accept these assertions. China's leaders face many substantial internal challenges. China's economy, heavily weighted to debt-financed investment spending and highly reliant on exports, has its own vulnerabilities and may face the same kind of debt crisis that has hobbled Japan, Europe, and the United States.[60] China's leaders face immense challenges managing a rapidly evolving economy and society and would seemingly have good reasons to focus their time and resources on these internal challenges instead of an arms race against the United States and its allies. The CCP's position may be equally precarious; according to official Chinese government reports, there were more than 90,000 protests in each of the past three years, in the face of China's large and strict internal security apparatus.[61] A fragile political position could induce CCP leaders to adopt a risk-averse external strategy.

Then there are the deep economic and financial linkages between China and the United States and its allies in the Asia-Pacific region. As mentioned earlier, China's economy is highly dependent on the exports it provides to customers in these countries and the nation would seem to have little appetite for taking risks with this vital aspect of its economy. Deep economic and financial linkages among the belligerents before World War I did not prevent the outbreak of that great war. But policymakers on both sides of today's Pacific are certainly aware of the grave economic consequences of conflict.

Finally, China, the United States, and other countries in the Pacific benefit from their current cooperation on a variety of security activities. These include cooperation on counterterrorism and counterpiracy, patrolling on both ends of the Indian Ocean, and cooperation on proliferation issues. The U.S.-China relationship in no way resembles the Cold War relationship between the United States and the Soviet Union; diplomatic contact is nearly continuous and covers a broad range of issues.

However, China's leaders will increasingly labor under the security concerns that come with being a great power with global interests. They will not be able to avoid attending to these concerns and, in doing so, will be forced to take risks with the conditions that are supporting their nation's development.

Internal and external forces will exert pressure on China's leaders to be more assertive regarding China's security concerns. Within China, rising nationalism, already visible, is likely to intensify. Per capita income in China is rising and has resulted in a higher standard of living compared to China's previous state of mainly rural subsistence. China's recent development has also increased urbanization, education levels, and greater awareness of the world beyond its borders. Somewhat paradoxically, these trends also correlate with rising awareness of China's historical grievances and expressions of nationalism, a phenomenon observed not only in China but in many other societies and cultures that have experienced rapidly rising incomes.[62]

It is thus possible that China's leaders will come under increasing pressure from an aroused population demanding greater respect for China's great-power status.[63] China's leaders may find internal political rewards for responding to these nationalist appeals. Conversely, nationalism may be a technique China's elites will use for social control, if other forms of their legitimacy falter.[64] President Xi Jinping has adopted the slogan "China Dream" as a theme of his presidency. Although the definition and implications of "China Dream" are murky, the slogan may amount to merely a stirring of Chinese nationalism, with possibly troublesome consequences in the future.[65]

China's analysis of its external security requirements may also result in more assertive behavior than exhibited thus far. The starting point of this concern is China's traditional fear of encirclement by potentially hostile powers. The long-standing remedy to this concern has been to increase

China's military power and to expand its zone of influence beyond the core territory, creating more defensible space.

China's leaders are likely well aware of the "paradox of power," that is, the more assertive China is and the more it builds its military strength, the more its neighbors will respond with their own military buildups and the containment of China.[66] Indeed, China's leaders must know that their higher assertiveness that began around 2008 has led to a backlash in the region. Yet when given the choice between military weakness and strength, policymakers invariably choose strength as the least risky option, if only because they are unwilling to bet on the good intentions of potential adversaries. As explained in chapter 4, China has clearly chosen the path of increasing military strength.

As discussed earlier, China's expanding role in the world has resulted in new vulnerabilities its leaders must mitigate. Regarding China's maritime interests in the Pacific, the first among these vulnerabilities is China's reliance on the Strait of Malacca to provide energy for its economy. Although China is attempting to develop alternate pathways for oil imports, including a pipeline through Burma, pipelines from central Asia, and perhaps a canal through Thailand's isthmus, these alternatives come with their own vulnerabilities and, in any case, will not remove China's dependence on the massive flow of tankers and merchant ships through the Strait of Malacca (China receives 85 percent of its crude oil imports through the strait, a quantity that pipelines from Central Asia will not be able to replace).[67]

It is disturbing to note that while China has settled eleven land border disputes with six of its northern and western neighbors since 1998—in many cases ceding more than half of its original claims—it has accelerated its demands for its maritime claims in the East and South China Seas.[68] China is thus not opposed on principle to settling territorial claims. If, for example, China's main interest in the Near Seas was the exploitation of their vast hydrocarbon potential (an important strategic interest for China), it would seem a straightforward matter to set aside sovereignty questions and instead negotiate deals with Japan, Taiwan, Vietnam, the Philippines, and others to develop and share the seas' oil and gas. The fact that China has done little to pursue this course indicates its unwillingness or inability to achieve mutually advantageous agreements with its maritime neighbors. Instead, China has chosen to build up its naval, air, and land-based missile power, aimed at maritime dominance (see more about this in chapter 4). It is alarming that China has chosen a confrontational path, backed by increasing military power, rather than a negotiated path that would be mutually beneficial and that China has used for disputes with other neighbors.

Finally, China's leaders undoubtedly conclude that they must hedge against uncertainty over America's future position in the region. The first concern of China's military planners is the potential for military-technical breakthroughs that could suddenly expose China to unforeseen danger. Like other observers, China's leaders were stunned by the technical and tactical efficiency displayed by U.S. military forces in Iraq in 1991, in Afghanistan in 2001, and again in Iraq in 2003.[69] Since 1945, U.S. military-technical breakthroughs—nuclear weapons, intercontinental missiles and bombers, stealth technology, and precision-guided munitions—have appeared to have stunning geopolitical consequences, at least to military planners responsible for countering U.S. military capabilities. These and other technical breakthroughs gave U.S. military planners and policymakers the freedom to fashion competitive military strategies that overcame adversary advantages and allowed the United States to achieve its geostrategic goals at reasonable costs.[70] With the United States thus viewed as a source of frequent strategic surprise, China's leaders undoubtedly view energetic military modernization as the least risky course of action.

China's leaders must also hedge against the possibility of a precipitous U.S. withdrawal from the region. A U.S. withdrawal would lead to a scramble for security by the other powers in the region, with unpredictable consequences (discussed in chapter 2). For China's leaders, the natural hedge to this contingency is the same: broad-based military modernization, with an emphasis on the high-technology components of modernization, such as missiles, aircraft, warships, electronics, and space systems. From the perspective of Beijing, the purpose of this modernization is to allow China to peacefully expand its zone of security, especially in the maritime domain, while continuing to enjoy the benefits of the open global economic and financial system.

Are There American "Red Lines" in the Pacific?

Based on China's actions and behavior, we can assume that China's leaders now believe that rapid military modernization and the acquisition of maritime "breathing space" in the western Pacific is the proper way to defend China's expanding interests and to hedge against uncertainty. But this logic has brought China into conflict with the interests of the United States and its allies.

From the perspective of policymakers in Washington and in the region, China's assertions in the East and South China Seas appear to be an attempt to rewrite international law and norms and to settle territorial disputes, if not by overt military force, then by material strength and intimidation rather than negotiation. The United States has a strong interest in defending the rules-based international system it helped establish. That system and U.S. interests would suffer damage should China succeed in unilaterally imposing its will.

China's claims for the Senkaku Islands, the Paracel Islands, Scarborough Reef, and the Spratly Islands are not the only worry. These claims, combined with China's interpretation of EEZ rights (an interpretation agreed to by only a handful of other countries), would permit China to exclude foreign warships from waters extending from the Strait of Malacca right up to Japan's home islands. Although the Chinese government insists that its broad territorial claim in the South China Sea will have no bearing on the free transit of commerce through those waters, free commercial navigation through the sea, currently valued at $5.3 trillion per year, would transpire at the whim of the Chinese government. China's leaders could point out their discomfort at relying on the U.S. Navy's whim; however, American officials can point to at least seven decades of U.S. support for an open global commons in the region.

Finally, U.S. officials must concern themselves with the credibility of the security promises they have made to their allies, not just in Asia but also elsewhere in the world. Should China be viewed as gradually undermining the existing U.S. security architecture in the western Pacific, the reliability of the United States as an ally elsewhere would come into question.

The stage is thus set for a security dilemma in the western Pacific, where leaders in both China and the United States will conclude that the least risky hedge for each is to reinforce its military power. Indeed, this competition has already been under way since at least the 1990s, when China shifted its military investments from land power toward aerospace and naval power and developed a military strategy designed to exploit U.S. vulnerabilities. These developments occurred while U.S. force structure shrank after the Cold War and while the United States was engaged in ground campaigns in the Middle East and Central Asia.

So even a decline in the U.S. military capacity to attack China, which occurred during the two decades after the Cold War, did not dissuade China's leaders from pushing forward their plans for military modernization. China's policymakers and military planners must reckon with America's potential future military power and the possibility that U.S. intentions—along with the intentions and capabilities of China's neighbors—could change at any time for any number of reasons. And so it is also for U.S. policymakers: as long as conflict is at least plausible, these policymakers and their military planners should prepare for China's actual and potential military capabilities.

That task will become increasingly expensive, especially when connected to a strategy that maintains a strong U.S. presence in the western Pacific. America's forward presence in the Pacific is a legacy inherited from World War II. As the cost of that policy rises, many will wonder whether there is a better approach, the subject that chapter 2 will discuss.

 *Chapter 2*

IT MATTERS WHO RUNS THE PACIFIC

The previous chapter discussed why U.S. and Chinese interests in the Asia-Pacific region are bound to clash, and why a security competition between the two countries is the regrettable, but likely inevitable, result. For many in the United States, it is not obvious why the region's security should be an American responsibility, or why a forward U.S. military presence in the region is a desirable policy.[1] These skeptics wonder whether the United States could avoid expense and risk if it simply left the region's security to the countries in the region, which, as noted earlier, are rapidly gaining the wealth to provide for their own defense.

This argument merits a full examination. As chapters 3 through 5 explain, the costs and risks of the current U.S. policy for the region are rising rapidly. These chapters also show that U.S. policymakers have not formulated a feasible strategy to credibly maintain America's position in East Asia. U.S. policymakers thus face some fateful decisions about what interests the United States can realistically defend, what price the country should be willing to pay, and what risks policymakers can accept to defend these interests.

Are there alternatives to the U.S. forward presence in the region, a presence that risks a costly clash with a rising China? As the costs and risks of forward presence grow, some policymakers in Washington, along with many skeptical constituents, will increasingly ask whether there are other policies that can avoid the burdens and risks of forward presence.

This chapter will examine different paths the region's security structure might take, along with alternatives to the current U.S. forward presence strategy; and this examination will conclude that for all of its costs and risks, forward presence is the least risky and, in the long run, least costly choice for the United States. The fact that the costs and risks of forward presence are rising does not challenge this conclusion. Even as the costs of the strategy rise, the benefits from a stable and prosperous Asia-Pacific region are too important to U.S. interests to risk with any other approach. Further, without a U.S. forward presence, the risk of regional conflict rises substantially. A conflict in this wealthy and rapidly growing region would be ruinous to America's standard of living and would inevitably result in U.S. military intervention anyway, an outcome that forward presence is designed to avert.

Four Paths Forward for Asia

In December 2012 the U.S. National Intelligence Council released *Global Trends 2030: Alternative Worlds*.[2] Beginning in 1996, and shortly after each U.S. presidential election since, the U.S. intelligence community has published a *Global Trends* report. The purpose of these reports is to "stimulate strategic thinking by identifying critical trends and potential discontinuities."[3] Each *Global Trends* report has sought to project economic, political, social, military, and scientific trends that could create significant transformations for global affairs. *Global Trends* is written by senior analysts in the U.S. intelligence community but relies heavily on contributions from researchers and practitioners in academia, business, finance, science, and other governments.

Global Trends 2030 had much to say about alternative futures for the Asia-Pacific region. The report described four possible pathways for Asia's strategic order over the next several decades.[4]

The report's first pathway is an extension of the present order, which assumes that the United States will continue its forward presence and engagement in the region. Under these conditions, the scenario assumes a continuation of rules-based cooperation and peaceful competition within existing regional structures. The scenario envisions the continued expansion of Chinese military power, various mischief created by North Korea, and the potential for other security competitions. However, the consequences of these problems would be mitigated by the U.S. presence in the region and by the cooperative security architecture the United States would maintain with its partners. The Obama administration's "rebalance" to the Asia-Pacific region, rolled out in the winter of 2011–12, aims to sustain and reinforce this pathway.

The report's second pathway is the most ominous and will be a focus of this chapter. This scenario envisions a Hobbesian scramble for security among the region's major and minor powers, sparked by U.S. disengagement from its security presence.[5] In this scenario, the region's countries struggle to establish a stable balance of power, resulting in rivalries, shifting and reforming alliances, and internal and external maneuvers among countries to find security. Nuclear weapon and missile races are likely as countries strive to compensate for the security vacuum left in the wake of America's departure from its previous security role.

The report's third pathway for the region envisions the development of a pluralistic and peaceful East Asian community, resembling the better aspects of the European Union (EU) that have emerged since World War II. This scenario assumes substantial political liberalization in China, universal respect across the region for the autonomy of Asia's smaller countries, and a dissipation of nationalist sentiments. If Western Europe's development over the past three decades is the model, this scenario also implies acceptance of the region's existing security structure (presumably still largely guaranteed by the United States), some demilitarization, and a focus on economic integration, fostered by the buildup of EU-like regional institutions.

The report's fourth pathway is a hierarchical Sinocentric order, with China establishing a sphere of influence over the region. Under this scenario, the role of the countries around China would be to support a regional political and economic structure designed and coordinated from Beijing. This structure would be centered on Asian trade, development, and cooperation rather than open transpacific trade and engagement, which has been the norm since World War II. This scenario assumes an end to America's forward security presence in the region, with security and the region's foreign policy under the direction of the leadership in Beijing. For China, this scenario would be a return to the "Middle Kingdom" system that existed in China's ancient past, whereby China's small neighbors are harmonious subordinates to China's leadership. In this scenario, China's neighbors would lack independent security options and would thus "bandwagon" with Beijing in order to obtain protection.

Which Path Will the Region Take?

The first pathway, the current rules-based system, characterized by increasing security competition but defended by forward U.S. power, is the familiar base case. However, China's growth, its security needs and ambitions, and its military modernization are making this pathway increasingly costly and risky for the United States. This pathway also creates numerous problems for U.S. policymakers: They must convince partners in the region that the United States won't abandon them, while also avoiding the underwriting of risky behavior by these partners that could ensnare the United States in an avoidable conflict. Constituents in the United States will complain about "free-riding" behavior by these security partners and ask why these wealthy countries won't do more for their own defense. Finally, for some, the rise of China's power is so compelling that it seems quixotic to attempt to resist or balance it. Given the costs, risks, and difficulties of the current approach, it is little wonder that many are looking for alternatives.

The report's third pathway, a pacific and demilitarized region focused on development and regional institution-building, would seem to be an ideal long-term goal for U.S. policy. Such an outcome would represent the triumph of the model the United States has promoted since World War II, with rules-based institutions, respect for rights and autonomy, and peaceful development. It would also permit a gradually declining U.S. security burden in the region as a more cooperative political culture takes hold, as it has in Europe.

Regrettably, this third scenario is undoubtedly the least likely to occur, at least within any relevant planning horizon. Unlike in Western Europe, the catastrophe of World War II did not burn out national and ethnic grievances in Asia. These grudges still linger, with rising living standards in China possibly fueling some of these feelings to burn hotter.[6] Western European unity after World War II was catalyzed by the Soviet threat and bolstered by the U.S. security presence. After World War II, old adversaries in Europe cooperated on building the North Atlantic Treaty Organization (NATO) and on trade and economic institutions that eventually led to the EU. East Asia has no similar accomplishments in its postwar record. Asia's security structure after the war was much more complicated, involving not just the USSR, but also Mao's China, a hot war in Korea, and postcolonial struggles in Southeast Asia that went on for decades. The U.S. security presence in Asia kept the Soviet Union at bay but did not douse many of the region's other lingering grievances.

China's political liberalization, denoted by pluralism and a truly open society, would seem to be a necessary (if insufficient) condition before China's neighbors could overcome their anxiety about China's rising power. But Western-style political liberalization is hardly the goal of the Chinese Communist Party (CCP). Indeed, in one of his first speeches to PLA generals after assuming his position as leader of party in 2012, Xi Jinping discussed the Soviet army's failure to protect the Soviet Communist Party before the Soviet Union's breakup in 1991 and vowed that that would not be allowed to happen in China.[7] With authoritarianism in China, and arms races, nationalism, and unresolved grievances still present across Asia, the Kantian future described by the report's third path seems an unlikely dream.

Nor do the odds favor the smooth arrival of the report's fourth scenario: the reestablishment of a Chinese Middle Kingdom, with the region's other nations a supporting cast in a Sinocentric hierarchy. China's leaders will certainly never declare this scenario as their preferred end state, any more than U.S. leaders would say out loud that a liberalizing political revolution inside China is a U.S. policy goal (in this regard, we should probably consider the Chinese foreign minister's agitated outburst about the proper places of "big countries" and "small countries" at the ASEAN Regional Forum conference in Hanoi in July 2010 as perhaps a revealing gaffe).[8] China's stated aspirations call for "peaceful development" not the reestablishment of the ancient tributary system. Yet the correctness for many in China of a Sinocentric hierarchy is something that seems to result from five millennia of recorded Chinese culture.[9]

Whether a Sinocentric structure in Asia is a subconscious Chinese goal or not, there are enough lingering fears elsewhere in the region about this prospect to create active resistance to the concept. Simply put, we should expect Japan, India, Vietnam, the Philippines, and many others to resist the establishment of a new Middle Kingdom. Should the United States scale back its security role in the region, that resistance would also occur, only in more unstable and dangerous forms.

It is important to discuss why China's neighbors tolerate—indeed, even welcome—U.S. security hegemony in the region and why, by contrast, these same countries would strongly resist Chinese hegemony. There is a structural reason why this is so, and it relates to geography and is therefore enduring: China is a large neighbor in the region and the United States is not. Because the United States has to project its presence across a vast ocean, it requires the permission of most countries in the region to continue its role as the security hegemon. The United States requires bases, access rights, and negotiated agreements with local governments to fulfill its security guarantees. If these governments withdrew their permission due, say, to bad American behavior, the United States would find it difficult and costly to sustain its presence across the ocean in the face of broad resistance.

China, by contrast, is a permanent presence in the region that the neighbors can never dislodge. Should China engage in the same bad behavior, these countries cannot make China go away. They can only fight or accept China's treatment. It is therefore easier for the countries in the region to enter into a security contract with an outside power, knowing they have some bargaining leverage and an escape clause. When dealing with a powerful neighbor like China that isn't going anywhere, the only way to achieve the same bargaining leverage is to match that neighbor's power, especially its military power. And that implies arms races and spiraling security dilemmas.[10]

Thus, hegemons are not all created equal. It is easier to strike a bargain with an outside hegemon than with a local one—an immutable reason why the U.S. security presence will be welcome in the region. Even more crucially, U.S. service as the region's security hegemon is much more likely to result in stability than if the region were left alone to find its own stable structure (more on this below). Adding to America's attractiveness as an outsider are the United States' seven-decade record of keeping the region's commons open for all and its not having territorial disputes with countries in the region. The logic behind why most countries in the region welcome the United States as the security hegemon, and why most would resist China attempting to play the same role, is a strong argument for maintaining this arrangement.

Which brings us to *Global Trends'* second pathway, the Hobbesian scramble for security, as the most likely outcome should the United States opt to reduce its costs by withdrawing from the region. As this chapter will later explore, this outcome would very likely trigger multisided missile and nuclear arms races across the region, with unpredictable and unstable consequences. The risk of military disaster inside the most important economic region in the world would rise abruptly. The U.S. economy and standard of living would not escape the risks and costs of these developments.

It is easy to see how the absence of the United States as an outside security provider could result in a dangerously unstable security competition in East Asia. The rapid rise of China's military power would create the logic for an offsetting alliance by most of its neighbors. Some however (perhaps, e.g., a future unified Korea) may choose to bandwagon with China instead, especially if historical grievances make allying with some of China's adversaries politically unacceptable. Bandwagoning by some would increase the security anxiety of the remainder that don't. Finally, some significant powers (e.g., Russia) might choose to remain unaligned, which would compound the region's uncertainty because the players would have to ponder how these neutrals would eventually act during a regional crisis. Should one or more countries conclude that stability was unachievable and conflict inevitable, the calculation would then turn to the logic of security trends and time pressure and the possible advantage gained by striking first rather than waiting for adversaries to grow even stronger in the future.

Critics of this line of analysis will note that the region's high degree of economic interdependence would make such a security competition illogical and therefore unlikely (although high economic interdependence among Europe's belligerents did not prevent war in 1914). Critics will also point out that awareness of the destructive power of modern armaments should be all that statesmen need to avoid provoking a conflict and finally note that state-on-state war is widely thought to be passé, an artifact of a thankfully bygone era.

We can hope that these notions are true. However, they don't remove the serious security concerns that Japan or the Southeast Asian countries would feel should China and the PLA obtain hegemony over the western Pacific and the commerce that runs through it. China, Korea, Russia, and others would likewise become alarmed should Japan, in its perceived self-defense, become a substantial missile and nuclear weapons state and rebuild its navy to protect its overseas interests. The result would very likely be several multisided and unstable security competitions that would leave decision makers in the region with great uncertainty and little response time during crises.

One would hope that the destruction caused by the twentieth century's wars and by the even greater destructive potential of modern nuclear weapons would provide a deterrent to aggressive behavior by today's statesmen. But while fear of the modern capacity for destruction may provide a deterrent to some leaders, for others, this same fear is leverage to be used against adversaries during a crisis. We may hope that we live in a more enlightened era, but that hope may be a consequence of the post–World War II *Pax Americana* era in Europe and East Asia that has lasted so long and that now seems taken for granted by many.

U.S. policymakers will thus have to choose whether to shoulder the costs of maintaining an ever more expensive forward presence or to take the risk of allowing the Asia-Pacific region to construct its own self-enforcing stability, with the knowledge that if that effort should fail, the consequences to the United States and the rest of the world would be ruinous.

Nuclear Asia—It Could Get Much Worse

Of the ten known, suspected, and impending nuclear weapon states (the United States, Russia, United Kingdom, France, China, India, Pakistan, North Korea, Israel, and Iran), six have military forces in the Asia-Pacific region. Should the *Global Trends* Hobbesian scenario occur due to a withdrawal of the U.S. forward security presence, the number of nuclear weapon states would almost certainly rise. That outcome would assuredly result in greater instability, as multisided security competitions would very likely break out. Military planners in the region would have to defend against multiple and possibly shifting adversary alliance combinations. The addition of more nuclear players would result in the need for greater preparation and stockpiling by all, because previously safe levels of nuclear munitions would no longer be safe enough. New players would mean further reductions in warning time during crises. Some leaders might conclude that striking first at the hint of crisis is the only way to survive. Under the Hobbesian pathway, the odds of nuclear disaster would rise substantially.

Should the United States withdraw its forward military presence, Japan has the capacity to rapidly become a large nuclear weapons state. Japan has decades of experience with its nuclear enterprise, which operates fifty electrical generation reactors and has fully developed nuclear fuel reprocessing facilities and expertise.[11] Japan already possesses roughly nine tons of weapons-usable plutonium, enough for about two thousand nuclear weapons—more than the number of strategic nuclear weapons allowed on active service by the United States and Russia under the New START Treaty.[12] In April 2013 the Japanese government decided to proceed with the opening of the Rokkasho reprocessing facility, which will have the capacity to produce an additional nine tons of plutonium annually from spent fuel at Japan's nuclear power plants.[13]

As a world leader in industrial machining and electronics, there is no doubt that Japan also has the ability to manufacture the other exotic components of nuclear weapons. Japanese officials remind observers concerned about its nuclear capacity that the country's nuclear enterprise is closely supervised by the International Atomic Energy Agency (IAEA). But it is also the case that Japan already has all of the ingredients required to quickly become a major nuclear weapons state should a change in the security environment in the region compel its leaders to make that decision.

Japan also already possesses the means to deliver nuclear warheads to targets anywhere in the region. Japan's civilian space agency has operated since 1955 and has deep experience with liquid- and solid-fuel missiles. Japan put its first satellite into Earth orbit in 1970 and has recorded scores of successful space launches.[14] Japan's experience with satellite construction and its participation in the International Space Station program demonstrate the country's expertise with payloads, sensors, telemetry, and space maneuvering.[15] Japan's current boosters, with the capacity to lift over ten tons into low earth orbit, show missile capacity easily exceeding that required for military intercontinental ballistic missiles.[16] In sum, Japan possesses the technical expertise and capacity to become an intercontinental missile power in short order, should a security vacuum created by a U.S. withdrawal from the region make that necessary.

Although South Korea would take more time than Japan, it too could become a nuclear weapons state. Indeed, some political leaders there have recently agitated for this course. If such action is taken, these leaders may be responding to popular wishes; after North Korea detonated its third nuclear device in February 2013, two public opinion surveys in South Korea showed that 64 to 66 percent of those surveyed believed that South Korea should have its own nuclear arsenal.[17] At the same moment, South Korean leaders pressed the U.S. government to modify an agreement between the two countries so that South Korea could build the same nuclear fuel reprocessing capacity that Japan has been allowed since the early 1980s. Such a capacity would allow South Korea to reprocess the spent fuel from its twenty-two nuclear power plants into weapons-grade plutonium.[18] As with Japan, South Korea possesses the industrial and electronics expertise to fashion the other components required for deliverable nuclear weapons. South Korean officials deny that the government is interested in nuclear weapons and remind observers that the country's nuclear enterprise remains under IAEA supervision. But the country is just a few steps away from having the capacity to produce substantial amounts of bomb-grade nuclear material, a capability that a large majority of the public seems to support.

South Korea recently demonstrated a new class of cruise missile with a one-thousand-kilometer range. In a 2013 exercise, the South Korean navy scored hits on targets with the new cruise missile launched from a destroyer and a submarine.[19] During the 1980s the United States fitted similar cruise missiles with nuclear warheads, and Israel is thought to have done the same with its submarine-launched cruise missiles.[20] Launched from ground positions inside South Korea, the missiles have the range to reach not only all of North Korea, but also Tokyo, Beijing, and Shanghai. When deployed on South Korean submarines, an even greater number of targets come in range.

Thus, although South Korea would take longer than Japan, it already has most of the nuclear enterprise and missile capacity it needs to become an effective nuclear weapons state. Perhaps equally important for political leaders responsible for such a decision, the South Korean public backs such a move. It seems rational to surmise that the intensity of such a view would only increase should either the United States reduce its security presence or Japan acquire its own nuclear arsenal.

India is already a substantial nuclear and missile power and has the capacity to further expand its capabilities and inventories. India is thought to have eighty to one hundred nuclear weapons based around plutonium cores (India conducted three underground nuclear tests in 1998). The nation also possesses up to 11.5 metric tons of reactor-grade plutonium in spent nuclear fuel which in theory could be reprocessed into enough bomb-grade plutonium for at least two thousand additional weapons.[21]

India has an active missile program and is adding new missiles to its inventory that will allow India to deliver nuclear strikes across the Asian region. In April 2012 India tested the Agni-5 missile, with additional testing in 2013.[22] The missile has a range of five thousand kilometers—sufficient to reach targets throughout China and into the western Pacific.[23] India is also testing a submarine-launched ballistic missile, the deployment of which would increase the survivability of India's nuclear capacity.[24] India will thus soon have the capability to deliver military power into the western Pacific, should its interests require it to do so—a development policymakers and military planners in the region will have to take into account.

Taiwan presents perhaps the least likely, but also the most provocative, case of nuclear weapons potential in the region. In the 1970s and again in the 1980s, Taiwan launched clandestine nuclear fuel reprocessing programs aimed at providing it with its own nuclear deterrent against mainland China. Both times, the United States forced Taiwan to abandon these programs.[25] Taiwan has stored spent nuclear fuel at three two-unit nuclear power plants, which could be reprocessed into bomb-grade plutonium if Taiwan built a facility to do so, as it attempted to do clandestinely in the 1970s and 1980s. Taiwan also possesses the industrial and electronics expertise to assemble a deliverable nuclear weapon.

Taiwan is developing an indigenously produced long-range land-attack cruise missile that in theory could be armed with a nuclear warhead. The missile, named Cloud Peak, has a range of 1,200 and possibly 2,000 kilometers and will be mounted on mobile transporters.[26]

The leadership in Beijing would view a decision by Taiwan to acquire nuclear weapons as highly provocative and quite possibly a casus belli. Beijing would likely view such a development as tantamount to a declaration of independence, something that Beijing in the past has stated it would resist with force. Under current circumstances, Taiwan appears to have no interest in this course. But a withdrawal of the U.S. security presence would be a different matter, especially if it led to nuclear and missile races elsewhere in the region. In that event a Taiwanese nuclear program could go from being a highly remote case to perhaps the most likely path to war in the region.

The Case against Offshore Balancing

There are several well-respected scholars who view nuclear proliferation in the region, especially for Japan, as a favorable path, not a course to dread. These scholars argue that the United States should reduce its costs and risks by extracting itself from its commitments to the region. Should countries such as Japan then require a large nuclear weapons capability as something necessary to establish an intra-region balance of power, these scholars assert that such an outcome is both logical and should be encouraged.

In his book *The Peace of Illusions: American Grand Strategy from 1940 to the Present*, Christopher Layne, professor of international affairs at

Texas A&M University, makes the case for a policy of offshore balancing. According to Layne, the offshore balancing strategy assumes that the only American strategic interest at stake in Eurasia is preventing the emergence of a Eurasian hegemon, an event that Layne asserts could (but might not) threaten U.S. interests.[27] According to Layne, wars between Eurasian great powers should not otherwise draw in the United States. Under a policy of offshore balancing, the United States would extract itself from its present security commitments in the Asia-Pacific region (and from Europe also) and then expect the great powers in Eurasia to manage their own security. According to Layne, this strategy would isolate the United States from the effects of conflicts in Eurasia and preserve America's freedom of action.[28] To many observers, offshore balancing appears to offer an attractive alternative to the rising costs and risks of forward engagement, especially as China's military capacity and its geopolitical interests expand.

Offshore balancing seeks to reduce America's risks by forswearing security commitments and thus creating freedom of action for U.S. policymakers. However, offshore balancing would require U.S. policymakers to take on a different set of risks and to accept some questionable assumptions. For example, in *The Peace of Illusions*, Layne is little concerned with the prospect of multisided and destabilizing nuclear and missile races that would surely occur in the wake of a U.S. withdrawal from the region. He asserts, "Great power wars in Eurasia don't happen often," a view that dismisses the stabilizing role the United States has played over the past seven decades and that ignores the much greater destructive potential that would reside in the region under the regime he prefers, should another war occur.[29] Layne similarly downplays the consequences to the U.S. economy from a catastrophic war in Asia, setting aside the more than 8 percent of U.S. output that is sold to the region, not to mention the second- and third-order effects to the global economy from a great power conflict in the region.[30]

As mentioned earlier, offshore balancing is premised on the possibility that the United States might need to intervene in Eurasia in order to prevent a hegemon from establishing a position that would threaten U.S. interests. Offshore balancing would not only increase the likelihood that the United States would have to return during a conflict to restore stability (because without a U.S. forward presence, the likelihood of major power conflict rises), the strategy ensures that the U.S. would have to do so under very unfavorable circumstances. Offshore balancing is premised on the United States intervening on the losing side during a conflict, if it appears that an undesirable hegemon might triumph. The three times the United States performed this task during the twentieth century (World War I and the European and Pacific sides of Eurasia in World War II), the costs of doing so were very high. In all three cases, U.S. intervention occurred after the potential hegemons had weakened the Allies the U.S. intervened to support and after the potential hegemons had built up their military power and captured forward positions. In these cases, an offshore balancing policy sacrificed an opportunity to prevent conflict in the first place and ensured that subsequent U.S. military campaigns to restore balance from offshore were costly in treasure and blood for U.S. soldiers.

Those painful experiences have led all U.S. presidents since World War II, and the vast majority of U.S. policymakers from all political persuasions, to reject offshore balancing and to support forward presence instead. Proponents of offshore balancing assert that the strategy reduces America's risks. In fact, it merely exchanges one set of risks for another. Since the 1940s U.S. policymakers have found the risks of forward engagement more subject to their management and adjustment—a preferable position compared to voluntarily opting out of any influence on international events. And when offshore balancing was actually employed during the first half of the twentieth century, the results were horrific. With the proliferation of nuclear weapons and missiles (a policy actually supported by offshore balancing advocates), the results of a hypothetical offshore balancing strategy could be even more catastrophic. It is little wonder that U.S. policymakers across the political spectrum have had little use for the approach.

Can the United States Safely Accommodate China's Rise?

There is only one answer to that question: the United States must—it has no choice. China is a great power, with rapidly expanding economic, diplomatic, and military power. The United States is obviously a great power too, and its economic and military power will also expand in the future, in absolute if not relative terms. Both countries have an obligation, for both practical and moral reasons, to find a way to coexist.

The problem is how, exactly, this mutual accommodation will occur. What will be the terms and conditions that might lead to a stable and mutually satisfactory arrangement in the Asia-Pacific region? As this chapter has argued, it is a question that China and the United States cannot decide by themselves; the other powers in the region will have their say, whether they are included in the conversation or not.

In his book *The China Choice: Why America Should Share Power,* Hugh White, a professor of strategic studies at Australia National University and a former official in the Australian government, proposes a framework for accommodating China's rising power.[31] White asserts that China's future power and its desire to use that power to guarantee its security interests will make the sustaining of America's primacy in the Asia-Pacific region untenable. He points out that China is already the most formidable country the United States has ever faced and concludes that an attempt by the United States to defend a position that is no longer sustainable will lead to a conflict that is unnecessary and that would cripple America's interests. At the same time, White rejects offshore balancing and a U.S. abandonment of the region. According to White, the United States, China, and other great powers in the region need to fashion a new and sustainable security order.

White proposes a "concert of powers" that would negotiate a stable arrangement that satisfies the security interests of the region's great powers.[32] White proposes that the United States, China, India, and Japan negotiate "spheres of influence" loosely modeled on the great-power negotiation after the Napoleonic wars that stabilized Europe's security for much of the remainder of the nineteenth century. White concedes that the Asia-Pacific's medium and small powers—including his own Australia—would be left out of the process and would be forced to accept their position in any new structure. But White asserts that for such medium and small nations, this outcome would be better for them than the likely alternative, a great-power conflict. White argues that U.S. leaders will have to accept that America's status in the region is no longer one of primacy but rather equality with the three other great powers, a reckoning he admits will be exceptionally difficult for the U.S. political system. For White, equality for Japan also implies the end of the U.S.-Japanese alliance and Japan's emergence as a nuclear and regional missile power.

This formulation makes several rather optimistic assumptions. It assumes that there will be a convenient convergence between what each of the four great powers is willing to concede as nonvital to its prospective sphere of influence, and what the other great powers will find acceptable for their security interests. The hoped-for outcome is mutually acceptable and non-overlapping spheres of influence.

For example, White suggests that the Japanese and U.S. spheres of influence would center on maritime interests in the western Pacific, while India and China would be satisfied with purely continental domains. But why would a Chinese sphere of influence restricted to, say, Indochina, have any relevance to China's concerns about the exposure of its economy to the South China Sea, the Strait of Malacca, and the Indian Ocean? It is simply that the vital interests of most of the region's powers, great and non-great, overlap and cannot be neatly divided up by contiguous spheres of influence. This is especially the case for the region's vast maritime areas and is a cardinal reason for the concept of the global commons and free international transit through it.

White admits that there would be immense practical difficulties in actually implementing his vision of a great-power "Concert of Asia." He has proposed it because he believes that the alternative, attempting to sustain U.S. primacy, is even more dangerous. But White's proposal still doesn't resolve the underlying conflicts. On the one hand, he assumes that China cannot be persuaded to accept the current rules-based international system in the region, even though the country has accepted this system thus far, and greatly to its benefit. On the other hand, White assumes that China will find its security interests satisfied with the concession of a sphere of influence that does little to advance the interests that are vital to it.

White's attempt at accommodating China would achieve little good while inflicting great harm. The result, as with offshore balancing, would be the region's descent into a multisided, Hobbesian security competition resembling the pre–World War I instability that finally resulted in a great-power war. With vital interests overlapping in so many areas, there is no chance of negotiating stable spheres of influence. Although White sees the 1815 Congress of Vienna as his model, the 1938 Munich Agreement, by which Europe's great powers agreed to dismember Czechoslovakia on the eve of World War II, is more fitting. It is highly likely that many of Asia's middle and small powers would not accept an arrangement that hands them their fate without their consent. Resistance would be likely and destabilizing. Finally, the pullback of U.S. security guarantees, combined with Japan's emergence as a nuclear weapons state, would surely catalyze disruptive arms races that would thwart the very stability White's "concert of powers" envisions. White is right to ask whether the status quo, guided by U.S. primacy, is sustainable. Unfortunately, his proposed solution would only increase the region's danger.

Despite the Costs, U.S. Forward Presence Is the Best Approach

As later discussed, the costs to the United States of maintaining the existing rules-based international order in the Asia-Pacific region are going to rise substantially. Past U.S. policymakers and military planners have not prepared adequately for this challenge. The Obama administration's "rebalance" to the region is the right idea, but it has come late and without the resources and strategy to be effective. Even so, the policy of U.S. primacy in the region, supported by a forward military presence, is the least risky and ultimately least costly of all of the alternatives.

Under these circumstances, the goal of the U.S. forward presence strategy will not be just to maintain stability in the region and circumvent the arrival of a Hobbesian security competition. Added to these long-standing missions is a new task: persuading China's leaders to continue accepting the status quo in spite of China's rising global security interests. This task will require the United States and its partners in the region to both reassure China that the existing rule-based system will continue to work for China's benefit while also dissuading China from attempting to unilaterally change the region's order in a way that would harm the interests and sovereignty of the United States and its partners. The United States and its friends will need a long-term and sustainable strategy to accomplish these goals, issues to be later explored in depth.

There are alternatives to this approach, as examined above. Proponents of these alternatives are seeking other strategies that will reduce America's exposure to risk, cut its security costs, or fashion a diplomatic solution that will avert a clash of interests among the region's great powers. However, these alternatives to forward presence will not achieve these aims. Offshore balancing aims to reduce America's exposure to risky entanglements and to reduce the costly burden of forward presence. Proponents claim that this approach will give U.S. policymakers more freedom of action, including the option to reassert U.S. power in Eurasia to prevent the arrival of a hegemon that could threaten U.S. interests. However, this strategy only assures dangerous great-power instability in Eurasia that will very likely result in a costly U.S. return under highly unfavorable circumstances. The U.S. experience with offshore balancing during the first half of the twentieth century was very expensive, with two world wars and the three costly U.S. military campaigns required to restore stability. It is little wonder that no U.S. president since World War II has returned to offshore balancing.

Others call for allowing China a sphere of influence in the hope that this will accommodate China's security concerns and thus avoid conflict. But the sphere that China will want will very likely overlap with interests vital to both the United States and its partners in the region. Accommodation is thus unlikely to avoid conflict. What it would do is spark an intense regional arms race after it became clear that the United States was willing to abandon its security commitments. The late nineteenth and twentieth centuries showed that regional great-power arms races can end very badly.

The *Global Trends 2030* report discusses substantial changes to the global energy markets and the prospect that increased U.S. hydrocarbon production may result in the elimination of U.S. crude oil imports within ten to twenty years.[33] Some have asserted that this development would allow the United States to reduce its global security responsibilities. While that argument might have bearing on future U.S. strategy in the Middle East (a topic outside the scope of this book), the prospect of U.S. energy independence does not alter America's strategic calculation for East Asia.

Indeed it is China's growing dependence on crude oil from the Middle East, combined with the rest of East Asia's already-heavy dependence, that will only amplify the region's looming security competition.

All of East Asia, especially China, will have increasing dependence on the maritime oil traffic that runs from the Middle East, across the Indian Ocean, through the Strait of Malacca and Indonesia's other straits, and up through the South and East China Seas and the western Pacific. In spite of hydrocarbon exploration in Central Asia and eastern Russia and the construction of additional pipeline capacity in those areas, the countries in East Asia (including China) will continue to heavily depend on crude oil from the Middle East and Africa. For example, the U.S. Energy Information Administration forecasts that in 2020 Asia will consume 34 million barrels of crude oil and other liquid fuels per day while producing only 8.8 million barrels per day, thus requiring daily imports of 25.2 million barrels to fill the gap.[34] Net exports of crude oil from Russia and the Caspian Sea region in 2020 are expected to total 8.7 million barrels per day.[35] Even if all of this production were to go to Asia (an unlikely outcome, as Russia currently sends 78 percent of its crude oil exports to Europe, resulting in geopolitical leverage over Europe that future Russian leaders will no doubt wish to maintain), Asia will continue to rely heavily on oil shipped by tankers from the Middle East and Africa.[36] The oil demand from East Asia is too large and the production capacity from Central Asia and Russia too small by comparison for any other outcome to occur. This will be the result for Asia whether the United States is an oil importer or not.

Developments in the global energy markets in the years ahead will not reduce the security competition in East Asia. None of the countries in the region will be able to escape dependence on oil tanker traffic from the Middle East and Africa and thus they will remain wary of military developments that might threaten that vulnerability. America's strong interest in Asia's stability will persist, if only because of the strong linkage between the U.S. economy and the region, a relationship that will continue even if the United States achieves energy independence. Developments in the global energy markets will not change the requirement that the United States remain East Asia's security guarantor in the decades ahead.

Finally, there is the impulse to conclude that China will simply become too powerful to either confront or dissuade and that it will eventually become foolish to even try. At the same time, China's neighbors should be powerful enough to collectively defend themselves without requiring the United States to entangle itself in a problem that these countries should fix for themselves.

The U.S. forward presence strategy in the Asia-Pacific region is not charity work. The United States has performed this task for seven decades in order to protect U.S. security, to avert more costly great-power wars that would inevitably involve the United States, and to bolster America's standard of living by promoting the security and growth of its trading partners in the region. Most crucially, as an outsider to the region with no territorial claims, the United States is trusted to be the security guarantor, a role the countries in the region would never grant to one of their neighbors. That is why the forward presence approach has worked so well for so long.

The price of continuing this success is now going up. China's rise, an inevitable fact, is shaking up the region's long-standing security structure. In spite of the Obama administration's "rebalance" to Asia and its pledge to maintain security spending in the region,[37] there are indications that many in the region have doubts about the future of America's forward presence. As mentioned above, a majority in South Korea believe that country should have nuclear weapons. Parliamentary elections in Japan in 2012 and 2013 strongly supported a more nationalist government that is expanding Japan's defense spending and its military doctrine. And the region's non-Chinese defense spending is expected to leap 55 percent over the next five years ending in 2018.[38] These may be early signs that the *Global Trends* Hobbesian scenario is unfolding, in response to faltering confidence in America's security commitment to the region.

The United States has no choice but to sustain its forward presence strategy. Although costly, all of the other alternatives are worse. Sustaining forward presence, however, will require making major changes to how the U.S. military equips, trains, and deploys its forces in the region. The most important role for U.S. military forces is to deter conflict by compelling potential adversaries to conclude that they would lose if they used force against U.S. interests. China's military modernization, combined with U.S. complacency in East Asia, is now calling the sustainment of this deterrence into question. Why this happened and what the implications will be for U.S. strategy are subjects of the next chapter.

 *Chapter 3*

AMERICA'S ARCHAIC MILITARY MACHINE IN THE PACIFIC

W hy a forward presence of U.S. military forces in East Asia is the least costly and least risky strategy for protecting U.S. interests was explained in chapter 2. Forward presence is also the strategy the United States has consistently implemented since the end of World War II. Examining the history of how U.S. policymakers, military commanders, and planners have implemented this strategy reveals remarkable stability in doctrine, equipment, training, and tactics, even as adversaries have changed and disruptive military technologies have appeared.

The extraordinary constancy in how the United States has implemented forward presence in the region could be attributed to the simple axiom "If it ain't broke, don't fix it." The goal of forward presence has been to protect stability and prevent the outbreak of a war between major powers. Since the region has not experienced a significant war between major powers since 1945, the means and ways by which U.S. policymakers and military planners have implemented forward presence over the past six decades appears successful. With that record of success concerning an issue of such grave national importance, it is natural to conclude that the United States should continue with an approach that has brought such good results.

That conclusion is now dangerously wrong (as asserted here and in the next chapter). China's military modernization program, begun in earnest after PLA planners carefully studied the results of the 1991 Persian Gulf War and the 1995–96 Taiwan Strait crises, has been specifically designed to exploit vulnerabilities in U.S. force structure, doctrine, and planning. Assumptions that U.S. commanders have long taken for granted will no longer be operative by the end of this decade. Under these conditions, U.S. military forces in the region, while on paper still the most formidable, will be vulnerable to frustration and defeat in a potential conflict against China. Should China's policymakers and military planners reach this conclusion, it could result in greater Chinese aggressiveness during a crisis and an increased chance of conflict. U.S. policymakers and planners need to urgently implement reforms to defense strategy, doctrine, acquisition, and war plans if they hope to maintain America's forward presence in the region.

Simply put, military doctrine, long-ingrained service cultures, and defense acquisition practices have resulted in U.S. military forces that are far too heavily weighted toward short-range weapon systems unsuited for the vast operational distances in East Asia. Military commanders and planners have become too comfortable with the assumption that their lines of communication between forward theaters and the continental United States will remain as unchallenged as they have been since 1945. Finally, U.S. military planners continue to assume that they will be able to sustain in future conflicts the "American way of war," centered on maximizing the number of combat aircraft sorties from centralized air bases and aircraft carriers, just as their predecessors have consistently done since 1945.

China's military planners have studied U.S. operating methods and have developed weapon systems and plans of their own to thwart them. By next decade, China will have the capacity to inflict substantial damage on U.S. forces in the western Pacific, out to about two thousand kilometers from China's coast. China's carefully designed strategy thus threatens to overturn the assumptions and doctrine that U.S. planners have taken for granted for so many decades.

The Origins of U.S. Military Strategy in the Western Pacific

To understand why U.S. forces in the western Pacific are becoming increasingly vulnerable, we must examine the history of America's forward presence in the region. The current array of U.S. bases and patterns of operations in East Asia trace their lineage to the middle of World War II, when the United States was still close to the beginning of its bloody march across the Pacific toward Japan and eastern Eurasia. Seven decades later, and in the face of remarkable changes in alliances and military technology, it is extraordinary how closely the current U.S. basing and operational architecture in the region resembles the postwar visions outlined by military planners during World War II.

In 1943 planners at the Joint Chiefs of Staff (JCS) in Washington prepared a classified postwar basing study. Titled JCS 570/2 and approved by President Franklin Roosevelt on November 23, 1943, the study identified sixty-six foreign sites where planners concluded access was required to meet the postwar mission requirements contemplated at that time.[1] Roosevelt's approval of the basing plan occurred immediately prior to the Tehran Conference, at which Roosevelt discussed postwar planning with British prime minister Winston Churchill and Soviet leader Joseph Stalin.[2]

In the Pacific region, the authors of JCS 570/2 foresaw basing requirements across the main island chains in the central Pacific and then all the way to the Eurasian mainland itself. At the western perimeter, the list included sites in Bangkok, the Philippines, Formosa, Hainan Island, mainland China, the Ryukyu chain, Japan, Korea, and the Kurile Islands.[3] The planners' stated assumptions included the defeat of the three Axis powers, the continued postwar solidarity of the anti-Axis alliance (which in 1943 included the Soviet Union and China), and the requirement to conduct postwar peace enforcement missions. The planners also assumed that the United States would have ongoing postwar security interests in the central Pacific and East Asia.[4]

The designers of JCS 570/2 and its successor plans did not envision establishing large basing hubs and garrisons at these locations. Rather they sought access rights, mainly for U.S. airpower, in order to be in a position to project power if needed and to retain the flexibility to respond to uncertain contingencies. The planners also sought to deny these sites to others by gaining access rights first.[5] The broader strategy behind the basing plan was to establish a "perimeter defense in depth," the border of which would roughly correspond to the Allied military positions in central Europe, the Middle East, South Asia, and the Far East at the conclusion of the war. Inside this perimeter, the United States expected to have complete control, especially over the Atlantic and Pacific Oceans.[6]

We can thus see that as early as November 1943, policymakers and military planners in Washington had disposed of offshore balancing as a future security strategy for the United States. At that point in World War II, Allied gains in the Pacific were limited to New Guinea and the Solomon and Gilbert Islands, with most of the bloodiest fighting still ahead. In the European theater, Allied forces still struggled to suppress Germany's two access denial threats—its submarine fleet and air defense network over northwest Europe. Ground fighting for the U.S. Army was confined to southern Italy. Again, the worst fighting in Western Europe had yet to occur.

But U.S. policymakers and planners had seen enough to conclude that after the war they were not willing to forfeit the sea and air control they were currently paying so much to achieve. They further concluded that in the future, America's first line of defense would be on Eurasia itself; the nineteenth-century notion of oceanic protection had proved to be a folly. Finally, U.S. policymakers at that time already perceived that U.S. military

power in the postwar era must be ready to respond to unknowable con-
tingences on both ends of Eurasia. These planning assumptions reflected
a conclusion by Washington policymakers: the United States would better protect its interests if it maintained a forward military presence on the
perimeter of Eurasia. For the U.S. policymakers who struggled with the
costs of fighting that great war, World War II killed the concepts of "splen-
did isolation" and offshore balancing as credible national strategies.

In October 1945, JCS 570/40, a successor to JCS 570/2, added basing
requirements in Indochina, India, and Pakistan. The updated plan also recognized that the Soviet Union's occupation of the Kurile Islands would rule
out U.S. bases there.[7] However, this plan and its successors remained out of
reach to U.S. military commanders and planners for the five years after the
Axis defeat. Resistance from both the State Department and several Allies
prevented the U.S. military from immediately establishing the perimeter-
defense-in-depth approach first laid out in 1943.[8]

The Soviet Union's break with the West, the triumph of the PLA in
China's civil war in 1949, and the outbreak of the Korean War resuscitated
the Joint Chiefs' overseas basing vision. However, rather than an archipelago of largely ungarrisoned access rights envisioned in JCS 570/2 and
JCS 570/40, the war in Korea and the standoff against the Soviet army in
central Europe resulted in the construction of large main operating bases
in Germany, South Korea, and Japan. Large supporting bases in the United
Kingdom, Italy, Turkey, and the Philippines sustained the expected front
lines in these two theaters. JCS 570/2 and JCS 570/40 contemplated an
array of air and naval access points that would support flexible and responsive expeditionary forces. Instead, the Korean War and the Cold War face-
off in Europe resulted in massive garrisons of ground forces, supported by
tactical airpower, and present on the terrain where they expected to fight the
next war.[9] This arrangement of bases, alliance relationships, and associated
training operations remained largely unchanged for the next four decades.

Coagulation around Korea

The Cold War, and particularly the Korean War, swept away any remaining resistance, either in Washington or in most host nations, to the strategy of U.S. forward presence in Eurasia.[10] By the mid-1950s U.S. planners
obtained either permanent bases or base access to support two broad missions. The first mission was strategic nuclear deterrence against the Soviet
Union. This mission required access to air bases that would support U.S. Air
Force bombers, tankers, and reconnaissance aircraft around that country's
long periphery.[11] The second mission was defending Western Europe from

a possible surprise attack by the large Warsaw Pact forces based in central Europe. In Asia, U.S. forces remained on watch in South Korea and Japan in the wake of the Korean War's murky ending.

The second mission, the ground defense of Western Europe, South Korea, and Japan, resulted in the permanent basing of hundreds of thousands of U.S. troops on both ends of Eurasia. The specific tactical missions in both theaters resulted in these forces being concentrated in a few frontline countries. By 1957 over 244,000 U.S. troops were based in Germany, over 150,000 in Japan (including Okinawa), and over 71,000 in South Korea. Back from the two fronts but in support of them were substantial garrisons in Great Britain, France, and the Philippines.[12]

In East Asia, U.S. military power began the Cold War era overwhelmingly concentrated in the northwest corner of the Pacific Ocean, poised for renewed combat in Korea. These forces have remained concentrated there up to the present. The one substantial excursion from this rule was the U.S. intervention in Vietnam, which saw large commitments from all four military services from 1965 to 1972.[13] The U.S. decision to fight in Vietnam was guided by the perimeter-defense-in-depth theory first drawn up in JCS 570/2 in 1943, which identified ongoing U.S. security interests in Eurasia and called for the flexibility to respond to unpredictable security contingencies.[14] Although the military campaign in Vietnam failed to achieve U.S. strategic objectives, no U.S. administration since has given serious consideration to abandoning the concept of perimeter defense and forward presence in Eurasia.

The end of the Vietnam War brought the pattern of U.S. military positioning in East Asia roughly back to the status quo antebellum, namely highly concentrated in South Korea and Japan. In addition to the concentration of ground and tactical air forces for South Korea's defense, commanders and military planners began developing plans to employ the U.S. Pacific Fleet to strike Soviet military facilities in Russia's Far East in the event of a wider war against the Warsaw Pact.

In the late 1970s Adm. Thomas Hayward, then-commander of the U.S. Pacific Fleet (and previously commander of U.S. Seventh Fleet, responsible for the western Pacific), promoted Project Sea Strike, which would greatly alter the wartime strategy of the Pacific Fleet. In the event of a war in Europe, previous war plans called for the Pacific Fleet to transit to the Atlantic to reinforce naval operations there. During his time as Pacific Fleet commander, Hayward argued for keeping the Pacific Fleet in the Pacific and employing the fleet's aircraft carriers for conventional strike operations targeting Soviet military facilities in Petropavlovsk, Vladivostok, and the Kurile Islands.[15]

Hayward reasoned that this horizontal escalation of a European-centered conflict would stretch Soviet military resources, prevent redeployment of Soviet assets from the Far East to the European theater, absorb Soviet decision-making attention, and degrade the ability of Soviet forces in the Asian theater to conduct offensive action. The naval offensive action in Operation Sea Strike strongly influenced the development of the Navy's overall maritime strategy that appeared in 1986.[16] As for the disposition of U.S. military power in the Pacific, Sea Strike and the later 1986 maritime strategy only added to the already high concentration in the northwest Pacific.

The collapse of the Soviet Union in 1991 did not lessen the concentration of U.S. military power in the northwest Pacific; it paradoxically increased it. In 1992 the Philippines government ordered the United States to vacate the large air and naval bases it used on the western side of Luzon Island. After serving as critical support facilities during the Vietnam War, these bases were well located to support U.S. air and naval patrolling of the sea lines of communication in the South China Sea, the value of which would greatly expand in the decades to follow. While the Cold War persisted, Filipino policymakers had reason to be wary of Vietnam, a Soviet client and frequent host of detachments of Soviet naval and airpower. But after the Soviet collapse in 1991, domestic hostility to a perceived quasi-colonial American presence at the bases became the top priority for these leaders. The ejection of U.S. forces from the facilities inevitably reduced the frequency and magnitude of U.S. forward presence in the South China Sea and further increased the concentration of U.S. forces around Korea and Japan.

But as discussed in the introduction and chapter 1, conflict flashpoints are now apparent in the East and South China Seas, in some cases over three thousand kilometers south of the main U.S. military concentration around Korea. Equally problematic is the easy proximity of these flashpoints to China's airpower and naval power. China has numerous basing options to project military power over these disputed territories, whereas U.S. options are comparatively constrained.

Over the past several years, U.S. diplomats and military planners have scrambled to improve basing options for U.S. military forces in the southwest Pacific. For example, the United States is establishing rotational deployments of four Littoral Combat Ships (LCS) to Singapore and battalion-sized Marine Corps air-ground task forces to Darwin, Australia.[17] The Philippine government has reversed its previous objections to U.S. military forces and now again hosts their presence, albeit for temporary training deployments only.[18] Finally, the U.S. Defense Department is expanding its basing capacities on Guam and neighboring islands Tinian and Saipan to support additional submarines, aircraft, and a brigade-sized Marine Corps

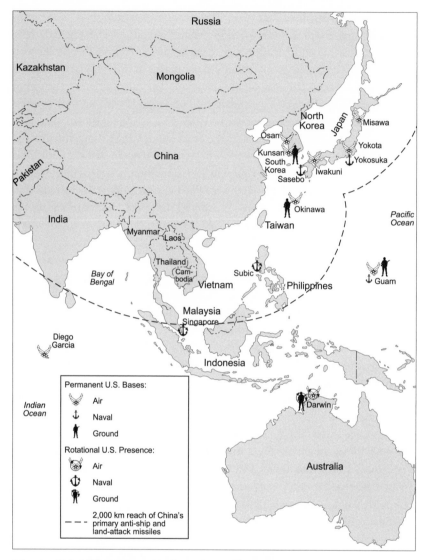

Map 3:   U.S. Military Bases in the Asia-Pacific Region

air-ground task force to be relocated from Okinawa.[19] Although the move-
ment of Marines from Okinawa to Guam actually takes them farther away
from the East and South China Seas, expanding the facilities on Guam and
neighboring islands increases the capacity to respond to contingencies in the
southwest Pacific and diversifies basing risk.

The recent efforts to diversify basing options in the western Pacific and
to expand the U.S. military presence in the southwest Pacific are helpful.

But by themselves, these moves will not be enough to staunch the deterioration of the U.S. military position in the region. The remarkably constant concentration of U.S. forces in and around Korea leaves these forces misplaced for the increasing security problems and flashpoints well to the south.

The congealing of U.S. military power in bases in the northwest corner of the Pacific would not matter so much if that military power itself were more flexible and able to deliver its effects from longer ranges. Alas, that it not the case, due to institutional cultures and preferences that became ingrained during the long and static Cold War. Along with basing geography, the institutional culture of U.S. military forces in the region is another part of the history that has led to the strategic problems policymakers and commanders now face.

Cold War Stasis Creates Its Own Military Culture

Tasked with defending Germany and South Korea against the possibility of a large, high-intensity mechanized blitzkrieg (the preferred conventional military doctrine of the former Soviet Union and most of its satellites), U.S. defense planners set about building forces, doctrine, and training to thwart this prospect on these two fronts. These planners also soon came to realize that these would not be fleeting planning requirements; as the Cold War congealed on these fronts, the missions in these two theaters became open-ended.

The long duration of the military missions in Germany and South Korea caused the U.S. military to develop a specific tactical culture that influenced the design and procurement of generations of weapons, warfighting doctrine, training, and personnel selection and promotion policies. Over time (and not hardly in a straight-line fashion), these ingrained cultural habits succeeded in producing a joint military force that displayed impressive tactical and operational competence, at least when deployed against adversaries that mimicked the anticipated high-intensity Soviet threat.

U.S. joint and combined arms operations in Panama in 1989, the Persian Gulf in 1991, and Iraq in the spring of 2003 displayed this tactical and operational (if not strategic) competence. Those three missions were well suited for the particular military force the United States established for combat in Germany and South Korea during the long Cold War. But as we will see, long-standing practices built up over many decades have resulted in a U.S. military posture in East Asia that is not prepared for the challenge China will present by 2020.

China is exploiting a revolution in conventional missile and sensor technology that is greatly expanding the ability of its forces, mostly land based, to threaten even well-defended warships and military targets thousands of kilometers from its territory. The naval dimension of this technical revolution actually began in the Soviet Union in the 1970s, with worrying consequences for U.S. naval planners and others in the 1980s.[20] The rapid maturation and falling costs of the technology associated with the missile and sensor revolution is allowing the PLA to greatly expand on the techniques and tactics the Soviets began developing four decades ago (explained further in chapter 4).

To cope with China's emerging capabilities to dominate land and naval targets far into the Pacific Ocean, U.S. military forces would themselves need the ability to strike effectively at greater ranges. Regrettably, the trend across all four military services over the past five decades has been declines in long-range strike capacity and an ever greater weighting in weapon system portfolios on highly capable but short-ranged platforms. These harmful trends, a consequence of service cultures that hardened during and after the Cold War, will leave U.S. forces in the Pacific highly vulnerable by the end of the decade.

We can thus trace, at least in part, the origin of the current U.S. military culture, and its resulting preferences regarding weapon systems procurement, warfighting doctrine, training, and personnel policies, back to JCS 570/2 and the assumptions and policies embedded in that plan for post–World War II basing and operations. JCS 570/2 and its successors assumed that the United States would have command over the Atlantic and Pacific Oceans and thus would have an unhindered ability to move forces and their support from the continental United States to forward bases in Eurasia.

Under this assumption, the starting point for tactical operations would be any of the numerous U.S. bases around Eurasia. With the archipelago of bases around Eurasia that the U.S military created in the decade after World War II, the range that tactical forces would normally have to travel from a base to combat was assumed to be relatively short. These assumptions proved to be sound; from Korea in 1950 through to Afghanistan in 2014, U.S. forces for the most part operated at short distances from logistics hubs and tactical air bases and had unimpeded access to these bases across the oceans. As these assumptions were repeatedly confirmed over many decades and conflicts, U.S. procurement, doctrine, and training increasingly conformed to these conditions, eventually becoming a part of the services' cultures.

How the Air Force's Reach Got So Short

Since World War II, airpower has played a major role in U.S. military doctrine. U.S. military commanders and planners have viewed airpower as a U.S. competitive advantage and thus a function worthy of considerable funding. At the beginning of this period, long-range and short-range airpower both played prominent roles in doctrine and planning, and both were substantially represented in Air Force budgets. However, over the decades since, long-range strike capacity has suffered a sharp decline, with short-range tactical airpower capacity enjoying overwhelming dominance in policymaker attention and resources. This outcome has resulted in part from acceptance of the assumptions behind JCS 570/2 and its successors and in part from the habits formed from repeated access to overseas bases close to required action. Up to the present, commanders and planners have formulated decisions with these assumptions and cultures seemingly unquestioned, even as the strategic situation in the western Pacific is now a stark departure from these expectations.

In 1960 the U.S. Air Force operated 2,194 bombers and 5,488 short-range fighter and attack aircraft, a fighter-to-bomber ratio of 2.5 to 1. The arrival of long-range Air Force and Navy strategic nuclear missiles in the 1960s allowed the Air Force to retire the medium-range bombers that had performed nuclear deterrence up to that point. Thus by 1980 the number of bombers dropped to 414, resulting in a fighter-to-bomber ratio of 9.2 to 1. By the 1990s and the end of the Cold War, strategic arms control agreements, and the association of the bomber with now-déclassé nuclear weapons, resulted in a further withering of the bomber fleet down to 163 aircraft by 2009, with a resulting fighter-to-bomber ratio of 13.9 to 1.[21]

Comfort with the assumption of large, modern, and secure air bases close to the conflict—a requirement for a force so heavily weighted to short-range fighters—was confirmed by the 1991 Persian Gulf War, interventions in the Balkans later in the 1990s, the intervention in Iraq between 2003 and 2010, and the few large air bases the U.S. Air Force and U.S. Marine Corps established in Afghanistan over the past decade. The U.S. military's aircraft investment plan through 2022 assumes more of the same; the number of bombers will continue to drift down to 154, with Air Force fighter-to-bomber ratio predicted to be 12.3 to 1 by 2022.[22]

Of course the assumption that the Air Force would have access to close-in bases wasn't the only reason for the service's focus on short-range fighter aircraft. One of the main goals of airpower doctrine is to establish air superiority, the condition in which friendly air forces can attack the enemy without serious opposition, while simultaneously preventing enemy air forces the ability to mount serious attacks on friendly forces.[23] According to U.S. military doctrine, air superiority is a necessity: "no country has won a war in the face of enemy air superiority, no major offensive has succeeded against an opponent who controlled the air, and no defense has sustained itself against an enemy who had air superiority."[24]

Since World War II, the U.S. Air Force has looked to its fighter aircraft as the principal tools for establishing air superiority. They are viewed as flexible platforms for destroying adversary aircraft in the air and on the ground and for defending friendly airspace against adversary air attack. Other tools, including missiles and bombers, are also used for establishing air superiority. But for the Air Force, the first required tool for air superiority is possession of the world's best fighter, which will achieve dominance over all second-ranking opponents.

Until the 1990s, airpower planners considered adversary aircraft the most serious threat to their own air operations. Before precision-guided missile technology began to proliferate, missiles armed with conventional warheads were not deemed to have the accuracy necessary to threaten friendly air bases that hosted tactical fighter-attack aircraft within a combat theater. Only enemy aircraft employing pilot-aimed bombs and rockets could pose such a threat. For this reason the U.S. services and planners have put great weight on having the best fighters and antiaircraft missiles, in order to establish air superiority and preserve airpower as a U.S. competitive strength. U.S. air bases in Vietnam, Iraq, and Afghanistan did occasionally come under ground attack, either from mortars or infiltrators.[25] But such attacks have heretofore been viewed as nuisances, not a significant threat to continuing air operations.

Having emphasized the acquisition of first-rate fighter aircraft, and having them based at secure bases accessible to close-by targets, the Air Force's next logical priority was to establish a command and logistics system that would support the generation of a high and sustainable rate of combat sorties. Sustaining tactical fighter wings at a high operating tempo requires a high-capacity supply chain that flows fuel, ordnance, spare parts, and many other provisions to the bases. The logic of economies of scale has typically resulted in the Air Force preferring fewer large bases over a dispersion of smaller bases, which would be more difficult to supply for high sortie rates. Host nation limits and better physical security have also been factors resulting in the Air Force typically operating from a few large bases.

Concentration at a few large bases describes the current U.S. Air Force basing position in the western Pacific. The Air Force relies on six bases—two in South Korea, two on Japan's home islands, one on Okinawa, and one on Guam—to support its operations in the western Pacific. This concentration has resulted from the factors previously discussed. Economies of scale, host nation political constraints, and easing the task of physical security have led the Air Force to consolidate its operations at these few sites. Although the bases host aircraft covering the full range of functions (e.g., Air Force special operations and transport aircraft on Okinawa and a bomber contingent on Guam), the bases (with the exception of Guam) are sited within fighter range of the Eurasian landmass, a requirement for an Air Force so heavily weighted with short-range fighter aircraft. U.S. Navy and Marine Corps airpower in the western Pacific is also located on Japan and Okinawa, with all of these strike aircraft being short-range fighters.

The current structure and basing of land-based U.S. airpower in the western Pacific is thus a product of its history in the region and the service cultures that have solidified since World War II. Beginning with the planning for peace enforcement after World War II and extending up to the present, the design of U.S. airpower has assumed that U.S. airpower would have access to bases in Eurasia and that there would be little or no constraint on supplying those bases across the oceans. Air commanders planned to keep these forward bases operational and to generate high sortie rates through centralized logistics and by maintaining air superiority. Enemy aircraft were long thought to be the only substantial threat to these bases. As long as the United States had the best fighter aircraft, U.S. air planners believed they could thwart the most serious threat to their forward bases. These air war assumptions were confirmed through every conflict from Korea in 1950 to Afghanistan six decades later.

What began as planning assumptions after World War II has now transformed into service culture. The Air Force now has more than twelve fighters for every bomber in its inventory. It is thus of little surprise that one of the Air Force's top acquisition priorities is another short-range fighter-attack aircraft, the F-35A.[26] Meanwhile, recapitalizing the Air Force's old and still-shrinking bomber fleet remains a lesser priority; the Air Force acquired the newest of its B-52H models, which comprise 76 of its 159 bombers, in October 1962.[27] The Air Force's Fiscal Year 2014 budget allocated just $400 million for a research program for a future new bomber, the hypothetical appearance of which will not occur until the next decade.[28]

The rapid proliferation and falling costs of precision-guided missiles and munitions, coupled with the expanding range of these weapons, is a dramatic change to the operating conditions under which the Air Force has long operated. These changes are a growing threat to the service's operating procedures, especially in the western Pacific, a topic chapter 4 will explore.

The Navy's Range Comes Up Short, Too

Just as the Air Force's culture, inferred from its institutional behavior, is centered on its fighter community, the Navy's culture places a very heavy weight on its aircraft carriers and associated carrier air wings, which are also dominated by short-range fighter-attack aircraft. The Navy's submarine fleets are also prominent inside Navy culture; indeed, the deterrence provided by the Navy's ballistic missile submarines could arguably be the most consequential mission the U.S. Defense Department carries out every day. But the Navy's own institutional behavior suggests that Navy culture values its aircraft carriers above all else. In 1989 at the end of the Cold War, the Navy battle fleet numbered 592 ships, 14 of which were aircraft carriers.[29] In 2013 the Navy operated 284 ships, a 52 percent reduction from 1989. Of these vessels, 10 are aircraft carriers, rising to 11 when USS *Gerald R. Ford* joins the fleet in 2015, a 21 percent fall by comparison from the number in 1989.[30] The Navy's large force of cruisers, destroyers, and supply ships (with the exception of a handful assigned to national missile defense duty) exist to support and defend the aircraft carriers in wartime. Ranking lower in priority is their support to amphibious forces and the Marine Corps.

The Navy's culture, built up over decades of experience in a particularly stable and unthreatening maritime environment, has resulted in a strong institutional preference for aircraft carriers. The Navy's aircraft carriers won the war at sea in the Pacific during that war's critical early phases, when the Navy lacked many alternatives. Over later decades, the aircraft carrier proved itself highly effective at projecting power against land targets. Aircraft carriers have seemed to be excellent investments, with service lives running up to five decades. Navy planners have adapted them to changing times by altering and recapitalizing the air wing with constantly improving aircraft. For all of these reasons, Navy commanders and planners have reasonably concluded that the aircraft carrier has been a dominant U.S. competitive advantage and a proven benefit worth sustaining into the future.

But just like the Air Force, the Navy's assumptions and institutional culture are facing new challenges. China's expanding ability to project its shore-based military power far out to sea is already presenting tough challenges to the ways the Navy has long done business.

Aircraft carriers convincingly displaced battleships as the decisive warship after the 1942 fleet battles against Japan in the Coral Sea and near Midway Island. During those battles, Japanese and U.S. aircraft carriers showed that they could find and sink any warship and do so from much longer ranges than could battleships. The lesson for the U.S. Navy was that maintaining superiority in aircraft carriers and their aircraft would ensure superiority over adversary fleets and thus control of the seas.

But after World War II, the U.S. Navy found itself without any naval challengers and thus without an apparent justification for maintaining a strong aircraft carrier force in the postwar era. Meanwhile the pressing strategic task at the start of the ensuing Cold War was to deter the Soviet Union. The Air Force proposed the solution, a large fleet of long-range bombers armed with nuclear weapons, and requested scarce postwar defense money to build this capability.

The Navy was on its way to losing this interservice funding squabble when North Korea's surprise invasion of South Korea in June 1950 presented an opportunity for the Navy's carriers to demonstrate their utility. The North Korean army quickly overran most of the friendly air bases in the south, leaving the beleaguered U.S. and South Korean defenders of the Pusan perimeter without airpower. The U.S. Seventh Fleet quickly arrived to provide the airpower the ground forces inside the perimeter needed to repel the North Korean assault.[31] From that moment up to the present, power projection against land targets, rather than fleet battles in deep blue water, would be the main role—and justification—for the U.S. Navy's aircraft carriers.

During the remaining three years of the Korean War, eleven different large deck aircraft carriers served in combat. Naval aircrews from the Seventh Fleet's Task Force 77 flew 275,000 sorties during the war, amounting to 53 percent of the close air support and 40 percent of the interdiction sorties flown by U.S. combat aircraft from all four services.[32]

During the Vietnam War, the U.S. Navy once again demonstrated its capacity to project power ashore from aircraft carriers. It re-formed Task Force 77 at Yankee Station in the South China Sea in order to participate in sustained air campaigns such as Rolling Thunder and Linebacker.[33] From 1964 to 1973 Task Force 77 aircraft flew hundreds of thousands of attack sorties against targets in North and South Vietnam and had major roles in the war's air campaigns.

Operation Desert Storm, the 1991 campaign to drive the Iraqi army out of Kuwait, presented another opportunity for the U.S. Navy's aircraft carriers to demonstrate their power-projection capabilities. In January and February 1991 the Navy gathered 6 aircraft carriers and over 400 aircraft into the Red and Arabian Seas as part of the coalition air campaign.[34] The Navy's aircraft carriers have remained in the region, participating in both the Iraq and Afghanistan conflicts.

In all of these naval air campaigns, the Navy's aircraft carriers were able to sail close to the adversary's coast with little to fear. Once in this position, the priority for commanders and planners shifted to maximizing the task force's sustainable sortie rate—the same operational imperative for

Air Force planners operating from ostensibly secure air bases ashore. In the Navy's case, supply ships sailing across unchallenged oceans continuously reprovisioned the carrier task forces with fuel, ordnance, spare parts, and other required supplies.

Only once during the long era between World War II and the present did the Navy have to plan for a significant threat to this familiar routine. Beginning in the 1970s the Soviet Union appeared to be mastering the elements of the "reconnaissance-strike complex," a development that might have menaced the Navy's aircraft carrier strike groups before they could come within range of Soviet land targets.

The "reconnaissance-strike complex," the Soviet long-range and land-based threat to the Navy's aircraft carriers, entailed three components: ocean surveillance satellites, submarines, and reconnaissance aircraft that would find the American aircraft carriers; the Tu-22M Backfire maritime strike bomber; and the Kh-22M Kitchen supersonic antiship cruise missile. Operating from land bases near Murmansk or the Soviet Far East, the Backfire had a combat radius of about 5,000 kilometers.[35] Added to this was the Kitchen's range of about 460 kilometers. Carrier strike group commanders had to reckon with a Soviet adversary that outranged the carrier's strike aircraft by a factor of at least four.[36]

In the late 1970s and extending into the Reagan administration in the 1980s under then–secretary of the Navy John Lehman, Navy commanders and planners acquired platforms, weapons, and tactics to fight back against the threat presented by the Soviet reconnaissance-strike complex. These acquisitions included the F-14 air superiority fighter, armed with the long-range Phoenix air-to-air missiles; the Aegis combat system and new surface-to-air missiles on its cruisers and destroyers for fleet air defense; and tactics designed to find and shoot down the Backfires before they could launch their antiship missiles.[37] Because the Cold War ended without a shootout between the Backfires and the U.S. Navy, we will never know which side had the advantage.

The Navy plans to continue a fleet designed primarily around aircraft carrier strike groups. Although the Navy continues to modernize its amphibious assault and submarine forces, aircraft carriers, new aircraft for its air wings, and surface combatants and munitions to defend the carrier strike groups continue to dominate the Navy's budget plans.[38] Navy officials assert that the next-generation aircraft carrier, the *Gerald R. Ford*–class, will generate more combat power at a lower lifetime cost than the *Nimitz*-class carriers it will replace.[39] These officials point to the responsive and flexible roles aircraft carriers have played over many decades, and how carrier air wings will continue to adapt to changing circumstances.

For the military balance in the western Pacific, the issue for the future of carrier airpower is whether these improvements, while notable, will keep pace with the dramatically improved reconnaissance-strike complex the PLA is now fielding (chapter 4 will discuss this in detail). In order to cope with the emerging land-based threats to sea power, the carrier air wing needs to greatly increase its range in order to keep the carrier strike group out of harm's way. Unfortunately, as large as U.S. aircraft carriers are, they are limited to hosting short-range tactical strike-fighters, which are fated to be outranged by land-based aircraft and missiles. The institutional culture inside the Navy that understandably promoted the aircraft carrier's role as an effective platform for projecting power ashore must now reckon with a missile and sensor technical revolution that previous commanders did not have to face in actual combat.

The Navy is introducing two new aircraft over the next two decades to modernize the carrier air wing. Although in many ways dramatic improvements, these upgrades won't be sufficient to overcome the inherent limitations imposed on carrier aircraft compared to their land-based competition. For example the new F-35C strike fighter, in many ways a remarkable technical achievement, has a maximum combat radius of about 1,100 kilometers, roughly matching the combat radius of the F/A-18 E/F it will join on Navy carrier flight decks.[40] Even when armed with standoff missiles, these combat radii won't be adequate to keep the aircraft carriers out of range of land-based threats to warships that are now emerging and will be common by the next decade.

In 2013 the Navy successfully tested the X-47B experimental unmanned combat aircraft. The goal of the X-47B program was to demonstrate that an unmanned strike aircraft could launch from an aircraft carrier, autonomously perform various missions, and then land on the carrier. Without the physiological limitations of a human crew and with aerial refueling, the X-47B experiment held out the promise of greatly extending the range of the carrier air wing. For the Navy, the X-47B concept held out some hope of making the carrier air wing relevant again against land-based adversaries that possessed long-range antiship capabilities. In 2013 the Navy successfully launched and landed the robotic aircraft on the aircraft carrier USS *George H. W. Bush*, demonstrating that an unmanned carrier-based reconnaissance and strike aircraft is feasible.[41]

Although the X-47B does enjoy a longer combat radius than both the F-35C and F/A-18 E/F (about 1,900 kilometers versus 1,100 for the two manned jets),[42] that greater range still won't be sufficient to allow either the carrier strike group or vulnerable air refueling tanker aircraft to operate outside the range of next-decade's land-based threats.

Of course the X-47B was an experimental program, not an actual combat aircraft meant for production. The intention is to take the technology from the experiment and transfer it to a future unmanned carrier-based combat aircraft. However, the X-47B itself provides a rough estimate of the future combat radius of its successor. The X-47B was a large aircraft, with a wingspan at least 39 percent wider than that of both the F-35C and F/A-18 E/F.[43] Aircraft range is highly correlated with aircraft size (the range of the Air Force's large bombers is many times that of fighter aircraft). The Navy's carrier-based aircraft have reached their size and range limits; if aircraft carriers could accommodate substantially larger and therefore longer-ranged aircraft, the Navy would have already acquired them. There is not that much room for the X-47B's successors to grow and thus acquire the range they will need to strike land-based targets while also keeping the carrier out of harm's way.

Indeed the Navy's desired performance specifications for the Unmanned Carrier Launched Surveillance and Strike aircraft (UCLASS, the X-47B's first successor) are surprisingly modest and add little long-range strike capability, especially inside defended airspace like China's. A May 2013 Navy document listed UCLASS's desired "key performance parameters."[44] The Navy wants UCLASS to be primarily a reconnaissance aircraft, with a weapons payload of only one thousand pounds, no better than the payload of World War II–era carrier aircraft. For surveillance, the Navy wants UCLASS to be able to perform one search orbit up to about 2,200 kilometers from the carrier.

The Navy does not expect UCLASS to have the same level of stealthiness as the F-35 or B-2, implying that UCLASS will not support these aircraft on missions inside defended airspace.[45] Finally, the Navy wants UCLASS to have a "limited ability" to strike targets in lightly defended airspace at a range of 3,640 kilometers.[46] That specification more accurately describes counterterrorism operations over underdeveloped countries rather than China's heavily defended airspace. Finally, the Pentagon's top-level Joint Requirements Oversight Council (JROC)—chaired in 2013 by Vice Chairman of the Joint Chiefs of Staff Adm. James Winnefeld (a career naval aviator)—specifically downgraded UCLASS's required performance, relegating it to surveillance and counterterrorism missions in low-threat airspace.[47] Subsequent to that decision, officials in the Navy's air warfare office have promoted a larger UCLASS, an aircraft with greater fuel and payload capacity than that approved by JROC.[48] Such a concept, if approved by top-level Pentagon officials, would imply a new aircraft design, which would likely delay the arrival of UCLASS well into the 2020s and would entail large technical and program management risks, risks that JROC seems unwilling to take. By contrast, the Navy's air warfare office sees the need to take those risks, a view that reveals the substantial vulnerabilities Navy officials admit U.S. aircraft carriers will face in the years ahead.

In addition to its carrier-based aircraft, the Navy can also strike land targets with Tomahawk cruise missiles. Navy submarines, cruisers, and destroyers are capable of launching Tomahawk land-attack missiles at targets up to 1,600 kilometers away.[49] The Navy's cruisers and destroyers launch the Tomahawk from Mark 41 Vertical Launch System (VLS) cells (there are 127 VLS cells on each Navy cruiser and 96 cells on each destroyer). VLS cells are also used for missile and air defense interceptors and antisubmarine weapons. In addition the Navy's attack submarines can carry up to 12 Tomahawks. The Navy's four guided missile submarines (two of which are assigned to the Pacific Fleet) each carry 154 of the missiles.[50] With a range of 1,600 kilometers, U.S. Navy surface ships launching Tomahawks against Chinese targets would have to approach within China's antiship missile perimeter (more on this in chapter 4).

The number of VLS cells in the U.S. Pacific Fleet represents the maximum theoretical land-attack cruise missile capacity of the Navy. The Defense Department has tasked the Navy to assign 60 percent of its warships to the Pacific by 2020.[51] According to the Navy's long-range shipbuilding plan and accounting for new construction, ship retirements, and the "60 percent to the Pacific" guidance, the Navy expects to have 9 cruisers, 43 destroyers, 29 attack submarines, and 2 guided missile submarines in the Pacific Fleet by 2020.[52] If so, by 2020 the Pacific Fleet would have a total of 5,927 VLS cells for air and missile defense, antisubmarine warfare, and Tomahawk land-attack missiles.

The Navy does not openly report how it actually allocates VLS cells among the various missions. By one report, the "baseline" loading of VLS cells allocates just four cells on cruisers or destroyers to Tomahawks, with almost 92 percent of the VLS cells allocated instead to air and missile defense.[53] Such an allocation reflects the main task of the Navy's surface combatants: defending the aircraft carriers against air and missile attack. If "baseline" loading is standard routine, the U.S. Pacific Fleet would have 864 Tomahawk missiles available across all its ships and submarines, each able to strike one aim point. The VLS system affords commanders and planners the flexibility to alter this loadout. But substantially increasing the allocation to Tomahawks would come at greatly increased risk to surface forces operating within range of adversary antiship weapons. In addition the Navy does not have the capability of reloading VLS cells while a ship is at sea. Although reloading VLS at sea is a Navy aspiration, its cruisers, destroyers, and submarines must return to port to rearm expended VLS cells.[54]

Although a highly useful weapon when used as part of a larger air operation (e.g., Tomahawks have been employed against adversary air defense systems at the start of air campaigns), the Navy's Tomahawk capacity by itself is insufficient for a sustained campaign against a significant opponent. For example during the six weeks of the 1991 air war against Iraq, coalition air forces attacked 35,085 targets (often consisting of more than one aim point), of which 11,655 were "strategic" targets (all other than Iraqi ground forces).[55] It is reasonable to presume that the potential target set in a hypothetical conflict with China will be larger than the target set in Iraq in 1991. Thus, although the Navy's Tomahawk inventory would be a critical tool during a conflict with China, the potential target set in China will certainly be at least one and perhaps as much as two orders of magnitude greater than the Tomahawk inventory available in the Pacific.

With no significant adversary since 1945 to challenge it on the high seas, the Navy found a mission for its aircraft carriers—power projection against land targets. During the numerous power-projection campaigns the Navy has waged since the Korean War, its adversaries also lacked the means to prevent the Navy's aircraft carriers from coming close to shore and setting up for long bombardment operations. Occasionally opponents had other ways of resisting; North Vietnam's dangerous air defense system claimed 900 carrier aircraft and 881 naval aviators killed or captured.[56] But over the decades and numerous engagements, the Navy perfected a method for sustaining air campaigns from its aircraft carriers, a technique that orchestrates task force tactics, an ocean-wide logistics chain, and integrated training and personnel systems.

This metasystem for naval power projection, combined with repeatedly favorable operating conditions, established an institutional culture supporting the aircraft carrier. That culture now seeks to sustain itself with new and improved components such as the *Ford*-class aircraft carriers and the F-35 strike fighter. Most of the Navy's senior leaders understand that the favorable operating assumptions and conditions that have supported this institutional culture for so long are now rapidly deteriorating. What remains to be seen is whether the Navy can make the difficult adjustments necessary to remain relevant for the entirely new era that looms in East Asia and elsewhere.

A Treaty Removes the Army's Long-Range Punch

Beginning in the 1950s the U.S. Army developed and maintained a variety of battlefield and theater ballistic missiles. The Army's missile capability reached its apogee in the 1980s when it deployed 108 Pershing II intermediate-range ballistic missiles in Europe. The nuclear-armed Pershing II missile was highly accurate and was designed to hold at risk Soviet leadership and command bunkers. At the same time, the Air Force deployed 464 equally accurate ground-launched cruise missiles in Europe, with the same mission as the Pershings': pinpoint attacks on Soviet command bunkers. A parallel purpose for these deployments was to compel Soviet leaders to agree to a treaty that would bilaterally remove intermediate-range nuclear forces from the European theater. Soviet leaders were apparently so agitated by the prospect of the two missiles delivering pinpoint nuclear strikes aimed at them personally that they soon agreed to the treaty after the United States completed the contentious deployments of the missiles.[57]

In December 1987 the U.S. and Soviet governments concluded the Intermediate Nuclear Forces (INF) Treaty. This treaty banned the two countries from possessing land-based missiles with ranges between 500 and 5,500 kilometers. By 1991 both countries had complied with the treaty by dismantling their land-based medium- and intermediate-range missiles and support equipment.[58]

As a result of the INF treaty, U.S. (and Russian) military planners are left in the odd position of merely observing while China builds and deploys thousands of land-based short-, medium-, and intermediate-range ballistic and cruise missiles. In the past, these planners were not so concerned that they were forbidden by the INF treaty from deploying land-based, theater-range missiles in the region. The long-standing ability of U.S. airpower to roam widely was thought to be all the capability the United States would need. However, we will see that China's military modernization is disrupting those assumptions, with consequences for U.S. strategy.

The Pershing and ground-launched cruise missiles (this cruise missile was based on the Navy's Tomahawk missile) provided an effective and inexpensive way of holding at risk targets that an adversary valued highly. Both missiles were mounted on mobile transporter-erector-launchers, allowing them to disperse and relocate during crises, making enemy targeting of the missiles much more difficult. Compared to the latest-generation strike fighters and warships, these missiles were cheap to produce and field. During the Cold War, the United States armed them with nuclear warheads in order to allow them to attack hardened and deeply buried targets, such as command bunkers. With their very high accuracy and armed with conventional warheads, these missiles could be effective against a broad range of other targets. With all of these characteristics, it is no wonder that the PLA finds its versions of these weapons so appealing. It is a strange historical anomaly:

the Cold War–era INF Treaty has denied this capability to the United States in East Asia, alarming in light of the deteriorating security situation there.

Why Is the U.S. Military Falling behind in the Pacific?

By 2020 China's military modernization will place U.S. military forces, doctrine, and plans in East Asia under great stress. With the Defense Department possessing a large budget, leading technology, and experienced commanders and planners, why is such a disturbing outcome looming?

There are many reasons for this unwelcome result, most because of bureaucratic culture. The services' cultures reward officers who support their traditions and continuity with the "installed base" of current programs, organizations, and policies. This is especially true when those programs, organizations, and policies are commonly accepted as having worked. As mentioned previously, the Air Force's fighter aircraft are recognized as having ruled the skies, while the Navy's aircraft carriers have ruled the seas. To argue against this success from inside the institution is to risk being branded an eccentric, even if the conditions that led to those favorable results might be quickly disappearing.

Second, economic and political interests reinforce inertia regarding military programs and doctrine. Political interests and defense contractors will seek to maintain current military bases and operational patterns, along with the defense industrial base that supports these practices.

An additional problem for those officials and planners responsible for designing U.S. military forces involves the broad range of tasks assigned to these forces. The Obama administration's Defense Strategic Guidance, issued in January 2012, assigned ten broad missions to the armed forces, ranging from nuclear deterrence and global power projection to "providing a stabilizing presence" and distributing humanitarian relief.[59] Designing and funding military forces for such a wide range of geographic and functional responsibilities will inevitably result in forces that are generally capable of many things but that are not optimized to be the best at certain narrowly focused tasks.

The PLA, by contrast, can focus its energy and resources, at least at this moment in China's history, on a very specific mission—preventing U.S. military forces from safely operating in or near China's Near Seas. China has concentrated on that specific task for two decades and by 2020 will field well-designed forces to accomplish that discrete mission (see chapter 4). The United States will need to design a response, which will likely be equally specialized. But paying for that unique response is likely to subtract resources needed for responsibilities elsewhere in the world.

Regarding the design of the latest generation of U.S airpower, it is possible that an excessive, and in retrospect, mistaken focus on contingencies in Europe resulted in today's new combat aircraft being unsuited for the vast distances in the Asia-Pacific theater. For example the Air Force was busy in the 1980s designing a replacement for its F-15 air superiority fighter.[60] During this time the Cold War military competition with the Soviet Union was climaxing, with the NATO Central Front the focus of contingency planning. That front was characterized by a relatively small geographic area and access to dozens of potential air bases for fighter operations. The result of these planning assumptions was the F-22, highly capable but short-ranged, which suited the requirements of the European theater.

But what was adequate for Europe, is not for the Asia-Pacific. If we define the NATO Central Front with a rectangle extending from the Bay of Biscay to Warsaw and Rome to Copenhagen, such a rectangle would fit into the Philippines Sea, which is just one portion of the Asia-Pacific theater with which U.S. airpower must cope. Add to that the six main air bases from which the U.S. Air Force operates in East Asia (not dozens as in Europe). Cold War Eurocentrism, at least as it relates to airpower design, has very likely detracted from the U.S. military position in the Pacific.

The F-35 Joint Strike Fighter program illustrates several of the institutional maladies discussed above. In the 1990s the Air Force, Navy, and Marine Corps pursued plans to replace their legacy strike fighter models: F-16 and A-10 for the Air Force, older F/A-18s for the Navy, and F/A-18 and AV-8B for the Marine Corps. Acquisition officials at the Pentagon perceived an opportunity to potentially reap large economies of scale, both in acquisition and maintenance, by using a common design for all of these replacements. The F-35 is a post–Cold War concept and should have been an opportunity for officials and planners to make a fresh assessment about what capabilities would be required for future, post-European conflict areas. The vastness of the Asia-Pacific theater should have indicated a need for strike aircraft with vastly more range than the four strike fighters to be replaced. Instead the three services agreed to the F-35, which while much more sophisticated than the legacy aircraft, has inadequate range to be very useful in the Asia-Pacific region.

Why did this happen? First are the incentives to perpetuate the services' institutional cultures: the F-35 provided continuity for each service's fighter community. Second, and related, is the cultural supremacy of the aircraft carrier inside the Navy. As mentioned above, conforming to the size restrictions imposed on carrier aircraft meant that the Navy's F-35C would be limited to a combat radius of about 1,100 kilometers. After Defense Department officials opted early on to pursue economies of scale for the joint program, the Air Force and the Marine Corps had to use the same airframe for their versions of the F-35.

For the Air Force, this removed the option of a larger medium-range strike aircraft such as a replacement for its current F-15E (combat radius of about 1,600 kilometers) or the Air Force's retired FB-111, which had a combat radius of about 2,300 kilometers. As a result of these pressures for conformity, the three services are getting a highly sophisticated strike aircraft with, regrettably, a range too short to be useful in the Asia-Pacific theater.[61]

At the genesis of the F-35 program in the 1990s, acquisition and strategy officials inside the Pentagon missed an opportunity to choose other options. Until the 1991 Persian Gulf War, air planners relied on fighter-attack aircraft to deliver precisely aimed bombs, either through pilot skill in a low-altitude attack or by using a laser to designate the target for a guided bomb. Large bombers like the B-52 still delivered conventional bombs in long, unguided "carpet bomb" strings. But later in the decade, those rules changed. By the late 1990s and into the 2000s, the Air Force repeatedly modified its three large bomber types to precisely deliver conventional bombs through satellite, inertial, and laser guidance. After these modifications, the military's small strike-fighters no longer had a monopoly on precision strike capability.

The deployment of a B-1 heavy bomber wing in 2012 to support the war in Afghanistan illustrated how long-range aircraft can now do the strike missions previously considered restricted to smaller fighter-attack aircraft. During a six-month deployment to southwest Asia, the Air Force's 7th Bomb Wing flew over 770 combat sorties and maintained at least one bomber continuously over Afghanistan during the entire deployment, in order to provide a rapid response to ground forces needing air support. The wing responded to over five hundred troops-in-contact requests for air support and delivered over four hundred precision-aimed weapons, sometimes within three hundred meters of friendly forces.[62] We can see that long-range strike aircraft can perform all of the air-to-ground missions fighter-attack aircraft perform, but at more than five times the combat radius.

The shortcomings suffered by the U.S. force design in the Pacific should require U.S. defense officials to think about airpower design from first principles. The late 1990s, when the bomber upgrades began and the first decision on the Joint Strike Fighter loomed, was an opportunity for these officials to think about airpower in a creative way. Regrettably for the current balance of power in the Pacific, they and their successors did not take advantage of the chances they were offered.

Avoiding Unpleasant Thoughts

The emergence of the Chinese missile threat over the western Pacific has sprung up as rapidly as China's economy has grown, that is to say, very fast. In the 1990s, with the Cold War over, the United States an unquestioned global hegemon, and its economy and confidence booming, most viewed China as an interesting emerging customer for U.S. exporters, not a looming security challenge.

Of course there were exceptions to this complacency. Around the turn of the century, analysts at the Pentagon's Office of Net Assessment, think tanks such as the Center for Strategic and Budgetary Assessments, scholars at the Naval War College, and others were increasing their focus on possible "anti-access and area denial" challenges in the western Pacific resulting from China's military modernization. Still, China's "smile diplomacy" of that period, and the continued adherence by China's policymakers to Deng's dictum of hiding intentions and biding time, made discussion of a hypothetical Chinese threat sound alarmist.

The 2006 edition of the Defense Department's Quadrennial Defense Review finally explicitly mentioned the potential Chinese threat. Under a section of the report titled "Shaping the Choices of Countries at Strategic Crossroads," the report stated, "Of the major and emerging powers, China has the greatest potential to compete militarily with the United States and field disruptive military technologies that could over time offset traditional U.S. military advantages absent U.S. counter strategies."[63] Four years later the 2010 Quadrennial Defense Review was even more explicit about China. The report listed eight areas of concern regarding China's military modernization, which it concluded were "raising a number of legitimate questions regarding [China's] long-term intentions."[64]

The 2010 report directed the services to develop a "joint air-sea battle concept," in response to the challenges adversary missiles are increasingly posing to the U.S. military's freedom of action.[65] But to some, preparing for a deteriorating security situation in the western Pacific, or even hinting in public that China could pose a security problem, was something that policymakers should avoid. In June 2012 James Cartwright, then the recently retired vice chairman of the U.S. Joint Chiefs of Staff, said, "AirSea Battle is demonizing China. That's not in anybody's interest."[66] Cartwright's remark implied that U.S. officials best not anger China lest its leaders remember the dramatic military modernization they have designed and implemented over the past two decades, a modernization specifically designed to thwart U.S. expeditionary forces in East Asia.

Many organizations suffer from institutional biases that cause them to make systemically poor assessments. One such bias is a tendency to conclude that an outcome, if unpleasant or unfamiliar, is therefore unlikely.[67] There are few things more unpleasant to contemplate than war between China and the United States. But avoiding or suppressing the topic does not make the prospect go away.

Complacency, institutional cultures, and the avoidance of unpleasant thoughts have caused the United States to get a late start on preparing for the security competition in East Asia. Fortunately, the history of U.S. strategy over the Cold War shows that when U.S. policymakers and the defense community focus their attention and resources on an important security issue, they can usually achieve a favorable outcome. The same can be true in East Asia. But getting there will require a different approach than has been tried thus far.

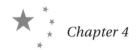

Chapter 4

CHINA'S STRATEGY:
SALAMI SLICING AND THE MISSILE REVOLUTION

China's approach to its territorial claims in its Near Seas (the East and South China Seas), combined with its carefully designed military modernization program, will present a particularly challenging threat to the U.S. position in East Asia and to the core interests of the United States and its allies. China's leaders are pursuing a patient, long-term approach that seeks to gradually achieve the nation's security objectives without triggering a conflict.

China's behavior suggests the use of "salami slicing" to gradually settle its claims in the Near Seas. Salami slicing is the slow accumulation of small changes, none of which in isolation amounts to a casus belli, but which can add up over time to a significant strategic change. China's application of steady pressure and increasingly persistent presence on and around disputed claims in the Near Seas is evidence of salami slicing at work.

At the same time, the buildup of Chinese air and naval power, particularly its missile forces, is creating a military capability that will deter adversaries from attempting to later roll back the nation's accumulated gains. China's military modernization program is greatly extending the missile and sensor revolution that the Soviet Union and the United States both pursued in the 1970s and 1980s. China's growing military muscle is designed to defend itself and its accumulated gains from adversary expeditionary forces.

This approach will present the United States and its allies in the region with a difficult quandary. They will have to summon the stamina to match China's persistence and the will to occasionally risk brinkmanship with another great power. Meanwhile they will have to understand the threat China's military modernization poses to U.S. and allied forces in the region and then be willing to make substantial reforms to those forces in order to defuse China's strategy. Neither of these efforts will be easy.

China's Salami Slicing in the Near Seas

China's strategy for establishing control over its territorial claims in the East and South China Seas is based on patience, the slow accumulation of incremental gains, and the avoidance of overt conflict. China is employing salami slicing in its dispute against Japan over the Senkaku Islands and against rival claimants in the South China Sea.

China's regional diplomatic strategy has attempted to support salami slicing in the Near Seas. Judging from China's behavior, its diplomatic strategy aims to weaken the role the Association of Southeast Asian Nations (ASEAN) plays regarding the South China Sea disputes. One of ASEAN's missions is to defend the interests of its members, including those around the South China Sea, several of whom have conflicting claims with China. ASEAN thus stands as a potential political and diplomatic impediment between China and its claims in the sea.

China's attempt to weaken ASEAN dramatically spilled out into the open in 2010. The July 2010 ASEAN Regional Forum conference in Hanoi met to discuss security issues in the southeast Asian region, including the ongoing territorial disputes in the South China Sea. Both China's foreign minister Yang Jiechi and then–secretary of state Hillary Clinton attended the conference.

ASEAN's tradition is to resolve disputes through consensus of all its members. For China, this means that the South China Sea disputes would have to be resolved with ASEAN as a bloc, and not bilaterally with each small country, as China would prefer. At the conference Clinton endorsed ASEAN's preferred concept of multilateral, noncoercive negotiations regarding the South China Sea's maritime disputes. She also spoke up for the principle that the sea is international waters and part of the global commons.[1] Those seemingly uncontroversial remarks resulted in a furious and public outburst by China's foreign minister, who had to leave a room at the conference to compose himself. Apparently frustrated by ASEAN's resistance to China's assertions, he soon returned to lecture Singapore's foreign minister about the proper places of "big countries" and "small countries."[2]

There were two important results from the 2010 ASEAN Regional Forum conference in Hanoi. First, the conference's verbal fireworks burst out from behind the meeting's closed doors and into the global media, revealing in a dramatic fashion the disputes between China, ASEAN, and the region's smaller countries. Second, Clinton's strong public support for

ASEAN and China's small neighbors displayed U.S. resistance to China's attempt to take advantage of its size in the region's territorial disputes.

In 2012 China would score a temporary success at weakening ASEAN's unity. China's ally Cambodia, ASEAN's chair that year, for the first time ever blocked ASEAN from issuing a consensus position on the South China Sea's territorial disputes.[3] Whether ASEAN's divisions in 2012 will recur remains to seen. But China's diplomatic strategy of attempting to weaken ASEAN so that the nation can bring its strength to bear against its small neighbors individually remains clear.

Salami Slicing in the South China Sea

Although China's claims in the South China Sea, denoted by the "nine-dash line" (see chapter 1), reach back to the Nationalist Government that preceded the founding of the Peoples' Republic in 1949, those claims lay dormant and largely unmentioned until late in the first decade of this century. There were however, two highly opportunistic exceptions to this dormancy. In 1974 China seized Woody Island in the Paracel Islands group from a dying South Vietnam, a seizure that Vietnam has protested ever since. In 1995 China occupied Mischief Reef in the Spratly Islands, over protests from the Philippine government.[4]

China's systematic salami slicing in the South China Sea was visible in 2012 as China made it increasingly clear its claims were no longer dormant. In June 2012 China declared the establishment of "Sansha City" on Woody Island. China intends Sansha to be the administrative center for all of China's claims in the South China Sea, including the Spratly Islands and Scarborough Reef, both claimed by the Philippines. China also announced its intention to send a permanent military garrison to the area.[5]

In April 2012 Chinese maritime law enforcement and Philippines coast guard vessels engaged in a protracted standoff over Scarborough Reef, located about 230 kilometers from the Philippines. The Philippine coast guard eventually retreated, and China's enforcement vessels have remained at the reef since.[6] What's more, Chinese vessels have prevented Philippine fishermen from returning to the reef.[7] Beginning in 2013, China announced its intention to have its police vessels in the South China Sea board and search vessels it considers illegally in Chinese territory.[8]

With these actions, Chinese authorities hope to systematically establish legal legitimacy for its claims in the South China Sea. It has set up a local government that will command a military garrison, both traditional indicators of state authority. These actions challenge the claims of Vietnam and the Philippines and are moves that these countries may lack the maritime resources to replicate or counter. China's leaders may be hoping that such moves to establish a more substantial presence than those of other claimants will, over time, bolster the legal legitimacy of China's claims.

China's attempts at economic development in the South China Sea are another indicator of its attempts to assert its sovereignty in the area. In June 2012 China National Offshore Oil Corporation (CNOOC), a huge state-owned oil developer, invited foreign oil drillers to bid on blocks of the South China Sea that are inside Vietnam's EEZ. In fact some of these blocks had previously been put up for lease by Vietnam.[9] At Reed Bank near Palawan Island, China and the Philippines have similarly clashed over oil and gas drilling rights.[10] With the much larger resources it commands in entities such as CNOOC, China will eventually be able to maintain a more widespread and persistent hydrocarbon exploration presence across the South China Sea.

China will employ the large and growing resources of its paramilitary maritime enforcement and coast guard establishments to persistently defend these claims and actions.[11] China's leaders likely hope that such a presence will eventually bolster its sovereignty claims in the region, especially if the other claimants lack the resources to display a similarly persistent presence around the disputed islands and reefs.

Salami Slicing in the East China Sea

China is similarly making assertive use of its paramilitary and nonmilitary maritime resources to establish a persistent presence around the Senkaku Islands. According to Japan's Ministry of Defense, incursions by Chinese government ships in Japan's territorial waters around the Senkaku Islands accelerated in late 2012 and averaged about five incursions per month during the beginning of 2013.[12] China's establishment of an air defense identification zone encompassing the airspace above the disputed Senkaku Islands would seem to be another incremental assertion of China's sovereignty claims in the East China Sea.

China has used nonmilitary forms of maritime power—civilian fishing fleets, coast guard cutters, and the China Maritime Surveillance Agency (CMS)—to press its presence near the Senkakus in a manner that U.S. and Japanese military forces find politically difficult to respond to.[13] China would gain a media advantage and possibly a legal one if Japan is forced to respond with armed warplanes and warships to the recurring presence of Chinese fishing boats and fisheries administration vessels. Should a confrontation occur, it would certainly be recorded and replayed on global media outlets, in an attempt to portray Japan as militarily aggressive.

China may hope that its superior resources will allow it to maintain a more persistent presence of fishing vessels, oil rigs, and coast guard and EEZ patrol vessels. China's superior numbers and material advantages could wear down Japanese coast guard and naval establishments that over time may not be able to keep up with China's operational tempo.[14]

Why Salami Slicing Is Hard to Resist

China's moves to patrol the two seas, protect its fishing fleets, set down offshore drilling rigs, and establish administrative offices and garrisons are acts that create "facts on the ground" that gradually legitimize its legal position. Over time, China will be able to build up its military and nonmilitary maritime power to a point where it will be able to have a continuous presence at the most important sites—a presence its rivals in the region won't be able to replicate without gaining access to greater resources to sustain their own maritime presence. At the end of this road would be China's claimed right to exclude foreign warships from its EEZ, as it attempted in March 2009 when five Chinese ships harassed the surveillance ship USNS *Impeccable* in international waters south of Hainan Island.[15] Under this scenario, China would assert the right to exclude foreign warships from the Strait of Malacca all the way to Japan's home islands.

China's salami-slicing tactics place its rivals in an uncomfortable position. Each of China's actions is calibrated to be too small to amount to a casus belli. China's adversaries will be forced to draw red lines and engage in brinkmanship over actions the rest of the world will perceive as politically trivial. Over time, China's leaders are counting on this inertia to result in their achievement of de facto and operational sovereignty over their claims. China's small rivals or the United States may find themselves having to contemplate making the first military move against a prepared adversary—difficult political and military decisions to make.

Carefully controlled salami slicing also means that China won't have to choose between expanding its area of control and continuing its participation in the international system from which it benefits. China's leaders will reason that they can have both. If China's neighbors or the United States wishes to stop the salami slicing, they will have to be the ones taking risks with the global commons and continued open commerce, not China. As China builds both justifications for its sovereignty claims and the military power to defend them, its leaders are likely concluding that time is on their side.

The Origin and Goals of China's Military Modernization

The Chinese military force emerging in the second decade of this century traces its origins to the early 1990s. Several incidents during that decade guided China's subsequent force planning and catalyzed its pace of modernization.[16] The first catalyst was the 1991 Persian Gulf War, which displayed for China's military planners and policymakers the stunning battlefield effectiveness of airpower, precision-guided munitions, and a modern intelligence and command infrastructure. The PLA of the 1980s, by contrast, was still dominated by a bloated and largely immobile army, supported by obsolete aircraft and warships. After witnessing the rapid and lopsided rout inflicted by the U.S.-led force against Iraq, PLA leaders knew drastic reform was urgent.

Next came the Taiwan Strait crises of 1995–96, prompted by China's attempts to influence Taiwan's election through PLA missile tests aimed into waters off the island. The Clinton administration countered this attempt at intimidation by sending two U.S. Navy aircraft carrier strike groups near Taiwan, without much fear of China's antiship capabilities. China's impotence at this American show of force was a further accelerant to PLA modernization.

Since then the PLA has embraced the missile and sensor revolution and applied it to the modernization of its forces. The goal of this modernization program is to build forces and supporting infrastructure that will give China the military capacity to dominate a deep air and maritime buffer zone beyond its coast. In wartime, this capacity would prevent the arrival of adversary strike and expeditionary forces into the western Pacific.

Since the 1990s China's leadership has taken several steps to achieve these results. First came rapid and continuous increases in defense spending; according to the U.S. Department of Defense, China's defense spending rose an average of 9.7 percent per year (after inflation) between 2003 and 2012.[17] Next, China reallocated defense resources from its land forces to its naval, air, space, and missile forces. China settled territorial disputes to its north and west, which permitted it to focus on naval, air, space, and missile modernization (see chapter 1). Finally, China's industrial development has enabled the establishment of a high-technology research and industrial base to support its military modernization.[18]

China has enjoyed remarkable success meeting its modernization objectives (detailed below). Indeed, it is now clear that China possesses formidable scientific, engineering, industrial, and organizational capacity and has in many cases delivered military platforms and capabilities faster than U.S. intelligence officials have expected.[19] These surprises include earlier-than-expected arrivals of long-range antiship cruise missiles, an anti-ship ballistic missile, stealthy aircraft prototypes, and space reconnaissance capabilities.

Studies of past military modernization programs and the application of emerging "revolutions in military affairs" (e.g., the current missile and sensor revolution) have consistently shown the most successful programs are those in which planners had a specific future adversary to study and a specific operational task to achieve.[20] That describes perfectly China's military modernization program, which is intently focused on preventing U.S. naval and aerospace power from operating effectively in or near China's Near Seas during a conflict. The specificity of China's planning task contrasts sharply with the broad and vague set of missions for which U.S. military forces must prepare. As discussed in chapter 3, this lack of focus for the United States has left its forces less and less prepared for the challenge China presents.

China thus far has concentrated the vast preponderance of its military resources and attention on achieving its security objectives in the Asia-Pacific region. China's ability to project military power out to the rest of the world beyond its home region is very limited and has heretofore not been a planning priority.[21] China's plans to acquire aircraft carriers, large cargo and refueling aircraft, and its small-scale participation in multilateral naval missions such as those off Somalia may foreshadow future out-of-region ambitions. Even so, China's most dramatic military developments are confined to its ability to exert substantial naval and aerospace power within its home region.

Although geographically focused, China's emerging military capabilities will still have global consequences. As discussed in chapter 2, a Chinese attempt to achieve hegemony in East Asia would result in a dangerous and destabilizing security competition among the region's large and small rivals that could result in conflict and great damage to the global economy and security system. So even though China's military modernization retains a largely regional focus, that is worry enough, and should be no comfort to the United States or other outside observers.

China's Vision to Rule the Sea from the Land

China plans to defend its interests in the western Pacific with a military doctrine it calls "active defense" or "counter-intervention" (military analysts in the United States term this doctrine "anti-access/area denial," "A2/AD," or "access denial").[22] This doctrine and related acquisition programs foresee China using a wide variety of ballistic and cruise missile types, land-based aircraft, missile-armed coastal patrol craft, submarines, surface warships, and naval mine warfare to dissuade U.S. and allied naval forces and air-power from approaching the Near Seas during hostilities.

China will attempt to use its continental position to achieve the limited goal of controlling the seas adjacent to its shores. The success of this "anti-navy" approach will thus not depend on the PLAN achieving operational parity with the U.S. Pacific Fleet.[23] Elements of the PLAN, specifically its submarines, missile-armed surface ships, and mine warfare capability, will make specific contributions to the PLA's overall counterintervention, or access denial, war plans. But most of China's access denial capacity will reside in land-based platforms and capabilities. In this sense, China will attempt to rule the sea from the land.

The hypothetical battle China's air and naval modernization is preparing for pits China, a continental power, against the United States and its allies, which would be expeditionary powers attempting to project their air and naval power against China's positions on the continent and in the Near Seas. The game-changing technological advance favoring China in this face-off is China's emerging capability to project precise and high-volume missile power into the western Pacific, a threat the U.S. Navy has not had to worry about since the height of the Cold War over a quarter of a century ago. China's force design combines these technological developments with its advantageous continental position in a way that will pose a great challenge to U.S. forces and plans.

China's position as the continental power in this competition affords it several important advantages. First, China's continental position provides it a much wider variety of basing options compared to those of the United States, the expeditionary power. For example, a study published by RAND Corporation in 2011 identified twelve major Chinese air bases in southeast China from which its air force could conduct air operations using fighter-bomber aircraft.[24] Eleven of these bases feature advanced air base hardening techniques such as underground aircraft hangers and support facilities, reinforced concrete shelters, revetments, and camouflage. In addition to those air bases in China's southeast, China's airpower can take advantage of basing options along the entire length of its long coast and deep into its interior. China's airpower basing options far exceed those available to U.S. commanders in the region, greatly complicating the task of coping with China's air threat to U.S. forces and plans.

China's continental position similarly supports its land-based missile strategy. The U.S. Department of Defense asserted that China operates the most active missile program in the world.[25] The vast majority of China's land-based ballistic and cruise missiles are mounted on mobile transporter-erector-launchers (TELs), truck and trailer combinations that allow China's missile commanders to move, hide, and constantly relocate their missile forces inside the country's vast and complicated terrain. This ability to disperse and hide, combined with China's integrated air defense system, will make it difficult for U.S. forces to suppress the missile threat. And as discussed in chapter 3, the 1987 Intermediate Nuclear Forces Treaty prohibits the United States (and Russia) from similarly possessing land-based ballistic and cruise missiles with ranges from 500 to 5,500 kilometers, weapons that could be useful counters to China's missiles.

As a continental power, China's military forces have the advantage of land-based logistic and communication networks. As the "home team" operating from interior lines, China's military supply network can be resilient, redundant, and positioned for enduring operations. Its military communications system can make use of terrestrial links, including underground fiber-optic cable, while U.S. forces will be more reliant on satellite and radio links that are more vulnerable to disruption.

In the matchup of continental versus expeditionary forces, the land-based power will usually be able to employ weapon platforms with longer ranges and heavier payloads compared to what expeditionary naval forces can support. Below, we will see how China could employ this advantage against U.S. and allied naval forces.

Finally, China's missile-based strategy (encompassing all land-attack, antiship, and air defense missile systems) allows China to take advantage of its status as a low-cost industrial producer. For example, an advanced long-range cruise missile costs the U.S. Defense Department about $1.5 million; it is reasonable to assume that China's production costs for similar models will be lower. A modern U.S. destroyer or amphibious ship will cost at least $1.5 billion and likely much more.[26] China will be able to acquire hundreds of antiship missiles for the cost of single ships in a hypothetical U.S. expeditionary force. Marginal costs similarly favor offensive missiles versus missile defense interceptors, which cost at least an order of magnitude more than the attacking missiles they have to intercept.[27] In a race between China's missiles versus U.S. platforms and missile defenses, it will be easier for China to stay in the lead.

China Has Its Vulnerabilities

In spite of these significant structural advantages, China labors under some substantial weaknesses. China's most significant strategic weakness may be its lack of allies and friends in the region. China can count only North Korea as an ally—and one of questionable value. In Southeast Asia, China has strategic relationships with Laos, Cambodia, and Burma. But Burma's leaders are now opting to open up to the United States and its partners in the region, a sign that these leaders want more options than their previous reliance on Beijing. Laos and Cambodia, which have occasionally provided diplomatic support to China at ASEAN Regional Forum conferences, are otherwise weak and limited partners.

By contrast, nearly all of the countries around the South China Sea are increasingly stiffening their resistance to China's assertions there. Despite Taiwan's openness to commercial and cultural détente, it still resists China's political and security encroachments. And China's contentious activity directed at the Senkaku islands has provoked a nationalist backlash in Japan and stepped-up preparedness by Japan's defense forces.[28] China is the strongest power in the region and its power continues to expand. It should be no surprise that virtually all of its neighbors are increasingly concerned about their security in this regard and are now taking diplomatic and military steps to counter this development.

Geography in the western Pacific presents obstacles to Chinese military operations. The First Island Chain, extending from Japan's home islands to the Philippines and Malaysia, are potential sites for U.S. and coalition sensors, air defense systems, antiship missile systems, and positions for undersea surveillance and operations. Positioning sensors and weapon systems along the First Island Chain could inhibit China's warships from accessing the wider Pacific Ocean, or channel their passage into corridors favorable to the coalition. Such positions could also threaten the freedom of Chinese air operations. Chinese commanders must grapple with the unpleasant fact that all of the First Island Chain is currently possessed by U.S. allies and partners.

The PLA lacks modern combat experience. Its last major combat operation was the 1979 punitive expedition into northern Vietnam. Having observed U.S. military operations over the past two decades, China's military leaders understand their lack of experience.[29] Although it is improving, the PLA continues to face deficiencies in interservice cooperation.[30] China similarly has limited experience operating with coalition partners. Its lack of significant allies in East Asia holds out little hope of improvement in this area.

Finally, China's internal political fragility is a possible risk factor for its decision makers and might be a vulnerability that adversaries could exploit. We should expect that Chinese nationalism, especially as it relates to unresolved grievances with Japan and other neighbors, would bolster support for China's political and military leadership, at least during the early stages of a potential conflict. However, wars develop in unexpected ways and China's leaders face even greater uncertainty about enduring domestic political support than do leaders in other countries, such as the United

States, who have more recent experience with wartime leadership. China has one of the largest and most pervasive internal security structures in the world, a force that currently must cope with over 90,000 protests per year. In his inaugural address in November 2012 as China's top leader, President Xi Jinping acknowledged that the CCP "faces many severe challenges," mentioning corruption and its officials being divorced from the people (see chapter 1).[31] China's leaders must reckon with the prospect of increased internal stress during a prolonged conflict, with uncertain consequences.

U.S. and allied policymakers and military planners will have to discern which of China's weaknesses are likely to be enduring and which that nation can repair through the application of resources, leadership, and time. For example the PLA can narrow the gaps in military training, joint doctrine, and staff efficiency by making these issues a top priority for the PLA's leadership. These leaders can then seek improvements by applying resources for better training ranges, challenging and realistic exercises, and experimentation with military doctrine. It is feasible that by the end of this decade, the PLA's tactical and operational performance can more closely match that of the United States, especially if U.S. proficiency slips during the same period due to constraints on funding for training.

China's weaknesses with regional allies and internal political stability, by contrast, are likely to endure and even intensify. These enduring weaknesses should be targets of a competitive strategy for the United States and its allies, a topic addressed in later chapters.

China's Emerging Air Superiority in the Western Pacific

Achieving air superiority is a well-known requirement for military success. China intends to achieve air superiority over the Near Seas by employing its land-attack missile power and by exploiting the U.S. military's overreliance on relatively short-range tactical aircraft, a U.S. weakness discussed in chapter 3.

The United States can rightly claim to have the best tactical combat aircraft in the world. The U.S. Air Force's F-22 air superiority fighter has no peer in air-to-air combat. Over the next fifteen years, the Air Force, Navy, and Marine Corps will receive versions of the F-35 Joint Strike Fighter, a multirole aircraft that in some situations will greatly boost the air combat power of those services. Several U.S. allies in the Pacific are also purchasing the F-35, with the intention of integrating their future airpower capabilities with those of U.S. forces.

However, the excessive allocation of short-range tactical aircraft in the U.S. inventory has created substantial handicaps for U.S. operations in the broad Pacific theater (discussed in chapter 3). Most crucially for the design of China's military strategy, these excellent aircraft are of no value if they are unable to get into the air to fight. China's adoption of the missile and sensor revolution over the past two decades is designed specifically to attack the handful of air bases in the western Pacific on which advanced U.S. tactical aircraft, and U.S. airpower strategy in general, depend. If successful, China's strategy could nullify the technological advantage U.S. combat aircraft possess and leave China, operating from its continental position, in command of the skies over the Near Seas.

China's land-attack missile forces very likely possess the capability of shutting down or severely suppressing the sortie generation rates of five of the six major U.S. air bases in the western Pacific (two in South Korea, two on Japan's home islands, and one on Okinawa).[32] In 2012 China's ground-based missile forces consisted of 1,000 to 1,200 short-range ballistic missiles with ranges up to 1,000 kilometers, putting them within range of the air bases on Okinawa and South Korea. China has an additional 600 ground-launched cruise missiles and medium-range ballistic missiles, with ranges from 1,500 to 3,000 kilometers, as well as 550 bomber and attack aircraft capable of employing new long-range cruise missile types.[33] Many of China's submarines are also armed with a variety of cruise missile types, adding another threat to U.S. air bases in the region.

According to the U.S.-China Economic and Security Review Commission, China's land-attack missile forces have the capability to overwhelm the defenses and shut down all six U.S. bases except the one on Guam.[34] China's bomber and submarine forces, armed with long-range land-attack cruise missiles, threaten the large U.S. Air Force base on Guam. China could use a portion of its land-attack ballistic and cruise missiles in coordinated attacks on the U.S. bases to suppress their operations. With surviving U.S. aircraft grounded, China's fighter and bomber aircraft could execute other combat missions without much opposition, while employing air-launched land-attack cruise missiles to keep U.S. bases suppressed.

The China Commission's conclusions about U.S. air base vulnerability match the finding of a Cold War exercise conducted by the U.S. Air Force. Called "Salty Demo," the 1985 exercise at Spangdahlem Air Base in Germany simulated strikes by thirty to forty missiles and bombs on the base, which the Air Force termed an attack of "moderate severity."[35] The result was severe degradation of sortie generation, an outcome that came as a "shock" to Air Force officials. Salty Demo's conclusion of severe degradation from thirty to forty impacts on the base was confirmed with similar findings from the China Commission study and from the 2011 RAND study referenced above.[36] Those studies concluded that thirty to fifty

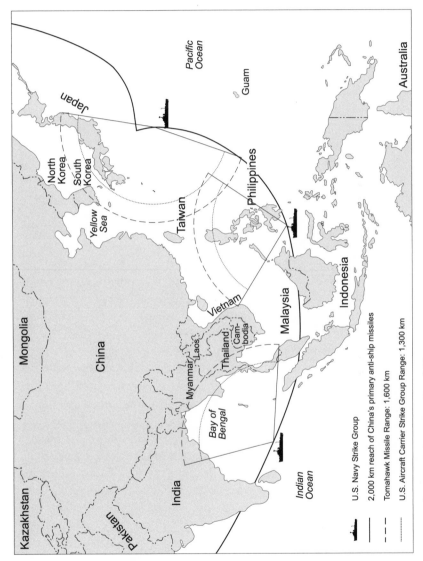

Map 4: China's Anti-Access Capability

U.S. Navy Strike Group
2,000 km reach of China's primary anti-ship missiles
Tomahawk Missile Range: 1,600 km
U.S. Aircraft Carrier Strike Group Range: 1,300 km

impacts would render even a large U.S. air base unusable. The Salty Demo exercise also tested the ability of air base personnel to repair damaged facilities and restore sortie generation. In the case of U.S. air bases in the Pacific, China will have the missile inventories to periodically restrike the six bases on Japan, South Korea, and Guam, its task made easier by having such a small target set to focus on.

Chinese missile attacks on U.S. air bases in Japan and South Korea would result in horizontal escalation of a hypothetical conflict, a result China's decision makers may in some circumstances wish to avoid. To the extent this is the case, the forward presence of U.S. airpower at these bases enhances regional deterrence. However, it is also possible that in a conflict with China, a nonbelligerent (say, e.g., South Korea) may prohibit U.S. forces from engaging in military operations against China from its territory. In this case, such bases would be "knocked out" with no missiles fired. Thus, forward bases can be both a deterrent to expanding aggression but also an unreliable asset for military operations.

China's Airpower Modernization Adds Range

Over the past decade, China has dramatically improved the equipment, training, and readiness of its airpower. China's various airpower components—the People's Liberation Army Air Force (PLAAF), the airpower component of the navy, and the Second Artillery's long-range missile forces—have been transformed from poorly equipped and trained organizations into increasingly capable fighting forces. Given continued rapid increases in China's military spending and the increased attention top policymakers are giving to the PLA's combat readiness, this trend of improvement should continue and likely accelerate. U.S. military planners should anticipate that by 2020, China will be one of the top airpower countries in the world.[37] According to a 2011 report prepared by RAND Corporation for the U.S. Air Force, by 2015 China's inventories of modern fighter aircraft and surface-to-air missile batteries will make China's air defense capacity "highly challenging for U.S. air forces."[38] Similarly, according to the RAND report, those same modern fighters, along with ground-launched conventional ballistic and cruise missiles, cruise missile–carrying bombers, and aerial refueling aircraft, will enable China to conduct offensive operations far into the western Pacific. So from both defensive and offensive perspectives, China's airpower will present an increasingly daunting challenge to U.S. military planners in East Asia.

The modernization of China's tactical airpower centers on its expanding inventory of variants of the Russian Su-27/30 Flanker multirole fighter-attack aircraft. China bought its first Su-27s from Russia in the early 1990s and in the 2000s purchased the upgraded Su-30MKK. China acquired a license from Russia to build Flankers in China and continues to build its indigenous version of the Flanker, the J-11B, outside the license agreement.[39] The later variants of the Flanker are true multirole fighter-attack aircraft, designed for both air superiority and precision ground attack missions, with performance roughly matching the U.S. Air Force's F-15E Strike Eagle fighter-bomber.[40] According to the RAND defense think tank, China will operate about 342 Flankers of all types by 2015 and will add about 14 to its inventory every year, putting China's potential Flanker inventory at over 400 aircraft by 2020.[41]

China's Flanker fighter-bombers present a particular challenge to the United States and its allies because of their relatively long combat radius. The Flanker variants have an unrefueled combat radius of at least 1,500 kilometers.[42] Five of the six U.S. air bases in the western Pacific (two in South Korea, three in Japan) lie within the combat radius of China's Flankers. U.S. Air Force tanker and airborne early warning and control aircraft, large and prominent targets, would be immediately vulnerable after taking off from any of these five bases. As a result, these bases (assuming they were not suppressed by Chinese missile impacts) would not be able to safely host the tanker and early warning "enabler" aircraft on which U.S. tactical aircraft depend. U.S. Air Force operations in the Pacific would then depend on Guam, creating a risky single point of failure and a focus for Chinese targeting. The next available bases to the east are in Hawaii and Alaska, far beyond the physiological endurance limits for a single pilot in a small tactical aircraft. Geography and the limits of being the expeditionary power thus create structural problems for U.S. planners. U.S. air bases in the Pacific are both too close to China and too few to compete against the continental power.

U.S. tactical aircraft—such as the F/A-18 E/F and the F-22 and F-35 in their stealthy configurations—have combat radii after their last refueling point of about 1,100 kilometers. If the United States did operate from dispersal and expeditionary air bases, say in the Second Island Chain roughly on the same longitude as Guam, U.S. Air Force tanker refueling aircraft could in theory sustain these fighters on long flights toward China from the east. But the last refueling point for U.S. tactical aircraft before entering combat would have to be at least 1,500 kilometers away from a Chinese Flanker's last refueling point, otherwise the ponderous and vulnerable U.S. tankers would risk being shot down by the Flankers. Unfortunately for U.S. planners, this would place the last refueling point for U.S. tactical aircraft beyond their combat radii to targets inside China or to much of the area west of the First Island Chain. Thus, the range advantage that China's Flankers enjoy will sharply limit U.S. tactical airpower in a conflict.

By early next decade, the range problem for U.S. tactical aircraft will get worse. China's J-20, a new stealthy fighter-attack aircraft, is thought to have a combat radius of two thousand kilometers.[43] The PLAAF is expected to begin forming J-20 squadrons by 2018. Although China still needs to improve the reliability and performance of the J-20 engine (a problem China suffers elsewhere in its aircraft inventory), the stealthy J-20 will be an even greater threat to U.S. airborne early warning and tanker aircraft than the Flanker. It will also push the last refueling point for U.S. tactical aircraft even farther east, further reducing the utility of these aircraft in the western Pacific.

With U.S. tactical aircraft either stranded on damaged air bases or pushed east out of range of Chinese targets, U.S. commanders would then have to rely on the Navy's Tomahawk cruise missiles and the Air Force's long-range bomber force as their remaining airpower tools. These tools would face China's integrated air defense system.

China continues to expand its inventories of long-range, advanced ground- and sea-based surface-to-air missile (SAM) forces, which the U.S. Department of Defense describes as "one of the largest such forces in the world." China operates the S-300 system, the most advanced SAM system exported by Russia, along with the similar and indigenously produced HQ-9 SAM system. China's mobile ground and naval SAMs have an operating range up to 150 kilometers and will provide a challenge to U.S. and allied air forces.[44]

The U.S. long-range bomber force has shrunk to 159 aircraft. Non-stealthy B-52 and B-1 models number only 139 and would have the most difficulty coping with China's air defense system (discussed in chapter 3). U.S. bombers would face hundreds of SAM launchers, providing mutual support with interlocking coverage. The U.S. aircraft would also face China's nearly 400 Flankers, along with hundreds of other interceptors armed with air-to-air missiles, all operating from scores of available air bases inside China.[45] U.S. Air Force flight crews and strike aircraft are normally well trained for overcoming adversary air defense networks. But the density and sophistication of China's air defenses would be unlike anything U.S. airpower has faced since the Vietnam War, when it lost hundreds of fixed-wing aircraft to air defenses.

The U.S. Navy's Tomahawk missile force in the Pacific will be one of the most effective tools available to U.S. commanders. However, their numbers are likely to be too few to have a substantial effect on the PLA's capabilities.

As the continental power with vast and deep territory, China will have too many targets for the Navy's Tomahawks to cover. This finding points up the difficulties an expeditionary power faces against a continental power; it also illustrates the consequences of the Intermediate Nuclear Forces Treaty for U.S. strategy in the Pacific.

The Influence of Missiles on Sea Power

China has similarly aimed the missile and sensor revolution at the sea. China has fielded a variety of missile-based strategies with the goal of keeping adversary surface warships, including U.S. aircraft carriers, away from its Near Seas. These strategies again exploit China's continental position and the basing and range advantages it provides.

By next decade, the missile and sensor revolution will allow China to dominate the sea from the land out to unprecedented distances. China plans to control its maritime approaches without having to match the U.S. Navy warship for warship. A side-by-side comparison of the two fleets is not the relevant measure of naval power and, therefore, the likelihood of strategic success. What matters is what the U.S. Navy can do to cope with China's antiship missile coverage, which by next decade will extend two thousand kilometers from China's coast.

China's possesses a wide variety of antiship cruise missile (ASCM) types, whose range, speed, and performance will increasingly threaten U.S. surface ships. China employs ASCMs from aircraft like the Flanker, surface ships, submarines, small fast patrol craft, and land-based mobile TELs. U.S. surface naval forces will thus encounter a thickening defense of ASCM launch platforms as they approach China's coast.

Chinese Flanker aircraft, armed with the latest models of ASCMs, will present one of the first, and perhaps most dangerous, threats to U.S. surface ships, such as those in carrier and expeditionary strike groups. As mentioned above, China's Flankers have a combat radius of 1,500 kilometers. They can be armed with up to six ASCMs, including the highly capable Russian SS-N-22 Sunburn supersonic ASCM, with a range of about 250 kilometers, or the Chinese-built YJ-91/12 ASCM, with a range of up to 400 kilometers.[46] The Flanker-ASCM combination can thus attack targets 1,750 to 1,900 kilometers from the Flanker's last refueling point.

China's most advanced ASCM models—the Sunburn, the Russian submarine-launched SS-N-27 Sizzler, and the YJ-91/12—are especially dangerous to adversary surface warships. These missiles approach their targets at wave-top heights to avoid detection and fly at supersonic speeds while executing very sharp terminal attack maneuvers to thwart ship defense systems.

These missiles use both inertial and satellite navigation and acquire their targets with active radar, infrared tracking, and homing on the target's own electronic emissions.[47] There are grave doubts about the capacity of U.S. warships to defend themselves against ASCMs that have acquired their targets, especially when launched in coordinated, multi-axis volleys.[48]

China's acquisition of long-range air-launched ASCMs like the Sunburn and YJ-91/12 has greatly increased the danger to U.S. carrier strike groups. Previously, when China's air-launched ASCMs had ranges under one hundred kilometers, U.S. aircraft carriers and their air defense escorts would be able to prepare for the incoming attackers and employ the full range of the strike group's defenses. The carrier's early warning aircraft and combat air patrols could detect incoming formations of enemy aircraft many hundreds of kilometers from the strike group. This would allow the carrier time to launch more interceptors to battle the incoming attackers before they reached a launch point for their ASCMs. Even worse for the adversary, that launch point would be well within the range of the strike group's surface-to-air missiles, directed by the powerful Aegis combat system.

But the addition of the YJ-91/12 has shifted the advantage to China. The four hundred kilometer–range of this missile places its launch point beyond the range of the Aegis and its missiles. It also allows very little time for the carrier to get more interceptors into the air to battle the inbound Flankers before they reach the four hundred–kilometer launch point. A hypothetical attack by two Flanker regiments would involve forty-eight aircraft, about 12 percent of China's Flanker inventory in 2020. These two regiments could approach the carrier strike group from at least two axes. Since such an attack could arrive at any time, the strike group could maintain a continuous combat air patrol of only a few interceptor aircraft. Although the strike group could rush a few more interceptors to the air defense perimeter before the Flankers reached their missile launch points, the Flankers would heavily outnumber the defenders and would likely approach from more axes than the Navy fighters could defend.

Accepting that the strike group would shoot down some Flankers before they launched their antiship missiles, the strike group would still have to contend with 125 to 200 incoming ASCMs, which would make wave-top, supersonic approaches to the U.S. ships. In past engagements of antiship missiles against alerted surface warships, 32 percent of attacking missiles scored hits.[49] If only 5 percent of the ASCMs scored hits, the carrier strike group's ships would still receive five to ten missile impacts, likely causing enough damage to render the group ineffective and possibly defenseless against another attack. Even if few or no ASCMs achieved hits, the carrier strike group would still very likely have to retire, having exhausted its defensive missile magazines.

U.S. naval forces will also have to contend with Chinese attack submarines armed with ASCMs and wake-homing torpedoes. In 2012 China possessed twenty-nine attack submarines, each armed with up to eight advanced ASCMs. Eight of these submarines are Russian-built Kilo-class boats armed with the supersonic Sizzler ASCM.[50]

China's attack submarine force will continue to expand, with two indigenous models the focus of production. The Type 041 Yuan-class is a new diesel-electric submarine. The Yuan-class submarine is expected to have air-independent propulsion (AIP), for sustained and very quiet subsurface operations. Unlike nuclear-powered submarines, diesel-electric submarines like the Type 041 are not well suited for long-range operations. But AIP-equipped diesel-electric submarines present a particular challenge to antisubmarine forces, especially when operating in the relatively shallow waters such as those in the First Island Chain zone.[51] The Yuan boats are armed with new models of long-range land-attack and antiship cruise missiles, wired-guided and wake-homing torpedoes, and naval mines (China has over fifty thousand naval mines). The Congressional Research Service estimated that China added five Yuan submarines to its fleet in 2012, presumably with a similar production rate in the future.[52]

In 2015 China is expected to begin production of a new Type 095 nuclear-powered attack submarine, which will feature improved quieting technology. Although somewhat easier to detect than the Type 041 Yuan, as a nuclear-powered boat the Type 095 will be capable of wide-ranging missions in the Pacific, including intelligence gathering and land-attack strikes on bases in the Second Island Chain (e.g., Guam) and beyond. China's total attack submarine force is expected to reach more than seventy units by 2020 and become increasingly modern and well armed, as new models replace obsolescent types.[53]

China also operates thirteen destroyers and twenty-two frigates armed with ASCMs. Four of China's destroyers are the Russian-built Sovremenny-class ships, each armed with sixteen of the supersonic Sunburn ASCMs. Closer to shore, the PLAN operates over eighty fast attack craft, each armed with eight ASCMs. In almost all cases, the ASCMs China deploys on surface ships outrange the U.S. Navy's Harpoon ASCM. In a hypothetical surface engagement, U.S. warships would have to endure missile volleys from China's surface forces before they closed to the Harpoon's range. Finally, China's land-based ASCM batteries, deployed on TELs, will be able to strike naval targets out to 160 kilometers.[54]

China's layers of ASCM launch platforms thus present a substantial challenge to the U.S. Navy's long-favored method of projecting power ashore. Since the closing months of World War II and up through the employment of carrier-based strike aircraft over Afghanistan, U.S. fleet commanders have enjoyed the freedom to sail their aircraft carriers close to an enemy's shore, confident that these adversaries had little or no capacity to interrupt the carriers' flight operations. With the missile and sensor revolution, the rules have changed dramatically. In a conflict with China, it will be highly dangerous for U.S. aircraft carrier strike groups to operate within 1,100 kilometers of China, the maximum combat radius of the carrier's strike aircraft. We should expect the missile and sensor revolution to continue, with ASCM ranges increasing, pushing the U.S. Navy's airpower capability even farther from shore.

China's antiship ballistic missile (ASBM) program is perhaps the most dramatic example of the PLA's strategy to control the Near Seas from its continental position, if only because the PLA is implementing a maritime strike technology no other country has mastered. The DF-21D missile is China's ASBM and is a modified version of an existing medium-range ballistic missile (MRBM) in the Second Artillery's inventory. The DF-21D has a range of up to 1,500 kilometers and employs a maneuvering reentry vehicle armed with a unitary or submunition warhead. The reentry vehicle likely receives midcourse updates from the Second Artillery's command network, with the warhead's terminal guidance to a target provided by active radar and infrared homing. With the employment of midcourse countermeasures, high hypersonic speed, and warhead maneuvering, the DF-21D warhead is thought invulnerable to existing missile defenses.[55] China's annual production of MRBMs, the missile class used for the DF-21D ASBM, is estimated at ten to eleven per year, with the capacity to perhaps double this rate during a surge in production.[56] By the end of the decade, the PLA could possess at least eighty DF-21Ds mounted on mobile TELs, a force large enough to execute many multimissile volleys against adversary naval task forces. Along with its cruise missile cousins, China's antiship ballistic missile program is another aspect of the missile and sensor revolution that calls into question surface naval operations within a useful range of China and its Near Seas.[57]

China's Maritime Reconnaissance Complex

China's antiship missile systems and strategies will only be as good as the intelligence, targeting, and command systems that support them. The PLA operates complementary and redundant C4ISR (command, control, communications, computers, intelligence, surveillance, reconnaissance) networks that by 2020 are likely to fully support China's missile forces.

China operates land-based sky- and surface-wave over-the-horizon radars capable of detecting the rough position of surface naval forces as far as three thousand kilometers out to sea.[58] To identify specific surface ships, such as U.S. aircraft carriers, for targeting by China's submarines, antiship ballistic missiles, or Flanker regiments, China would employ its growing constellations of reconnaissance and navigation satellites. China has roughly fifteen imaging satellites useful for military reconnaissance missions, employing electro-optical, multispectral, and synthetic aperture radar sensors, capable of remote sensing by day or night and in all weather conditions.[59]

In 2013 this imaging satellite constellation was not sufficiently numerous to provide the PLA with continuous coverage of the maritime areas out to the Second Island Chain. However, steady launches of additional imaging satellites should give China the targeting capability the DF-21D requires within the next five to ten years.[60] For example China's synthetic aperture radar satellites provide all-weather, day and night coverage, with imaging resolution of five meters or less, sufficient to detect any U.S. Navy warship. By 2020 China's reconnaissance satellite constellations are likely to be capable of revisiting targeted areas every thirty minutes, frequently enough to track adversary naval task forces under way.[61] China's planned constellation of communications and data link satellites will reliably connect the imaging satellites to PLA commanders by 2020.[62] In addition, China's Beidou-2/Compass global navigation satellite constellation will be complete by 2020, giving China's aircraft, ships, and missiles an independent and highly accurate navigation and timing capability.[63]

China's attack submarine and surface naval forces, including the Type 052D guided missile destroyer equipped with long-range phased array radars, will be other sources of information on adversary naval and air forces. China also operates ocean-bottom sonar beds in its Near Seas, similar to the antisubmarine listening networks the United States operated during the Cold War.[64] In the air, China has adapted the indigenously produced Y-8 cargo aircraft for airborne early warning, electronic surveillance and warfare, and communication relay missions.[65] China will also likely use its civilian maritime patrol craft and even fishing vessels to spot adversary naval targets for its reconnaissance and command network.[66]

Finally, in the future China will use its continental position to develop an extensive land-based unmanned aerial vehicle (UAV) capability for patrolling the Near Seas and conducting other military operations such as data relay, electronic warfare, deception, and direct attack. The PLA is establishing a broad research and industrial base for UAV development, customized for the requirements of the Second Artillery, the air force, and the navy.[67] Over the next decade, China will very likely deploy medium- and high-altitude long-endurance UAVs deep into the western Pacific Ocean for surveillance, targeting support for antiship missiles, data relay, and electronic warfare.[68] Such a land-based UAV capability will supplement and provide critical redundancy for China's satellites and will likely possess capacity and resilience that expeditionary U.S. and allied forces will have trouble matching.

Will China Achieve What the USSR Failed to Achieve?

At the height of the Cold War military competition in the mid-1980s, the U.S. Navy and Air Force also faced a very disturbing cruise missile threat from Soviet maritime strike bomber aircraft and submarines. What Soviet planners termed the "reconnaissance-strike complex" prompted the U.S. Navy to invest in the Aegis combat system for its air defense cruisers and destroyers, the F-14 Tomcat and its long-range Phoenix air-to-air missile, antisubmarine warfare technology and equipment, and an anti-satellite program to blind Soviet ocean surveillance satellites. The U.S. Navy carrier strike groups also practiced deception and masking tactics, to avoid detection while approaching close enough to Soviet targets. The Soviet cruise missile threat forced the Navy to expend substantial resources on defensive measures, which detracted from the carrier strike group's offensive capacity.

Since the U.S. Navy's war against the Soviet reconnaissance-strike complex was never fought, we will never know whether the Soviet cruise missile threat was severe enough to jeopardize the viability of U.S. surface forces. What we do know is that China's version of the reconnaissance-strike complex has greatly benefited from the technology improvements that have occurred over the past three decades.[69] China's satellites have vastly improved electro-optical and radar sensors compared to the Soviet versions. China's antiship cruise missiles benefit from better targeting sensors than those on Soviet missiles several decades ago. China's antiship ballistic missile is armed with a maneuvering warhead that the Soviets were never able to field. Finally, and perhaps most crucially, China seems able to produce highly threatening quantities of platforms and munitions without burdening the Chinese economy to the point of collapse.

The U.S. Navy's defenses against missiles have also benefited from technological advances. The modern Aegis system and its surface-to-air missiles are superior to their 1980s versions. U.S. warships also have better point defensive systems. However, Navy deception and masking tactics have deteriorated since the Cold War. The Navy long ago retired the F-14 and the long-range Phoenix missile. And aircraft carriers and other Navy surface ships are as large and noticeable to optical, infrared, and radar reconnaissance as ever. Thus it is likely that the offensive reconnaissance-strike complex has benefited more from technological advance than have its targets.[70]

Why the Conventional Measures of Military Power in the Pacific Are Flawed

Some observers, many with only superficial knowledge of the military balance in the Pacific, have a sanguine view of the potential threat posed by China's military modernization. They will point to well-regarded sources like the Stockholm International Peace Research Institute, which noted that in 2012 U.S. military spending exceeded China's by a factor of four ($682 billion versus an estimated $166 billion for China, at market exchange rates).[71] Skeptics will also note that the United States has ten aircraft carriers in operational service compared to China's one (still in development), that the U.S. nuclear submarine force in 2012 outnumbered China's ten to one, and that the United States is the only country with operational stealthy bombers and fighter aircraft.[72]

These skeptics will also note that the United States has extensive combat and operational experience while China hasn't fought a war in over three decades. Indeed, the PLA, like all large organizations, suffers from a lack of cooperation among departments, bureaucratic jealousies, and staff inefficiencies.[73] In a May 2010 speech to the Navy League, former U.S. defense secretary Robert Gates noted that the U.S. Navy could carry at sea twice as many aircraft as the rest of the world's navies combined and that the U.S. fleet's missile capacity exceeded that of the next twenty navies—and that most of those navies were allies or friends of the United States.[74] The implication of such side-by-side comparisons is that U.S. military strength remains overwhelming and certainly enough to deter any conventional adversary.

However, such analyses are facile and disregard the critical comparisons that actually bear on the military balance in the western Pacific. For example such comparisons usually neglect China's many thousands of ballistic and cruise missiles with ranges exceeding five hundred kilometers; the United States has no such missiles on land opposing China and at best a few hundred available at sea in the Pacific.

Superficial side-by-side comparisons of the two arsenals don't reveal the very low number of bases on which U.S. forces in the theater are concentrated or the vulnerability of these bases, along with U.S. aircraft carriers, to missile attack. Considering these factors will largely remove U.S. tactical airpower from the tally sheet. Not including China's stealthy diesel-electric submarines neglects another substantial threat to U.S. surface warships operating near the First Island Chain, certainly a factor in the naval balance. Thus even though a count of platforms seems to reveal a U.S. advantage, a closer examination of the tactical circumstances in the region largely erases that ostensible U.S. advantage.

China's military planners have made an intense study of U.S. forces and capabilities and have designed their forces to achieve the missions these planners need them to accomplish, given the characteristics of U.S. forces. Although in most respects U.S. military forces remain more advanced, experienced, and capable in the aggregate, China's planners have still discerned notable shortcomings, which their strategy, doctrine, and investments exploit.

In a mid-ocean battle between Chinese and U.S. fleets, the U.S. side would undoubtedly prevail, due to its advantages in submarines, aircraft carriers, and operational experience. But that is not the battle China is preparing for. Using salami-slicing tactics, China aims to slowly establish its physical and legal presence over its claims in the South and East China Seas. Should the United States and its allies attempt to roll back this presence, they will have to make the first military move, a difficult political act.

From a military perspective, U.S. and allied forces will have to confront China's naval forces, optimized for missile and submarine combat in its Near Seas, and China's land-based air and missile power, also specifically structured for an "anti-navy" campaign out to two thousand kilometers. U.S. airpower, heavily weighted to short-range platforms, will find its few bases in the region vulnerable to missile attack. U.S. surface naval forces, including its aircraft carrier strike groups, will be vulnerable to missile attack long before coming into range of Chinese targets. U.S. long-range striking power, from submarine-launched cruise missiles and long-range bombers, will be too few in number or too vulnerable to China's integrated air defenses to be decisive against China's dispersed and mobile forces.

In his speech to the Navy League, Gates also made note of these asymmetric threats to U.S. platforms and doctrine and called on military planners to reexamine their assumptions.[75] During his time at the Pentagon, these planners and other analysts stepped up their attention to China's military challenge. But as we will see in the next chapter, they have much more work to do.

Chapter 5

AMERICA PIVOTS TO ASIA, THEN STUMBLES

By 2010 officials and military planners at the U.S. Department of Defense were fully engaged with the access denial problem posed by China's military modernization. The 2010 edition of the Quadrennial Defense Review, the department's periodic strategy assessment, explicitly discussed the military threat posed by China and directed the Air Force and Navy to establish a coordinated response.[1] In January 2012, under the signature of Joint Chiefs chairman Gen. Martin Dempsey, the Pentagon's Joint Staff issued the Joint Operational Access Concept (JOAC), an attempt at a capstone, all-service response to the access denial problem.[2] Two months prior to the arrival of that document, the department established the Air-Sea Strategy Office, staffed by officers from all four services and tasked with developing operational concepts and doctrine to counter access denial threats.[3] Between the "rebalance" to the Asia-Pacific region and the increasing focus of staff attention on theater access, a scramble was on inside the Pentagon in response to China's employment of the missile and sensor revolution.

The Pentagon's responses have become controversial and for many, unconvincing. This controversy should not be surprising. The challenge posed by China's missile-centered military strategy would seem to be a familiar problem for U.S. military planners and one well suited for the U.S. Defense Department's traditional strengths in technology and weapons platforms. The United States overcame a more virulent adversary in the Soviet Union and, in doing so, developed the research and technology defense culture that should be a good match for the problems posed by China. Finally, China is much more exposed to global commerce than was the Soviet Union and should thus be vulnerable to apparent U.S. advantages in naval and airpower, a form of leverage the United States could not employ so easily during the Cold War.

But as we will see, the current U.S. responses to China's military challenge are incomplete, uncompetitive, and impractical. The military responses are too narrowly focused and thus fail to take advantage of a full range of options that could be available to policymakers and commanders. Many of the U.S. responses under consideration are either dismissive of allies and potential partners or risk creating adversaries instead of eager supporters. Most crucially, the most commonly discussed U.S. response, the Air-Sea Battle Concept, concentrates expensive U.S. defense resources at China's strengths rather than its vulnerabilities. Although some aspects of Air-Sea Battle will be necessary in an effective response to China, the concept by itself is uncompetitive and therefore an insufficient answer to China's military modernization.

In order to formulate an effective strategy in response to China, we should first understand what is wrong with the current responses. This chapter will explain the shortcomings of the current concepts and clear the way for a better strategy.

Worrying Once Again about the "Reconnaissance-Strike Complex"

Using military power in an attempt to deny an adversary access to a region or territory is as old as warfare itself. In naval history, epic engagements such as Salamis (480 BCE), Gravelines (1588), and the campaign against the German submarine fleet in World War II (1939–45) are notable examples of adversaries clashing over theater access in order to enable, or prevent, further decisive operations ashore. The Battle of Britain, the fight in August and September 1940 between the British and German air forces for control of the airspace over southern England, is another classic example of an access denial effort against an expeditionary force. China's development of an access denial capacity thus fits within a long stream of military history.

That said, each example of an access denial challenge holds its own aspects of tactics and technology, which commanders and military planners must master and shape for their purposes. China's access denial strategy, based on the latest developments of the missile and sensor revolution, has its unique features, which are now the object of intense scrutiny.

Andrew F. Krepinevich, president of the Center for Strategic and Budgetary Assessments (CSBA), lays claim to the first discussion of the access denial problem, at least in its current form. In November 1993, while serving as an analyst at the U.S. Defense Department's Office of Net Assessment (ONA), Krepinevich completed a draft report that forecast the consequences of adversary long-range missiles and precision weapons. Once these adversaries acquired the precision-guided munitions and targeting capabilities U.S. forces had recently demonstrated in the 1991 Persian Gulf War, Krepinevich concluded that such capabilities would threaten U.S. forward military bases and the ability of U.S. forces to project power in traditional ways into combat zones.[4]

Early awareness in the 1990s of the potential for adversary access denial was no doubt informed by the 1970s Soviet "reconnaissance-strike complex" concept (see chapters 3 and 4).[5] The combination of the Backfire bomber and Kitchen antiship missile warranted the great concern it generated inside the U.S. Navy at that time. But the quiet ending of the U.S.-Soviet competition relegated the Soviet "reconnaissance-strike complex" to a theoretical abstraction.

However, the precision-guided rout inflicted on Iraqi forces in 1991 by U.S. and coalition airpower was no abstraction. The Persian Gulf War was the first large-scale demonstration of the damage a wide-ranging intelligence and command network and precision-guided munitions (the envisioned components of the Soviet reconnaissance-strike complex) could inflict on adversary command and control, air, and land forces. Subsequent to that episode, Krepinevich and others at ONA and CSBA began to contemplate the threat a modern adversary reconnaissance-strike complex could pose for forward-deployed and expeditionary U.S. naval and airpower. It has taken two decades, but what began as a thought experiment by Krepinevich is now a real-world dread for U.S. military commanders and planners in the western Pacific.

JOAC Lays Out the Problem, But Not the Answer

As mentioned above, Gen. Martin Dempsey, soon after he became chairman of the Joints Chiefs of Staff in 2011, ordered the JCS and other military experts to write the JOAC. JOAC was issued under Dempsey's signature in January 2012.[6] The monograph was an attempt to fashion a top-level, capstone perspective on the access denial challenge, to show that the problem was not a concern just for the Navy and Air Force, and to reassure the defense bureaucracy that all four services would be included in the solutions the department would pursue.

The authors of JOAC performed a notable public service by honestly describing the challenges U.S. military forces would increasingly face in merely obtaining access to war zones, let alone prevailing against adversaries. Even more notable was the authors' blunt candor concerning the risks and barriers U.S. policymakers and military planners will face when attempting to fashion practical solutions to the access challenge, especially those posed by peer competitors such as China. JOAC described the military problem. But it was not very sanguine about an easy solution.

The authors of JOAC asserted that *cross-domain synergy*, "the complementary vice merely additive employment of capabilities in different domains [land, sea, air, space, and cyber] such that each enhances the effectiveness and compensates for the vulnerabilities of the others," should be the central operating tenet for U.S. and allied forces attempting to prevail against adversary access denial capabilities.[7] An example of cross-domain synergy would be employing submarine-launched cruise missiles to suppress enemy air defenses in prelude to an air campaign; another would be the use of cyber weapons to disrupt an adversary's space-based reconnaissance and command network. JOAC also calls for U.S. and coalition forces to achieve cross-domain synergy at lower levels in an organization. The goal is to enable U.S. forces to generate the speedy decisions and actions necessary to exploit fleeting local vulnerabilities in adversary forces and systems. Faster decision making and exploitation of opportunities will more likely occur if low-echelon commanders are empowered to act independently and if they have the cross-domain tools envisioned by the concept.[8]

JOAC's description of the sophisticated challenges to theater access matches the description of China's military modernization discussed in chapter 4. JOAC's list of looming access barriers includes precision-guided and long-range cruise and ballistic missiles; long-range and integrated surveillance and targeting networks; anti-satellite weapons that threaten U.S. space systems; and a submarine fleet capable of holding at risk sea-lanes that U.S. forces would use to transit to an operational theater.[9] As we have seen, these are all capabilities that have been top investments of the PLA.

One of JOAC's purposes is to guide the development of joint warfighting doctrine for overcoming access barriers. JOAC offers up a list of precepts for future authors of doctrine and war plans involving access denial challenges. Unfortunately most of these precepts are either facile, impractical, or counterproductive. For example JOAC's suggested precepts include "maximize surprise," "disrupt enemy reconnaissance and surveillance efforts," "prepare the operational area in advance," "exploit advantages in one or more domains to disrupt enemy anti-access/area-denial capabilities in others," and "create pockets of local domain superiority."[10] These are hardly original ideas for trained commanders and planners of any military background.

On the other hand, JOAC's suggestions to "maneuver directly against key operational objectives from strategic distance," "attack enemy anti-access/area-denial defenses in depth," and "attack the enemy's space and cyber capabilities" may either be beyond the capabilities of U.S. and allied forces, or may create unfavorable escalation risks—points discussed in more depth below.

In the concluding portions of JOAC, the JCS authors soberly lay out the steep challenge facing both policymakers and military planners as they contemplate the implications of China's military modernization. JOAC lists thirty operational capabilities U.S. military forces should possess if they expect to succeed in a high-end access denial environment. The list includes capabilities such as

1. The ability to perform effective command and control in a degraded or austere communications environment.
2. The ability to locate, target, and suppress or neutralize hostile anti-access and area-denial capabilities in complex terrain with the necessary range, precision, responsiveness and reversible and permanent effects while limiting collateral damage.
3. The ability to conduct and support operational maneuver over strategic distances along multiple axes of advance by air and sea.
4. The ability to mask the approach of joint maneuver elements to enable those forces to penetrate sophisticated anti-access systems and close within striking range with acceptable risk.[11]

Many of these required capabilities are operations few if any U.S. or allied commanders have ever had to execute, at least outside of scripted training events. The United States has not faced large-scale opposed access to the global commons since 1945. Today's commanders and their staffs thus face the disorienting task of having to discard long-standing assumptions and procedures related to strategic maneuver, engagement ranges, logistics support, and force protection, among many other considerations. As we saw in chapter 3, discarding long-standing ways of doing things has not been a notable characteristic of U.S. military culture for many decades, especially in the Pacific theater.

JOAC's authors performed their highest public service when they listed ten risks that if not addressed could compromise the joint access concept and presumably the viability of access operations by U.S. and coalition forces.[12] In this risk analysis, the authors frequently discussed the possibility that U.S. and allied forces would fail to achieve sufficient cross-domain synergy, the key tenet of the concept. This failure could occur because of an adversary's success at degrading the coalition's command and control network, thus preventing the effective integration of domain capabilities. China's cyberwarfare and counterspace capabilities are notable concerns in this regard. Failure could similarly occur because the systems in the various domains are unable to integrate their operations or because particular operational demands make it too complicated to do so.

JOAC calls for cross-domain synergy to occur at low organizational levels in order to speed up actions and take advantage of fleeting opportunities. However, low-level commanders and staffs may be untrained, ill equipped, insufficiently connected, or lack the authority to achieve the cross-domain synergy JOAC's authors intend. Once again, these are supposed to be priorities for the Air-Sea Battle Office and ongoing training, but improvements may require difficult disruptions to resistant service cultures.

Perhaps even more critical, JOAC's authors posited that U.S. and allied forces may simply lack the proper systems and capabilities to implement some the concept's required precepts and tasks. In addition, policymakers may conclude that it is too expensive to acquire these systems and capabilities. For example the concept calls for employing deep and precise strikes to attack deeply inside an adversary's systems and networks. U.S. and coalition forces may not be able to acquire at a reasonable cost the capabilities needed to acquire and target mobile and stealthy adversary platforms operating from deep continental positions. Similarly planners may find it impractical to logistically support the concept at strategic distances through contested lines of communication (chapters 7 through 9 discuss these challenges).

Finally, and perhaps most crucially, JOAC's authors suggest that policymakers may not want to execute some of the concept's essential features. Deep strikes against enemy systems and networks could greatly increase escalation risks, in ways unfavorable to U.S. interests. For example policymakers may blanch at bombarding the homeland of an adversary armed with intercontinental-range nuclear forces. In addition, attacks on an adversary's space and computer systems would likely lead to retaliation against U.S. systems, an escalation that could impair U.S. forces more than it would the adversary's forces.

JOAC's formal title—*Joint Operational Access Concept, Version 1.0*—emphasizes the "first draft" nature of the document, likely no accident for Dempsey and the authors. It was a reminder of how little work has been done by the U.S. military on the access problem, how much more needs to be done, and, by implication, how late the Defense Department arrived at the issue. Dempsey deserves credit for putting his signature on a document that candidly discusses the operational risks U.S. forces face and thus how ill-prepared and ill-equipped his forces are for the high-end access challenge they will soon face in the western Pacific. The first step for fixing a problem is admitting that it exists. JOAC did that. JOAC also hopes to move the immense and largely inert defense bureaucracy to adapt before an access crisis strikes. That would be out of character for the Pentagon, yet not a completely forlorn hope.

Why Air-Sea Battle Is Both Wrong and Right

Well before General Dempsey had the JCS draft JOAC, an action that ensured all four services would have a role in the access denial problem, staff planners at the Air Force and the Navy had been at work on the Air-Sea Battle Concept. That concept in its current context traces back to the 1990s with theoretical analysis occurring at the Pentagon's Office of Net Assessment, the Center for Strategic and Budgetary Assessments, and the Naval War College among other places. In a 2010 study titled *AirSea Battle: A Point-of-Departure Operational Concept*, CSBA formally defined Air-Sea Battle and explained how the Defense Department might implement the concept in an effort to overcome the PLA's access denial programs.[13] Completing the concept's institutionalization, the Defense Department's 2010 Quadrennial Defense Review made explicit mention of the Air-Sea Battle Concept and called on the department to implement its tenets.[14]

Even before it received formal blessing by top officials in the department, Air-Sea Battle sparked a backlash from critics. The secretive nature of the concept and those planning it, explained as required for operational security, raised suspicions. Those suspicions were taken up by advocates for the ground forces, who saw the Army and Marine Corps still at war and yet threatened with having the future budgets of the ground forces gutted in order to pay for the exotic technology Air-Sea Battle would likely require. Finally, many strategists were skeptical about a concept that openly relied on large-scale bombardment of a nuclear-armed peer competitor like China. These critics foresaw a boondoggle of spending that would enrich certain defense contractors but would result in weapons and capabilities that could never be used in the real world.

In response to this skepticism, in February 2012 Gen. Norton Schwartz, then–chief of staff of the Air Force, and Adm. Jonathan Greenert, chief of Naval Operations, jointly wrote an essay on Air-Sea Battle for *The American Interest* journal. Their essay described the military problem that the concept is designed to address and explained some of the concept's operational methods. In doing so, Greenert and Schwartz also attempted to squelch some of the misunderstanding that the previously secretive concept had spawned.[15]

Schwartz and Greenert's description of the military problem closely matched that found in the JCS's JOAC monograph. They surveyed past examples of adversary access denial efforts, such as the German submarine campaign in the Atlantic during World War II and the Soviet blockade of Berlin in 1948, and explained how ad hoc interservice cooperation (what JOAC calls "cross-domain synergy") overcame these adversary attempts at exclusion. They described how Army Air Corps long-range bombers coordinated their actions with Navy sub-hunting destroyers and escort carriers to eventually defeat the German submarine threat. In Berlin, Air Force cargo aircraft persuaded Soviet leaders that a land blockade of Berlin was fruitless.

According to Schwartz and Greenert, the access denial problem is becoming a pervasive syndrome—not just a one-off situation in the western Pacific. They assert that ad hoc solutions designed for specific episodes, such as the antisubmarine campaign in the Atlantic in World War II, won't be adequate in the future. Instead the Defense Department requires, by their reckoning, a permanent and wide-ranging organization, both at the Pentagon and at field commands, to ensure comprehensive interservice integration. Far from being a power and budget grab by the Air Force and Navy, the Air-Sea Battle concept was defended by the two officers as sensible planning and coordination to cope with an increasingly omnipresent problem and the very kind of prudent action Defense Department officials should be taking.

After making that reasonable case, Schwartz and Greenert then proceeded to explain how Air-Sea Battle would actually work in combat. However their discussion of the concept's three lines of effort only served to expose the concept's shortcomings. Instead of rebutting skeptical strategists, the two officers raised doubts about the concept's practicality.

At its essence, Air-Sea Battle is about protecting U.S. and allied warships and bases from adversary missiles (submarine torpedoes are also a consideration). In their *American Interest* article, Schwartz and Greenert described three lines of effort designed to thwart precision missile attacks: (1) *disruption* of adversary reconnaissance and command networks; (2) *destruction* of adversary missile-launching platform such as submarines, aircraft, and ships, to reduce the missile threat to allied forces; and (3) *defeating* adversary missiles before they impact allied targets. The officers discussed how a networked and integrated joint force, able to operate at great depth, will be required to execute Air-Sea Battle's three lines of effort.

Disrupting adversary reconnaissance and command networks, in other words, disrupting that adversary's ability to locate and target opponents, involves a variety of passive and active measures, some of which are as old as warfare itself. Ancient passive measures, all still used today, include camouflage, hiding out of sight, and employing decoys. Over the past century, combatants have disrupted enemy surveillance by shutting down their radios and radar (called operating under electronic emissions control or

EMCON) and employing deception such as fake transmitters. More recent forms of disruption include electronic attacks on adversary sensors and thwarting enemy sensors through stealthy designs and materials.

More controversial would be kinetic attacks on China's reconnaissance satellite constellations and cyber attacks on the PLA's communication and computer networks. The PLA has strived to emulate the U.S. military's ability to operate under "conditions of informatization." As commanders on both sides know, such a capability, while greatly enhancing command efficiency, also increases vulnerability to command disruption.

U.S. military forces have become highly dependent on space and computerized global communication systems, especially expeditionary forces that would be "playing an away game" in the western Pacific (discussed in chapter 3). At the same time, China has already acquired a high level of expertise with both space and counterspace operations and with cyberwarfare.[16] U.S. strategists contemplating cyber and kinetic attacks on China's space-based surveillance and communication networks should reckon with the possibility that China enjoys escalation dominance in these domains.

This means that China could benefit from war in the space and cyber domains because of the greater reliance by U.S. military forces on space and computer capabilities and the relative difficulty the United States will face establishing alternatives to this reliance. By contrast, China's position as the continental power improves its position in this regard. As a large continental power in a hypothetical conflict against U.S. expeditionary forces, China will have a much easier time operating a land-based manned and unmanned aircraft reconnaissance network to supplement and substitute for a space-based intelligence and communications system. In a hypothetical war over space-based networks, China will have an easier time fielding substitutes, at least for military operations over China's Near Seas, than will the United States. Thus for technical and geographic reasons, the United States may find it imprudent to disrupt China's reconnaissance and command networks if doing so invites Chinese retaliation on U.S. networks, which the United States would have a much more difficult time replacing or working without.

Schwartz and Greenert's second line of effort contemplates destroying adversary platforms such as submarines, aircraft, and ships to reduce the missile threat to allied forces. If this battle were to take place over neutral ground, U.S. forces would enjoy advantages in both technical sophistication and operational experience. However, for battle over the control of the East and South China Seas, China's land-based "anti-navy" air and missile forces will increasingly give it an advantage over U.S. expeditionary forces.

As discussed in chapters 3 and 4, by next decade, China's land-attack and antiship missile forces will make it too dangerous for U.S. short-range tactical airpower, which constitutes the vast majority of U.S. striking power, to get close enough to suppress China's land-based aircraft and missile forces. China's airpower will operate from scores of air bases, most hardened against air attack and heavily defended by a sophisticated air defense system. China's land-based antiship missiles will operate from mobile TELs, which will use China's expansive and complex terrain to hide from U.S. sensors.

With its heavy reliance on short-range tactical airpower, the United States has the wrong mix of forces to execute Schwartz and Greenert's second line of effort. The United States lacks the number of long-range platforms and weapons required for a sustained campaign against China's land-based air and missile power. The 1991 Persian Gulf War indicated the rough order of magnitude of such a campaign, namely tens of thousands of individual bomb aim points.[17] To attack this target set, the United States would be limited to a handful of B-2 bombers (the only aircraft with the range and stealthiness to operate inside China's air defense system) plus Navy Tomahawk cruise missiles numbering in the hundreds rather than thousands.[18] Finally, the INF Treaty, which prohibits the United States from matching China's massive missile forces, completes the portrait of China's looming missile dominance in the western Pacific. "Killing the archer before he shoots the arrow," Air-Sea Battle's second line of effort, will very likely be beyond the capacity of U.S. forces when facing the PLA in the next decade.

The inability of U.S. commanders to get their otherwise highly capable short-range airpower into effective range of China's bases explains the shortfall in U.S. strike capacity. But why should China alone benefit from air base hardening and air defense systems? Can't the United States also harden its bases in the region, add air and missile defenses, and disperse its forces to additional sites, just like the PLA?

The United States in fact intends to make all of these improvements to its basing posture in the region, and will be wise to do so.[19] Strengthening the forward presence of U.S. military forces in the region sends a political message to both America's partners and China that the United States is deepening its security commitment to the region. As important, the presence of these forces, even though they will be vulnerable to Chinese missile attack, establishes "first strike deterrence." This means that if, during a conflict, PLA commanders decided to remove these threats to Chinese operations, China would have to escalate the war by attacking more countries, presumably bringing them into the conflict against China.

In spite of these realities, geography, China's continental position, its marginal cost advantages, and the INF Treaty result in a structural advantage in China's favor with respect to basing options. As the continental power operating from a large country, China's air and missile forces will have scores of basing options. The United States, by contrast the expeditionary power, is limited to what its allies allow it and by the relatively few choices available on islands in the western Pacific. In this respect, U.S. bases are either too close to the PLA's firepower or too distant to be practical for short-range tactical aircraft.

U.S. planners realize that Guam, while developing as an important hub for U.S. air and naval power, is also becoming a vulnerable single point of failure for U.S. strategy in the region. The United States intends to build additional base facilities on neighboring sites such as Saipan, Tinian, and elsewhere along the Second Island Chain. But these new bases will provide only modest risk diversification for U.S. forces. China will be well aware of these facilities and will simply allocate additional missiles to target these sites. China will benefit from its marginal cost advantage; the declining relative cost of precision missiles will overcome the higher costs to the United States of adding hardened aircraft shelters and missile defense systems.[20]

A logical U.S. response to the Chinese missile threat to U.S. air bases in the region is to increase the number of missile defense systems such as Patriot and Theater High Altitude Air Defense (THAAD). Another response is to improve air base hardening by locating air base support services underground and by fabricating hardened aircraft shelters. A 2011 RAND report examined these options and concluded that although these measures would require the PLA to expend more missiles to achieve its goals, missile defenses and hardening are unlikely to keep the bases in action if China were determined to suppress them.[21] It will be cheaper for China to add additional attacking missiles than for the United States to add interceptors. Attacking missiles will always be able to crater runways and puncture aircraft shelters. U.S. commanders will face the prospect of placing very expensive aircraft at risk of further Chinese bombardment in the hope of finding brief periods of air base availability.

An alternative approach is to move U.S. tactical aircraft to dispersal and expeditionary air bases across the region. The Salty Demo exercise (discussed in chapter 4) noted that during the Cold War, the U.S. Air Force in Europe responded to the Soviet threat to its main fighter bases by establishing agreements to operate from an additional sixty dispersal bases in wartime. For the NATO Central Front, where the main Soviet attack was expected, the Air Force would call on thirty dispersal air bases, in addition to the twenty main bases it operated in that region. The hope (never tested) was that with so many basing options, the Air Force would be able to maintain effective sortie generation in the face of Soviet air and missile attacks on its bases.[22]

Unfortunately the United States and its allies won't be able to apply this example in the western Pacific. During the Cold War in Europe, NATO was a continental power, facing off against another continental power. Both sides enjoyed territorial depth, highly developed military infrastructures, and a high concentration of forces in a relatively small theater of operations (NATO's Central Front would fit into the Philippine Sea). In the Pacific, China is the only continental power. The United States and its allies are operating from islands or from warships, which is why they are limited to so few bases. Political barriers and the lack of available land mean there is little prospect of creating a reserve of dispersal bases such as the Air Force enjoyed in Europe. Indeed the United States and Japan have bickered for over fifteen years over the construction of a new small air base on a remote part of Okinawa, an issue that still hasn't been resolved. In a hypothetical conflict, existing civilian airports could be used as dispersal air bases. But with no hardened aircraft shelters or support facilities, they and the aircraft parked there will be very vulnerable to missile attack.

Nor are expeditionary air bases an attractive option. Some countries have planned to use stretches of highway or other large concrete pads as improvised air bases. The U.S. Air Force rejected this option in Europe during the Cold War because it concluded it could not organize the logistics system necessary to support a meaningful amount of combat sorties.[23] Fighter aircraft operations require a large and sustained flow of fuel, ordnance, spare parts, maintenance and support personnel, and the housing and supporting facilities required to maintain these personnel and operations (see chapter 3). That is why air forces have preferred large, fixed bases. Expeditionary bases would likely be difficult to supply and therefore unlikely to generate many combat sorties. Remotely located expeditionary bases may be outside the coverage of air and missile defenses and if hastily established, could be vulnerable to ground attack by special operations direct action teams. Finally, such bases are unlikely to have any hardened facilities and, once discovered, would be highly vulnerable to missile attack. For these reasons, commanders are unlikely to be comfortable parking billions of dollars' worth of advanced fighter aircraft at expeditionary sites.

For all these reasons—geography, China's continental position, marginal costs, and difficulties with dispersing forces—China will enjoy structural advantages in the competition over "killing archers."

That leaves Schwartz and Greenert's third line of effort: defeating adversary missiles before they impact their targets. Chapter 4 examined the steep challenge faced by U.S. air bases and naval task forces attempting to defend against saturation missile attacks. The current era of technology favors offensive missiles compared to passive and active defensive measures.

Over the next decade, the falling relative cost of guided munitions will greatly expand the number of incoming missiles with which defenders must cope. Falling relative missile costs will similarly reduce the value of passive defenses. With cheap but precise missiles, rationing by the attackers will be less necessary; attackers will simply strike more and more suspected, if unconfirmed, adversary targets. The same technological progress will improve sensor fidelity and reduce sensor costs, resulting in their ubiquity on and around the battlefield—increasing ubiquity and fidelity of sensors will make passive defenses such as deception, dispersion, and camouflage less useful.

Advancing technology should logically also benefit defenders. But for the next decade, active defenses, such as missile interceptors, will be much more costly than offensive missiles, making a race between attackers and defenders a cost contest defenders will lose. Emerging technologies such as electromagnetic rail guns and free electron lasers hold out the hope of swinging the military balance back to defenses (chapter 9 will discuss this topic). But such technologies, if successful in the laboratory, won't see the battlefield until the second half of the 2020s.[24] This means that for at least the next ten years, the United States and its allies in the western Pacific face a deteriorating security balance—the consequence of today's missile and sensor revolution.

The technical advantages currently enjoyed by the attacker, and thus the vulnerability of forward-deployed forces, increases the risk of instability during crises. During a crisis, decision makers may view their own vulnerable forces from a "use it, or lose it" perspective, increasing the temptation to strike first before the other side employs missile power to disarm the opponent. The fact that U.S. forces have such short range, are located so close to Chinese firepower, and are so vulnerable to sudden attack only increases the level of crisis instability and the pressure that U.S. policymakers would face during a crisis.[25] This perceived "first-mover advantage" and the vulnerability of forward-deployed forces to a surprise disarming strike is yet another disturbing parallel with the decision pressures faced by policymakers and military commanders in Europe during the summer of 1914.

The U.S. military's perception of Chinese military doctrine would further add to crisis instability. According to that perception, China's doctrine emphasizes secrecy, deception, offensive action, and the benefits of surprise attack.[26] Combining this perception with the vulnerability of forward-deployed U.S. forces in the region magnifies concerns about crisis instability. A remedy for this dangerous condition is a reformed U.S. force structure that would not be as vulnerable to surprise attack and that would thus not create a "use it, or lose it" situation. The United States should retain some forward-deployed forces as a signal of its security commitment to the region and to establish first strike deterrence. But a large majority of its power-projection capacity should be in long-range forces that would be much less vulnerable to Chinese preemptive attack and would thus provide greater stability during a crisis. Chapters 8 and 9 will address these reforms.

The Air-Sea Battle concept, at least as described by Schwartz and Greenert, is an uncompetitive response to China's access denial strategy. It is uncompetitive because it focuses expensive U.S. and coalition military resources at China's strengths rather than its vulnerabilities. As we have explored, all three of Air-Sea Battle's lines of effort have flaws that would impair their practicality in wartime. Should there be a conflict between the United States and China, Air-Sea Battle does not look like a winning approach for the United States and its allies.

Although Air-Sea Battle won't be a path to success, some elements of the concept are valuable and will be essential features of a truly competitive U.S. response to the security competition in East Asia. Chapters 6 through 10 discuss the design of competitive strategies and how U.S. policymakers and military planners should fashion a design for the region.

Why a Blockade Is Not an Easy Answer

We have seen that the JOAC, the U.S. Defense Department's current top-level thinking on the access denial problem, is more of an aspiration than a description of real military capacity. JOAC's authors discussed a long list of required capabilities, many of which the United States won't be able to achieve in the western Pacific by the end of the decade. They also listed some significant risks that stand in the way of achieving the concept's goals.

Air-Sea Battle, a precursor to JOAC and now subsumed within it, also has its flaws and critics. Its three lines of effort—disrupting adversary sensors and command, destroying an enemy's missile-launching platforms, and defeating those missiles after launch—are increasingly impractical tasks, especially against a future peer competitor like China.

But for many strategists, Air-Sea Battle's most glaring weakness is its implicit call for widespread bombing of China. For many experienced strategy advisers, bombing a peer nuclear power would lead to escalation risks that no U.S. president would be willing to face. By this view, a strategy based on this premise will be stillborn and thus not a credible option or deterrent.

These views have sparked a search for alternative ways to achieve leverage over China during a conflict without creating dangerous escalation risks. That search has logically led to China's trade-dependent economy, which appears to be a tantalizing vulnerability and an exposure ripe for exploitation. Economic sanctions or even a maritime blockade would seem to offer a way of creating leverage without having to bomb China proper and risk the grim possibility of escalation against a formidable nuclear weapons state.

For some strategists, a distant blockage or "offshore control" is a promising strategy. Dr. T. X. Hammes, a senior research fellow at the U.S. National Defense University, has recommended this approach. Under offshore control, Hammes recommends using U.S. air, maritime, and ground forces to impose a distant blockade of Chinese commerce, as an alternative to a seemingly expensive and risky direct assault on China's homeland contemplated by Air-Sea Battle.[27]

Blockade advocates see several advantages compared to Air-Sea Battle's call for large-scale attacks on China's military forces and space assets. They note the Chinese economy's high exposure to seaborne commerce, both for raw material imports and for finished goods exports. Hammes posits that China's economy would have a tough time adjusting to a cutoff of seaborne trade. A distant blockade, implemented at the Indonesia archipelago and the First and Second Island Chains, would, to China's detriment, take advantage of these permanent geographical features. In addition, the enforcement of the blockade by U.S. and coalition surface forces would largely occur outside the range of China's land-based air and missile power. Closer to China's shore, the United States would use its advantage in submarines to tighten the blockade.

Equally important, in Hammes's view, is what offshore control would not do. It would not require a buildup by the United States of long-range striking power, which he doesn't believe will be affordable. Next, offshore control would explicitly rule out kinetic and cyber attacks on China's homeland, space assets, and other command networks. Hammes asserts that such forbearance would avert risky and self-defeating escalation and would make it easier for policymakers on both sides to find a path to negotiated war termination. Finally, Hammes believes that offshore control will be more acceptable than Air-Sea Battle to U.S. allies in the region. Some of these allies will likely be reluctant to openly join up with an aggressively offensive military strategy against China. Further, most of the region's military forces are not prepared for the high-technology battle contemplated by the Air-Sea Battle concept.

Thus Hammes and other blockade advocates conclude that a distant blockade is a more sensible and less risky approach than Air-Sea Battle. It takes advantage of geographical advantages and U.S. maritime strengths while avoiding China's air and missile power. It attacks a particular vulnerability in the Chinese economy. Perhaps most important, it is a slow-moving approach, allowing policymakers on both sides to avoid dangerous escalation and to find a way to resolve a conflict without losing face.

Although formulated to avoid Air-Sea Battle's drawbacks, offshore control contains its own weaknesses, which inhibit its practicality. A blockade suffers from two major weaknesses. First, a blockade will threaten to inflict almost as much economic damage on U.S. allies and neutral countries as it would on China. This will make a U.S. blockade highly unpopular across the world and likely politically unsustainable for very long. Second, the huge volume of commerce and shipping involved in a blockade of China is almost certainly beyond the capacity of the U.S. military to manage in an orderly way, making the implementation of a blockade impractical.

Hammes assumes that a conflict with China would last for years and would result in massive damage to the global economy. Indeed, he asserts that these characteristics are favorable to the United States and a competitive weakness for China.[28] Hammes reasons that in a long conflict structured on a blockade and global trade disruption, the United States would be less vulnerable than China and in a better position to adapt by building new commercial shipping routes. He concludes that the United States would thus gain negotiating leverage and a favorable position to end the conflict.

This is not likely to be the case. A military blockade against China would make the United States an aggressor against the global economy, since the damaging effects of the blockade, as Hammes points outs, would be felt everywhere. This premise will especially be the case if the United States is forced to act in response to Chinese "salami slicing," by inciting a crisis over China's small actions that many will view as not serious enough to warrant brinkmanship. It is questionable whether the United States would be able to politically sustain a blockade for the time required to compel a change in Chinese policy, especially when some of the greatest unintended damage from a blockade would fall on U.S. allies in Asia, Europe, and Latin America.

Economic damage inside the United States and China would also be severe. As an authoritarian country, with strict censorship controls and a large internal security apparatus, it is reasonable to presume that the Chinese Communist Party and government would stand a better chance of outlasting the domestic and global political backlash from the blockade's consequences. This outcome is even more likely when one considers both the high level of nationalist feeling inside China, compared to that in the United States, and the memory of the Chinese population concerning foreign economic exploitation. It is questionable to conclude that a prolonged and economically devastating blockade would favor the United States.

A U.S. blockade would also damage the U.S. diplomatic position, especially with key relationships around Eurasia. In response to a seaborne blockade, China would attempt to reroute trade through Russia and Central Asia. China would not be able to use the old "Silk Road" to regain what it lost in seaborne traffic. But the blockade would boost geopolitical ties between China and Russia and greatly increase Russia's overall geopolitical and economic role, a result not in America's interest. Europe's trade with China would go through Russia, which could cause Europe to strategically drift away from the United States. In essence, a distant blockade would cut the United States away from Eurasian affairs, increase the power of U.S. adversaries there, and inadvertently push its Eurasian allies away.

Next, the U.S. military is neither equipped nor organized to execute the distant blockade that offshore control will require. Enforcing a distant blockade would be an immense task. For example, over 60,000 ships transit the Strait of Malacca every year, a rate of over 164 ships every day.[29] It would not be politically feasible in the modern era for U.S. submarines to simply lie off China's ports and sink all incoming merchant ships. Such "unrestricted submarine warfare," and the resultant casualties to third-nation civilians, would be even less politically sustainable today than it was for Germany and its submarine strategies in the twentieth century. The U.S. military would thus have the task of boarding and searching thousands of container ships at a variety of distant points in the Indian and Pacific Oceans, finding cargo bound for China, and somehow diverting that cargo while minimizing disruption to the rest of the global economy.

This task would require the Navy, Marine Corps, and Army to mobilize hundreds of platoon-sized visit, board, search, seizure (VBSS) teams and support them at sea for a potentially open-ended duration. For example, staffing two-hundred platoon-sized VBSS teams on an ongoing rotational basis could require the Marine Corps and Army to commit at least ten regiment- or brigade-sized units to the task. An additional combat support organization would be required.

The U.S. Navy operates thirty-three amphibious ships.[30] Sustainable maintenance practices typically permit the Navy to operationally deploy at best no more than a third of such a force at any one time. The Navy's amphibious ships, with troop berthing quarters, helicopter space, small-boat facilities, and command suites, are well suited for blockade enforcement. Leased commercial ships, even if available in the numbers required, generally do not have these features and would likely be unsuited for prolonged VBSS operations, which would require billeting troops for months at sea and supporting helicopter and small-boat detachments. Other Navy ships such as littoral combat ships and joint high-speed vessels could supplement the thirty-three amphibious ships.

But that addition would still be trivial compared to the immense search and boarding requirement, which could amount to hundreds of ships per day. The Navy's amphibious fleet, even if supplemented with improvised support, would lack the capacity to sort through the thousands of commercial ships sailing in and out of East Asia. The offshore control strategy is almost certainly beyond the capacity of the U.S. Navy to execute and would leave the United States with little reserve amphibious or ground combat power for other contingencies.

Nor should U.S. planners count on host nation support from countries in the Indian and Pacific Oceans for enforcement of such a blockade. As mentioned previously, the economic effects of the blockade would render the U.S. policy unpopular and likely unsupported by many neutral countries, let alone allies.

Limiting the blockade to just the crude oil trade and the large tankers that transport crude oil from the Middle East and Africa also won't work. China could respond to such an oil blockade by seizing outright the maritime territory it already claims in the East and South China Seas and then using its access denial forces to defend these seizures from counterattack and, likely, from commercial transit by the United States and allied countries. As mentioned in chapter 1, the U.S. government estimates that these two seas hold enough crude oil to supply China's future needs for perhaps seventy-five years.[31] If the United States and its allies in the region sought to recapture the seas and restore freedom of navigation to the western Pacific, doing so would require robust military forces and the willingness to attack China, conditions that advocates of offshore control are hoping to avoid.

There would be additional political and geostrategic consequences to an indefinite distant blockade of China. The global blockade imposed by the U.S. military would be vulnerable to irregular warfare methods and propaganda exploitation. Cargos bound for China would be mixed on container ships with cargo bound for many other countries in the region.[32] U.S. board and search operations would be blamed for the delays in the arrival of cargo to these third-party countries, which would certainly increase hostility toward the United States. U.S. boarding parties would eventually encounter armed resistance, a video of which would quickly appear in global media, damaging the U.S. diplomatic position.

Finally, U.S. policymakers should not expect that a blockade would impair the PLA or its ability to sustain military operations. China, especially considering its authoritarian government, would be able to redirect sufficient resources from the civilian economy to the PLA in order to supply its operations.[33]

Although at first glance a seemingly appealing option, imposing a blockade on China would actually encounter immense logistical, economic, and political barriers. These barriers would make the offshore control strategy impractical. The strategy's greatest drawbacks for the United States are political; offshore control would inflict pain on U.S. allies and alienate the United States in terms of global public opinion. A blockade would compel the United States to engage in an opened-ended political-military struggle, an approach that would spark resistance and insurgency, this time at sea. As U.S. policymakers have witnessed repeatedly over recent decades, such conflicts have not gone well.

Offshore control by itself is not a war-winning strategy. However, U.S. military forces should nonetheless prepare to implement many of its features. U.S. military planners should be prepared to monitor and if necessary control seaborne traffic through the Strait of Malacca and Indonesia's other straits. The U.S. Marine Corps and Army should be prepared to stand up and deploy large numbers of VBSS teams. And the United States and its allies should visibly rehearse these preparations.

Why? The skills needed for offshore control are similar to those needed for maritime counterpiracy, counterterrorism, and search and rescue—missions that all countries in the region understand and support. Preparing for these missions, especially in a multilateral context, benefits all. When the U.S. military can also display the ability to greatly expand the scope of such an effort, it will show China and other potential adversaries that the United States is ready for a blockade, as one element of a more comprehensive strategy. Transmitting that signal to China's decision makers will boost deterrence and thus regional security.

Needed: A Competitive Strategy for the Asia-Pacific Region

This chapter has explained why the current U.S. military responses to the growing security competition in East Asia—the Joint Operational Access Concept, Air-Sea Battle, and a distant blockade—fall short of what will be required to stabilize the foreboding trends the United States and its partners in the region now face.

These three approaches suffer from some common flaws. They take little account of America's best asset in the region: its allies and partners. The security interests of these countries closely overlap with those of the United States. They are key to any successful military strategy—the United States cannot implement any significant military operations in the region without partner support. U.S. allies and partners provide powerful diplomatic and legal legitimacy to any effort to resist China's encroachments on its neighbors' sovereignty. And China is utterly lacking in a similar network of partners, which makes America's partners a substantial and enduring competitive advantage. Yet JOAC, Air-Sea Battle, and offshore control give insufficient attention to the potential contributions of these partners and could turn some of them into adversaries. That is not the makings of a good strategy.

The three approaches are uncompetitive. They call for focusing valuable U.S. resources at China's strengths rather than its vulnerabilities and weaknesses. In the case of JOAC and Air-Sea Battle, U.S. policymakers and planners have to reckon with the fact that as the expeditionary power, its power-projection forces will be more expensive than China's anti-access forces. Thus, a military strategy premised on a high-technology battle of attrition will not favor the expeditionary force, especially when it goes up against a continental rival with nearly equal technology and clearly lower costs. As the continental power, China will enjoy other enduring advantages such as more redundant surveillance and command systems, better dispersion and concealment, and longer-range platforms and missiles. Strategies that are directed at China's best enduring advantages are not likely to succeed.

A distant blockade, by pitting the United States against the global economy, would similarly turn a Chinese weakness, its lack of allies and popularity, into a strength. A U.S. blockade would alienate America's friends in the region, its friends in Eurasia, and many neutral countries, likely pushing some into China's camp.

Finally, these three approaches lack a theory of success. What is the specific connection between the approaches' recommended actions and their desired results? Do the approaches even clearly identify what outcomes they seek to achieve? Ultimately, conflict is about persuading adversaries to settle disputes on favorable terms that will endure. In order for military action to achieve lasting success, it must connect to this concept. How the approaches discussed in this chapter specifically make the connection between military action and war termination is not clear. Commencing military action without a clear end state and without a theory of how the proposed action will achieve that end state is a recipe for frustration.

These criticisms illustrate a larger problem. Strategists coping with the security challenges in East Asia need to step back and view the problem from first principles. They should undertake a thorough approach to strategy formulation—one that makes a comprehensive assessment of all the players, declares what the strategy must achieve, devises a theory of success, and then crafts competitive and effective policies and programs for achieving the desired outcomes. The remainder of this book will lay out this prescription.

 *Chapter 6*

A Competitive Strategy for the Pacific

The United States faces an open-ended contest with China over influence in the Asia-Pacific region. Policymakers on both sides of this contest will have to get comfortable with the fact that this competition will occur even as the two countries mutually benefit from trade and financial linkages. U.S. policymakers will have to prepare for the likelihood that the resources available to China, for example its military budgets, will continue to ascend rapidly while those available to the Pentagon and elsewhere in the U.S. government will be constrained. Planners and policymakers in Washington and the Pacific will need better strategy choices than those currently contemplated if they are to preserve stability, guide China's behavior in a favorable direction, and prevent a destabilizing regional security competition from breaking out.

Finding a better strategy begins with finding a good strategy formulation process. And that begins with defining what a strategy is. Richard Rumelt, a veteran strategy consultant and UCLA business school professor, defines a strategy as "a coherent set of analyses, concepts, policies, arguments, and actions that respond to a high-stakes challenge."[1] A strategy is not simply setting goals or establishing aspirations for an organization, essential as those tasks are. A successful strategy must also include a realistic set of programs, policies, and resources designed to achieve the organization's goals and aspirations in a competitive context.

For example, the 2010 National Security Strategy of the United States is an admirable description of American aspirations. But its title is a misnomer. It is not a strategy because it contains little discussion of how the U.S. government will organize its resources to achieve these aspirations (previous versions issued by other U.S. presidents were no better in this regard).[2]

Stating goals is relatively easy. Designing realistic ways to achieve the goals, marshaling the necessary resources, and convincing an organization to effectively implement the design are much harder tasks.

The output of a strategy process could be a set of documents describing the organization's new program, policies, and supporting resources that will guide the way forward. But this work product is incomplete and is unlikely to result in success even if brilliantly crafted. Completion will occur when the organization's culture accepts the strategy process and enthusiastically implements the results. To increase the odds of success, organizations should seek not just a strategy—which inevitably will become stale with time—but a strategy process that becomes a permanent feature in the organization's routine operations and culture. A strategy process includes implementation, evaluation, critique, and guidance for the next strategy iteration. The goal of this process is continuous adaptation and improvement.

Most organizations face challengers, which make strategy design and execution even more difficult. In the business world, organizations face competitors seeking a bigger market share at the organization's expense. Businesses also face potentially hazardous changes to the economic and legal environment. Military forces face enemies on the battlefield. All organizations face resource constraints. Strategy design in competitive situations thus requires leaders and planners to find advantages in the operating environment, to discover their organization's comparative strengths, and to reveal the vulnerabilities left exposed by their competitors. A competitive strategy will include these factors in its design while also building in hedges for the risks the organization must face. With these additional complications, it is no wonder that so many business ventures fail and that other large and immensely endowed organizations such as the U.S. Department of Defense struggle to achieve their goals, evidence that they have failed to design competitive strategies.

Why Bother with Strategy?

One purpose of strategy is to help an organization adjust to changes in the world in which it must operate. Changes can come through the slow accumulation of social or economic trends, the shifting preferences of clients, or through the disruptive arrival of innovative or better-resourced competitors. A formal strategy process is only one method by which organizations attempt to cope with change. Many either rely on the intuition of the organization's top leaders or simply muddle through, making small adjustments to immediate problems. These techniques may appear to work for a time. But without a systematic method for thoroughly evaluating the organization's changing world, an organization risks finding itself set adrift by change.

Implementing a new strategy means making changes to an organization's processes, the duties and status of the organization's managers, and even the organization's culture. Making changes almost always creates winner and losers, not to mention disorientation when employees are required to either do their jobs differently or are even cast aside. A strategy process, if it is meaningful, must lead to disruption—something organizations naturally resist.

An effective strategy process thus must battle against an organization's strong preference for inertia. Resistance can be cultural or bureaucratic. Small or young organizations are typically led by a founder who, if the organization has survived its childhood, has gained the respect of the organization's stakeholders and has likely created a unique culture that serves to reinforce loyalty and cohesion among employees and clients. The organization will likely see its culture as being a valuable attribute and will resist a strategy process that could bring on introspection and change. Many charismatic founders may similarly resist a process that would expose the founder's judgment to scrutiny or supplant his or her authority.

For larger organizations such as military establishments, resistance to a formal strategy process will come from bureaucratic interests protecting their status, programs, and budgets. Threatened elements within, say, the U.S. Defense Department, will find powerful allies in Congress and in large defense contractors, allies who are likely in many cases to conclude there is lower risk to them in perpetuating existing programs and structures than in betting on hypothetical programs that may be required to adapt to disruptive change. In spite of these obstacles, adaptation may occur. However, it may occur too slowly to keep up with disruptions in the operating environment.

A formal strategy process must thus labor against ingrained and powerful institutional obstacles. In spite of these obstacles, a thorough strategy process remains the best hope for adjusting to a changing world.

Strategy Begins with Assessment

An effective strategy process has four steps: assessment, design, execution, and evaluation. We will discuss these steps, in the context of searching for a competitive strategy for the Asia-Pacific region.

Strategy should begin with an assessment of the players in the competition and the environment in which they will compete. The assessment phase will collect the baseline data and analysis on clients, competitors, partners, and the operating environment that will inform the remainder of the strategy process.

Assessments should begin with customers and clients, past, present, and future. For businesses, this is an obvious place to begin, for there is no business without understanding who the business's potential customers are, what they will want from the business, and how the business can reach them.

Military organizations like the U.S. Department of Defense and U.S. Pacific Command have clients too. Most obvious is the chain of command above, leading to the president. The service chiefs and senior officials in the Pentagon understand very well that Congress is another critically important stakeholder. Military commanders and planners should remember too that the public will also form its judgment on their plans and how well they are implemented, in the end making the public perhaps the most important client of all.

History provides numerous examples of military commanders and planners who failed to remember that they too should strive to understand their customers and to fashion solutions suited to their needs and constraints. On the eve of World War I, war planners on all sides were focused entirely on the technical aspects of mobilization, the rapid assembly of mass combat formations along their frontiers, and the urgency of striking first in order to gain the initiative and disrupt enemy preparations. Ignored completely was the idea that the military instrument and military planning should support statecraft, foreign policy, or even negotiations during a crisis. When such a crisis erupted in the summer of 1914, attempts by political leaders to settle the dispute were ignored by military planners, whose focus on mobilization and obtaining the first-move advantage trumped all other considerations. The result was disaster.[3]

Top-level U.S. commanders and military planners must answer first to their chain of command, leading up to the president. But they must also cope with the requirements and limits of their two other clients, Congress and the public. To do otherwise similarly flirts with disaster. The requirements and limits of all three clients should figure into strategy.

This seems like an obvious point until one ponders how it has routinely been ignored. Even after public opinion had soured on the manpower-intensive and casualty-ridden stabilization strategy used in Iraq, in 2009 policymakers pressed for the same unpopular strategy for Afghanistan, charting out an operational time line they should have known exceeded the support of all three clients.[4] With minimal political support remaining for the strategy, the United States is withdrawing from Afghanistan with little confidence in having achieved a positive result.

For the competition with China, the United States needs a strategy that will sustain broad appeal and that will thus endure across political administrations. It must be a strategy that sustains U.S. public support for an open-ended period. This implies a strategy that maintains stability with a low risk of combat, has a reasonable financial cost, and supports commonly accepted American values, such as playing by the rules and protecting the weak from bullying. Sustained American public support will also require partners in the Asia-Pacific region to make a substantial effort in their own defense.

Assessment next requires a deep study of the competition, with the goal of understanding its current and future interests, capacities, strategies, strengths, and vulnerabilities. There are countless examples of organizations failing because they failed to understand their competition. Nearly every week brings a story of some major business that did not understand or did not take seriously the cumulative effect of a competitor's continuous improvements or the disruption caused by the emergence of an innovator in the marketplace.

Examples similarly abound in military history. British officers planning the defense of Singapore in 1941 largely dismissed the idea that a major threat could arrive down the Malay Peninsula. When a Japanese army forced Singapore's surrender in 1942 from this very approach, the result was the worst disaster in British military history. More recently, many U.S. policymakers and planners underestimated the risk of insurgency in both Iraq and Afghanistan, even though the U.S. government had supported a successful insurgency in Afghanistan just fifteen years previously.

The assessment phase must also consider the interests, strategies, and attributes of partners. For businesses, partners include suppliers, financiers, distributors, product allies, and employees, among others. For national security strategists and military planners, partners include other agencies in the government, foreign state allies, nonstate partners, and contractors. For U.S. national security planners, the interests and attributes of partners should be a central consideration. Whether the task is irregular warfare in the Middle East and Central Asia or establishing a modern security architecture in the western Pacific, America's partners will be both essential for success and also one of the most troublesome planning factors.

Assessment should include research on the future operating environment, with a search for trends and potential disruptions that could affect strategy design. The U.S. National Intelligence Council's *Global Trends 2030* report is one example of an attempt to comprehensively discern relevant and potentially disruptive economic, technological, and social trends that may occur over the next two decades.[5] In the mid-1990s several assessments of security trends correctly anticipated the falling costs and broadening diffusion of mid-level military technology, which resulted in the missile and sensor revolution that is now so threatening to U.S. military forces and doctrine.[6] These are examples of analysis of future trends that bear on strategy design.

The final and most crucial assessment is the organization's appraisal of its own strengths, vulnerabilities, capacities, and interests. This self-assessment should result in a realistic description of the *means* available to the organization, an essential input in the strategy design process. Objective self-assessment is asking a lot from members inside an organization, who are themselves engaged in a competition with their peers for status and advancement. Under such circumstances, it is difficult to expect an organization's members who are participating in the strategy process (ideally, the organization's line managers and staff) to openly discuss their units' weaknesses and shortcomings. For this reason, many organizations employ outside consultants to perform internal assessments that the organization's own staff cannot be counted on to do itself.

Once again, history finds innumerable examples of organizations that failed as a result of their inability to recognize their own limitations. For example, the German army's war plans for the Western Front in 1914 and for the invasion of the Soviet Union in 1941 badly overestimated the ability of the army's supply services to deliver adequate supplies to massed mobile formations operating far beyond forward railheads. The result in both cases was disastrous, as the offensive capacity of forward units withered at climactic moments in these two campaigns. Policymakers responsible for strategy in Afghanistan have relied on NATO's assumption that it could create a large, effective, and resilient Afghan security force, a skill that NATO planners have likely overestimated, with baleful consequences for NATO's campaign plan.

Assessment is mainly a research task. But if performed badly, it will cripple the rest of the strategy process. Assessment is fraught with trouble. It is information gathering and analysis, the output of which will only be as good as the researchers doing the work. Assessment involves forecasting, always a hazardous venture. Assessment is almost guaranteed to involve blind spots and embarrassing errors of exclusion and distortion. The assessment process may result in an indigestible mountain of data. Finally, and perhaps most frequently, the assessment phase may include a bias that consciously or unconsciously predetermines the results of the entire strategy process.

In view of the resources needed to perform a thorough assessment, one may wonder, given the potential for error and misdirection, whether such an effort is worth the expense. However, effective strategy design is not possible without a systematic examination of the competitive world in which the organization must function. That examination is the purpose of the assessment phase.

Designing a Competitive Strategy

Having achieved an understanding of the operating environment, the needs of clients, the strengths and weaknesses of competitors, and the resources and constraints of their organization, leaders are now in a better position to formulate a coherent way forward. With their assessments in hand, strategy designers are equipped to proceed through the next steps.

Strategists next need to make assumptions about the future. Ideally, the facts and analysis produced during the assessment phase would be sufficient to form a clear picture about the future operating environment. But this will never happen—such facts and analysis will always be insufficient. Assumptions are required to complete the picture. They are unavoidable and implied in any plan; they also introduce into any strategy risk and the possibility of great error. It is thus best to make assumptions explicit and subject them to open critique.

Assessments plus assumptions equal the strategist's vision of the future operating environment. With that vision, the strategist has a basis to formulate realistic goals and, later, the programs and policies to achieve those goals.

Organizations pursue goals (or at least they should) in order to solve specific problems. So before enumerating goals, an organization should understand and clearly state the core problems it needs to solve. In his book *Good Strategy/Bad Strategy: The Difference and Why It Matters*, Richard Rumelt listed "failure to face the problem" as a key indicator of bad strategy.[7]

Rumelt calls on strategists to dig beneath the surface to find the true underlying problem. For national security strategists and military planners, the problem is usually deeper than just figuring out how to inflict damage on an adversary's military forces. Ending a war on favorable terms requires compelling an adversary, both its leaders and its foot soldiers, to accept conditions they would likely have rejected at the start of the conflict. In this sense, the true objective is not a city, a hilltop, the destruction of a tank regiment or a fleet but rather changing the calculations occurring inside the adversary's minds. Armed coercion may be only one aspect of reaching this true underlying objective.

Rumelt also warns against choosing impractical or unattainable objectives.[8] It is pointless for business or government policymakers to expend scarce resources on goals that clearly are beyond their reach. In the realm of military strategy, policymakers must consider the costs required to achieve the desired ends.

Considering costs may seem like an obvious proposition, but it actually becomes murky in execution. Strategy accrues costs in both the short run and the long run, and attempting to minimize one often leads to increasing the other. Early in World War II, Allied leaders agreed on a policy of unconditional surrender of the Axis powers. Removing the possibility of a negotiated settlement greatly increased the short-run cost of the war, since a policy of unconditional surrender would undoubtedly require the complete destruction of Axis military forces. The idea was to minimize long-run costs, even at the price of increasing them in the short run. In making this decision, Allied leaders were seeking to avoid the negotiated armistice that ended World War I. That truce left Germany's military potential intact and thus a source of large long-run costs for the Allies, as an embittered but still capable Germany soon restored its military capacity. In the 1991 Persian Gulf War, the United States and its coalition partners opted to minimize their short-run costs by signing a ceasefire with Iraq, leaving it to their successors to manage the long-term costs and consequences, which ended up being considerable. When deciding on the *ends* of a national security strategy, policymakers will have to envision a sustainable end state, the costs and practicality of achieving that end state, and the ongoing costs of maintaining that end state.

The strategist's next step is to spell out the *ways*—the policies, programs, organizational changes, deployment of resources, and other measures—that will employ the organization's *means* (identified during the assessment phase) to achieve the strategy's *ends*.

But before beginning a detailed enumeration of the strategy's ways, the strategist must clearly describe the strategy's *theory of success*. A theory of success should describe in a simple and convincing manner why, in the context of the assessment and assumptions, the means applied by the strategy's ways will achieve the desired ends. The theory of success is the logic underpinning the strategy.

After the May 1863 Confederate victory at Chancellorsville during the American Civil War, Confederate leaders met to discuss their war strategy. At this conference, Gen. Robert E. Lee successfully argued for an invasion of the North. His theory of success supporting this strategy was that a convincing Confederate victory deep in Northern territory would provide a psychological shock to Northern policymakers that would compel them to negotiate a settlement. For Lee, continuing to play defense in Virginia, even if it conserved Southern resources, lacked a theory of success because in his view, it did not hold out the hope of changing the calculations of the North's policymakers—the condition that was ultimately required to end the war on favorable terms.

Two documents, George Kennan's July 1947 article in *Foreign Affairs* titled "The Sources of Soviet Conduct" and *NSC 68: United States Objectives and Programs for National Security*, authored by the State Department's Policy Planning staff and signed by President Harry Truman in April 1950, established the foundation of U.S. Cold War policy.[9] Both documents envisioned open-ended resistance of Soviet expansionist pressure. Both also contained a theory of success that reassured readers that the resistance of Soviet pressure would not have to last into perpetuity. Kennan asserted, "[T]he United States has it in its power to increase enormously the strains under which Soviet policy must operate, to force upon the Kremlin a far greater degree of moderation and circumspection than it has had to observe in recent years, and in this way to promote tendencies which must eventually find their outlet in either the breakup or the gradual mellowing of Soviet power."[10] Likewise *NSC 68* stated, "The only sure victory lies in the frustration of the Kremlin design by the steady development of the moral and material strength of the free world and its projection into the Soviet world in such a way as to bring about an internal change in the Soviet system."[11] For both documents, the theory of success was containment of Soviet expansion and the support of Western strength, until the Soviet Union's weaknesses led to its "mellowing" or internal change. The assumptions underlying this theory of success would occur but only after four decades of perseverance.

Specifying the strategy's ways leads to the drafting of organizational changes, budgets, programs, and incentives for the organization's operational units. With resources always limited, policymakers will have to make decisions on priorities, sequencing, and synchronization, both internally and with outside partners. In late December 1941, a few weeks after the United States entered World War II, President Franklin Roosevelt and British prime minister Winston Churchill agreed that the defeat of Germany should be the alliance's top priority and should receive adequate resources to achieve this sequencing. Within the European campaign, wresting control of the Atlantic Ocean's sea lines of communication from Germany's submarine forces was a required first priority, followed by a strategic air campaign against Germany's airpower, military-industrial capacity, and transportation infrastructure. These two campaigns were capital- and technology-intensive and also required high levels of crew training and experience. They also had to succeed before the Allies could complete the destruction of Germany's armed forces on the European continent. The Allies' virtual absence of capacity in these areas at the start of the war delayed the war's culmination by at least two years and thus added greatly to the war's total costs.

Risk is an inescapable feature of strategy. Resources are always limited. Therefore, policymakers must choose priorities that will get the first call on resources, leaving lower priorities underfunded and exposed to risk. For example, U.S. defense policymakers must periodically choose between, on the one hand, keeping the current force ready for combat by expending limited resources on equipment maintenance and realistic training and, on the other hand, preparing for future adversaries by spending more now on research to develop weapons for the future. Making that choice requires assessing whether current threats or future threats are more problematic.

In many cases, policymakers will conclude that they have sufficient knowledge to assess the risks they must choose among and then to make rational choices within the context of their objectives. During the early decades of the Cold War, the top defense priority for U.S. policymakers and planners was preventing nuclear war with the Soviet Union while also resisting Soviet expansion. During this period, defense plans, research budgets, and procurement focused on this goal, which resulted in large spending on Air Force and Navy strategic nuclear programs and systems. One can conclude that, having seemed to prevent nuclear war through deterrence, this strategy worked.

However, the Soviet competition observed and adapted. It employed proxy and irregular warfare to sustain its competition with the West in ways that bypassed the focus of the U.S. defense program. U.S. military forces entered Vietnam in the 1960s without a warfighting doctrine, organization, or training necessary to succeed against that irregular warfare challenge. This U.S. risk exposure occurred because U.S. defense policymakers, arguably rationally, focused more attention at that time on preventing nuclear war and other major war challenges than on devising programs and policies for thwarting irregular adversaries. Pentagon planners achieved their first priority: deterring nuclear war and avoiding Soviet nuclear blackmail; but that which did not receive much attention initially—irregular warfare and how ground forces might deal with it—became the risky vulnerability. This is a reminder that strategy is almost always a competitive contest involving thinking adversaries.

Risk management should be an explicit feature of strategy design. Through the assumptions and choices they make, strategists and policymakers should understand where they are increasing their risks. Awareness should be possible even when hedging may not be. If known risks later develop into problems, the policymakers will at least have a head start on mitigation, having pondered the risk already.

A Soviet Tu-22M Backfire bomber with the Kh-22 Kitchen anti-ship cruise missile in 1983. In the 1970s and 1980s, this was U.S. Navy's first brush with the modern land-based "reconnaissance-strike complex." *(Defense Imagery, photographer unknown, 1983)*

Adm. Thomas Hayward, USN, chief of naval operations in 1980. While commander of U.S. Pacific Fleet and later as CNO, Hayward pushed for aggressive aircraft carrier strikes against Soviet land bases, in spite of the Backfire threat. *(U.S. Navy, Jim Preston, July 1980)*

Secretary of the Navy John Lehman at the retirement of Adm. Hyman G. Rickover in 1981. As Navy secretary, Lehman incorporated Hayward's ideas into the U.S. Navy's war plans of the 1980s. We will never know if these plans would have worked. *(U.S. Naval Institute, January 19, 1982)*

A Chinese Su-27 Flanker fighter-bomber on a training exercise over Anshan Airfield, China, in 2007. By 2020 China will have more than four hundred Flanker variants, which will bring Chinese airpower deep over the western Pacific Ocean. *(U.S. Defense Department photo, SSgt. D. Myles Cullen, USAF, March 24, 2007)*

U.S. Carrier Strike Group 8 under way in the Atlantic Ocean in 2012. Can the defenses of these strike groups fend off more than one hundred incoming supersonic cruise missiles at once? *(U.S. Navy photo, MC2 Julia A. Casper/Released)*

A U.S. Army Pershing II intermediate-range ballistic missile in Germany, 1987. The 1987 Intermediate Nuclear Forces Treaty between the United States and the Soviet Union banned this system and remains in force today. China's missile programs are unconstrained by the treaty. *(U.S. Army photo, Bob Crossley, June 1987/Released)*

A U.S. Air Force Ground Launched Cruise Missile from the 1980s, also currently banned by the INF treaty. Reintroducing the mobile launcher with modern long-range land-attack and anti-ship missiles could help even the missile balance in East Asia. *(General Dynamics)*

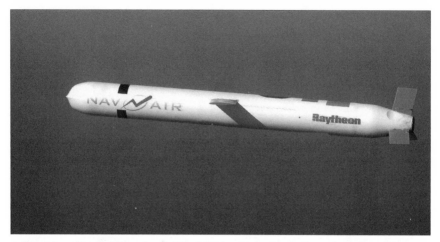

A U.S. Navy Tactical Tomahawk Block IV land-attack missile undergoing testing off California in 2002. This missile used to be the U.S. military's best "first-hour" weapon. Now its range is too short for the Asia-Pacific theater. *(U.S. Navy photo/Released)*

A U.S. Navy Harpoon anti-ship missile launched during a training exercise from USS *Cowpens* (CG 63) in 2012. The Harpoon is now outclassed in range and speed by several Chinese anti-ship missiles, and Navy commanders in the Pacific have pleaded for a replacement. *(U.S. Navy photo, MC3 Paul Kelly/Released)*

The USS *Ohio* guided missile submarine (SSGN 726) under way in the Pacific Ocean in 2008. The U.S. Navy's accidental "Arsenal Ship" faces retirement next decade. *(U.S. Navy photo, MC2 Clifford L. H. Davis/Released)*

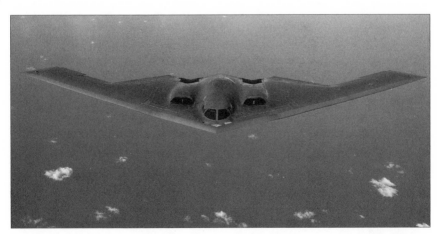

A B-2 Spirit long-range bomber on a training flight over the Pacific Ocean in 2006. The B-2's development costs ran out of control, resulting in only twenty-one purchased. Will the new bomber's program managers do better? *(U.S. Air Force photo, SSgt. Bennie J. Davis III)*

Two MQ-4C Triton unmanned reconnaissance aircraft parked at a Northrop-Grumman facility in Palmdale, California, in 2013. The U.S. Navy will use this very long-range unmanned reconnaissance aircraft to patrol the ocean and compensate for a shrinking number of U.S. warships. *(U.S. Navy photo courtesy of Northrop Grumman, Chad Slattery/Released)*

An F-35C, the U.S. Navy variant of the Joint Strike Fighter, on a test flight near Patuxent River, Maryland, in 2012. The stealthy strike fighter has advanced electronics, but its range is too short to keep its aircraft carrier base away from China's anti-ship missiles. *(U.S. Navy photo courtesy Lockheed Martin/Released)*

The X-47B unmanned demonstrator aircraft on the flight deck of USS *Theodore Roosevelt* (CVN 71) in 2013. Dashing the hopes of many, UCLASS is not likely to keep U.S. aircraft carriers in the game against China's land-based missile power. *(U.S. Navy photo, MCSR Kris Lindstrom/Released)*

Artist's conception of a U.S. Air Force Global Positioning System (GPS) Block IIR satellite in orbit around the Earth. In a war, combat is likely to extend to space, where networks of imaging, navigation, and communication satellites will be vulnerable to attack. *(U.S. Air Force Space Command/Lockheed Martin)*

Finally, the strategy process ends—and begins again—with an evaluation of the strategy's performance. This should lead to a new assessment phase and a renewal of the strategy process.

For most organizations, life is much more complicated than the simple strategy outline discussed here. All strategy models suffer from inescapable frailties. Leaders must attempt to assimilate a daunting amount of detail about the world in which they function. That mountain of data, no matter how voluminous, will still very likely miss many critical considerations. Strategies are about the future, which requires forecasts and assumptions, many of which will be wrong. Finally, strategy implies change, which all organizations are bound to resist in some way.

Is a strategy process worth the effort? What is the alternative? "Muddling through" almost guarantees an organization's collision with a changed world for which it will not be prepared. Muddling through and an institutional resistance to new ideas and the changes they imply have resulted in a U.S. strategy that is unprepared for the rapidly evolving security situation in the western Pacific region. The United States needs a competitive strategy for the region—and that will come from a better strategy process.

A Competitive Strategy for the Pacific

Let us now apply this framework to the challenge the United States and its allies face in the Asia-Pacific region. Chapters 1 through 5 provided, at least in summary form, an assessment from which to design a strategy. The next step is to use this assessment to formulate the following assumptions that will underlie a strategy:

1. *In order to protect its growing interests and hedge future uncertainty, China will continue its buildup of air, naval, missile, and military space capabilities with the goal of eventually establishing control over its maritime lines of communication, beginning with those in East Asia.* China's security interests, within the region and beyond it, will continue to expand. Regardless of how China's economy evolves in the years ahead, it will still retain a high dependence on exports markets and imports of raw materials. China's commercial deals with Russia and central Asian countries indicate its attempts to reduce its dependence on sea lines of communication across the Indian Ocean, through the Strait of Malacca, and through the Near Seas. But even if these attempts are successful, China will still retain a very high exposure to seaborne trade, a disturbing risk from Beijing's perspective.

2. *Even as China's economy expands and the standard of living of China's citizens improves, economic, social, and political volatility inside China are likely to increase.* Rising internal instability will be the likely consequence of growing public dissatisfaction with corruption, inequality, the stresses caused by economic adjustment, and pollution. Rising nationalism is another likely consequence, brought on by both rising expectations inside China and by the elite's use of nationalism as a means of social control.

3. *As they observe China's rising nationalism and military modernization with increasing alarm, China's neighbors will step up their internal and external balancing.* The first preference for most of these countries will be a deepening of their security relationships with the United States. But if the United States isn't able or willing to play this role or to maintain a credible forward presence, most of these countries will pursue aggressive military modernizations of their own, which for a few could include long-range missiles and nuclear weapons. A few countries may agree to bandwagon with China, which will cause those countries that don't to further accelerate their military buildups.

4. *The security competition in the Asia-Pacific region will be open-ended.* Even as the United States and its partners compete with China over security concerns, they will simultaneously be large and expanding trade and financial partners with China. In spite of this duality, all of the players will face the prospect of sustaining their competitive positions for an indefinite period.

5. *China will continue to enjoy the advantages of its continental position, lower production costs, and an increasingly narrow gap between its military technology and training standards and those of the United States.* In addition, China's military spending is likely to continue its robust upward trajectory, while U.S. military spending, including on research and procurement, will likely stagnate for the rest of this decade.

6. *Even if China's various bureaucracies pursue their own interests during peacetime, in a crisis China's central leadership will exert command and control over China's military and paramilitary forces.* In light of Edward Luttwak's analysis of China's strategy and command structure,[12] this assumption is worth evaluating. If this assumption is not valid, then U.S. and allied policymakers and planners need to prepare for how they might directly influence the behavior of subordinate decision makers in China.

7. *China's leadership will respond to incentives.* Regarding large and consequential decisions, China's leaders will evaluate the costs, benefits, and risks embedded in those decisions. If this assumption is true, it provides an opening for the United States and its allies to increase the costs for those courses of action they do not want China to pursue and also for them to increase the benefits to China for those actions they favor. If this assumption is not true, the United States and its partners in the region will need to generate the methods and resources to protect their interests regardless of China's decision-making process.

8. *China has weaknesses and vulnerabilities that the United States and its allies in the region can use to influence China's behavior.* These weaknesses and vulnerabilities are discussed below in more detail. The purpose of studying these is to generate leverage that can influence China's behavior during an open-ended peacetime competition. Should conflict occur, the United States and its allies would seek to use these weaknesses and vulnerabilities to increase China's costs and attempt to settle the conflict on more favorable terms.

With an assessment and assumptions determined, what should be the goal, or ends, of America's Asia-Pacific strategy? Broadly, it should be the same goal that the United States has pursued for decades, namely to preserve the rule of law, the open commons, and respect for sovereignty in the region. The issue in the current context is to dissuade China from employing its formidable military potential, either directly or indirectly, in an attempt to change the existing international system in ways that would substantially diminish the sovereignty and benefits enjoyed by the United States and its partners in the region. And if this attempt at dissuasion fails, the strategy should provide U.S. and coalition policymakers with effective options for settling a crisis or conflict against China on favorable terms.[13]

A Theory of Success

The strategy's theory of success rests on assumptions stated above, namely that China has weaknesses and vulnerabilities that U.S. and allied policymakers and planners can form into leverage that can influence China's peacetime behavior in favorable ways. Should conflict occur, policymakers and planners would attempt to use this leverage to resolve the conflict on favorable terms.

In an open-ended peacetime competition, policymakers should employ techniques that raise China's costs for unfavorable behavior while providing the nation with benefits for favorable choices. Military planners should prepare techniques and tactics that will increase the costs to China of employing its favored strategies and that will deny China benefits from military action. Ideally these measures should be transparent to the extent possible, in order to influence China's peacetime decision making. Finally, in the event of conflict, the United States and allies should prepare for escalation on terms and in domains that would increase China's pain compared to that of the coalition, in an effort to achieve conflict resolution on favorable terms.

Looking for vulnerabilities, developing leverage, and designing plans to impose costs on a competitor are long-standing methods of pursuing a security competition. Yet, outside a relatively small network of researchers and analysts at a few war colleges and defense think tanks, few policymakers in the United States seem to be considering how to engage in a sustainable security competition in the Asia-Pacific region.[14] Among the reasons for this neglect are that most of these policymakers have yet to admit that such a competition with China is even occurring, or they worry that taking actions to prepare for a peacetime security competition would spark a competition where none previously existed.

These concerns are a manifestation of the uncomfortable duality of the U.S.-China relationship, which contains growing security concerns that exist alongside deep commercial and financial linkages.[15] It is little wonder that there is debate and confusion about how the United States should proceed. However, resistance to at least preparing for a security competition is very likely to fade, as China's capacity to dominate the western Pacific's sea lines of communication at a time of its choosing becomes undeniable and as China's territorial assertions in the region very likely intensify. As these realities become universally accepted, policymakers will call for an intensive search for competitive responses to China's challenge.

Implementing this theory of success requires a deeper understanding of China's vulnerabilities. This endeavor will mean finding what assets and conditions its leaders value most and then fashioning ways and directing resources to reach these vulnerabilities.

In an essay in the October–November 2012 issue of *Survival*, published by the International Institute of Strategic Studies, Michael Pillsbury discussed sixteen potential areas of strategic vulnerability for China's leaders.[16] Pillsbury, a senior fellow at the Hudson Institute and a former top planner for China and Asian issues at the U.S. Department of Defense, also called for stepped-up research on China's strategic decision-making process, similar to the research on Soviet decision making analysts in the West conducted during the Cold War. Pillsbury's "sixteen fears" can be grouped into several broad categories:

1. Fear of internal instability, riots, civil war, and terrorism
2. Fear of a blockade or other maritime disruption
3. Fear of Taiwan independence or a lack of PLA capacity to deal with Taiwan
4. Fear of a land invasion, of the military capacity of regional neighbors such as India, Russia, Japan, and Vietnam, and of China's territorial dismemberment
5. Fear of bombardment from long-range bombers or aircraft carriers
6. Fear of attacks on important strategic assets such as China's missiles forces, its anti-satellite capability, its computer and telecommunications network, and its pipelines
7. Fear of escalation and a loss of control

In his essay Pillsbury discussed unilateral actions the United States could take to reassure China's leaders, with the hope of decelerating China's military buildup. These actions include the United States making a "no first use" pledge regarding nuclear weapons, voluntarily capping its long-range missile defense program to thwart China's need for an expanded strategic nuclear force, reassuring China about its access to sea lines of communication, and downgrading the U.S. commitment to Taiwan. In Pillsbury's estimation, bilateral arms control negotiations have little hope until China agrees to more transparency regarding its military forces and doctrine.[17]

Although U.S. policymakers should pursue reassurance efforts with China, they should not expect such actions by themselves to resolve the growing security competition. In the long run, unilateral American assurances are unlikely to be persuasive to Chinese policymakers and military planners. From Beijing's perspective, U.S. assurances can change rapidly, especially during a crisis, when they would be most valuable. For example, a U.S. reassurance regarding China's concerns about sea lines of communication will hold little weight with naval planners in Beijing who watch U.S. and Indian fleets patrolling the Indian Ocean through which most of China's oil imports must pass.

Thus, dissuasive and cost-imposing approaches must necessarily play a major role in a competitive strategy. Pillsbury's list of Chinese fears can serve as a starting point for fashioning some dissuasive and cost-imposing courses of action. These courses of action would serve at least four purposes.

1. Increase the political and diplomatic costs to China for, say, continuing its salami slicing in the East and South China Seas
2. Impose costs and deny China the rewards from any successes it might enjoy through expansion or from the intimidation of its neighbors

3. Dissuade China away from assertive policies by holding at risk assets and conditions valued by China's leaders

4. Reduce the value of China's military modernization by instituting U.S. and coalition defense reforms that will negate China's current military strategy in the region

As concerns rise over how to cope with China's increasing military capacity and assertiveness, U.S. strategy during the Cold War is receiving renewed examination. Much of this attention focuses on how the Pentagon's Office of Net Assessment, established in 1973 and led since its inception by Andrew W. Marshall, assisted a succession of U.S. Defense secretaries in formulating competitive strategies aimed at managing the long-term competition with the Soviet Union.[18]

Marshall's office, along with many other military planners between 1973 and 1990, fashioned approaches that attempted to match U.S. comparative advantages against Soviet weaknesses, with a goal of either diverting Soviet resources away from threatening capabilities or weakening the Soviet Union's overall military capacity. Notable examples include U.S. bomber and cruise missile programs from the late 1970s, which aimed to divert Soviet defense spending into air defenses; the aggressive U.S. maritime strategy from the mid-1980s, which sought to draw Soviet naval power away from allied sea lines of communication; and, perhaps most famously, the Strategic Defense Initiative, which threatened to negate the huge Soviet investment in intercontinental ballistic missiles (ICBMs).

Since the Soviet Union did subsequently collapse, it is appealing to conclude that the U.S. competitive strategy approach made a major contribution to that result. Indeed, Marshal Sergei Akhromeyev, chief of the Soviet General Staff at the end of the Cold War, later concluded, "The Soviet Union could not continue the confrontation with the United States and NATO after 1985. The economic resources for such a policy had been practically exhausted."[19]

Akhromeyev's conclusion matches a widely held supposition regarding the Soviet Union's demise. However, the exact role, if any, played by U.S. competitive strategies bears further research. Indeed whether the competitive strategies employed by the United States during the Cold War had predicted effects on Soviet behavior and its economic and social outcomes requires investigation before such effects can be asserted with high authority.[20] But even assuming we cannot connect every link between a particular competitive action and a hoped-for dissuasive or cost-imposing outcome, the logic for at least preparing, and in some cases employing, competitive strategies against China remains strong.

Pillsbury's list of Chinese fears provides a starting point for developing a list of targets that, if held at risk by U.S. forces, could dissuade Chinese leaders from pursuing an aggressive external policy. An important theme in Pillsbury's list is the strong control leaders of the Chinese Communist Party wish to maintain over the PLA, the government, and Chinese society at large. Attacks that threaten to weaken that control, for example, strikes against the leadership of China's internal security forces, could be compelling. Attacks against the personal assets of upper echelon CCP leaders could provoke dissention inside China's leadership.[21] A U.S. capability to remove perceived strong Chinese leverage, such as China's anti-satellite capability, might also provide effective dissuasion. The threat of irregular, information, and unconventional warfare methods that held out the possibility of creating instability in, say, Tibet or Xinjiang provinces are more examples of holding at risk conditions China's leaders value.

These are merely a few examples of ways to create dissuasive leverage against China's policymakers. This topic is in need of much greater research; but it is reasonable to conclude that China's leaders and the system they lead have vulnerabilities the United States and its partners can reach.

Taking advantage of these vulnerabilities will require a broad portfolio that will include political, diplomatic, economic, and military capabilities. Useful military capabilities will run the full spectrum from special and unconventional warfare to high-end maritime, air-, and space power. This call for a full range of coercive capabilities, including such controversial notions as creating internal instability and the capacity to strike targets deep inside China, contrasts with the view of advocates of offshore control, who wish to focus on just China's economic vulnerabilities and who explicitly rule out targeting China's homeland.

As mentioned, economic warfare options should certainly be part of the portfolio of coercion. But history suggests that such a narrow approach is by itself unlikely to be sufficiently compelling against a determined adversary. In addition, a narrow strategy, especially when declared in advance, allows the adversary much greater scope to implement adaptive strategies. Just as in the past, success—either as a deterrent or in a conflict—is likely to require a broad range of coercive capabilities. By developing and quietly displaying these capabilities to Chinese decision makers, the United States and its partners will stand a better chance of dissuading assertive Chinese behavior.

It may be the case that China's top leaders don't calculate costs and benefits with the same parameters as do American strategists; or it may be that China's top leaders are not actually in control of wayward elements of the PLA or other bureaucracies (although that trait could be a vulnerability open for U.S. exploitation). If either of these cases is true and conflict nonetheless occurs, the United States and its allies in the region will again need these tools and tactics for exploiting Chinese weaknesses and vulnerabilities. So whether one believes in the theory of dissuasion or not, the case for preparing competitive strategies remains.

Finally, there are some analysts who believe that pursuing competitive approaches with China will merely create an enemy where one does not exist. Better, from this perspective, to find negotiated solutions to the various clashes over interests.

It is very likely that all such clashes will be resolved through negotiations. The issue will be what leverage each side brings to the talks. With its military modernization on track to achieve dominance of the Near Seas out to two thousand kilometers by 2020, China's leaders are likely to conclude that they will possess the most leverage, at least over the medium term. The U.S. pursuit of offsetting leverage, through the development of its own competitive strategies, would improve, not diminish, the prospects for useful talks with China's leaders.

How, specifically, should the United States and its allies develop that leverage? The remainder of this book will discuss reforms and new ideas—the strategy's means and ways—that constitute an improved competitive approach. Also discussed will be alliance relationships, new military doctrines and organizations, and defense procurement reforms that will take advantage of U.S. and coalition strengths, while exploiting China's weaknesses and negating its strengths. With a better and more competitive approach, the United States and its allies will stand a better chance of guiding China and the region toward a peaceful and mutually beneficial future.

Chapter 7

A New Approach to America's Pacific Partnerships

A merica's allies and partners in the Asia-Pacific region are an indispensable component of any successful U.S. strategy. These relationships are vital, both for the political legitimacy of America's regional strategy and for supporting any military strategy. As discussed in chapter 2, supporting security and development in the region is not charity work for the United States, since trade with the region is an enormous benefit to U.S. workers, consumers, and investors. Equally important, supporting and defending these interests also bolsters long-standing U.S. principles such as the rule of law, open trade and commerce, freedom of navigation, and respect for sovereignty. The success and advancement of these principles, which define the region's development since World War II, boost America's prestige and diplomatic power and advance U.S. interests around the world.

Most of America's partners in the region view their relationship with the United States as critical for their security. Although the importance of these security relationships faded for some in the decade after the Cold War, rising fears of terrorism, soon followed by China's military expansion, reawakened the importance of security cooperation with the United States. China's recent assertions in the East and South China Seas have accelerated this renewal.

With the interests of the United States and its allies aligned in most cases, it would seem a simple matter for diplomats and military officials to extend and deepen security ties between the United States and others in the region. Indeed, U.S. security relationships in the region are extensive and date back many decades. As an example, the U.S. Pacific Fleet conducts 170 exercises and 600 training events with more than twenty allied and partner countries in the Asia-Pacific region every year.[1] America's long effort at building relationships in the region is a clear success. But these relationships are burdened with many dilemmas, which will test the patience and nerve of all sides. China's rising presence, while clarifying the stakes for some, will also add stress to many of these relationships.

America's partnerships in the region are perhaps its most important competitive advantage. This means that U.S. policymakers and military planners will need to get more out of these relationships in order to maintain the region's stability in the face of China's ascent. For those policymakers coping with the dilemmas of partnership, demanding more from the relationships will not always be welcome. U.S. officials will thus need new approaches for getting more out these critical partnerships while maintaining their cohesion under increasing stress.

What America's Partners Can Contribute to a Competitive Strategy

In order to keep up with China's growing influence and military capabilities, U.S. policymakers will inevitably press America's partners for greater contributions to the region's security. China's strategy—salami slicing, military modernization, and creating commercial and financial dependence with others in the region—is multidimensional and requires a similarly broad-based response. This section describes ways America's partners, with U.S. support, can contribute to a competitive response to China's strategy. These responses will resist China's salami slicing and attempt to counter elements of China's military program. As we will see, many of these approaches come with risks and objections.

★ ★ ★

First, America's partners must promote their legal cases against China's territorial assertions. A central element of China's salami slicing is to gradually build up the legal legitimacy of its territorial claims by incrementally, but firmly, accumulating ever more "facts on the ground" to support its claims. America's partners must resist this by supporting their own legal claims. China's "nine-dash line" and its legal position regarding EEZ restrictions are weak legal claims and they find little acceptance in the international community. But China's persistent salami slicing, if not resisted, could still prevail. The United States could help its partners, and its own interests, by leveraging existing law and institutions.[2]

For example, the United States and its partners in the region should support use of the United Nations Convention on the Law of the Sea (UNCLOS) as a dispute resolution method. The Philippines is pursuing such a case against China, with China resisting the legal authority of this procedure. Building a large multinational front supporting the Philippine UNCLOS gambit will reduce the legitimacy of China's claims.[3]

The U.S. government should continue its support of ASEAN's unity and its role in promoting a binding Code of Conduct for resolving disputes in the South China Sea. Achieving this unity and establishing such a code would constitute resistance to China's salami slicing and would reduce the legitimacy of China's strategy. Supporting the Trans-Pacific Partnership (TPP) free trade negotiations is another method the United States and its partners can use to build up multilateral cooperation and the broader concept of a rules-based system—a visible contrast to China's unilateral assertiveness.

Second, America's partners around the East and South China Seas need to match China's maritime presence. China's salami-slicing strategy is supported by its economic and industrial power, which Beijing believes will sustain a growing and persistent presence of civilian, paramilitary, and if necessary, military vessels on patrol around the disputed claims in the two seas. Chinese planners are counting on their material advantages to wear down the other claimants, with Chinese fishing boats and patrol craft establishing new "facts on the ground," which they hope will eventually be accepted by the international community. Japan, the Philippines, Vietnam, Malaysia, and other claimants need to match China's persistence with their own, otherwise they risk conceding the seas to China.

The United States has a strong interest in supporting a matching presence by the other claimants. Should China's salami slicing eventually result in recognition of the nine-dash line, the burden could eventually fall on U.S. military forces to restore the status quo ante in a crisis—a situation U.S. policymakers and military commanders greatly wish to avoid. In order to assist the other claimants with their maritime patrolling presence, the United States should organize a multilateral group to support the claimants, especially the smaller countries around the South China Sea. The United States should quietly rally Japan, Australia, and India, the other three big powers in the network, to assist and subsidize a matching maritime presence in the two seas.

The civilian component of maritime presence should have the lead in such an effort. The private-sector fishing fleets of Japan, the Philippines, Vietnam, and Malaysia should do more to match those from China. A subsidy fund organized by the United States, Japan, India, and Australia could support the capacity and endurance of fishing fleets from the smaller countries, for the sole purpose of strategic competition with China. Foreign assistance from these four countries should also support paramilitary maritime capacity in the South China Sea, such as coast guard cutters, fisheries enforcement craft, police patrol boats, and other maritime policing activity. The program could establish technical support relationships, for example, Japanese maritime patrol forces supporting their Philippine counterparts and Indian units supporting Vietnam.[4]

The goal of this program would be to build up the sustained civilian maritime capacity of the other claimants, demonstrated by fishing fleets and paramilitary patrolling that match China's presence. Should these claimants succeed in matching China's maritime presence, it would demonstrate resistance to the notion that China is succeeding in establishing new territorial facts on the ground in the two seas. This effort, at relatively little cost, could stymie China's salami slicing, raise political costs to China, and boost the confidence of the U.S. partnership network.

Boosting the maritime presence of the claimants opposing China will increase both the risk of maritime incidents and clashes and the risk of an accident or miscalculation that could lead to a conflict entangling the United States. Dissuading China from continued salami slicing will unavoidably require the United States and its partners to assume a heightened risk of confrontation. There is a perception that the United States stepped away from such a risk during the April to June 2012 standoff over Scarborough Reef that left Chinese paramilitary forces and fishing fleets in sole control of the shoal and left the Philippines locked out.

The desire by policymakers of the major powers to avoid a confrontation over uninhabited rocks is understandable. Regrettably that view only postpones trouble for the future, when China is likely to have a stronger hand to play. The United States and its partners will eventually have to face China's salami slicing. Preparing for that with legal, diplomatic, media, and security strategies will improve the likelihood of success when such a face-off occurs.

Third, America's partners in the region should improve their information operations and messaging to the global audience. Media outreach, information operations, and public diplomacy are critical elements of a successful strategy. In the contest with China over territorial claims in the two seas, America's partners should enjoy a comparative advantage in the realm of media and information operations: they have a stronger legal case to argue before the global audience. Even more compelling should be the impression that China, with its huge size and graceless moves, is a bully, intent on using its raw power to take possessions and rights from its much smaller neighbors.[5]

In a battle over media impressions, the small neighbors should have an advantage. For example, in the event of a clash between Chinese paramilitary patrol vessels and Philippine or Vietnamese fishing boats, the smaller countries should have an easier time portraying China as the bullying aggressor. This portrayal is even more likely if the small neighbors encourage crews of their fishing boats and coast guard cutters to record clashes when they occur, for later editing and display through global media channels. By making the case that China is bullying its neighbors, these countries will raise the costs of China's salami slicing, possibly to the point of making the tactic too painful to continue. The U.S. government, along with other partners in the region, can quietly support this line of effort through technical assistance and through its own indirect public diplomacy initiatives.

Fourth, the United States should expand and deepen its partnership network across Asia. There are at least three aspects to this initiative: (1) the United States should reach out to countries where there has been little security cooperation in the past, (2) U.S. security interests would benefit from deepening the security relationship with a few especially important partners, and (3) the U.S. government should extend the concept of partnership beyond just relationships with states and state-based organizations like ASEAN.

Burma's decision to break from China provided the United States with an opportunity to develop a new security partnership, an event the Obama administration quickly exploited. The United States should look for other opportunities to build security relationships around China that will complicate Beijing's security planning, increase China's security costs, and hold out the prospect for further cost increases should China pursue assertive behavior.

Central Asia, Russia, and the Himalayan countries merit consideration in this regard. The start of the U.S. and NATO campaign in Afghanistan in 2001 brought U.S. military and intelligence forces into Central Asia. Since then U.S. relations with the countries in that region have waxed and waned because of tension between U.S. concerns about human rights in some countries and the need for bases in the region to support the war in Afghanistan. China and Russia responded to the sudden arrival of U.S. power in the area by stepping up their own presence and influence. China's emergence as a naval and aerospace power in the western Pacific is predicated on maintaining the strategic tranquility Beijing thought it established along its northern and western frontiers in the 1990s. For little cost the United States could create concerns on China's western frontier, which China would have to expend time and resources to protect.

U.S. relations with Russia are troubled while China's relations with Russia seem on the rise. Xi Jinping's first foreign trip as China's president was to Moscow to negotiate deals on energy, weapons, and technology.[6] The Russian and Chinese economies are highly complementary, with

Russia a well-positioned supplier of energy and high-end weapons and China an eager customer. China has a strong interest in maintaining serenity to its north and west, while Russian sales of warships, submarines, and antiship missiles threaten U.S. maritime power in the Pacific, where Russia is not competing.

But this is a short-term calculation for Moscow. Longer term, China would seem a larger threat to Russia's interests than the United States or Europe; in particular, China's ballistic and land-attack cruise missiles are as threatening to Russia as they are to the United States and its partners in the Pacific. Russia is as constrained by the INF Treaty as the United States is. Given Russia's experience and comparative advantage with ballistic missiles, it would benefit even more than the United States would from the treaty's termination, should Moscow decide that it needs to respond to China's military buildup.

It may thus come to pass that Russia and the United States will find a mutual interest in either terminating the INF treaty or in negotiating an exception for missiles deployed in Asia. U.S. policymakers would be wise to quietly explore this possibility with Russia.

In response to possible Chinese aggression in the Himalayan region, expanding U.S. security relationships there could draw China's attention, stretch its security resources, and threaten to impose greater costs in the future.

The United States should seek to deepen its security relationships with India and Vietnam, two notable partners in the Asia-Pacific region. The U.S.-Indian military relationship has already advanced considerably over the past decade. Indeed India now conducts more military training exercises with the United States than with any other country and is purchasing billions of dollars of U.S.-sourced military hardware.[7] U.S and Indian security interests in the region overlap considerably and the United States is understandably interested in a deeper security partnership. But for reasons discussed below, there are cultural and political barriers to achieving this aspiration, at least at a rapid pace.

Regarding China's assertiveness, the United States and Vietnam similarly share overlapping interests. The military partnership between the two countries is deepening but has begun from a minimal base.[8] As with India, cultural and political obstacles are likely to slow the progress of this relationship.

U.S. policymakers and planners should remember that partners should include nonstate actors. With their experience in Iraq, Afghanistan, and elsewhere in recent years, U.S. military commanders are well aware of the role of nonstate actors and have learned to exploit this aspect of irregular warfare. Irregular warfare and nonstate actors will be factors in the Asia-Pacific theater, something military planners for the region should keep in mind not only as threats but also as opportunities.

Fifth, the United States should lead an effort to build up basic maritime domain awareness and information sharing among its partnership network. The goal would be to develop an accurate and timely picture of China's maritime activities, of both its naval forces and its civilian and paramilitary patrolling. This network would then share this up-to-date picture with all its members so they could improve their responses to China's maritime actions. This initiative would not be a substitute for U.S. Pacific Command's current intelligence collection; rather it would be a complementary effort, designed to assist America's partners in the region and to improve cooperation among them.[9]

The partnership network would use a variety of sources to collect information on China's maritime dispositions. First are the normal contact reports from naval and paramilitary patrolling. Enhancements to partners' maritime presence capacity would add to this collection source. The four big powers in the network (the United States, Japan, India, and Australia) could also assist some of the partners in acquiring unmanned aerial vehicle capabilities to expand their maritime patrolling coverage. A similar effort could promote the emplacement of undersea sensors for detecting and monitoring PLAN submarine forces.

Equally important would be the use of civilian vessels, such as fishing boats with radios and satellite phones, as collectors of information on China's military and nonmilitary maritime activities. Chinese commanders will find it politically awkward to attempt to thwart the collection efforts of civilian vessels. And because of their protected status as noncombatants, these vessels may be able to go places their military and paramilitary counterparts cannot.

Partners contributing to the network's common maritime picture would share its output. In addition to the valuable information the program would produce, network participants would gain experience cooperating on a common task, experience that will bring benefits in other ways. Additionally this program will raise the costs to China should it attempt to attack the network's collection efforts. Although the network would not be a binding treaty, some members may view an attack on the network as an attack on all of its members, a position that may improve deterrence in the region.

Sixth, the United States should encourage its partners in the region to build their own access denial capabilities. China's rapid development of extensive access denial capabilities over the past two decades demonstrates that dangerous antiship and antiaircraft capabilities are accessible to countries (and even nonstate actors) not previously ranked as leading military powers. With moderate effort, it is within the capacity of some of China's neighbors to develop some of the access denial capabilities China has itself developed. The purpose of building partner access denial capabilities is to complicate the PLA's military planning, reduce its options, and raise China's potential costs for employing military force during future crises.

Japan's military forces are already near the leading edge of technology. In 2010 Japan acted to increase its submarine fleet by one-third, from eighteen to twenty-four boats, citing concerns about China's naval expansion.[10] Prime Minister Shinzo Abe expressed his desire to expand Japan's offensive capabilities, using platforms and doctrines not previously considered by Japan's policymakers. For example, Japan is a participant in the F-35 stealthy Joint Strike Fighter program, which will give that nation the capacity to penetrate a sophisticated adversary air defense system. In February 2013 remarks to Parliament, Abe said, "Can we continue to depend entirely on the United States to attack our enemy's bases? . . . If we're going to introduce F-35s, then we should consider fully utilizing their capabilities."[11]

Abe made these remarks in the context of the threat to Japan from North Korea. But the concept naturally applies in other contexts such as the rising threat from the PLA, which arguably was a major factor in Abe's return to power in 2012. And once the principle of Japanese offensive actions using F-35s is accepted, that principle can be transferred to more survivable platforms such as mobile cruise and ballistic missiles.

In 2009 Vietnam placed an order with Russia for six Kilo-class diesel-electric submarines and received the first of these in 2013.[12] The version of the *Kilo*s Vietnam will get may be more advanced that the Kilo submarines operated by the PLAN. It remains to be seen what armament for the Kilos Russia provides to Vietnam; in theory, Vietnam's Kilos could be armed with the same supersonic antiship cruise missiles and wake-homing torpedoes that make China's submarines a threat to the U.S. Navy. Although it will take many years for Vietnam's submarines crews and maintenance personnel to transform this Kilo program into a significant military capability, with persistent effort and support such an outcome is realistic. When that occurs, Vietnam's submarines will have a short transit to patrol positions off Hainan Island and other PLAN bases.

There are more initiatives the United States and its partners could support that would build up the access denial capabilities of China's neighbors. Vietnam, the Philippines, and others could acquire frigates and patrol boats armed with antiship cruise missiles, torpedoes, and antiaircraft weapons. The technology involved with these capabilities is relatively modest and is accessible to small countries.[13] These countries could also acquire land-based antiship cruise missiles and air defense systems mounted on mobile TELs.

The United States and its partners could attempt to get more out of their submarine fleets by increasing cooperation among them. The planned expansion and modernization of China's submarine fleet is perhaps the most important part of its naval program, and, as mentioned, Japan and Vietnam are responding with their own submarine acquisitions. Australia also plans to completely renew its submarine fleet in the years ahead.[14] With these countries recognizing the importance of submarine warfare, they may also see the benefit of coordinating their efforts in order to achieve a better return from the investments they make in these assets. The U.S. Navy, with its comparative advantage in submarine warfare, could be in a good position to develop this concept with these partners.

The United States could work still further with Japan, India, and Australia in sponsoring solutions and in providing ongoing technical assistance for these access denial initiatives. Working through a multilateral group will improve the political legitimacy of such a program and allow the participants to practice cooperation that will be useful in other contexts.

Vietnam, the Philippines, and others in the region are obviously not going to match the PLA's military capacity. The Philippines in particular is beginning its military reforms from a very low base. The PLA's missiles and airpower are daunting enough for the United States and Japan, let alone the other small countries in the region (see chapter 4). In a conflict sparked by, say, a confrontation over maritime claims in the South China Sea, the military forces of the small countries would suffer badly under a determined PLA assault.

The purpose of building regional access denial capabilities is not only to raise the political costs of potential Chinese mischief but also to make such hypothetical PLA military operations more complicated, more risky, easier to detect in advance, and ultimately more costly to China. Raising China's political and military costs at the margin, and making it more difficult for the PLA to achieve operational and tactical surprise, should reduce the utility of the military option for China's leaders and thus improve deterrence. The United States and its partners can achieve this important benefit at relatively little cost and with benefits to all the countries in the network.

Seventh, the United States and its partners should prepare for irregular warfare. Much of the discussion about the various military competitions in the Asia-Pacific region centers on high-end conventional and, occasionally, nuclear forces. This is understandable given the growth in spending on these capabilities over the past two decades. However, all sides, especially China, will prefer to use their conventional military capabilities for signaling and intimidation rather than actual employment—that is, to achieve their political and security objectives without kinetic combat. Against this backdrop, it is likely all sides will look to a variety of irregular warfare techniques to enhance political advantage and to wear down their opponents.

The recent wars in the Middle East and Central Asia have focused the minds of U.S. policymakers on defending against an adversary's use of irregular warfare. The United States and its allies in the Asia-Pacific region may face this prospect, either through China's expanded use of its nonkinetic "Three Warfares" doctrine (media, psychological, and legal techniques) or through its employment of proxies, nonviolently or kinetically.[15] Should these tactics transpire, the United States and its partners will once again have to fashion ways to parry them.

However, U.S. and allied planners should also plan for their own offensive use of irregular warfare. Irregular warfare is commonly associated with the weaker players in a security competition—the side that does not have the advantage in military hardware and organization and that would not gain from conventional military escalation. A decade from now, when China's reconnaissance, missile, aircraft, and submarine programs mature, the United States, with its defense effort lagging by comparison, might end up as the second-ranking military player in the region and thus the player on the losing side of potential conventional escalation. In that case, the United States and its allies may have to resort to irregular warfare in order to change the rules of the competition in their favor.

The intent of this approach would be to impose costs on hypothetical Chinese expansion and to deny China the benefits it seeks should it eventually achieve its territorial goals through salami slicing or other means. Examples of irregular warfare in the maritime domain could include more aggressive media and information operations directed against China's actions, clandestine emplacement of sea mines targeting Chinese naval and paramilitary ships, sabotage of Chinese oil facilities in the South China Sea, and sabotage of undersea data cables connecting to China.

Other forms of irregular warfare might include covert action and unconventional warfare aimed at creating trouble for the CCP in Tibet and Xinjiang province and also mobilization of resistance to China's economic and political presence in Central Asia, Africa, and Latin America.

These are controversial measures that policymakers should not employ without very careful consideration. But merely preparing for their employment could be a powerful and low-cost deterrent to possibly aggressive Chinese behavior. The United States and its allies should prepare offensive irregular warfare options and do so quietly yet within full view of China's intelligence collection system. The intent would be to show resolve and the capability to impose costs and deny benefits to China, should it seek to expand its authority in the region at the expense of its weaker neighbors.

These seven security initiatives would accomplish several important goals. They would improve the political and security cooperation of the countries affected by China's assertions by giving them specific security tasks such as working together to develop a common maritime operating picture; the countries in the region could similarly cooperate on access denial techniques and information operations. Greater cooperation among the partners would result in better security and greater legitimacy for the initiative.

Next, the initiatives call for the other big powers in the region besides the United States to take a role in coordinating regional security. The United States would still have a very large role in most of these programs; but the greater the role played by the other powers, the more the overall effort will be viewed as legitimate.

Perhaps most important, these initiatives show how the small countries in the region can take actions that threaten to impose costs on potential Chinese misbehavior. Effective dissuasion will result in improved regional stability and the avoidance of conflict. When all of the partners in the network are contributing to that effort, the results will be more enduring.

Expanding the U.S. Security Force Assistance Mission

Implementing these initiatives would require an expansion in the already prominent U.S. security cooperation program for the region. Security cooperation and security force assistance with partner military forces are core missions of U.S. Pacific Command, which has ongoing security relationships with dozens of countries in the region.[16] The U.S. State and Defense Departments have well-established and wide-ranging programs for exports of military equipment to partners in the region, ongoing technical support for that military equipment, training and education programs for foreign military officers at U.S. war colleges, and numerous large and small bilateral and multilateral training exercises with partner military forces in the region.

The U.S. Army's Special Forces have had a lead responsibility for conducting foreign internal defense training with partner militaries, with the Army's 1st Special Forces Group assigned to the Asia-Pacific region. The Special Forces have long-established missions in many countries and have built up relationships and trust with soldiers and officials across the region. Special operations forces from the U.S. Navy, Air Force, and Marine Corps are also active in the region, building relationships and training partner forces in their areas of expertise.

One particularly successful recent example of special operations relationship-building is Joint Special Operations Task Force Philippines (JSOTF-P). Established in 2002, JSOTF-P is a small multiservice detachment headquartered in Zamboanga City, with a mission of assisting the Philippine government and military with their operations against Islamic militants in the southern Philippines.[17] Although not directly related to the security challenge posed by China, JSOTF-P is an example of U.S. special operations forces extending a relationship with an ally, improving the capabilities of its armed forces and thereby improving the larger security environment in the region. While security challenges in the southern Philippines continue, the task force is a model for how U.S. forces can establish long-term productive relationships with partners in the region. U.S. special operations forces have also recently expanded training missions with special forces and counterterrorism units in Cambodia, Bangladesh, and Indonesia and have numerous relationships with other partners across the region.[18]

With the U.S. government's stepped-up attention to the Asia-Pacific region and the drawdown of U.S. forces in the Middle East and Central Asia, a competition has broken out inside the U.S. military, especially among the ground forces, to show which can best demonstrate its relevance to the region. In 2011 Gen. James Amos, commandant of the Marine Corps, announced, "The main focus of effort is going to be the Pacific for the Marines."[19] Not to be outdone, Lt. Gen. Robert Brown, commander of the U.S. Army's I Corps (which is also earmarked for missions in the Pacific region), coauthored an article explaining why his command, populated with conventional ground troops, is the best for security force assistance missions in the region, a conclusion that no doubt raised eyebrows among his Special Forces colleagues inside the Army.[20]

Although the largest U.S. military challenges in the region are maritime and aerospace, U.S. ground forces will have a critical role in a successful strategy. Seven of the ten largest armies in the world are located in the region, and twenty-one of twenty-seven Pacific nations have an army officer as chief of all defense forces.[21] These facts imply that U.S. Army and Marine Corps officers and units should be present, both in relationship-building and for security force assistance missions, if the U.S. military is to establish and maintain credibility with these partners.

But the seven initiatives described previously, designed to dissuade potential Chinese assertiveness, suggest that the U.S. Army and Marine Corps will have to expand into new areas the roles they play with partners. For example, establishing a cooperative domain awareness and intelligence collection and dissemination enterprise will require sharing expertise with unmanned aerial vehicle operations, sensors, and communication networks.

Building local access denial capabilities will require the U.S. Army to share its expertise with air and missile defense (which it has) and its experience with land-based, truck-mounted antiship missiles (which it completely lacks). Building partner capacity in psychological and information operations, and the black arts of offensive irregular warfare, covert action, and unconventional warfare are clearly the work of special operations forces and intelligence agencies. In short, U.S. security force assistance in the Asia-Pacific region will need to shift its focus to external security threats, a change from the focus on mainly internal threats that has predominated over the past decade.[22]

U.S. forces are thus eager to expand their forward presence in the region and their security force assistance missions. They are seeking out these roles because the leadership in Washington has declared the region to be the top security priority and because the services need to show their relevance as the overall defense budget comes under pressure in the years ahead.

However, this urge to demonstrate relevance has exposed some shortcomings. First, the services will need to expand their security force assistance expertise into new areas and fill in knowledge gaps, for example with shore-based antiship missiles, which are currently lacking. Second, the overall success of the security force assistance mission for the region would benefit from greater participation from other countries, which will have expertise and cultural knowledge the United States lacks. Greater participation will also boost the effort's political legitimacy. Finally, and perhaps most crucially, an expanded security force assistance effort will have to overcome numerous dilemmas, as explained below.

The Dilemmas of U.S. Security Cooperation

At first glance, it would seem straightforward to implement the seven initiatives described above that would expand the role played by America's security partners in the region. These partners would benefit from the resulting improvements in security and the expanded cooperation built into the concepts. The United States would similarly benefit, not only from improved regional security but also from the status it would gain from successfully leading such an effort. And U.S. military forces, looking for useful work during a time of austerity, would be eager to contribute.

However, numerous dilemmas both in the region and in Washington stand in the way of improved security cooperation, multilateral coordination, and deeper security relationships between the United States and its partners. Any reformed security cooperation effort will have to recognize and overcome these dilemmas.

America's partners in the region certainly want better security; but deeper security ties with the United States come with costs and risks some of the leaders of these countries often find unpleasant. For example, although the United States has pledged to increase its security presence in the region, this will almost always take the form of temporary training visits and rotational deployments and not new permanent bases or larger garrisons at existing ones. Indeed, existing U.S. bases in Japan and Korea are unpopular and politically corrosive; the current trend in both places is to reduce the overall U.S. troop level and to move as many as those bases that remain from urban to rural areas. This trend was demonstrated in 1992 when the Philippines government tossed out the large U.S. Navy and Air Force presence in Luzon, a response to intense public opposition. The Chinese threat has caused the Philippines to invite U.S. forces back, but for training visits, not at permanent bases; thus, an increased presence of U.S. military forces, even if on temporary or rotational terms, could create cultural frictions that some leaders in the region may find too risky.

Similarly, political leaders in most partner countries do not want to give the appearance that their country is a mere auxiliary of the U.S. military, in service to Washington's foreign policy. In many cases, when a partner's security interests might closely overlap those of the United States, it will be too risky politically for that partner to openly collaborate with U.S. military forces, especially if the collaboration takes on the appearance of preparation of mainly offensive operations that might be unrelated to the partner's security interests. As a result, many countries in the region will limit their training alongside U.S. forces to humanitarian relief and disaster assistance scenarios, with some nations adding counterpiracy and counterterrorism readiness. The U.S. military engages in high-intensity combined arms training with South Korean and Japanese militaries, but this training is tied to the ongoing security threat from North Korea that those countries face. Elsewhere in the region, the sensitivity of security cooperation will limit the level of interoperability many partner countries will be able to achieve with U.S. forces.

Countries may wish to limit their security engagement with either the United States or with a wider regional security network to avoid getting entangled in a conflict not connected to their interests. During the Cold War, neutral countries such as Sweden, Switzerland, and Ireland benefited from NATO's stand against the Warsaw Pact, even though these countries did not participate in the alliance. Staying outside the alliance may have required them to spend more on defense than they would have had they been inside NATO (or maybe not), but it did allow these countries greater freedom of action and the avoidance of entangling commitments during a potential crisis. By this logic, some countries in the Asia-Pacific region will resist participation in even a loose security network, at least until they conclude that their security requires it.

Likewise, many leaders will not want to risk committing to a course of action that would limit their options in the future, especially if they had doubts about the success of such action. Specifically, many may resist committing to a U.S.-led security architecture for the region that the United States may subsequently abandon. U.S. commitments of prestige and military investments may not be wholly convincing, especially when decision makers consider U.S. disengagements from other commitments in recent memory when trends turned badly.

The logical conclusion for these decision makers will be to hedge their bets. For example, in April 2013, Australia and China formally entered into a "strategic partnership" that resulted in a schedule of regular high-level meetings between the two governments, an arrangement Australia does not have with the United States, a formal security treaty ally.[23] Australia's deep dependence on China's purchases of Australian raw materials is likely the main motivation for this arrangement. Leaders in Canberra likely view a deeper Australia-China relationship as completely compatible with Australia's security relationship with the United States and a U.S.-led security network in the region. For Australian leaders, there seems little downside to hedging.

At least there should be no incompatibility when security tensions are low. But should China's territorial assertions accelerate, the United States and many of its other partners will observe Australia's response and draw conclusions accordingly. Policymakers in Canberra likely conclude that they can deal with such a hypothetical situation if it arises. In the meantime, they will conclude that they have kept their options open. By contrast, the view in Washington and elsewhere may be that Australia's hedging might encourage greater Chinese assertiveness, which could result in a crisis that might well have been deterred.

Thus the greatest diplomatic fear in Washington (and perhaps elsewhere in the region) is that Chinese diplomacy, bolstered by China's overwhelming economic presence and perhaps the feeling that its regional dominance is inevitable, will erode the security network that officials in Washington and elsewhere in the region might wish to build. This would open the way for more salami slicing in the Near Seas, the establishment of new "facts on the ground," and perhaps the de facto completion of China's territorial goals, which the PLA could effectively defend with its access denial military investments. Washington's renewed attention to the region aims to avert this scenario; the seven initiatives discussed earlier would boost America's odds. But the dilemmas discussed here show why it won't be simple for the United States and its partners to succeed.

Indeed, should the United States succeed in establishing a more robust security cooperation architecture, such an achievement would come with new problems attached. For example, the more successful the overall network would become, the greater the incentive for individual members to "free ride" by economizing on their own contribution.

Free riding has been a perennial challenge for U.S. policymakers charged with defending foreign security commitments, as constituents back home frequently remind them. These policymakers fear that the more the United States spends on the region's security, the more free riding there could be. On the other hand, if the United States doesn't take the lead in organizing a security network, it very likely won't get built given the still-simmering animosities lingering among many of America's security partners in the region. The result would be an open field for Chinese salami slicing and a divide-and-conquer approach, followed soon after by an unstable arms race as the other large powers in the region mobilize to protect themselves. The United States has little choice but to be the security leader in the region, for the protection of its own interests above all else (discussed in chapter 2). But as the United States has experienced with its European partners in NATO and elsewhere, free riding will be a continuing concern.

At the same time, a successful security network could result in an opposite concern—encouragement of excessively aggressive behavior by partners who may conclude that, should conflict break out due to their behavior, the United States would be compelled to support them or risk losing the security architecture, something they may conclude the United States could not tolerate. U.S. policy tries to make it clear to partners which events would trigger U.S. intervention and which would not. A North Korean invasion of South Korea would invoke the U.S. security guarantee; an unprovoked South Korean missile attack on the North would likely find Washington attempting to disengage from the resulting conflict. At least this is what U.S. officials have communicated to their counterparts in Seoul.

The United States employs ambiguity to dissuade its partners from pressing their territorial disputes with China. U.S. officials regularly explain that the U.S. government does not take a position on disputed territory claims in the East and South China Seas, other than to insist that disputes be resolved without force or coercion. The United States does not take a position on the question of sovereignty, but it does generally pledge to defend the status quo. This position in favor of the status quo mostly favors the interests of America's partners, who are in most cases the incumbents on the rocks, shoals, and islets under dispute. But U.S. officials still prefer ambiguity in order to keep partners uncertain about what behavior they might get away with. The goal is to avoid U.S. entanglement in an undesired conflict. Unfortunately, such ambiguity in some circumstances might also encourage adversaries and weaken deterrence.

It remains in question whether the United States will be able to maintain this cautious and restraining ambiguity should China's assertiveness and salami slicing accelerate. It is understandable that U.S. officials would want to avoid getting entangled in a conflict whose origins begin outside their control. This is especially a concern in a region that still harbors highly charged nationalist sentiments and unresolved grievances, which could quickly compel local leaders into aggressive actions. In 2010 Secretary of State Hillary Clinton made a clear statement committing the United States to the defense of the Senkaku Islands in case of armed conflict. By contrast, U.S. support to the Philippines was nowhere to be found during the 2012 confrontation that nation had with China over Scarborough Reef, which ended up in China's possession, at least for now. For some observers in the region, ambiguity might be another word for inconsistency or even abandonment.

Part of the competitive strategy discussed here calls for the small countries opposing China's assertions to do more to defend their interests. This line of effort is competitive because it places China in the position of being the large bully, a winning propaganda position for the small countries and a position that raises China's costs for its assertive behavior. Further, the only way to halt China's salami slicing is to have the small countries around the Near Seas step up their civilian, paramilitary, and military presence, to match China's presence and material advantages. Many of the small countries won't be willing to take this risk while the United States still maintains ambiguity on the sovereignty issue. In this regard the small countries would be right to fear later abandonment by Washington.

Dissuading China's salami slicing is essential to averting a larger and more serious confrontation later. But such action may require Washington to rethink its purposely ambiguous position on sovereignty, a step that has its own risks and that will surely worsen relations with Beijing.

How to Resolve the Dilemmas

These dilemmas are eternal features of security partnerships, as familiar to today's strategists as they were to Thucydides during the Peloponnesian War. Statesmen can only hope to manage them, not avoid them completely. There are several reforms the United States could make to its approach to its security relationships in the region that would mitigate some of the harmful consequences of these partnership dilemmas.

First, although the United States should lead the establishment of a broad security network in the region, it should attempt to maintain a modest profile and encourage others to have equally prominent leadership roles. The idea behind this notion is to diffuse the perception that the purpose of the security network is merely to enlist auxiliaries to execute America's foreign policy agenda. Such an awkward (and incorrect) impression will be easier to refute when the United States shares the leadership responsibilities broadly. Leaders in the partner countries will have more success generating domestic support for a regional multilateral security network if the network appears to really be a multinational rather than a U.S.-dominated group. Greater political legitimacy of the overall effort will result.

Second, U.S. Pacific Command should to the extent possible organize multilateral rather than bilateral training exercises and exchanges; this will create several benefits. It will create more opportunities for officials and soldiers to develop trusting relationships and exchange ideas. Multilateral exercises will promote greater military interoperability across the region. Multilateral events will tamp down the perception that the security network is centered on U.S. interests only. And multilateral exercises add to political legitimacy, both internally and in the eyes of outside observers.

Third, U.S. policymakers should keep in mind that military exercises with partners can serve many purposes and that planners should have these purposes forefront when developing and executing these training events. Military training exercises are obviously meant to improve soldier skills and interoperability among exercise participants. But exercises are also opportunities for political signaling to a wide variety of audiences. For example, humanitarian assistance exercises, perhaps the most popular among policymakers in the region, are a chance for local governments to display their value to their domestic audiences. U.S. policymakers who are struggling to justify foreign engagement to skeptical constituents might prefer more combat-oriented exercises, in order to show voters that America's partners in the region really are putting their troops at risk.[24] Planners should understand the domestic political consequences—good and bad—of a military exercise's format and then structure the exercise to achieve desired political goals.

Potential adversaries will also receive signals from training exercises. U.S. and South Korean training exercises are designed to signal to the leadership in Pyongyang a readiness for high-intensity combat. The U.S. government invited China to participate in the large multinational Rim of the Pacific exercise in Hawaii in order to show that the United States and its partners are not isolating China from the region's security arrangements. Planners also hope that China's officers receive the message that the United States and its partners are stepping up their military readiness. Should the

United States and its partners decide to make preparations for offensive irregular warfare, some of those preparations should occur in China's view, in order to send the message that they are preparing to impose costs on China if necessary.

Fourth, the United States and its partners may wish to consider designs that seek to negate the conflicting dilemma of abandonment and entanglement. Security arrangements that deliberately build in interdependence, or a "two-key system," could help mitigate these two dilemmas. As discussed in chapter 2 and above, interdependence is already present to some degree among the United States and its partners; however, only the United States has some of the high-end military capabilities—such as long-range bombers and extensive reconnaissance and military communication systems—that would be crucial in a hypothetical conflict with China. In this sense, the smaller countries in a security network will be dependent on the United States as the sole source of certain capabilities.

For its part, the United States, being an expeditionary power from outside the region, still requires the approval of its partners in the region to implement any effective strategy. But for those partners who are particularly sensitive to the possibility of abandonment or entanglement, combined military planning could incorporate a more specific segregation of tasks and duties, in order to reinforce mutual interdependency.

Finally, and perhaps most crucially, any security architecture created by the United States and its partners must take account of China's legitimate security concerns and ensure that these concerns are respected and protected. The overarching goal of the reformed strategy for the region is to dissuade China from using its power to attempt to change the existing international system in East Asia (discussed in chapter 6). In order for China to continue to accept the current system as its interests and power continue to expand, its leaders need to believe that the system will work for China in the future. The United States and its partners have a strong interest in making sure that this remains the case, not only to avoid Chinese resistance, but because they will all benefit from China's continued peaceful development.

Obtaining China's cooperative acceptance of the international system in East Asia will require ongoing consultation with that country's officials and military leaders. The purpose of these consultations will be to clearly hear China's concerns and ensure they are incorporated into security planning. Success will also benefit from China's participation in the region's cooperative security operations.[25] Such participation will give China a stake in the region's security. And knowing that China is included may make the security architecture more acceptable to some of the other partners in the region.

It is not a logical contradiction to invite China into the region's security architecture while simultaneously preparing for China's military modernization and possible Chinese aggressiveness. Achieving a peaceful and sustainable security balance in the region will require not only incentives for positive behavior but also the threat of costs for disruptive conduct. The United States and its partners should accept this duality and design policies that support it.

A New U.S. Diplomatic Approach: More Assertive, More Subtle

A new U.S. diplomatic approach to the Asia-Pacific region that is both more assertive, yet also more subtle has been described here. This diplomatic strategy would definitely acknowledge that the United States and its partners are engaged in a long-term security competition with China and that this network of partners needs to form an active and coordinated response to this challenge. Yet for this response to be successful, it will need to be multilateral, speak with actions more than words, and match its strengths against China's vulnerabilities. It also needs to take account of China's legitimate security interests and invite China to participate in the region's security.

This chapter also described how the U.S.-led partnership network can increase China's costs for assertive behavior and displayed how those costs can compound if necessary. U.S. diplomats and military planners working in the Asia-Pacific region are already implementing some of these ideas while others remain unused. Indeed many will consider some of these recommendations, such as increasing the risk of maritime confrontations, building up missile capacity among China's neighbors, and preparing for offensive irregular warfare, needlessly provocative and counterproductive.

Further, the recommendations here include having the United States seek out and deepen security relationships around China's entire periphery, including with Burma, India, the Himalayan region, Central Asia, and Russia. Some individuals, including nearly all in Beijing, will view this as an obvious containment strategy, treating China as if it was a rogue nation rather than a great power deserving respect.

These recommendations are not needlessly provocative. A major theme of this book is that the United States and its allies must reckon with the fact that China is both a security competitor and an economic partner and will be for the indefinite future. The United States and its partners, especially China's small neighbors with modest resources, need to fashion competitive responses to China. Such responses will necessarily require exploiting China's vulnerabilities, which will include propaganda, China's dependence on its maritime access, its long border, and its possible political fragility.

Nor are these recommendations a containment strategy. A real containment strategy would see China politically and economically isolated, as are Iran and North Korea. By contrast, the United States and its partners in the region want to see expanding trade and contacts with China. All benefit from this trade. But from the strategic perspective, positive interaction with China is part of an incentive structure that encourages behavior that benefits all players in the region, while holding out the prospect of increasing costs for unfavorable conduct.

The United States and its partners will face many dilemmas and hurdles managing their relationships during the long competitive challenge ahead. This chapter has discussed some ways to mitigate these dilemmas. The United States and its partners should expect China to add to the challenges, as, for example, it has done with its efforts to weaken ASEAN's role in the region.

The United States and its partners need each other if they are to achieve the security they seek. Thus any successful U.S. strategy must begin with the maintenance of its relationships in the region, including above all, America's relationship with China.

Getting diplomacy and security cooperation right will make a major contribution to success. But the U.S. Defense Department will also need to look inward to fix the flaws inside its programs and military strategies for the region. The next two chapters will address these problems.

 *Chapter 8*

THE FUTURE OF AIRPOWER IN THE PACIFIC

The Asia-Pacific region is often thought of as a primarily maritime theater for military operations. In the future, naval forces will undoubtedly play an important role. However, we have seen that the falling costs and rapid expansion of missiles and targeting sensors will make life for military forces on the surface—massed ground combat formations, air bases, and surface warships—increasingly risky. Surface forces within missile range of adversaries will spend more time and resources evading detection and less time doing their designed missions. Add in the submarine threat possessed by both China and the United States and one has to question the ability of surface naval forces on either side—including aircraft carriers—to "stand their ground" west of the Second Island Chain.

Thus, transient patrolling and raiding in the Near Seas, rather than a persistent presence and control, likely best describes the pattern of future warfare in the region, at least in the initial stages of a conflict. Patrolling and raiding will best be done by long-range airpower, which can attack and retreat better than naval and ground forces. In a theater dominated by long-range precision missiles, retreating after a raid will be critical for survival and ultimate success.

For these reasons, long-range airpower dominance will be the key to military success in East Asia. The structure of U.S. forces in the region has drifted far from this concept (as seen in chapter 3). Building a fleet of long-range stealthy aircraft adapted to a long list of missions beyond just "bombing" is necessary if the United States is to persuade China's decision makers that establishing Chinese regional hegemony won't be feasible.

The United States needs to redesign its military forces in the region in order to cope with China's military modernization. This redesign would have several goals: First, the capability to convincingly deny the PLA the ability to achieve exclusive military control over the Near Seas; second, the ability for U.S. and allied forces to hold at risk, with conventional strike operations, assets valued by China's leaders, in an effort to dissuade those leaders from coercive strategies; third, the ability to sustain U.S. and allied control over the global commons in the western Pacific; and finally, a force redesigned around long-range striking power that would reduce the dangerous "use it, or lose it" instability the current force structure, centered on short-range forward-deployed forces, has created.

In order to do these things, during wartime the United States needs the ability to employ conventional airpower with consequential effect anywhere in the region. Without changes to its programs and policies, the United States will struggle to retain this ability by next decade. As we have seen, the U.S. airpower force structure, with its excessive weighting to short-range platforms, is unsuited for the region. The main U.S. air bases in the region are too vulnerable to Chinese missile attack, and the vast preponderance of U.S. airpower has insufficient range to be effective in the region. U.S. military planners and acquisition officials need to look at airpower from first principles in order to reconfigure these forces so they can be effective in East Asia.

Doing so will require a creative approach to the full range of airpower attributes including aircraft, missiles, space operations, communications, warfighting doctrine, and coordination with other services and with allies. And this approach will require confronting service cultures and norms that suited the past but will not work in the future.

Needed: More Long-Range Aircraft, and Not Just for Bombing

Chapters 3 and 4 examined why the position of U.S. airpower in the western Pacific has deteriorated; for example, even while the United States operates some of the most capable tactical combat aircraft, these aircraft lack the range and bases to be present where they will be needed.

One example, as cited in chapter 4, is based on research from a RAND Corporation study of a hypothetical battle for the airspace over Taiwan. During a war with China, the U.S. Air Force would likely be restricted to operations from its air base on Guam, about three thousand kilometers southeast of Taiwan because it will be a simple matter for China's missile forces to suppress U.S. air operation from its bases on Okinawa, Japan, and South Korea, which are so close to China. U.S. Air Force F-22 air superiority fighters operating from Guam would require two midair refuelings to reach Taiwan and would be operating at the extreme limit of human physiology for a single-seat aircraft.[1]

The report concluded that even if the Air Force relocated virtually all of its F-22 fleet and supporting aircraft to Guam and dispersal airfields on neighboring islands, air planners would be able to keep only a handful of F-22s continuously over Taiwan. The PLA air force, operating from many bases much closer to Taiwan, could choose a time to overwhelm the small F-22 patrol over the island. And even though the superior F-22 would be expected to dominate Chinese fighters in air-to-air combat, the small force of F-22s would quickly run out of missiles, leaving the airspace over Taiwan in Chinese control.

For East Asia's vast distances, the United States needs a combat aircraft with the range, persistence, and payload capacity to be useful in the theater. Indeed the Air Force is developing (albeit at a seemingly leisurely pace) a new long-range strike bomber.[2] This development program is classified with little information in the public domain. In 2012 a senior Air Force acquisition official discussed the new bomber in general terms. He said the aircraft is being designed with Pacific scenarios in mind and will have the ability to persist inside defended airspace, implying that it will be a stealthy aircraft. The aircraft will be designed to perform missions with a human crew or as a remotely piloted drone. He also noted the aircraft will rely heavily on subsystems currently in use on other aircraft in order to reduce the program's technical risk and cost. Indeed program managers for the new bomber are allowing only already proven technology and are excising "nice to have" features from the design in order to reduce cost risk during development.[3] The Air Force is targeting a cost of $550 million per aircraft for a fleet of eighty to one hundred, a figure that if achieved would be substantially less than the cost of the B-2 bombers it would eventually replace.[4]

Large aircraft possess structural advantages that are denied to their small fighter-attack siblings, advantages that are especially important in the vast Asia-Pacific theater. Human physiology imposes a time limit on a fighter operated by a single crewmember. Although midair refueling extends the range of bombers and fighters, twelve hours of continuous flight duty (including pre- and postflight briefing) is the upper limit for the pilot of a single-seat fighter.[5] Larger bombers such as the B-2, by contrast, have two pilots. The crew space is capacious compared to a fighter and commonly includes a small galley, a lavatory, and space for one of the crewmembers to sleep. The Air Force's B-2s have thus routinely flown from central Missouri to the Middle East and Central Asia, round-trip missions lasting over thirty hours. As we have seen, the Asia-Pacific's distances and the basing constraints the United States faces will require the combat radii available to long-range bombers.

In addition, large platforms such as the Air Force's bombers have demonstrated an ability to adapt to changing circumstances and mission requirements and have had very long service lives as a result. For example, the B-52 bomber began its life in the 1950s as a strategic nuclear bomber designed to penetrate Soviet air defenses. Over the succeeding decades, the airplane was adapted for conventional bombing, as a standoff cruise missile carrier, for maritime patrolling and strike, and most recently for close air support for ground forces in Afghanistan. Small fighters, by contrast, typically lack the capacity to be adapted for new roles and thus must be discarded in favor of new (and increasingly expensive) generations of fighter aircraft.[6]

Although the need for greater long-range capacity for the Asia-Pacific region should be clear, a few years ago this clarity inside the Pentagon was absent. In April 2009 then–secretary of defense Robert Gates cancelled the Air Force's next-generation bomber development program.[7] Gates explained his decision in the context of uncertainties relating to U.S. strategic nuclear forces and related arms control issues—not in terms of usable long-range conventional strike capacity in regions like the Asia-Pacific. As a result of misperceptions like these—the result of Cold War–era mental framing—the arrival of added long-range strike capacity was delayed, a decision that could result in a dangerous shortfall of U.S. strike capabilities in the region by 2020.

Although the Air Force bomber development program is classified, there is some well-informed analysis in the public domain of the new bomber's potential characteristics.[8] These characteristics include a combat radius of about 4,500 kilometers (sufficient to reach any target in China from a secure refueling point); stealthiness and defensive systems in order to permit operations inside defended airspace; the ability to loiter inside defended airspace in order to find and attack mobile targets; and the ability to employ a broad range of munitions, including long-range land-attack and antiship missiles and large penetrating bombs for defeating hardened and deeply buried targets.

In 1977 the Carter administration cancelled the B-1 bomber program. It reasoned that long-range cruise missiles, an emerging technology at that time, offered a more economical way of attacking targets deep inside defended airspace when compared to the cost and risk of building a new penetrating bomber like the B-1 to replace the aging B-52 (the succeeding Reagan administration opted for both the B-1 and cruise missiles). Ever since these decisions, airpower analysts have debated the merits of penetrating bombers versus long-range cruise missiles launched from much cheaper "bomb trucks," cargo aircraft that loiter well beyond adversary air defenses.

The increasing prevalence of underground and hardened military facilities has resolved the debate for most in favor of maintaining the penetrating bomber. The discovery of a previously clandestine uranium enrichment facility deep underground near Fordow, Iran, reaffirmed the need for U.S. capability to strike such deep and hardened targets; however, the conventional warheads on long-range cruise missiles, typically 1,000 kilograms or less, are too small to hold such targets at risk. In the case of Fordow and other such deep bunker complexes, the U.S. Air Force has developed an upgraded Massive Ordnance Penetrator, a 30,000-pound guided penetrating bomb. The B-2 bomber is the only aircraft capable of delivering this bomb.[9]

With U.S. military planners largely restricted to considering only conventional munitions, the appeal to potential U.S. adversaries of tunneling and underground bunkers has increased. China in particular is making wide use of bunkers and technologically advanced underground facilities to protect its command and control structure, its logistics assets, its missile forces, and some of its naval assets.[10]

The United States will need large penetrating bombers in order to carry the large bombs needed to attack these targets. Indeed, retaining the ability to hold such targets at risk may be one of the most important components of a credible dissuasion strategy. China has spent considerable resources on tunneling and hardened bunkers because it places high value on the assets it wishes to protect in these facilities. Maintaining the capability to hold these assets at risk should restrain a temptation by China's leaders to act with impunity during a crisis.

Insufficient range and the inability of many current U.S. aircraft to operate inside defended airspace hamper not only the ability to strike targets on land, but hamper nearly the full range of airpower missions in the Asia-Pacific theater. The aircraft the Air Force is designing for long-range strike should also be considered for this much longer list of required tasks.

For example, the RAND study of air superiority over Taiwan discussed the employment of long-range air-to-air missiles on B-1 bombers to supplement the limited missile capacity of the Air Force's F-22 air superiority fighters. The report described the feasibility of loading such missiles into the weapons bays of the bombers, which would use their long endurance to loiter outside of Chinese fighter range east of Taiwan. The bombers could then employ long-range air-to-air missiles to prevent the Chinese air force from establishing air superiority over the island.

Standard U.S. Air Force air superiority doctrine calls for air-to-air engagements to begin beyond the visual range of enemy aircraft, using missiles such as the AIM-120 Advanced Medium Range Air-to-Air Missile (AMRAAM). Although also designed to be dominant in air combat maneuvering, the F-22's best comparative advantage is to use its stealthiness, powerful radar, ability to share data with other aircraft, and missiles such as AMRAAM to attack enemy aircraft from beyond visual range.[11]

The RAND study surmised that in a hypothetical air battle over Taiwan, U.S. Air Force F-22s would be vastly outnumbered by Chinese Flanker fighter-attack aircraft; the F-22s on patrol over Taiwan would expend all of their AMRAAM missiles before they could prevent the Flankers from achieving dominance over the island. The study also contemplated bombers such as the B-1 launching additional air-to-air missiles from beyond visual range, which either the bombers or other friendly aircraft such as F-22s would guide to Flankers not downed in the first round of combat.[12]

In the event Chinese ballistic and cruise missiles succeeded in suppressing most or all of friendly air bases west of the Second Island Chain, the United States, with its current force structure, would have limited ability to deny the airspace over the Near Seas to PLA aircraft. However, arming a large, stealthy, long-range aircraft such as the new bomber with long-range air-to-air missiles would restore some of this capacity and at the very least complicate Chinese air combat planning.

The new bomber—here used as an air superiority platform—would bring several advantages to this mission. First, its long-range and endurance would permit it to patrol a wide area and provide persistent coverage. As a large platform with ample electrical power, the new bomber could host a powerful radar, while its weapons bays could hold a large number of missiles and other munitions. The aircraft would have the communications capability to coordinate its actions with other aircraft and ships, and its stealthiness would achieve surprise over China's Flankers and other nonstealthy aircraft, while leaving it a mystery to Chinese planners as to which parts of the airspace were being patrolled.

To support this concept, the Air Force should develop a new air-to-air missile with a much longer range than that of the AIM-120D missile, the range of which is reportedly 181 kilometers.[13] The RAND study discusses various methods of adapting existing technology to produce air-to-air missiles with ranges over 500 kilometers.[14] Stealthy "bombers," armed with as many as thirty such long-range air-to-air missiles, could deploy in coordinated patrol lines near the First Island Chain and hold at risk Chinese aircraft groups attempting to operate in the same airspace.

This would be an air superiority capability the United States would not have if the PLA's land-attack missiles suppressed current friendly air bases in the area. It is also an air defense capability current U.S. Navy ships, such as the DDG-51 *Burke*-class destroyers, may also find it too dangerous to provide, given the antiship capabilities the PLA will possess by 2020. Thus we can see that the United States can employ a stealthy long-range aircraft for more than just attacking land targets.

The new bomber aircraft will have additional uses. Its use as a long-endurance reconnaissance platform, loitering in defended airspace and striking mobile targets of opportunity, has already been described. The United States has long employed this technique as a counterterrorism tactic in the Middle East, Central Asia, and Africa. The Air Force and Central Intelligence Agency have used the Predator and Reaper remotely piloted aircraft to establish dozens of "orbits" where these unmanned aircraft continuously monitor the terrain below for intelligence, occasionally striking targets with Hellfire air-to-surface missiles. However, the United States is able to perform these operations only because the airspace is undefended. The patrolling over Pakistan occurs only because the Pakistani government permits it; should it withdraw that permission, the orbits would halt—the Pakistani military would easily be able to shoot down the vulnerable Predators and Reapers. In 2013 the commander of the U.S. Air Force's Air Combat Command asserted that its Predators and Reapers were "useless in a contested environment."[15] The United States thus needs a stealthy long-range reconnaissance-strike aircraft to patrol where Predators and Reapers cannot.

After a small stealthy unmanned aircraft crashed in Iran, it was revealed the United States was monitoring that country with an RQ-170 Sentinel. A small aircraft, the RQ-170 had a short range and flew from an air base near Kandahar, Afghanistan, to observe neighboring Iran.[16] The U.S. government was willing to risk the RQ-170 over Iran because the intelligence the drone collected was thought important and presumably could not be obtained any other way, including by means of space-based assets. But should the United States lose access to nearby bases, it will also lose the use of the short-range RQ-170 as a stealthy reconnaissance aircraft. The unveiling of the RQ-170 in 2011, and the discovery of its limitations, provided another argument for building a fleet of long-range stealthy reconnaissance-strike aircraft.[17]

A stealthy long-endurance aircraft will have several maritime roles. The U.S. Navy is replacing its legacy P-3 Orion land-based maritime surveillance and antisubmarine aircraft with the P-8 Poseidon submarine hunter and the MQ-4C Triton unmanned aircraft for high altitude, long-endurance broad area maritime surveillance.[18] The P-8 is a modified version of the civilian Boeing 737 airliner, while the Triton is a version of the Global Hawk drone first acquired by the Air Force.

Although replacing the elderly P-3 fleet is a long overdue decision, neither of the new aircraft is stealthy and thus can't persist for long in defended airspace. For most of the maritime realm the Navy patrols, this is not an issue. But patrolling the western Pacific during a conflict with China will be a critical task, and we know that by the next decade, China will be able to contest that airspace with its Flankers and J-20s out to two thousand kilometers from its coast. Adapting a stealthy long-range aircraft for maritime surveillance and antiship strike would give the Navy a system for accomplishing this mission in defended airspace, a capability it wouldn't have with its current plans.

Finally, U.S. and allied special operations forces would benefit from a long-range stealthy aircraft from which they could clandestinely insert special operations teams through defended airspace. Special operation and irregular warfare capabilities will be important components of a broad portfolio designed to improve conventional deterrence and stability in the region (discussed in chapter 7). Over the past several decades however, U.S. special operations forces have almost always operated in undefended airspace. In a potential conflict with China, that is not likely to be the case. In addition, the long distances from friendly bases in the Asia-Pacific theater will be another feature unfamiliar to most current special operations planners. For many critical special operations missions, the capability to insert special operations forces clandestinely and at long distance through defended airspace may be highly desirable. Once again, the long-range stealthy "bomber" aircraft may be useful for this application.[19]

After completing the research and development phase of its new long-range stealthy bomber, the Air Force plans to acquire eighty to one hundred of the aircraft at a hoped-for price of $550 million per airplane.[20] However, given the usefulness of this aircraft for air superiority, reconnaissance, maritime patrol, and special operations missions in defended airspace, U.S. military forces will need such an aircraft for more roles than just "bomber." Both the Air Force and the Navy would benefit from this aircraft. By extending the production run for this larger set of purposes, both services would benefit from economies of scale and presumably lower prices. Both services could pay for the critical capabilities this aircraft would provide by redirecting some funding from currently planned purchases of F-35, MQ-4C, and P-8 aircraft, which would have only limited utility in the most contested areas of the western Pacific during a hypothetical war with China.

Closing the Missile Gap with China

In chapter 4 we saw how over the past two decades China has aggressively exploited the missile and sensor revolution. By 2020 China will have many hundreds of highly accurate medium- and intermediate-range ballistic and cruise missiles that will threaten U.S. and allied bases in the region. The INF Treaty prohibits the United States from possessing similar land-based missiles. China's antiship cruise missiles have superior range, sensors, and numbers compared to the legacy Harpoon missile used by the U.S. Navy. In a surface battle, China's ships would very likely get the crucial first effective shots, which U.S. ships would have to endure before the survivors could return fire. China is fielding a medium-range antiship ballistic missile; the United States has nothing like it (nor is permitted to under the INF Treaty). Most crucially, China gets to employ its diverse inventory of weapons from an advantageous continental position, while the United States must cope with the limitations of being an expeditionary power. In the past the U.S counted on its superior tactical airpower from land bases and aircraft carriers to offset all of these shortcomings; but, as we have seen, China has designed its forces to exploit America's excessive reliance on short-range aircraft.

Over the past few years, U.S. military leaders and acquisition officials have begun taking steps to close the tactical missile gap with China. Indeed, in July 2012 Adm. Jonathan Greenert, the chief of naval operations, asserted that an acquisition strategy centered on "payloads"—including, but not limited to, missiles—would be wiser than an acquisition strategy that relied mostly on "platforms" such as high-end ships and aircraft, to overwhelm an opponent. Greenert reasoned that with technology advancing so quickly, the latest model ships and aircraft would quickly become obsolete, but would be too expensive to replace; however, the missiles carried by these ships and aircraft could be upgraded quickly and cheaply by comparison. A strategy focused on payloads instead of platforms would be more flexible and realistic.[21]

The Air Force and Navy have several new tactical missile programs under way that will improve the U.S. position in the western Pacific. But even after the services field these new missiles, several critical gaps in capability will remain that PLA commanders will be able to exploit in a conflict.

The Air Force is now acquiring the AGM-158B Joint Air-to-Surface Standoff Missile-Extended Range (JASSM-ER). JASSM-ER is an air-launched cruise missile able to defeat a variety of fixed and moving targets after penetrating through defended airspace, and, important for the Asia-Pacific theater, has a range of over nine hundred kilometers. The B-1 is the only aircraft equipped to support JASSM-ER, but we should presume that the missile will also eventually be mated to most legacy strike aircraft, as well as the future new bomber.[22] The Air Force plans to acquire 2,500 JASSM-ERs.[23]

Although a joint service program, the Navy has apparently shown little interest in JASSM-ER. Instead the Navy uses the air-launched AGM-84K Standoff Land Attack Missile-Expanded Response (SLAM-ER), a cruise missile which is able to precisely attack fixed and moving targets at a range of 250 kilometers.[24]

Realizing that Chinese antiship cruise missiles such as the YJ-91/12 (four hundred-kilometer range) outranged U.S. counterparts, in 2008 the U.S. Pacific Fleet issued an urgent request to the Defense Advanced Research Projects Agency (DARPA) for a new long-range antiship cruise missile. In order to fulfill the request as quickly as possible and avoid the costs and delays of designing a completely new missile, DARPA is adapting JASSM-ER and its targeting system for antiship missions.[25] In August 2013 the first test flight of a JASSM-ER adapted as a long-range antiship cruise missile occurred.[26] The test missile was deployed from a B-1 bomber, the only platform currently equipped to support JASSM-ER. When operational, this new long-range antiship missile would make the Navy competitive with the PLAN's antiship missiles—assuming the Navy finally shows interest in adapting its platforms to the JASSM-ER missile.

But the trend across the region is for more missiles, with longer ranges, and improved sensors and systems. China's land-attack cruise missiles, both ground- and air-launched, can attack targets out to 3,300 kilometers.[27] This range is far beyond U.S. capabilities. Dissuading future potentially belligerent Chinese leaders from aggressive actions will require U.S. leaders to have credibly coercive options available. Among these options should be the ability to hold at risk through precise conventional weapons targets that China's leaders value highly. The Air Force's handful of B-2 bombers and the Pacific Fleet's submarines, hosting fewer than seven hundred Tomahawk missiles, are currently the sum total of this capacity. For the Chinese threat, much more is needed.

The United States, Russia, Japan, the Philippines, and other partners in the region should jointly request that China sign and comply with the INF Treaty; however, given the centrality of the PLA's Second Artillery missile forces to China's military strategy and doctrine, no one should have any expectation that China would do so. China will also assert that it cannot sign on to a treaty it had no role in negotiating. However, making the request, and having China reject or ignore it, would highlight the asymmetric legal advantage China currently enjoys with its missile buildup and would provide political cover for a subsequent U.S. intermediate-range missile deployment.

Ideally the United States should renegotiate the INF Treaty with Russia, allowing both countries to deploy missiles with ranges from 500 to 5,500 kilometers within specified longitudes encompassing the Asia-Pacific theater. Given the threat to Russia posed by China's missiles, that nation could very well agree to this treaty modification.

The United States could then reconstitute its Pershing II and ground-launched cruise missile forces, this time with conventional warheads. The United States could approach Japan, the Philippines, and perhaps Vietnam—those in the region most affected by China's territorial ambitions—to host these missiles. As with their deployment in Europe in the 1980s, these missiles, if based in the region, would create "first strike deterrence"—in order to remove this threat, China would have to strike these countries, a politically difficult act of horizontal escalation for China's leaders. If China did not attack them, the missiles (which would be mobile and concealable) would hold at risk important targets inside China and would enhance the very limited capability the United States currently possesses in this regard.

If U.S. policymakers are unwilling to modify or abrogate the INF Treaty, the United States has other options for enhancing its intermediate-range missile capacity in the region. In 1974 the U.S. Air Force demonstrated its ability to deploy and launch a long-range ballistic missile from one of its cargo aircraft.[28] In September 2013 the U.S. Missile Defense Agency deployed a medium-range ballistic missile from a C-17 cargo aircraft as a target in a missile defense test.[29] This is an example of the "missile truck" concept to which Adm. Jonathan Greenert referred in his *Proceedings* article cited above. During the Carter administration in the late 1970s, defense planners looked to cargo aircraft to carry large numbers of air-launched cruise missiles as an alternative to the B-1 program, which that administration cancelled (the Reagan administration revived it). Although penetrating bombers are required for real-time targeting and for striking deep and hardened bunkers, missile trucks will be useful for supplementing the bombers, for suppressing air and missile defenses with cruise missiles, and for providing a volume of missile fire that may not be available from other platforms.

Should the Air Force recognize this requirement, it may need to extend the production run of C-17 aircraft in order to support the capability. Equally important, the Air Force and Navy need a new land-attack cruise missile with at least double the range of the 1,600-kilometer Tomahawk. With China's J-20 stealthy air superiority fighters operating out to 2,000 kilometers from China by 2020, the launch point of the vulnerable Air Force missile trucks will necessarily be pushed far back from important targets in China's interior. In order to compensate for this range handicap, a new cruise missile with a much longer range is required.

Regaining Sea Control Will Require Autonomous Missiles

China's emerging ability to dominate the Near Seas with its land-based missiles and airpower places U.S. policymakers and commanders in a position they and their predecessors haven't faced in decades. The common conception is that it takes a navy to dominate the seas. It then typically follows that if your navy is superior to your adversary's, you will then dominate the seas. Head-to-head, the U.S. Pacific Fleet easily outclasses the PLAN, but that is not enough to establish sea control over the East and South China Seas and the western Pacific out to two thousand kilometers from China's coast. Establishing control over those waters will also require suppressing China's land-based missile and airpower that, by next decade, will contest U.S. and allied naval operations in the Near Seas.

This is hardly a new problem for naval planners. During World War II in the Pacific, U.S. naval task forces had to reckon with Japan's land-based aviation as they conducted their advance toward Japan's home islands. During the early years of the war, Japan's land-based aircraft outperformed the U.S. Navy's carrier-based planes. Over the course of the war, the U.S. Navy gradually overcame the starting advantage of Japan's land-based airpower by improving the quality of U.S. carrier-based aircraft. But even more important was the power of America's industrial advantage—the United States simply overwhelmed Japan with its massive production of warships and aircraft.

During the Cold War, the U.S. Navy faced the Soviet Union's "reconnaissance-strike complex" (discussed in chapters 3 and 4). The long-range, land-based supersonic Backfire bomber, armed with the dangerous Kitchen antiship cruise missile, threatened to track down and strike U.S. carrier strike groups long before their aircraft came in range of meaningful Soviet targets. The aggressive U.S. maritime strategy that emerged in the late 1970s and into the 1980s attempted to thwart the Soviet's continental advantage through stealthy tactics and improved fleet air defense technology. Since a U.S.-Soviet war happily never occurred, the outcome of this competition remains a mystery.

What we can surmise is that it will be much more challenging for the United States to employ these techniques against China. China's land-based aircraft continue to outrange the U.S. Navy's, and that gap is growing not shrinking. The United States cannot hope to outspend China as it did Japan and the Soviet Union—China has a very large economy and is the low-cost producer of military aircraft and missiles. Furthermore, the United States will be hard-pressed to replicate the stealthy naval tactics it employed against the Soviets; by next decade, China's maritime sensors, both space- and land-based, will be better and more numerous than those operated by the Soviets in the 1980s.

The United States will thus need new technology and tactics to suppress China's land-based "anti-navy" missile and airpower. The problem for U.S. military planners is that much of China's "anti-navy" missile and airpower is dispersed, mobile, and designed either to be hidden or sheltered in hardened and underground facilities. For example, China's DF-21D antiship ballistic missile is based on a medium-range missile that is moved about and launched from a TEL. Most of China's land-based antiship and land-attack cruise missiles are also mounted on TELs. China's maritime strike airpower, which includes most of its fleet of Flanker strike fighter aircraft, can be based at scores of air bases, most of which are hardened against attack, some to a very high extent.[30]

A fleet of new penetrating bombers, able to loiter and search for ground targets in defended airspace, is one method of addressing this problem. But this is also an expensive approach. The economics of this competition will not favor the United States; it will be cheaper for China to produce more missiles and TELs than it will be for the United States to produce more bombers. In this "finder versus hider" competition, the United States will need a cheaper strategy.

In the 1990s the U.S. Air Force developed the Low Cost Autonomous Attack System (LOCAAS), a program it successfully tested but later terminated. LOCAAS was a small (about one meter long) jet-powered unmanned aerial vehicle that was designed to autonomously search for specific targets on the ground and then attack them. LOCAAS would be launched from aircraft outside an adversary's air defense system. It would then fly to a predetermined patrol area and begin searching the ground for specific targets, such as TELs, using a precise laser-radar (LADAR) sensor, similar to sensors DARPA and others have tested on self-driving ground vehicles. Once LOCAAS located a target, it would dive on it, destroying it.[31] If LOCAAS failed to find a suitable target when it exhausted its fuel, it would self-destruct by crashing into a water feature or empty field. A set of four LOCAAS missiles could search up to a hundred square kilometers before exhausting their fuel.

LOCAAS was designed to equip U.S. military forces with the capability to safely search for important mobile targets inside an adversary's air defense system. U.S. forces would launch hundreds or even thousands of LOCAAS at any one time into suspected TEL operating areas, either destroying them or forcing them to shelter where they could not launch their missiles. The concept called for producing over ten thousand of the small robotic jets, with a marginal unit cost of about $70,000.[32] At that price, the United States would likely be on the winning side of a production competition, compared to the cost of additional Chinese cruise and ballistic missiles or passive and active Chinese air defenses.

LOCAAS's autonomous decision making was deemed an essential feature. Designers assumed that electronic warfare, jamming, and adversary attacks on the U.S. military communication system would prevent the many LOCAAS flying in combat from maintaining connections to a "man in the loop" at a rear command post. Thus, LOCAAS was designed to make its own attack decisions. In the early 2000s when the program was terminated, such lethal autonomy for robots was apparently a cultural barrier U.S. defense officials were unwilling to cross.[33] Even when LADAR achieved higher target identification accuracy than humans in an aircraft cockpit, cultural and political sensitivities concerning a robot's lethal decision making led to LOCAAS's cancellation.

However, the fact remains that the United States and its allies will not be able to safely operate their warships in the Near Seas—thus reestablishing freedom of navigation—until China's land-based "anti-navy" forces are suppressed. Note, the issue here is not China's navy, which U.S. submarines and standoff airpower should be able to dominate. Despite otherwise adverse trends, the United States should be able to deny the Near Seas to China's fleet. The issue is that China's land-based forces will be able to do the same to the surface naval forces of the United States and its allies. Thus, the United States will need something like LOCAAS as an affordable and competitive answer to China's mobile missile forces and dispersed and protected airpower.

The original 1990s version of LOCAAS, although a conceptual breakthrough, lacked the performance necessary to be effective in the vast Pacific theater. Its range was only around one hundred kilometers, with a loiter-search time limited to just thirty minutes.[34]

The next-generation LOCAAS needs a much greater range and loiter time, ideally thousands of kilometers and hours or even days of search time.[35] Long range is necessary so that vulnerable cargo aircraft can deploy large volumes of LOCAAS from beyond China's air defense perimeter, which would then penetrate and loiter deep inside Chinese territory. Whether such performance is technically feasible, and whether such specifications would cause LOCAAS to lose the competitive economics that made the concept so appealing, remain to be seen.

In any case the United States needs to revive the LOCAAS concept. Indeed LOCAAS could be a core (albeit not the only) element of a competitive strategy for the region. China's military strategy for the region is centered on forces designed to keep U.S. naval and airpower out of the Near

Seas and the western Pacific. The United States and its allies need a response to that move, one that will convince China's leaders that the United States and its allies have a credible way of thwarting that nation's strategy. An effective coalition response will require many lines of effort. LOCAAS, and its potential to thwart China's land-based "anti-navy" forces, could be an important part of the response.

Chapter 5 criticized the Air-Sea Battle concept (as described by Gen. Norton Schwartz and Adm. Jonathan Greenert) as impractical and possibly prone to risky escalation. Is the call in this chapter for new bombers and missiles capable of heavy strikes inside China reviving the most dangerous parts of Air-Sea Battle that should be left discarded?

No, there are important differences between Air-Sea Battle's vision (a vision also shared by the JOAC) and the strategy described in this book. Air-Sea Battle and JOAC envision thwarting an adversary's access denial capabilities in order to allow U.S. forces, as traditionally designed and fielded, to freely maneuver as they have since World War II. Air-Sea Battle and JOAC aim to achieve this condition by blinding the adversary's reconnaissance and command networks and by shooting down enemy missiles or the systems that fire them.

The strategy described in this book does not have these specific aspirations. Instead it calls for a broad range of persuasive and dissuasive capabilities—diplomatic, economic, and military (irregular and conventional)—designed to convince China's leaders that they will achieve no gains in the region from coercion. The strategy will do this by threatening to impose costs, creating resistance to coercive Chinese gains, and holding at risk assets and conditions valued by China's leaders. Unlike Air-Sea Battle or JOAC, the strategy does not call for first strikes on the adversary's reconnaissance and command systems. Nor does it expect existing U.S. forward bases in the region to be useful after war breaks out, or U.S. surface forces to operate for sustained periods inside the range of China's missiles. This strategy's theory of success is based on persuading and dissuading China's leaders, not on tactically rolling back China's access denial capabilities.

Perhaps most important, the proposed new structure of forces, heavily weighted to long-range striking capability rather than existing short-range systems, will allow U.S. and allied commanders a patient approach to operations, in contrast to the "use it, or lose it" pressure that the current force design will compel. Not only will this feature enhance crisis stability, it will greatly bolster deterrence by removing first strike options from Chinese military planners.

The strategy calls for weapons to attack inside China; these will be a few of the tools inside a much larger toolbox. The target for all the tools in the toolbox is the behavior of China's leaders and not, as with Air-Sea Battle, simply China's missiles and command networks.

Protecting Reconnaissance and Communications

Chapter 5 critiqued the Air-Sea Battle concept, noting the concept's call for U.S. disruption of an adversary's reconnaissance and communications network could be a foolish move if that led to a counterattack on the U.S. network. In the case of a conflict against China, Beijing would very likely benefit from such escalation. As the expeditionary power, U.S. military forces would be highly dependent on their space-based reconnaissance and communication networks, which would be particularly exposed to Chinese disruption.[36]

Operating at far distances from command posts and support, U.S. reconnaissance and communication networks would lack redundancy and would be more difficult to repair. China, by contrast, would benefit from fighting as the continental power. From that position, Chinese reconnaissance and communication networks would inherently have greater capacity and redundancy and would be easier to reestablish after attack (e.g., a network of land-based surveillance and communication unmanned aircraft would be much harder for the United States to duplicate from its more extended expeditionary basing position).

If Air-Sea Battle's guidance to disrupt China's networks is misguided, it logically follows that China's commanders might see the competitive benefit of attacking U.S. space and communication networks as soon as hostilities begin. U.S. policymakers should expect wide-ranging Chinese attacks on U.S. satellite constellations and command networks early in a conflict. China's commanders no doubt anticipate that the United States would retaliate against China's existing networks. But in making this calculation, China's commanders could also assume that they, due to their continental position, will be in a better position than U.S. forces to both continue operations without these assets and to reestablish surveillance and communications by other means.

The United States and its allies thus need a strategy that deters PLA commanders from drawing this conclusion. And should deterrence fail, the United States and its partners need a strategy and tools to reconstitute communications and reconnaissance in an effective and robust manner.

In January 2011 the U.S. government released its National Security Space Strategy (NSSS).[37] The unclassified document explained that "space is vital to U.S. national security and our ability to understand emerging threats, project power globally, conduct operations, support diplomatic efforts, and enable global economic viability."[38] Indeed, modern U.S. military operations are wholly dependent on satellite constellations for reconnaissance, weather forecasting, communications, and navigation. However, unlike terrestrial weapons platforms, space satellites transit well-known and predictable orbits, are unable to hide from an adversary's view, and generally have no ability to defend themselves against attack. As a result, satellite constellations are highly vulnerable to disruption.

By 2020 China will have its own space capabilities for all of these functions, at least enough to support operations in the Asia-Pacific region, if not globally (see chapter 4). In addition China is building a fleet of surveillance and communication relay unmanned aircraft that will provide redundancy for its space-based assets. Given the vulnerability of U.S. space platforms, the United States needs a strategy for protecting its military space operations and for continuing its operations if those assets are disabled.

The NSSS provided an outline for such a strategy. The first line of defense involved some clever soft power and diplomacy. Included was a call for a code of conduct and international norms against attacks on space infrastructure. Few would expect such codes and norms to restrain belligerents in a high-stakes conflict, but they could raise the political price for countries that chose to violate the norms first.

Bolstering such deterrence was the NSSS call for the United States to share its space platforms, including its military platforms, with other countries, including even non-allies. An attack on shared space platforms would thus affect all countries using the platforms, an act of horizontal escalation that adversary decision makers might prefer to avoid. If U.S. partners in, say, Europe and Latin America depended on space platforms targeted by the PLA, such attacks would surely damage China's diplomatic position and might thus create a deterrent.[39]

The NSSS realized that such soft power and diplomatic gambits might not suffice to protect U.S. space assets against opponents who are either unconcerned with diplomatic consequences or who conclude the benefits of knocking down U.S. reconnaissance and communication capacity would be worth the cost. As a hedge against this enemy calculation, the strategy called for alternatives to vulnerable space-based systems. Such alternatives will not be cheap for an expeditionary power like the United States operating in the western Pacific, but they will be essential if the United States is to have a credible military strategy for the region.

Here again we can see the importance of the new stealthy long-range strike bomber aircraft. China's direct-ascent anti-satellite missile, demonstrated against an old Chinese weather satellite in 2007, showed China's capacity to knock out U.S. Air Force reconnaissance and earth observation satellites in low earth orbit; in higher orbits are the communication and navigation satellites that China might attack with its own co-orbital satellites.[40]

Should these attacks on U.S. space assets occur, the United States will then depend on long-range aircraft to collect imagery and sustain communications. U.S. commanders would send out specialized platforms such as Global Hawk, Triton, and P-8 for maritime reconnaissance, and a variety of other aircraft for imagery and electronic reconnaissance. But for intelligence gathering over defended areas—which by 2020 will encompass the western Pacific out to two thousand kilometers from China—the United States will need a stealthy and long-endurance aircraft such as the new long-range strike bomber.

There are additional steps U.S. military planners and acquisition officials can take to reduce U.S. dependence on space assets. For example, the U.S. Air Force and DARPA have long been interested in designing advanced, highly accurate, and inexpensive inertial navigation systems that would free U.S. forces from dependency on the satellite-based Global Positioning System (GPS).[41] In addition the Air Force and Navy could employ high-altitude aircraft equipped with jam-resistant, narrow-beam, and high data-rate communication lasers to establish networks of communication relay points covering broad areas of the western Pacific.[42]

The technology for these alternatives to military satellite constellations is currently mature or will be soon. Pursuing these initiatives—both the diplomatic and soft power ideas suggested by the NSSS and the alternatives to satellite dependency—will greatly boost strategic stability in the region. Enhancing deterrence to attacks in space and implementing alternatives to space assets would remove a major Chinese competitive advantage during a potential conflict. China would lose the benefit of escalating the war into space and would lose the logic for striking U.S. and allied space assets early in the war.

Perhaps most important, by showing China that the United States and its partners are prepared to fight a high-intensity campaign under a variety of challenging circumstances, the coalition will improve its chances of dissuading China's leaders from ever contemplating this course of action. For good reasons, China's military strategists see space warfare as a trump card in a potential conflict. This is currently a great vulnerability for the United States and its friends. But it doesn't have to be. U.S. policymakers simply need to make these actions priorities for the government.

People, Not Just Hardware, Win Wars

The discussion thus far in this chapter has focused largely on new hardware U.S. airpower will need to regain an advantage in the Asia-Pacific theater. The current hardware mismatch—inadequate aircraft and missiles—has resulted from planners and acquisition officials not assigning a high priority to the region's unique range requirements and from policymakers' neglect of the Chinese military threat. As we have seen, current U.S. acquisition plans will not deliver enough of the capabilities that U.S. forces will need to sustain conventional deterrence in the next decade.

But hardware alone does not create military capability. People, organizations, training, doctrine, support, and many other factors are needed in equal measure. These factors for success need as much reform as the Pentagon's hardware acquisition plans.

The ability of the PLA to project strong anti-access capability out to two thousand kilometers from its territory has created a very unfamiliar military problem for most U.S. commanders. There are very few commanders and planners who have had to concern themselves with armed opposition in the global commons or with fighting to obtain access to a theater of operations; but these are now looming problems. Successful solutions will require not only new hardware, but also new approaches to training, new organizational structures, new tactics, and new processes for supporting forces in the field.

Large changes to organizations, training, and tactics will be needed to adapt to such a radically unfamiliar challenge. The magnitude of the required changes will undoubtedly inflict great stress on organizational cultures noted for their conservatism and inertia. Indeed the institutional pressures that resulted in the airpower hardware shortfall discussed previously are the same pressures that will resist the other adaptations required in organizations, training, support, and doctrine.

In November 2011 the U.S. Defense Department created the Air-Sea Battle Office, with a goal of sparking the conceptual thinking, experimentation, tactics, and service cooperation necessary to overcome access denial challenges like those the United States is now facing in the western Pacific.[43] The hope is that officers from all of the services can work inside this office to collaborate on effective solutions to the access denial problem.

Their work will only be effective if they can convince the bureaucracies of each of the armed services to implement the changes they will recommend. Field commanders must also be willing to change long-established procedures and routines. With no operational or budgetary authority, officers in the Air-Sea Battle Office may struggle to push through significant changes.

In *The Dynamics of Military Revolution, 1300–2050,* Williamson Murray carefully analyzed the sources of the German army's superior performance during its attack on France in May 1940.[44] Murray strongly argues that the German army's decisive success in that campaign was the result not of superior tank and aircraft technology, but rather of incremental and sustained organizational and doctrinal improvements that were built up over many years of experimentation and training.

Murray notes that this process of improvement began immediately after World War I concluded in 1918. At that time the German general staff organized fifty-seven committees to study specific military problems encountered during that war.[45] According to Murray, it was the German army's culture of self-examination and reform, and not the acquisition of any breakthrough technology alone, that resulted in its tactical and operational successes in the early years of World War II.

Those in the U.S. military responsible for airpower planning for the Asia-Pacific theater will need to embark on a similar journey of self-examination and reform if U.S. airpower is to meet the mounting challenges in the region. Indeed, given the gravity of those challenges and the shortfalls in current airpower, commanders would do well to examine from first principles the premises and assumptions underlying U.S. airpower in the region. Maintaining U.S. and allied airpower dominance in the region will require both the platforms and technology the theater requires and the organizational adaptation discussed by Murray. This chapter has posed some suggestions regarding how to extend the striking range, survivability, and flexibility of U.S. air- and space power for the region. The United States and its partners have much catching up to do, and little time to do it.

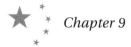 *Chapter 9*

THE STRUGGLE FOR CONTROL OF THE WESTERN PACIFIC

On January 31, 2013, Capt. James Fanell, the U.S. Pacific Fleet's top intelligence officer, shook up an audience at a naval conference in San Diego when he stated some unfashionably blunt views about Chinese maritime behavior:

> As the Pacific Fleet Intelligence Officer, I arrive at work every morning around five a.m. and by that time my officers will have prepared a book for me outlining the maritime events over the last twenty-four hours in an area of responsibility that stretches from the west coast of Hawaii to Africa. . . .
>
> At six, I will take an intelligence briefing, surrounded by the best Asian maritime analysts in the world, submarine specialists, aviation experts, governance specialists, imagery analysts, cryptanalysts and linguists, over two dozen of us as we probe the very latest intelligence and each other with questions and observations from forty-five minutes to an hour, every day. All countries are included in this analysis, Japan, Russia, North Korea, India, Southeast Asia, we cover all the bases, event by event. That being said, every day, it's about China. . . .
>
> Make no mistake, the PLA Navy is focused on war at sea and about sinking an opposing fleet.
>
> The PLA Navy's civil proxy, an organization called "China Marine Surveillance," has escalated a focused campaign since 2008 to gain Chinese control of the Near Seas, and they now regularly challenge the exclusive economic zone resource rights that South Korea, Japan, the Philippines, Malaysia, Brunei, Indonesia, and Vietnam once thought were guaranteed to them by the United Nations Convention on the Law of the Sea.

If you map out their harassments you will see they form a curved front that has over time expanded out against the coasts of China's neighbors, becoming the infamous "nine dash line" plus the entire East China Sea.

To put it another way, we do not see incidents or controversies around Chinese platforms off the coast of Guangzhou or Shanghai. No. China is negotiating for control of other nations' resources off their coasts. "What's mine is mine, and we'll negotiate what's yours."

China now has eight military installations on seven reefs in the Spratlys including one they seized 115 miles off the Philippine coast.

And China Marine Surveillance cutters now regularly patrol the entire region.

Incidentally, unlike U.S. Coast Guard cutters, Chinese Marine Surveillance cutters have no other mission but to harass other nations into submitting to China's expansive claims. Mundane maritime government tasks like search-and-rescue, regulating fisheries, ice breaking, and criminal law enforcement are handled by other agencies.

China Marine Surveillance is a full-time maritime sovereignty harassment organization, and they are still building their large cutters at an astonishing rate. By their own count, China Marine Surveillance tripled its patrols in the South China Sea since 2008.

I've just used the words "expand" and "expansive" and I know it's controversial for some in this room. And it even feeds the caricature of Department of Defense promotion of the quote-unquote "China Threat Theory."

But for those of us who have watched this on a daily basis over the last decade, there is no better description for what China's been doing.

The People's Republic of China's presence in the southern China sea prior to 1988 was nearly zero.

Now, in 2013, they literally dominate it. They are taking control of maritime areas that have never before been administered or controlled in the last five thousand years by any regime called "China." And the PRC is now doing it in an area up to nine hundred miles from the mainland and up to dozens of miles off the coasts of other nations.

In my opinion, China is knowingly, operationally, and incrementally seizing maritime rights of its neighbors under the rubric of a maritime history that is not only contested in the international community, but has largely been fabricated by Chinese government propaganda bureaus in order to quote-unquote "educate" the populace about China's "rich maritime history" clearly as a tool to help sustain the Party's control.[1]

Captain Fanell's candid remarks portray a Chinese maritime establishment, with both its military and paramilitary components, implementing the salami-slicing tactics discussed in chapter 4, while also preparing for a possible naval clash with its neighbors or even the U.S. Navy.

In response to the challenge described by Captain Fanell, the fundamental task for the U.S. Pacific Fleet is to retain sea control in the western Pacific, keeping open to global commerce the sea lines of communication that run through the East and South China Seas. In the past, the military analysis of this challenge involved the comparison of opposing fleets. Should those fleets actually fight for the control of particular seas, the outcome would depend on such factors as seamanship, "deckplate" leadership, ship and weapon technology, allies, tactics, weather, and the fortunes of war. Until recently, there was little question that sailors and ships (including ships that launched aircraft) determined which country would control the seas.

But the missile and sensor revolution has upset that analysis. With land-based "anti-navy" capabilities reaching farther out to sea, sinking the enemy's fleet is only the first step to establishing control of the sea. Also necessary—and now more difficult—will be the suppression or destruction of the enemy's land-based air and missile power.

Captain Fanell's presentation about China's growing naval power was bracing, but it describes only the beginning—and likely not the most difficult—portion of the problem for U.S. military forces tasked with maintaining the global commons in the Pacific. The U.S. Navy has not adequately adapted to the missile and sensor revolution and will struggle to achieve its most important mission: keeping open the global commons in the western Pacific. The Navy needs to implement dramatic changes if it is to remain relevant. The required revolution in U.S. naval power is the subject of this chapter.

The Problematic Prospects for Power Projection

By next decade China's land-based missile and airpower will be able to hold at risk surface targets out to two thousand kilometers (and in some cases farther) from China's coast (discussed in chapters 3 through 5). That means the U.S. Navy won't be able to operate in the manner it has become used to ever since its aircraft carriers arrived to rescue the beleaguered defenders of the Pusan Perimeter in the summer of 1950.

A clever and risk-taking U.S. carrier strike group commander might be able to pull off a single surprise air strike on the Chinese mainland.[2] But an extended campaign, in which the Navy's carriers lie off China's coast for weeks or months launching thousands of strike sorties, will be out of the question. Nor, as we have seen, will the Navy's limited numbers of Tomahawk land-attack cruise missiles be a replacement for what the aircraft carriers won't be able to do.

In a conflict with China, the U.S. Navy as it currently exists is largely out of the power projection business. China's continental position; its ability to regenerate land-based maritime reconnaissance in spite of U.S. attempts at disruption; and its dispersed, mobile, and relatively inexpensive missile and airpower will make it too dangerous in a conflict for surface naval forces to sail for sustained periods in the waters near China.

The Navy should logically have a very high interest in the development of a capability that could suppress China's land-based "anti-navy" forces. America's discontinued LOCAAS program in the late 1990s promised to produce cheap but smart robotic aircraft that would loiter for long periods over enemy missile and aircraft staging areas, attacking those targets when they revealed themselves (discussed in chapter 8). A new version, with longer range and endurance, might be able to aid in the suppression of Chinese land-based missiles and aircraft that menace the U.S. Navy's freedom of action. But first, officials in the U.S. Department of Defense have to commit to the LOCAAS concept.

Until U.S. forces acquire some sizable capacity to suppress enemy "anti-navy" forces on land—a capacity that is currently woefully inadequate—the Navy's surface ships must now rely on their own ability to defend themselves from missiles. However, by next decade the PLA will have the ability to organize air attacks with its Flanker strike fighters that could launch a hundred or more high-speed antiship cruise missiles from several axes at approaching U.S. naval strike groups. Even if ship defenses knocked down 95 percent of the attacking missiles (much higher than the historical rate), China's ability to saturate ship defenses would be telling. Even a few hits on a naval strike group would be shocking. And after fending off one such attack, the strike group would likely have few if any remaining defensive missiles to resist a follow-up attack.

Navy scientists hope that electromagnetic rail guns and free-electron lasers will swing the arms race away from missiles and back to missile defenses (discussed in chapter 5). But such weapons will require entirely new ship designs to support them and likely fifteen more years of research and development before an operational and integrated system is ready for the fleet.[3] Until then the advantage of the "anti-navy" forces is likely to only widen; the range and sensors of China's antiship missiles will continue to advance while the Navy's really useful ship defense systems struggle to emerge from the laboratory.

We must then conclude that with respect to power projection against China, the U.S. Navy's aircraft carriers won't play the role they have become accustomed to playing since World War II. Some have hoped that the arrival of unmanned carrier strike aircraft, such as successors to the X-47B, would extend the aircraft carrier's reach, making it once again relevant. But as we examined (chapter 3), aircraft carriers are limited to hosting small tactical aircraft and place an upper limit on the carriers' radius of action. Even with the somewhat longer-ranged unmanned strike aircraft, that upper limit will be too short compared to the ranges of the aircraft and missiles that threaten the carrier strike groups. Carrier aircraft have always faced inherent shortcomings compared to the land-based threats with which they must contend. The missile and sensor revolution has intensified these shortcomings to a degree that has removed U.S. aircraft carriers from a power projection role in facing China.

U.S. aircraft carriers will have a role in sea denial (discussed later), and they will have roles elsewhere in the world. But for power projection as it relates to the security competition in the western Pacific, China's access denial capabilities have upended the aircraft carrier–centered doctrine under which the U.S. Navy has operated for decades.

With aircraft carriers removed from consideration, are there other ways of restoring the Navy's ability to project conventional strike power against targets inside China? Naval analysts are revisiting the idea of "arsenal ships," surface ships with the primary mission of launching large numbers of long-range land-attack and antiship missiles. In the 1990s then–chief of naval operations Adm. Jeremy M. Boorda promoted the Arsenal Ship concept: a large, single-purpose surface ship that was envisioned to carry up to five hundred long-range missiles. The concept was abandoned when analysts concluded the ship would have concentrated too much capability in a single target and would have revealed its position to enemy sensors before it could complete its mission and escape a counterattack.[4]

Although the Navy rejected Boorda's concept, it did endorse the idea in a modified form. After the Cold War, the Navy converted four of its *Trident*-class ballistic missile submarines into cruise missile ships, each armed with 154 Tomahawk missiles. This gesture toward the Arsenal Ship concept resulted from an accident in history (the reduction in strategic nuclear forces after the Cold War) and was too expensive to expand into a capability that would match the sustained strike capacity of a carrier air wing.

However, the shortcomings of the aircraft carrier in the age of the missile and sensor revolution have resulted in renewed interest in large-capacity missile ships. Research supported by the U.S. Defense Department's ONA recently argued that surface missile ships could deliver firepower more cheaply than aircraft carriers.[5]

Previous research concluded that if an air campaign required striking only a relatively small number of targets, land-attack missiles such as the Tomahawk would be cheaper than the large capital costs associated with an aircraft carrier and its strike aircraft.[6] However, if the air campaign were long and required striking hundreds or thousands of aim points, aircraft dropping laser- or satellite-guided bombs would be the much cheaper option. Indeed, that describes many of the most notable air campaigns the Navy has conducted since World War II and the type of campaign U.S. naval strike aviation has prepared for. It should be little surprise that the Navy's power projection doctrine matches the analysis of what is most cost-effective, at least based on past air campaigns.

However, the ONA's new and contradictory conclusions are based on assumptions that are more realistic about future air campaigns. By these assumptions, heavily defended airspace (like China's) will force aircraft to employ, instead of cheap bombs, stand-off missiles like JASSM-ER, the cost of which matches Tomahawk's. Add in the cost of aircraft shot down—even if only a few, the cost efficiency of the carrier air wing disappears, according to this analysis. In addition, advocates of missile ships will point to the benefits of dispersing the land-attack missiles over many destroyer-sized surface ships. This will reduce risk and increase target coverage, especially when compared to the risk concentrated in one or a few large aircraft carriers.

Given the aircraft carrier's severe shortcomings in a China scenario, it is not difficult to make the case for missile ships as an alternative. However, the missile ship concept has its own weaknesses. The U.S. Navy's surface ships and submarines launch Tomahawk cruise missiles from vertical launch cells. This clever system expanded the missile capacity of these ships and allowed commanders to vary the missile loadout of ships depending on the anticipated mission. However, the cells cannot be reloaded at sea; surface ships and submarines must return to port, tie up at a dock, and have technicians and dock cranes carefully reload the expended cells.

This is a substantial contrast to decades of aircraft carrier operations where the Navy's underway replenishment ships resupplied carrier strike groups with fuel, munitions, food, spare parts, and other provisions, allowing the carriers to remain in combat for weeks or months at a time. Reloading vertical missiles cells while under way is an unmet aspiration and remains a severe limitation for the missile ship concept.[7] Why the Navy has not given more attention to this limitation remains a mystery, given the Navy's reliance on these launch cells for fleet defense against air and missile attacks. Given this well-known vulnerability, we have to conclude that missile cell reloading at sea faces such technical barriers as to make the procedure impractical.

Next, the Navy will need a new land-attack cruise missile with a much longer range than the 1,600-kilometer Tomahawk Block IV.[8] At that range, attacking even just coastal targets would place the Navy's surface missile ships within the radius of the PLA's maritime strike Flanker regiments. To threaten targets inland would require the Navy's cruisers and destroyers to expose themselves to not only the Flankers but also to the PLA's antiship ballistic missile force and cruise missile–armed fast attack craft. Until the Navy fields a land-attack cruise missile with, say, at least double or even triple the range of the current Tomahawk, surface missile ships won't have much usefulness for power projection against China.

This conclusion is based on the PLA's projected capabilities in 2020. The larger trend indicates that the range and targeting ability of land-based "anti-navy" forces will continue to grow. China's satellite and unmanned aircraft reconnaissance coverage will continue to thicken, with fewer and fewer U.S. and allied surface forces able to escape detection. The ranges of land-based aircraft and missiles will expand and their targeting sensors will sharpen. Missile costs will continue to fall relative to the costs of their intended targets.

The regrettable conclusion is that the danger of lingering on the surface will continue to increase. This trend strikes at the heart of the Navy's long-standing plans for power projection. It also threatens the Navy's ability to maintain control over the western Pacific's critical lines of communication.

Sea Denial, But Not Sea Control

Until the United States develops a much more substantial capacity to suppress land-based air and missile power (e.g., LOCAAS or penetrating bombers able to loiter and search for targets), Chinese "anti-navy" forces will make it too risky for U.S. surface forces to operate around the First Island Chain, within two thousand kilometers of China. But that hardly means that China will establish its own control over these waters. U.S. air and naval power will have the capacity to return the favor to China's surface navy. In a war, the Near Seas will thus become a "dead zone" for the surface forces of both sides.[9]

Even while the U.S. Navy's aircraft carriers won't be able to project their striking power onto China proper, they will be able to reprise the role they made famous in World War II, namely sinking enemy warships, at least those that venture away from land-based protection. Close to China's shore, the PLAN's warships will operate under the cover of the country's integrated air defense system and "anti-navy" missiles and aircraft that will push U.S. warships at least two thousand kilometers away.

The advantage for the United States is that as China's warships venture east into the Pacific, this overhead protection will thin. The First Island Chain will make it difficult for China's surface warships to sail east undetected; these ships will have to pass through channels that U.S. and coalition sensors will easily monitor. Aircraft from U.S. aircraft carriers cruising beyond the reach of China's land-based striking power will still be able to patrol some of the Near Seas and in most cases attack Chinese surface warships under their surveillance. Armed with standoff missiles such as SLAM-ER, the Navy's F-35C stealthy strike aircraft will be capable of attacking surface targets up to about 1,300 kilometers from the carriers. China's new Type 052D multimission guided missile destroyer is an impressive warship with modern air defense capabilities resembling those of the DDG-51 *Burke*-class destroyer, the mainstay of the U.S. surface fleet.[10] However, the Type 052D, China's most capable air warfare surface ship, would very likely struggle to survive against F-35Cs outside the protection of land-based cover.

The U.S. fleet's best trump card is its attack submarines. The 1982 Falklands War between Great Britain and Argentina demonstrated how intimidating modern submarines can be. Early in the conflict, HMS *Conqueror,* a British nuclear-powered attack submarine, sank the Argentine cruiser *General Belgrano.* The Argentine surface navy subsequently retreated to port and played no role during the remainder of the war.[11]

The PLAN will not have much capability to prevent U.S. attack submarines from operating at will against China's surface fleet. The U.S. Navy's *Virginia* and *Seawolf* classes of attack submarines are highly capable and very difficult to detect.[12] China has made a minimal investment in its antisubmarine warfare capabilities and thus will have little capacity to oppose the U.S. Navy's submarines.[13] The Navy's attack submarines will be free to patrol the Near Seas and the Philippines Sea in search of China's surface warships, whose hulls would likely soon be resting on the bottom. Thus, between the U.S. fleet's submarines and aircraft carriers, the PLAN's surface forces aren't likely to play much of a role, at least beyond China's immediate coast.

The question is, will the U.S. Pacific Fleet have enough submarines to ensure this outcome? The Navy's long-term shipbuilding plan forecasts forty-eight attack submarines for the entire fleet by 2020 and thereafter.[14] Allocating 60 percent of these to the Pacific would result in twenty-nine submarines hypothetically available for operations against China. Due to regular maintenance requirements, the number actually available for war at any given time would be less, probably fewer than twenty.

Those submarines would be tasked with a variety of missions in wartime. U.S. fleet commanders would send them to collect intelligence on Chinese operations and attack PLAN surface warships in the Near Seas and the Philippine Sea. U.S. submarines would also be the fleet's principal antisubmarine weapon, defending carrier strike groups and transit routes in the region from Chinese submarines. And aside from the Air Force's bombers and the Pacific Fleet's two guided missile submarines, the Navy's attack submarines, each armed with a dozen Tomahawks, would be the only other platform capable of striking inside China.

By 2020 the Office of Naval Intelligence predicts that China will have about seventy-two attack submarines, a force with increasingly more modern and capable boats.[15] The PLAN will use its quiet but short-range diesel-electric submarines to patrol the Near Seas near China's coast. Meanwhile China will attempt to use its long-range nuclear-powered submarines to search for U.S. carrier strike groups in the Philippine Sea and beyond, to interdict U.S. warships transiting to the western Pacific and to conduct cruise missile attacks on U.S. bases across the region.

China's wartime submarine availability will very likely be no better and probably much worse than that of the U.S. Pacific Fleet. But by 2020, the Chinese submarine force will likely outnumber the U.S. force two to one. In spite of their high capability, twenty-nine submarines for the U.S. Pacific Fleet are almost certainly too few, given the long list of responsibilities assigned to the force.

Undersea warfare is a comparative advantage for the United States and its Pacific allies.[16] The U.S. coalition holds an advantage in submarine technology, training, and experience. China, meanwhile, has devoted very few resources to antisubmarine warfare, further accentuating the allied advantage. The shallow water near China's coast will limit the ability of U.S. submarines to find and target China's submarines in those waters: the submarines on both sides will have a free hand to attack surface ships there, leaving the Near Seas a "desert" for surface naval forces.[17]

Deeper into the Pacific, the United States will have an easier time targeting China's submarines, although given the vast space and large number of assignments, U.S. submarines will be hard-pressed to fulfill all of their missions. A successful Chinese submarine attack on a U.S. carrier strike group or the suppression of Guam's air bases by sub-launched cruise missiles would be major setbacks to the coalition war effort. The U.S. attack submarine force will have the large responsibility of preventing these events.

That will be a challenge unless fleet commanders get more submarines than currently planned.

Does the United States Need a New Kind of Navy?

In the security competition with China, maritime success—indeed overall strategic success—will be defined by whether the United States and its coalition partners can maintain freedom of navigation throughout the Asia-Pacific region, especially the East and South China Seas, where China's anti-navy forces will be most powerful. The preceding discussion has revealed that the design of the U.S. fleet seems increasingly unsuited to achieving this objective. The U.S. Navy's aircraft carriers will have a role to play in deep-ocean naval battles but will be unusable close to China, either for establishing sea control over the Near Seas or for projecting power into China.

The Navy's high-end guided missile destroyers and cruisers are similarly becoming mismatched for the tasks the Navy needs to achieve. In spite of being the most technologically advanced multimission surface combatants, they are losing the race against precision antiship missiles, whose capabilities are rising even as their costs fall.[18]

In this sense, the Navy's *Burke* and *Ticonderoga* guided missile destroyers and cruisers are not only too expensive and overengineered to risk on sea control missions in contested waters but also not capable enough to survive against the threats menacing them in those waters. Their air defense capabilities, the "gold standard" for warships, will by next decade be inadequate to defend either themselves or carrier strike groups against determined saturation missile attacks.

Recent U.S. Navy officials know that the Navy needs to make a leap to dramatically new missile defense technology, such as electromagnetic rail guns and free-electron lasers.[19] But these solutions are still early in laboratory development and won't see the fleet until the second half of the 2020s at the earliest. Thus the Navy's two signature ships representing its maritime dominance—its aircraft carriers and guided missile surface combatants—find themselves out of place and increasingly sidelined when facing the PLA in the western Pacific.

As a result, some naval theorists have called for a radical redesign of U.S. naval power, in order to adapt to the missile and sensor revolution. In 2009 Wayne Hughes, a retired U.S. Navy captain and a professor of operations research at the Naval Postgraduate School in Monterey, California, proposed a "New Navy Fighting Machine" that would dramatically reshape the Navy.

Hughes's design steps away from a Navy organized around the large carrier strike group. He would cut the Navy's large nuclear-powered aircraft carrier fleet from eleven to six and build a force of smaller carriers hosting F-35B short-takeoff, vertical-landing jets. Hughes would also replace the Navy's sophisticated and expensive multimission guided missile destroyers with a wide variety of simpler, cheaper, and smaller single-purpose ships.[20]

Under Hughes's plan, the fleet would grow in numbers while smaller and relatively inexpensive single-purpose ships replace expensive, overengineered hulls. He asserts that the fleet would be more resilient in combat because it would be diversified over a wider number of ships. In addition, he believes there would be benefits for both the U.S. shipbuilding industry, since this fleet would require more shipyards than currently, and for Navy procurement, which would benefit from more competition among contractors. Finally, Hughes believes his plan would result in ships easier to maintain, with better training and command opportunities for the Navy's personnel.[21]

But would Hughes's New Navy Fighting Machine improve the ability of the Navy to maintain control over the East and South China Seas during a conflict with China? That is not clear. In his recommendations for naval strategy in the Near Seas, he recommends submarines, along with long-range unmanned aircraft and bombers, similar to our advice in this book.[22]

As for maintaining a presence on the surface, Hughes's counsel doesn't sound too hopeful. He recommends "affordable numbers of small, lethal combatants capable of demonstrating a commitment to defend" U.S. allies and partners around the two seas. Rather than providing serious military capability, such a force of small surface combatants—presumably ships no larger than patrol boats, corvettes, and frigates—would function as a sacrificial "tripwire," forcing the PLA to draw American blood and thus risk a large and costly war. Hughes sees the same function for the vulnerable U.S. airbases on Okinawa, Japan, and South Korea; the combat aircraft there hold China at risk and, in Hughes's view, force China into costly horizontal escalation. But he implies that in a prolonged conflict, these bases would have little tactical utility for the U.S. coalition, a conclusion we also reach.[23]

Robert Rubel, a retired U.S. Navy captain and dean of the Center for Naval Warfare Studies at the U.S. Naval War College, largely endorses Hughes's concept for how the U.S. Navy should approach China's Near Seas. Rubel asserts that these waters are no longer a place for the Navy's largest capital ships (aircraft carriers, cruisers, and destroyers).[24] Instead Rubel agrees with Hughes that the United States should maintain its surface naval presence in the Near Seas with small and inexpensive ships, backed by the menace of powerful deterrent forces over the horizon. Ruble argues that until the United States is willing to patrol the Near Seas with expendable "tripwire" ships, the Navy will be increasingly unwilling to risk its expensive capital ships in these waters, thus eventually ceding these seas to China's control.[25] Implementing the tripwire concept requires credibly menacing military power over the horizon, ready to intervene and retaliate after the small ships are attacked. But by next decade, this won't be something China will have to fear, once the PLA gains confidence in its ability to suppress U.S. forward bases and attack U.S. naval strike groups two thousand kilometers from China.

U.S. naval planners should not presume that small combatants will escape the wrath of China's antiship cruise missiles when sailing near China. By the next decade China's reconnaissance satellite constellations and unmanned surveillance aircraft will provide PLA commanders sufficient and virtually real-time data on surface targets out to the Second Island Chain (discussed in chapter 4).[26] All-weather synthetic aperture radar imaging resolution of five meters or less means small ships will not escape detection.[27] The declining cost and improving performance of antiship missiles relative to their targets will make it economical for PLA commanders to attack just about any detected combatant. For example the U.S. Navy's Littoral Combat Ship, its current low-end surface combatant, will cost $587 million per ship (excluding its required mission modules), a sum with which the PLA could purchase hundreds of antiship missiles.[28]

Hughes's proposed radical redesign of the U.S. Navy would achieve many benefits. It would diversify the Navy across many more platforms, reducing combat risk, and allow the Navy to be in many more places at any given time. Redesigning the fleet would compel the Navy to examine its culture and doctrines, thus catalyzing innovation and adaptation. The new design would strengthen the shipbuilding industrial base in the United States and lead to more competition among contractors. Finally, it would likely result in better officers and sailors since they would have to assume greater responsibility for all of these smaller ships at earlier stages of their careers.

In spite of these improvements, Hughes's radical redesign won't by itself provide a way for the Navy to maintain control of the East and South China Seas in the face of the PLA's land-based air and missile power. Maintaining or restoring the freedom of navigation to a global commons that is subject to Chinese interdiction would require achieving one of two conditions. First, U.S. and coalition military power would have to succeed in neutralizing China's land-based antiship forces. Given China's advantageous continental position, this condition will not be easily accomplished. But concepts such as LOCAAS and a significant number of penetrating stealthy bombers provide examples of how this might be achieved. Many years in the future, defensive shipborne technologies such as electromagnetic rail guns and high-powered free-electron lasers could swing the advantage away from missiles and back to ship missile defenses.

The second path would be to compel China's decision makers to refrain from employing their "anti-navy" capabilities. This would imply a permanent settlement of the strategic issues at the source of conflict on terms favorable to the United States and its partners. As with most conflicts, such an outcome would occur after China's leaders determined that the costs of prolonging the conflict would be too steep compared to likely gains.[29] And that condition would occur only after the coalition achieved substantial coercive leverage over China's leaders.

Indeed, it is this second path—attacks that target the adversary's leadership and its central processes of control and organization—that describes the best use of airpower in the view of many airpower theorists. John Warden, a retired U.S. Air Force colonel, chief planner of the 1991 Persian Gulf War air campaign, and noted airpower theorist, advises largely bypassing attacks on the enemy's forces in the field. Warden instead calls for focusing airpower on the enemy's leadership and on the processes essential for sustaining the enemy's internal control and military potential.[30] Warden points to the direct coercion NATO airpower achieved over Serbia's leadership in 1999, and the resulting settlement of the Kosovo conflict on NATO's terms, as an example of this theory's effectiveness.[31]

Warden's "Five Rings" theory is highly controversial among military strategists. Skeptics note the failure of Warden's 1991 air campaign against Iraq's strategic targets to compel Saddam Hussein's compliance; contrary to Warden's theory, a long campaign of attrition against Iraq's fielded forces was still required. But whether one believes in Warden's theory or not, the United States will still need the capacity to suppress China's land-based "anti-navy" forces directly or indirectly if it is to gain control over the South and East China Seas.

A Land-Based Future for the Navy

In the event of a conflict with China, policymakers in Washington will hold the Navy responsible for gaining and maintaining control of the western Pacific sea lines of communication. This condition would very likely be a key war aim and the prime indicator of U.S. and allied success. Unfortunately for the Navy, its force structure and operating doctrine are on the losing side of the missile and sensor revolution. If it is to salvage its position and stand prepared to achieve the missions that will be assigned to it, the Navy needs to undertake creative thinking and some disruptive organizational change.

In particular, Navy budget planners in Washington need to transfer significant funding from current systems that won't be useful in a conflict with China to new systems that are critically required. This would mean taking money away from shipbuilding and giving it to long-range airpower and missiles. Paradoxically, such a transfer from surface ships to long-range aircraft and missiles will actually benefit the Navy because it would improve the prospects of the Navy accomplishing its wartime missions. In light of the missile and sensor revolution, the Navy can no longer afford to continue its long-standing practices under the assumption that what has worked in past decades will also suit the future. Instead Navy leaders need to remember their maritime missions and then acquire the force structure that will be required to achieve those missions under the circumstances it will face in the future, not the past.

In order to wage a sustained campaign against China's land-based "anti-navy," the Navy should transfer funding away from its carrier-based strike aircraft, acquiring instead some of the long-range land-based strike aircraft currently under development for the Air Force. For example, sustaining the Navy's aircraft carrier fleet costs $15.1 billion per ship—an average of $11.8 billion for each of the new *Gerald R. Ford*–class aircraft carriers, plus an additional $3.3 billion for twenty-four F-35C strike fighters that will comprise part of the carrier's air wing.[32] As we have seen, it is the limited combat radius of the F-35C (about 1,100 kilometers) that forecloses a power projection role for the Navy's aircraft carriers in a China scenario.

For that sum, the Navy could purchase twenty-seven of the new long-range strike aircraft, at the planned unit cost of $550 million—aircraft that will likely each carry at least eight times the stealthy payload of an F-35C. Similarly, to protect its aircraft carriers, the Navy plans to acquire additional DDG-51 *Burke*-class destroyers at $1.6 billion each, a cost equal to that of three new long-range stealthy bombers.[33] With these stealthy bombers instead, the Navy would have maritime airpower that would actually be useful against China's navy under way in the heavily defended Near Seas and against the PLA's naval bases and "anti-navy" forces—missions too dangerous for the Navy's aircraft carriers and destroyers.

For many inside the Navy, it would be heresy to transfer resources from sea-based aviation in order to basically duplicate the Air Force's bomber force. Aircraft carriers and sea-based fighter-attack aircraft are what distinguish the Navy and are central to its purpose and culture. Yet in the one-hundred-year history of naval aviation, the Navy has also continuously operated land-based aircraft. Today the Navy is successfully modernizing its land-based maritime air fleets, with large-scale purchases of the P-8 Poseidon antisubmarine and MQ-4C Triton unmanned patrol aircraft. The Navy is establishing fifteen airborne electronic attack squadrons equipped with the new EA-18G aircraft; five of these squadrons will operate from land bases in support of joint service missions.[34] Indeed, in a somewhat heretical article, a Navy airborne electronic attack squadron commander asserted that land-based electronic attack aircraft provide more capacity, flexibility, persistence, and freedom of maneuver compared to basing these aircraft on an aircraft carrier.[35] Land-based aircraft have been an essential element of naval air-power and are an important part of the Navy's aviation heritage.

Even more important for Navy leaders should be the requirement to achieve the wartime missions they will be assigned. As we have seen, the Navy will need long-range strike capacity if it is to achieve control of the East and South China Seas in wartime. That should be all the incentive required for Navy leaders to make the necessary adaptations.

Why would the Navy need to acquire for itself long-range strike capacity the Air Force is also acquiring? After all, under the Air-Sea Battle concept, should not the two services coordinate their unique capabilities in pursuit of campaign objectives such as sea control? Isn't the suppression of China's "anti-navy" forces with Air Force airpower a quintessential example of the "cross-domain synergy" called for in the Pentagon's JOAC? Won't the Air Force's bombers be enough?

In spite of these questions, the Navy should still make the case for its own land-based long-range strike capability and retain the funding and authority to build such a force. Policymakers will hold the Navy responsible for achieving control of the seas, a core naval mission throughout recorded history. If the Navy is to be held responsible for achieving this mission, it should receive the resources, capabilities, and authority to do so.

Under the theories of Air-Sea Battle and joint operational access, it shouldn't matter which service, or combination of services, actually does the work. But in practice, the Navy will have the most intense interest both in maritime challenges, such as land-based "anti-navy" forces, and in development of the capabilities and doctrine necessary to cope with such challenges. Top-level policymakers interested in making sure the "anti-navy" problem is fixed will have a strong reason to assign the problem—and resources—to the Navy.

This implies that the new long-range strike bomber will become a joint Air Force–Navy program. Given the wide range of missions this aircraft could be assigned, a joint service program is a logical conclusion. Expanding the production run of the aircraft to meet the needs of the two services and its many potential missions should reduce its unit cost.

When setting priorities for the U.S. defense budget, building the capacity to neutralize or dissuade China from using "anti-navy" forces should rate at the top. It is true that the U.S. Defense Department has a whole world of responsibilities, but arguably none is more consequential to U.S. interests than stability and security in East Asia. Success or failure for the United States and its partners will be judged by whether they can maintain control of the western Pacific's sea lines of communication. Navy leaders need to have an open mind about acquiring the mix of forces necessary to accomplish that mission in the future.

This hardly means the end of the aircraft carrier. Carrier strike groups will still have critical roles to play in achieving dominance in deep-ocean areas and in projecting power against adversaries lacking antiship missile capacity. The U.S. Navy should retain a highly capable, if smaller, aircraft carrier fleet for decades into the future.

But the Navy also needs to reckon with its most challenging nemesis, the land-based "anti-navy" that threatens the global commons. Dealing with that nemesis will require the rebirth of a land-based naval strike warfare capability. This will challenge the Navy's cultural heritage but also provide an opportunity for the Navy to display its powers of adaptation.

The Marine Corps Grapples with the Missile Revolution

The U.S. Marine Corps has defined its strategic roles as responding to national security crises and assuring access to the world's littoral regions.[36] The Marine Corps is a naval service structured to respond to crises and to project power from sea bases and naval platforms.[37] Marine Corps planners believe that operating from Navy ships and sea bases provides advantages in flexibility and sustainability. Unfortunately, the missile and sensor revolution is as much a problem for the Marine Corps' operating concept as it is for the Navy's surface forces and for the Air Force's short-range tactical airpower. Marine Corps planners are well aware of this problem.[38] But until it is solved, the Marine Corps will have a difficult time assuring littoral access and contributing to sea control in the western Pacific during a high-end conflict with China.

The Marine Corps' misadventures with the Expeditionary Fighting Vehicle (EFV) program illustrate the service's reckoning with the missile and sensor revolution. Begun in the 1980s to replace aging amphibious assault vehicles, the EFV program was cancelled in 2011 after consuming more than $3 billion in development costs. In his remarks announcing the cancellation, then–U.S. Defense secretary Robert Gates noted that the planned $12 billion acquisition budget for the EFV fleet would "essentially swallow the entire Marine vehicle budget and most of its total procurement budget for the foreseeable future."[39] The EFV program failed because its designers and engineers attempted to keep ahead of the missile and sensor threat, a competition Marine Corps leaders eventually (and correctly) concluded they couldn't win.

To land Marines on a hostile beach, the Navy's amphibious ships must approach within a few miles of the shore and deploy the legacy amphibious assault vehicles transporting the landing forces for a slow swim to the beach. In the missile age, planners knew this model was no longer feasible. The Navy set a requirement for its amphibious ships to approach no closer than forty-six kilometers (twenty-five nautical miles)—the distance out of sight from the shore—for deployment of the new EFVs.[40] Marine Corps planners also sought to limit the time EFV passengers were exposed to the ocean to an hour or less; this meant the EFV was required to swim at roughly forty-five kilometers an hour, a highly challenging engineering requirement for a heavy armored vehicle.

Once ashore, the EFV was expected to then perform as a high-end infantry fighting vehicle, able to master most terrain, keep up with tanks, protect its passengers from bullets and chemical weapons, and provide fire support to dismounted troops. Escalating costs and reliability problems plagued development; however, it was the expanding missile threat that proved lethal to the EFV. A launch point of 46 kilometers out to sea was not sufficient to thwart the antiship cruise missile threat. In China's case, its mobile land-based antiship cruise missiles can strike 160 kilometers out to sea.[41] This is relatively simple technology that is also available to other potential adversaries, who with missile-armed ships or aircraft could extend the missile threat range much farther.

Top U.S. Navy officials explained that "the Navy-Marine team will never contemplate littoral maneuver until an enemy's battle network, capable of firing dense salvos of guided weapons, is suppressed. Consequently, the initial phase of any joint theater-entry operation will require achieving air, sea, undersea, and overall battle-network superiority in the amphibious objective area."[42] Achieving this dominance would remove the requirement for an amphibious assault vehicle to launch from over the horizon and race ashore at forty-five kilometers per hour. But achieving such superiority in the Near Seas during a conflict with China will, needless to say, be highly challenging.

There will be many important roles for the Marine Corps to play during the looming competition with China. But these roles will occur for the most part everywhere but during the battles for air and maritime superiority in the western Pacific, arguably the decisive episode of such a conflict. It is these roles for which the Marine Corps should prepare, as it turns its attention back to the Asia-Pacific theater.

"Left of Boom"—A Job for the Marine Corps

In the security competition with China, the U.S. Marine Corps can make its most important mark "left of boom," that is, in shaping and improving the security environment in the region before conflict occurs, and, in doing so, strive to prevent conflict from occurring in the first place.

America's allies and partners in the region are its most valuable assets. The larger and more confident the coalition of partners is, the more effective it will be at persuading China to work within the region's existing rules and norms rather than seeking to supplant them with new arrangements that favor that nation at the expense of others in the region. There is much more America's allies and partners should be doing to improve their security, increase regional security cooperation, and enhance local conventional deterrence. Fortunately the U.S. Marine Corps is already an institution well designed to assist these partners with these needed improvements.

The Marine Corps has a very long history of cooperative engagement with the military forces of many partners in the region. The end of Marine Corps combat operations in the Middle East and Central Asia will allow the Marines to increase their activities in the Asia-Pacific region, a shift the Marine Corps is eager to make.[43] The territorial clashes around the East and South China Seas involve disputes over water, islands, and surrounding airspace. This topography perfectly matches the Marine Corps' core expertise with littoral operations and amphibious warfare.

The Marine Corps possesses extensive competence with land, maritime, and air operations and knows how to combine its competency in these domains to build operational synergy.[44] The Marine Corps promotes its Marine Expeditionary Units (MEUs)—a battalion landing team and composite aviation squadron deployed on Navy amphibious ships—as a well-designed package for crisis response. MEUs can respond to crises, albeit small ones. An even more important role for an MEU is as a mobile security force assistance training unit, able to help partners develop their military skills. When countries such as Japan, the Philippines, Vietnam, and others are attempting to improve their capacity to defend their interests, the U.S. Marine Corps is very well positioned for the collaboration these forces need.

The Marine Corps should combine its experience with partner engagement; its growing forward presence in the region; and its knowledge of air, land, and maritime operations into a comprehensive strategy for regional security force assistance. The goal of this improved regional strategy should be not only to improve the capacities and competencies of each partner's military forces but also to improve multilateral military coordination in the region, among countries that heretofore have trusted the United States more than each other. China has exploited these historical animosities to degrade cohesion among countries that have common interests in resisting China's assertions. The Marine Corps, with a better security force assistance strategy, will be a trusted partner and can build a better regional security network through multilateral security force assistance missions and exercises.[45]

U.S. partners such as Japan, the Philippines, and, increasingly, Vietnam, need to improve their capacities for naval patrolling, littoral maneuver, amphibious operations, airpower coordination, and many other functions if they are to credibly resist China's salami slicing in the Near Seas. From a political and diplomatic perspective, these countries are best positioned to resist China's assertions, since they (especially the small countries around the South China Sea) are most likely to be viewed as victims of a large regional bully. The Marine Corps is well positioned to assist these countries to improve these military capacities. In implementing this security force assistance strategy, the Marine Corps will require support from all of the other services and from U.S. special operations forces.

During a potential conflict in the western Pacific, the missile threat against surface forces will greatly limit the Marine Corps' scope of action. But maritime irregular warfare, raiding, sabotage, special reconnaissance, and munitions guidance will likely play out in the Near Seas in wartime. Marine Corps, special operations, and coalition submarine forces should be prepared for these missions.

Finally, the Marine Corps and Navy should prepare to conduct a distant blockade of shipping bound for China. There are shortcomings to this strategy; also, it is not likely by itself to be an effective substitute for the full range of measures that success against China will require (described in chapter 5), however, U.S. policymakers are still likely to call for a blockade, at least as part of a broader campaign. Thus Marine Corps and Navy planners should be prepared for that call. In addition, rehearsing elements of a distant blockade in peacetime, in full view of the PLA's intelligence collection, will signal resolve and add doubt to the minds of Chinese decision makers. Such preparations will thus add to deterrence and regional stability.

A New Fleet Design?

The U.S. Navy has global responsibilities—preparing for a possible conflict with China in the western Pacific is just one mission for which the Navy must be ready. However, this mission is arguably one of the Navy's most important, perhaps second only to strategic nuclear deterrence in terms of its consequences for U.S. interests. Indeed the Defense Strategic Guidance, signed by President Barack Obama in January 2012, left little doubt that the Asia-Pacific region was now the country's top security priority.[46] So although the Navy needs to prepare for missions across the globe, policy guidance for the Navy directs it to place its preparations for Asia-Pacific missions at the top of its list.

In the Asia-Pacific region, the most essential mission, and one that falls squarely on the Navy, is maintaining freedom of navigation in the global commons, in particular, the East and South China Seas. This is where China's "core interests" (so described by top Chinese officials)[47] clash with those of its neighbors and the United States. And should the United States withdraw from this responsibility, a pre–World War I–style regional arms race and competition for security is highly likely, which would result in great risk to U.S. and global interests (explored in chapter 2).

The missile and sensor revolution has created a growing mismatch between the design of the U.S. fleet and the Navy's ability to accomplish its fundamental missions in the western Pacific. The Navy's decades-long practice of replacing legacy aircraft carriers, destroyers, and amphibious ships with more modern and sophisticated models no longer works in the missile and sensor age. The Navy's newest surface ships have lost the battle against the increasing capabilities and falling relative costs of adversary land-based missiles and sensors.

To achieve its fundamental missions in the East and South China Seas, the Navy needs its own technical revolution that will swing the advantage away from offensive missiles, something not likely to arrive in the fleet before the end of the 2020s, if then. At the same time, the Navy's fleet design is ready to face the PLAN away from Chinese land-based support, in the mid-Pacific or Indian Oceans; but the PLAN won't be ready for those battles until at least the late 2020s either. This is the other side of the mismatch between the Navy's fleet design and the military problem China presents over the next decade and a half: the Navy is buying ships that soon won't be able to achieve its most important missions in the western Pacific; meanwhile, these ships are prepared today for a fleet battle that isn't on the horizon for at least fifteen years.

In response to the missile threat, Wayne Hughes recommended a Navy composed of many more smaller, simpler, and single-purpose ships. According to Hughes, such a fleet design would diversify the Navy's combat risks over many more platforms and also complicate enemy planning. A recent study from the RAND Corporation on the naval balance in the Pacific endorsed a similar conclusion. That study called for the Navy to move away from striking power centered on the aircraft carrier, protected by expensive multimission destroyers, and proposed instead a "phantom sea power" design characterized by many small combatants, more submarines, unmanned aircraft and ships, and decoys and deception measures, all tied together by robust communication links.[48] By diversifying U.S. combat risk, the RAND study asserted, deterrence and crisis stability would be enhanced since the allure of a Chinese first strike against U.S. naval forces would be reduced.

The RAND study admitted that "eventually, breakthroughs in sensor technology may make any platform, anywhere, observable and vulnerable."[49] That is the basic problem for U.S. surface forces: the inability to hide while forward deployed in the face of thickening Chinese sensor networks. With antiship missiles costing a small fraction of even a small warship, the PLA would have no reason to hold back from attacking every threatening sighting its sensor network reveals. For U.S. and allied surface naval forces, the trends are headed in a bad direction.

While the Navy waits for high-powered lasers and electromagnetic rail guns to swing the advantage back to missile defenses, planners at the Defense Department need to consider how much money they should spend now buying additional targets for China's missiles. First priority for funding should go instead toward systems and concepts that hold out the hope of neutralizing China's land-based "anti-navy" missiles and aircraft. That means top funding priority for long-range strike aircraft, LOCAAS, long-range cruise missiles, and survivable sensor and communication networks.

This does not mean the Navy needs to lose funding to the Air Force. Naval aviation is not limited to aircraft carriers—the Navy has operated land-based patrol and strike aircraft since the inception of naval aviation a century ago. The Navy has a great incentive to expand its land-based air operations with its own fleet of new long-range strike bombers. The Navy will use this aircraft for maritime strikes over the heavily defended Near Seas and to attack China's land-based "anti-navy." In spite of the aspirations of service integration under the JOAC and Air-Sea Battle, the Navy should claim responsibility for these missions and build the capabilities it needs to accomplish them. The Navy can thus make a strong case that it needs its own force of long-range strike aircraft to achieve critical maritime superiority objectives, a core naval mission.

Next, the Navy needs enough submarines to ensure that China's navy will quickly go to the bottom if a war breaks out. Only after the neutralization of China's navy and "anti-navy" are well funded should the Pentagon then concern itself with more surface naval forces (and carrier aircraft) for the western Pacific.

Relegating surface ship modernization to the bottom of the priority list has implications for the Marine Corps, which uses the Navy's amphibious ships as its preferred way of performing its missions. As discussed above, the most important role for the Marine Corps regarding the security competition with China will be what the service can do to shape the region's security environment through engagement, security force assistance, and multilateral training exercises. Its shipping needs in this context will include some modern amphibious warships, littoral combat ships, and noncombat support ships such as the Joint High Speed Vessel and other useful transports.

As with the Navy, the Marine Corps has global responsibilities beyond China, naturally a significant planning factor. But China's missile threat should reduce expectations for the role the Marine Corps would play in a highly intense missile combat environment. Planners and program managers should relent from attempting to acquire amphibious ships, amphibious assault vehicles, transport aircraft, and other systems under the expectation that these systems would permit the Marine Corps to operate under a heavy missile threat. Such efforts won't succeed at a reasonable price and shouldn't be tried. Regarding China, the Marine Corps and its planners should focus their efforts "left of boom," on shaping regional security in peacetime and, by doing so, helping to prevent a war from starting.

For Americans, the Pacific has always been considered a naval theater. Almost immediately after the United States acquired Hawaii, Guam, the Philippines, and other possessions after the Spanish-American War, the U.S. Navy, under President Theodore Roosevelt, began planning for how to defend and, if necessary, retake the great ocean from Japan.[50] U.S. Pacific Command, based in Hawaii, has always had a U.S. Navy admiral as its commander. The United States has fought many wars in and around the Pacific and all of the armed services have suffered while doing so. But America's military history in the Pacific seems first and foremost a naval history.

From this cultural perspective, it is understandable that current and future policymakers will turn first to the Navy when they have concerns about U.S. security interests in the western Pacific. Open access to the sea has been a key American interest since the founding of the country, and the Navy has taken on protecting that access as one of its core missions.

The missile and sensor revolution has upset the long-standing link between naval dominance and the security of sea lines of communication. Highly capable and inexpensive missiles and sensors now allow continental powers to deny important regions of the seas to others, even when these powers have inferior navies. These land-based "anti-navies" will be able to thwart the most powerful fleets' regaining of control of these denied waters.

As a result, the American perception of the Pacific as a naval theater needs to change. It is now first an air and space theater. Control over these domains is required before control over the surface of either the water or land will be possible. And given the range and precision of "anti-navy" weapons, control of air and space needs to be broad, deep, and persistent, not just local and fleeting.

Accepting the notion that the Pacific is now an air and space rather than primarily a naval theater will allow policymakers and planners to recognize new structures and concepts for how to defend U.S. and allied interests in the region. The challenge for these officials will be understanding these changes and then leading their organizations down the new paths they must travel.

 *Chapter 10*

A New American Strategy for the Asia-Pacific Region

D esigning and implementing an effective strategy for China will be an especially demanding task for U.S. policymakers. Almost every dimension of the problem adds difficulty and complexity to the challenge.

Within a decade, China's economy, and the potential for that economy to support military power, will constitute a rival the size of which the United States has not faced since it emerged as a global player over a century ago. Comparisons with recent large military competitions reveal the size of the looming challenge. World War II required the United States to mobilize for a global war effort. But once it did so, its production, combined with that of its allies, including the Soviet Union, easily swamped that of the Axis powers.[1] By 1944 success in that war was not in doubt. During the Cold War, U.S. economic and technical advantages over the Soviet bloc permitted a military competition that little strained the United States but bankrupted the Soviet Union.[2]

With China, by contrast, the United States could by next decade face a rival with substantially equal economic output and potentially comparable military spending. Unlike the Soviet Union, China, with a much larger economy, will very likely be capable of sustaining an arms race on roughly equal terms for as long as it chooses. For the security balance in East Asia, China, as we have seen, gets much more out of its military spending because it is the "home team." The effectiveness of U.S. military investment by contrast is diluted both by U.S. global security responsibilities and by the nation's need to project its military power to a far-off "away game" in East Asia. The United States will be able to add the military potential of its partners in the region to its side of the ledger. But others in the region may bandwagon with China. The result is a security challenge in East Asia the potential magnitude of which U.S. policymakers have not faced in the modern era.[3]

Second, as much of this book has sought to explain, the structure of the military problem in East Asia seems only now to be dawning on policymakers in Washington responsible for the design of U.S. military forces. Overconfidence in an assumed lead in U.S. military technology and attention drawn to nearly two decades of small wars have led policymakers and planners to lose sight of technological developments—most of them ironically first developed by the United States—that are now nullifying previous U.S. military advantages in power projection and strategic mobility. With the PLA's military strategy now placing much of America's tremendous investment in naval and aerospace power at risk of irrelevance, U.S. military planners and commanders must now cobble together new ways of performing basic missions in a region they previously took for granted.

America's allies in the Asia-Pacific region are its most valuable asset; but they are also an especially challenging lot for U.S. diplomats. In Western Europe during the Cold War, former enemies were able to put the past behind them and coalesce around NATO and the concept of collective security. The bald Soviet threat, the brashness of which China has yet to fully replicate, certainly provided much of NATO's glue. France's early obstreperous behavior toward NATO is just one example that not all was harmonious inside the Atlantic alliance. But today's American diplomats would surely welcome that relative unity of purpose compared to what they must wrestle with in East Asia.

Unlike Europe, bitter memories in Asia from last century and before remain unforgotten, with multilateral security cooperation suffering as a result. Moral hazard, the temptation by allies to let America do the heavy work, remains strong; for all of the talk about China's military modernization, defense spending in frontline places such as Taiwan, the Philippines, and Japan is shockingly slight. Schizophrenia over either U.S. abandonment or entrapment in a military misadventure still plagues many of America's allies in the region.[4] With little prospect of any permanent and effective security institutions developing in the region, U.S. diplomats will continue to face uncertainty and ambiguity; partners may plead for U.S. protection while simultaneously hedging to keep their options open.

At home, the American public and policymakers have yet to sort out just what to make of the new China. A poll conducted in 2012 by Pew Research showed that while 52 percent of the U.S. general public viewed the emergence of China as a major threat, the concern centered on China's economy rather than its military potential; only 28 percent of the public rated China's military might as the greatest concern. A parallel poll of government executive and legislative branch officials found just 31 percent perceived China as a major threat.[5] A 2013 Pew poll asked respondents from the general public to rate various international security issues. While 59 percent assessed North Korea's nuclear program a major threat, 56 percent said the same of Islamic extremist groups; China's power and influence, number five on the list, was rated a major threat by 44 percent of the respondents.[6] With economic anxiety lingering in the United States in the wake of the recent economic recession, many in the U.S. public register more concern about China's economic competitiveness than its military modernization, a topic which has received scant media attention. So although we have argued in this book for major reforms to U.S. security strategy in Asia, most of the U.S. public seems unaware of the need for a change.

Adopting a more assertive stance toward China is also likely to create frictions inside the United States. The 2012 Pew poll showed a broad disparity of views between the general public and some elites regarding China. For example, 71 percent of the general public perceived a loss of U.S. jobs to China as a very serious problem, a view held by only 15 percent of the business and trade leaders Pew interviewed.[7]

Even as a security competition between China and the United States continues to grow, trade and financial linkages will continue to deepen. Commercial and financial interaction with China creates winners and losers inside the United States. Although overall economic welfare benefits from this trade, those losing from trade with China—say workers and investors in some industries—might view a more assertive stance against China favorably. By contrast, those who currently benefit—those with large exports and investments in China—may argue against a more assertive U.S. security strategy in the Asia-Pacific region. Because of the deepening trade and financial linkages between the two countries, a debate over U.S. security strategy in the region could pit many domestic interests against each other.

It has been two centuries since the United States last faced a country that was simultaneously a potential adversary and a large and vital trade and financial partner. The misbegotten War of 1812 divided the southern and western states, which saw the war as a chance to expand the country into Florida and farther west, against the New England states that had deep commercial and financial ties with Great Britain and that therefore strongly opposed President James Madison's war policy.[8] Strong economic ties to an adversary, concentrated in mainly one region of the country, resulted in a deep internal split over foreign policy. Should the security competition between China and the United States accelerate in the years ahead, we should expect to see interests and factions inside the United States clash over America's China policy. An internal competition over China policy will only increase the subject's complexity for political leaders responsible for fashioning that policy.

Finally, the gravity of U.S. interests at stake in the Asia-Pacific region will magnify the stress on America's policymakers. No less than America's standard of living, the future of its relationships around the world, and its status as a great power are in the balance. The Obama administration's "pivot to Asia" is both a reflection of this gravity and an antecedent for follow-on actions in the region by his successors. With the China security competition, U.S. policymakers will be forced to deal with a true peer competitor, a confounding military challenge, quarrelsome yet vital allies, clashing domestic interests, and a public that is understandably conflicted about the issues in play. Because the stakes are so large, no security issue will be more consequential for American interests. China policy will be a great challenge for a long time to come.

The United States Needs a New Approach

For the United States and its allies, the current trends are too dangerous to be allowed to continue. By early next decade, China's leaders could conclude that they, and not the United States and its partners, possess escalation dominance. Those leaders could perceive that China's leverage would improve during a crisis in the western Pacific, the more that crisis escalated. During such escalation, the PLA could put into readiness, and perhaps into action, more and more of its land-based access-denial air and missile power. Under these conditions, U.S. commanders would not relish the prospect of sending their naval and airpower into such tactically unfavorable circumstances. They would presumably have to report this analysis to policymakers in Washington, who would similarly have to ponder the consequences of a visible and substantial military setback. For the policymakers, attention would inevitably shift to face-saving de-escalation of the crisis, done with a lack of negotiating leverage.

Needless to say, such a scenario would be unfamiliar ground for U.S. policymakers and commanders who have held, in most cases since World War II, the advantage of escalation dominance. Policymakers in the Lyndon Johnson administration believed (incorrectly as it turned out) that escalating the employment of airpower and ground forces would compel North Vietnam to end its military operations in South Vietnam and its support for the Viet Cong resistance.[9] In the 1991 Persian Gulf War, President George H. W. Bush resisted attempts to arrange a negotiated settlement even after the monthlong preparatory air war had begun; Bush and his advisers wanted more escalation, with the employment of U.S. and coalition ground combat power against Iraqi forces.[10] In 2002 and 2003 President George W. Bush and his advisers again favored escalation in order to achieve the employment of what they believed was U.S. military superiority over Iraq.

Perhaps the most interesting and, for current U.S. planners, the most disturbing parallel, is the 1962 Cuban Missile Crisis. In that case, President John Kennedy and his team employed conventional military escalation—the visible buildup of air, naval, and amphibious forces opposite Cuba—to persuade Soviet leaders that a military clash in the Caribbean was hopeless for Soviet plans.[11] In this case, Soviet forces, in the role of the expeditionary power, faced poor odds against the American and continental "home team." The result was a withdrawal of the Soviet missiles from Cuba.

An adversary's possession of escalation dominance will be strange territory for U.S. policymakers, one that could lead to either costly miscalculation or an embarrassing climbdown in a crisis. Most dangerous of all would be a situation in which each side perceived it would benefit from escalation. In that case, a conflict would be virtually certain. By next decade, such a disturbing scenario in East Asia is plausible. By that time, PLA commanders might have great confidence in the missile and aerospace power they will have built. On the other side, the confidence of U.S. policymakers in a crisis could rest on comforting, but possibly mistaken, memories of military dominance. Needless to say, it can't be the case that both sides will benefit from escalation. We can hope that it won't take a clash of arms to prove this point.

Should U.S. policymakers and military planners take little effective action to change the current trajectory, we should expect other players at risk in the region to take their own actions, with unpredictable consequences. For example, in July 2013 the Japanese government, led by the nationalist prime minister Shinzo Abe, released a new defense policy white paper. Reflecting a trend of increasing Japanese anxiety about the regional security situation, the white paper called attention to China's "dangerous acts," including intrusions by Chinese air and naval forces into Japan's territory.[12] Perhaps most notable was the white paper's call for Japan to develop the ability to execute preemptive attacks on enemy bases abroad and an amphibious assault capability, presumably with the clashes over the Senkaku Islands in mind.[13] As a result, the Japanese government increased defense spending in 2013 and directed more of Japan's defense resources toward the Chinese threat to the Japan's southwest.[14]

U.S. policymakers should obviously be pleased that Japan is doing more for its own defense. The much more assertive content of Japan's 2013 defense white paper is largely a response to China's own military assertions, even into Japanese territory. As a consequence, Japan's defense policy is now much more hawkish, a substantial change in policy and military latitude from just a few years ago. This trajectory is likely to keep going should the security situation in the region continue to deteriorate. Without a new American strategy, the still-modest defense buildup now under way in Japan could metastasize into a much more intense regional arms race, with destabilizing consequences to follow. Indeed non-Chinese defense spending in the region is expected to leap 55 percent in the five years ending in 2018.[15] This budding arms race could turn dangerous should players conclude that they need more nuclear weapons and ballistic missiles or should they perceive that adverse trends and time pressure are eroding their strategic positions.

As discussed in chapter 2, it matters who runs the western Pacific. Because the United States is an outsider, most countries in the region trust it to be the region's dominant security provider, a role they will not trust to a local great power like China. As a corollary, it is very unlikely, and indeed too risky, to contemplate East Asia finding a stable balance of power on its own. The Asia-Pacific is the globe's economic dynamo and the direct source of nearly a tenth of America's economic output; the consequences of a large conflict in the region would be disastrous. Thus, the United States needs to maintain its security presence. But it also needs a new and better way to do so.

Sustaining an Effective Peacetime Competition

The goal of America's strategy for the region should be to preserve the region's security while also maintaining the existing rules-based international order. With China's interests and those of the United States and its partners increasingly coming into conflict, a successful strategy must first attempt to persuade China's leaders to accept—to China's benefit—the existing order and to dissuade China's leaders from attempting to replace it with an alternative that privileges China over its neighbors. Developing effective persuasive and dissuasive leverage will require a much deeper understanding of Chinese decision making. It will also require assembling a full range of political, diplomatic, economic, and military tools that can both provide rewards for favorable Chinese behavior while also threatening to impose costs for unfavorable actions. China has interests and vulnerabilities that can be sources of leverage for a competitive coalition strategy. U.S. and allied policymakers and planners need to understand these sources of leverage and design a strategy that takes advantage of them.

The first and most important element of an effective American strategy is America's partners in the region. In most respects, the security interests of the United States and its partners are in alignment; China's rising military power and its territorial assertions are a common concern. These partners in the region, especially those on the front line such as the Philippines, Japan, India, and Vietnam, add political legitimacy to the effort of resisting China's assertions in the region. The larger the partnership network, the greater its overall legitimacy and the more difficult the task for China's decision makers. No U.S. strategy can hope to succeed without the participation of these partners. For these reasons, the partnership network should be the key pillar of any U.S. strategy for the region. This means that all other elements should support this pillar. And in order to do that, U.S. policymakers and diplomats must listen carefully to the interests and concerns of the partners.

The United States and its partners face an open-ended competition with China. All the players have an interest in avoiding conflict. But that outcome will not happen without active "preventive maintenance" by policymakers. For the United States, that means creating persuasive and dissuasive leverage designed to influence Chinese strategic behavior along a favorable path. An effective and sustainable U.S. strategy will engage the partners to contribute to this effort.

Persuasive and dissuasive leverage comes in many forms. China's breathtaking economic growth over the past three decades should be evidence enough to China's leaders of the rewards for cooperating with the existing international system. That success has resulted in more diplomatic power for China and greatly increased prestige for the CCP. China's continued access to these benefits should be persuasive.

China's military modernization now hangs like a cloud over this universally beneficial success. This means the United States and its partners need to develop dissuasive tools that could impose costs on China and that would promise to negate much of the large investment China has made in its military strategy. The coalition's dissuasive tools should hold at risk those assets and conditions China's leaders value most. These dissuasive tools should encompass a very broad range, from political and economic pressure up through potential military options. As we have seen throughout history, the more the United States and its partners are prepared to employ these tools, the greater will be their credibility and thus the less likely their need to be used.

Much of the recent discussion inside Washington defense circles regarding China and the Pacific has focused on Navy and Air Force programs and plans. But regarding the peacetime security competition in the region and bolstering deterrence, the contribution made by U.S. ground forces—the Army, Marine Corps, and special operations forces—may be the most valuable. These services will have the lead role in assisting America's security partners in the region as they build their own capabilities to resist China's pressure and assertions. The actions of China's neighbors to defend their sovereignty will enjoy increasing political legitimacy and will be key to preserving the existing rules-based order.

U.S. ground forces can provide assistance with internal defense, building conventional combat power, air defenses, antiship missile systems, command and control, intelligence gathering and sharing, amphibious capability, and many other important military functions. Ground forces will also have an important role preparing for various forms of defensive and offensive irregular warfare, which could occur as the security competition intensifies. The assistance provided by U.S. ground forces will boost the confidence of America's partners while displaying to China's leaders the rising costs for potentially bad behavior. Such an outcome would bolster deterrence and improve regional security.

The U.S. Navy and Air Force naturally must prepare as well for a security environment in the western Pacific that now challenges the operating practices these services have long taken for granted. China's land-based air and missile power, and a "reconnaissance-strike complex" with ever-increasing range and targeting ability, have resulted in bleak prospects for the U.S. Navy's surface forces in the region, at least until advanced missile defense technology arrives at the end of the next decade. The Navy will thus increasingly rely on its submarines to hold China's navy at risk; the Navy must make sure that this remains the case.

Meanwhile the United States needs to ensure that it has enough long-range strike capacity to hold at risk those targets China's leaders value most. High on this list should be China's land-based "anti-navy" capabilities. The U.S. Navy will not be able to maintain freedom of navigation in the western Pacific without the capacity to suppress these forces. In addition U.S. long-range strike capacity should hold at risk targets and assets valued most by China's leaders. Creating these capabilities will be technically challenging and will not be cheap. Suspending the purchase of systems such as aircraft carriers and short-range tactical aircraft that don't have much use in the region could help pay the bills. Meanwhile, expanding America's long-range strike capacity will be an important dissuasive tool and will be critical to maintaining deterrence.

Why the Skeptics of Sustaining America's Presence in Asia Are Wrong

This book has argued that sustaining the U.S. forward presence in Asia is essential to America's interests. It has also shown that the current policies supporting that commitment are weak and are failing. Dramatic reform to the U.S. approach to the region is needed if the United States is to maintain the credibility of its commitments. Some of these reforms will be controversial because they will include measures that threaten to impose steep costs on China in the event Beijing pursues actions that would harm U.S. and allied interests.

Naturally there are skeptics who doubt whether it is wise or even practical for the United States to attempt to sustain its leading role in the region in the face of China's rapid rise.[16] It is important to rebut the skeptics' arguments.

Some skeptics assert that a visible and formidable response to China will only antagonize China, making an enemy where none previously existed.[17] But this ignores the fact that China's well-planned military modernization strategy began two decades ago and has followed a steady course since its inception. The U.S. "pivot to Asia" came long after and was clearly a response to decisions China's leaders had previously taken. The skeptics' view also presumes that China's leaders respond emotionally rather than deliberately, as is much more likely the case. The recent U.S. response to the changing security balance in the western Pacific will not spark a new military competition with China, because that competition has been already been under way for some time.

Many observers explain that it would be irrational for two countries as interdependent economically and financially as China and the United States to ever go to war. Others made the same assertion a century ago to explain why a war among the great powers in Europe would be similarly illogical.[18] In 1914 Europe's great powers were more intertwined by trade and financial linkages than are the United States and China today. But for the statesmen who made decisions in that fateful year, strategic considerations trumped economics and finance. We can hope that today's policymakers, chastened by the past century's wars, will be wiser. But now as then, decision makers might also conclude that it will be easier to recover from the economic consequences of conflict, which could be temporary, than from a grave strategic setback, which would more likely be permanent. By this reasoning, a temporary economic setback caused by conflict would be a price worth paying for the avoidance of a strategic defeat.

Perhaps more relevant in the current case is Beijing's view that it does not have to choose between peace and the achievement of its territorial and security goals. Through careful "salami slicing," China's leaders very likely believe they can have both the peaceful development they enjoy plus the enlarged security they seek. The risk, of course, is that China will eventually meet resistance that its leaders did not expect, resulting in a crisis fueled by nationalism and the perceived need by leaders to defend their country's prestige. Add in the possibility of miscalculations over escalation dominance and the result could be calamity. The United States and its partners can avoid this scenario by bolstering their deterrence capacity and by displaying early resolution against China's assertions, before possible misunderstandings accumulate.

Many skeptics assert that it is the responsibility of China's neighbors, and not the United States, to balance China's power. Under this view, these countries, having the most at stake, should bear the heaviest portion of the balancing task, instead of "free riding" on U.S. security guarantees. Other skeptics (notably Christopher Layne and others from the "offshore balancing" school) believe that U.S. security alliances in general expose the United States to unnecessary risks in exchange for minimal benefits.

This book has argued for a diplomatic strategy that would make America's security partners in the region the central pillar of this strategy and would arrange for them to play a larger role in regional security; but a leading U.S. role is also essential. Just as Europe witnessed in the years leading up to World War I, East Asia, too, will unlikely be able to peacefully establish on its own a stable balance of power. It is certainly too dangerous to take a risk with such an experiment, because the consequences of failure would be immense. By contrast we see how the opposite experiment, with the United States as the outside security provider, has allowed East Asia to become perhaps the most successful region in the world over the past seven decades. The United States has a strong interest in making sure that experiment continues to run.

Another criticism is that China's military rise is simply a natural consequence of its economic and political rise and its need to protect its growing interests around the world. It is argued that this is a reality U.S. policymakers must therefore simply accept. It is true China's military expansion is a consequence of its rising power and interests, but just because it is a natural and logical consequence of China's rise does not mean it is not also dangerous to regional stability. Indeed, the rise of Athens in ancient Greece, Germany in the late nineteenth century, and Japan during the first half of the twentieth century were similarly "natural" and all led to clashing interests and war. It will take more than merely accommodating or accepting China's rise as a great power to avoid similar disastrous results. Avoiding disaster will require astute policies that both actively balance China's power and create effective incentives for China and the other players in the region.

This book has called for numerous reforms to U.S. military forces for the region. These reforms include increasing U.S. long-range striking power, establishing the capability to suppress China's land-based "antinavy" air and missile forces, and holding at risk other assets and conditions highly valued by China's leaders. Many observers object to a strategy designed around the prospect of bombing China. They assert that such a plan only guarantees a large and damaging war, and potentially ruinous escalation.

The object of the strategy proposed in this book is preventing conflict in the region by bolstering deterrence. The proposed strategy is not a war plan. It is a strategy to manage a peacetime security competition in East Asia.

The strategy calls for preparing favorable and unfavorable consequences for China's leaders to consider as they fashion their nation's external policies. A credible U.S. strategy must include the ability to hold at risk those targets China's leaders value. The United States, with its tiny number of stealthy long-range bombers and relatively small capacity to deliver Tomahawk land-attack cruise missiles, currently lacks the needed capacity to threaten these targets during a conflict. China's leaders will take that into consideration during a crisis. Perhaps most important, the United States cannot achieve its most important mission in the region, defending the freedom of navigation in the western Pacific, while China's land-based antiship forces continue to threaten the sea lines of communication. A credible strategy will have to include the ability to hold these land-based targets at risk.

Finally, some will label a policy that responds to China's assertions as "containment" and thus a throwback to the Cold War. But the strategy proposed here in no way resembles Cold War–style containment. The West's containment of the Soviet Union during the Cold War was multidimensional. In addition to the military competition, the United States and the West battled the Soviet Union's ideology and isolated it (until late in the period) economically and financially. Diplomatic contact was sparse and trade was virtually nonexistent until near the end. In sum, containment was broad-ranging isolation, imposed until, as George Kennan predicted early on, the Soviet Union's internal weaknesses caused its ruin.[19]

The policies proposed in this book in no way resemble containment. China's economic and financial linkages with the world are large and expanding, trends the United States should welcome. There is no ideological competition with China, at least from the U.S. perspective (the leaders of China's Communist Party may have a different view).[20] Diplomatic contact between China and the United States is continuous and extensive. Far from containment, the strategy proposed in this book relies on positive (and negative) incentives to encourage China's leadership to choose a path that benefits China, its neighbors, and the United States. This book has recommended U.S. military reforms that counter China's military modernization and create a capacity to hold valuable Chinese assets and conditions at risk; but these reforms serve deterrence and regional stability and hardly amount to Cold War–style containment.

Those who are skeptical of maintaining America's leading role in the region are concerned that the cost of that role is going up, perhaps sharply. On this, the skeptics are right—the costs are going up. But so too would be the consequences to the United States for surrendering that role. It will not be easy for the United States to sustain its position. But the benefits of doing so are still great and will exceed the costs and risks.

The Barriers to a New Strategy

If a better approach to China was obvious and easy to implement, that approach would already be current policy. There are several reasons why the United States does not have the policies for the region that it should; overcoming barriers to a better approach will be a challenge and will require leadership from policymakers.

The first barrier is overcoming the reluctance to recognize that the U.S. strategic position in the western Pacific is quickly deteriorating, a syndrome seemingly few policymakers, let alone the public, yet appreciate. Media attention on China has focused on its economic growth, its financial influence, its cyber espionage activities, and some of its internal social problems. China's military modernization, by contrast, receives only occasional coverage in mainstream Western media. Most people inside the United States assume that American military power is still superior and free to roam as it has for decades; arguing that this will soon no longer be the case in East Asia is a novel thought to most observers and thus not easy to accept.

Next, U.S. policymakers, tasked with an entire world of security responsibilities, will struggle to decide how many resources to allocate to the growing security problems in the Asia-Pacific region. This book has focused narrowly on what the United States should do to respond to the challenge presented by China; it is explicitly not a template for how America should meet its global responsibilities. Many of the military capabilities proposed, such as new long-range strike aircraft, however, would be useful everywhere, not just in East Asia. Even so, policymakers will debate what draw on resources the China challenge properly merits. The Obama administration has identified the region as America's top security priority. But that does not settle how much of the security pie it should receive. That is a question that very likely will never be finally settled.

With resources finite, allocating more to meeting the particular challenges in East Asia means allocating less elsewhere. The good news is that whenever U.S. policymakers have given their consistent attention to certain security threats, they have usually been successful at mitigating those threats. Four decades of consistent attention to Soviet power deterred conflict, prevented war, and protected Western values and institutions. In another example, once the U.S. security bureaucracy fully mobilized after 2001 to face the terrorism threat, large-scale terror attacks inside the United States did not recur. Likewise, if U.S. policymakers really make security in East Asia the priority they say it should be, they should be able to prevent conflict in the region from happening.

However, in a world of zero-sum security planning, U.S. policymakers will necessarily have to take risks. Even while defense planners averted conventional and nuclear war with the Soviet Union, irregular and proxy conflicts occurred in Southeast Asia, the Middle East, and elsewhere, with damage to U.S. interests. Neglecting the terrorist threat before 2001 led to a decade of costly interventions. The security challenge posed by China is arguably the most consequential the United States faces and therefore warrants the first call on attention and resources. But that will likely necessitate more risk elsewhere.

The greatest barrier to a better security strategy for Asia is the existing bureaucratic and institutional interests that will resist changes to the programs from which they currently benefit. As discussed in chapter 3, there are large defense bureaucracies, industrial contractors, military bases, local constituencies, and supporting interest groups that have grown around the current defense posture and that will resist any radical change to it. Short-range tactical airpower and surface forces of all kinds are under increasing threat in the looming military environment. But these forces also constitute the overwhelming majority of the U.S. Defense Department's current program of record. In theory, reallocating the same defense dollars into more useful programs and systems could see existing personnel, contractors, and communities transition to those new programs and systems. But that reassuring message likely won't forestall bureaucratic and political resistance from risk-averse interests that fear change.

Overcoming these barriers to change will require persistent and bipartisan leadership from civilian political leaders and policymakers. These civilian leaders must learn about the quickly changing security situation in Asia and then formulate enduring policies that successive administrations will continue. Above all, success will require strong civilian leadership to implement the changes that numerous interests are likely to resist. That is asking a lot from America's political system; but that is what the China challenge will require.

Entering a Danger Zone

The delayed response by U.S. policymakers to China's military modernization has regrettably ensured that a period of danger for U.S. and allied interests will inevitably occur around the end of this decade. China's development of its space- and land-based reconnaissance and command systems, and its land-based antiship air and naval forces, will begin to fully flower around 2020 and thereafter. However, U.S. responses, such as directed-energy missile defenses and alternatives to space-based command and control, are not likely to arrive in force until the second half of the next decade. Military improvements begun recently by China's neighbors may similarly not mature until later next decade. New U.S. long-range aircraft and missiles could arrive sooner if made an urgent priority.

China's leaders may perceive a narrow window of opportunity during which they might believe they will possess escalation dominance. These leaders might conclude that early next decade will be the last opportunity for China to settle its claims in the Near Seas and to obtain any other regional security interests its leadership feels China requires. The leaders of Imperial Germany, facing similar concerns about Russia's growing economy and military power before World War I, felt themselves under pressure to employ their military option while it was still useful.[21]

The fact that an improved U.S. military and diplomatic strategy for the region will create time pressure for China's leaders is certainly not an argument that the United States should refrain from these reforms. Prolonging the period of danger—the consequence of further delaying or even rejecting reforms—makes no sense. U.S. military planners will attempt to get through this increasingly risky period by shifting more military assets into the region. This shift will increase the vulnerability of these mostly short-range forces to Chinese attack and will magnify the risk of "use it, or lose it" instability during a crisis. In order to escape these dangers, U.S. policymakers should urgently get on with the military reforms discussed in this book, reforms designed to increase the range and reduce the vulnerability of U.S. military power in the region.

In the long run, the Asia-Pacific region will avoid major conflict only after the players in the region establish incentives that reward cooperation and punish attempts to disrupt the existing rules-based system. For these incentives to be effective, they will have to endure changes in governments and policies as well as shifts in the region's allocation of power and influence. Sadly, history is filled with occasions when swings in the balance of power, national and ethnic grievances, or the sudden arrival of aggressive leaders brought an end to long episodes of regional stability.

The United States and its partners should firmly pursue their interests; this book has described how they can do that. As they do so, they must also treat China with respect and ensure that China has a clear path for continued success, a path that does not detract from the potential of its neighbors or the United States. The United States and its partners should bolster their defenses quietly, but in full view of the PLA and China's decision makers. The United States and its allies should do nothing to cause China's leaders to lose face. But these leaders should also be fully aware of the consequences of continued assertive behavior.

Preparing for the security challenge posed by China's growing military power is not an affront to China. Indeed, these preparations show respect for China's arrival as a great power. That arrival now threatens the region's hope for a rich and peaceful future. History is now calling on the United States to again lead its partners in a new effort to sustain the region's balance and prosperity, an endeavor from which all will benefit.

Notes

Preface

1. Joint Special Operations University's publications are available at https://jsou .socom.mil/Pages/Publications.aspx.

Introduction

1. Henry Kissinger, *Diplomacy* (New York: Simon and Shuster, 1994), 826.
2. Kevin Rudd, "A Maritime Balkans of the 21st Century?" *Foreign Policy,* January 30, 2013, http://www.foreignpolicy.com/articles/2013/01/30/a_ maritime_balkans_of_the_21st_century_east_asia?wp_login_redirect=0.
3. Kurt Campbell, "Threats to Peace Are Lurking in the East China Sea," *Financial Times,* June 25, 2013, http://www.ft.com/intl/cms/s/0/b924cc56-dda1–11e2-a756–00144feab7de.html#axzz2ZtGart72.
4. Joseph Kahn, "China, Shy Giant, Show Signs of Shedding Its False Modesty," *New York Times,* December 9, 2006, http://www.nytimes.com/2006/12/09/ world/asia/09china.html?pagewanted=all&_r=1&.
5. *Annual Report to Congress: Military and Security Developments Involving the People's Republic of China 2013,* U.S. Department of Defense (May 2013), 45, http://www.defense.gov/pubs/2013_China_Report_FINAL.pdf.
6. Michael Fabey, "U.S. Asian Allies Raise Regional Stakes with Military Spending," *Aviation Week and Space Technology,* July 22, 2013, http:// www.aviationweek.com/Article.aspx?id=/article-xml/AW_07_22_2013_p31–597837.xml.
7. *Sustaining U.S. Global Leadership: Priorities for 21st Century Defense,* U.S. Department of Defense (January 2012), 2, http://www.defense.gov/news/ Defense_Strategic_Guidance.pdf.

Chapter 1. A Three-Decade Drive to a Collision

1. *The World Factbook: China,* United States Central Intelligence Agency, Economy tab, https://www.cia.gov/library/publications/the-world-factbook/ geos/ch.html.

2. Alan Heston, Robert Summers, and Bettina Aten, *Penn World Table Version 7.1*, Center for International Comparisons of Production, Income and Prices at the University of Pennsylvania, July 2012, https://pwt.sas.upenn.edu/php_site/pwt71/pwt71_form.php.

3. *The World Factbook: China*, United States Central Intelligence Agency.

4. *People's Republic of China: 2012 Article IV Consultation Report*, International Monetary Fund (IMF Country Report No. 12/195) (Washington, DC, July 2012), 38, http://www.imf.org/external/pubs/ft/scr/2012/cr12195.pdf.

5. Lucy Hornby, "Record Imports Make China World's Top Importer of Crude Oil," *Financial Times*, October 12, 2013, http://www.ft.com/cms/s/0/75d94744–332b-11e3-bf1b-00144feab7de.html#axzz2juD5PhE3.

6. *China Country Analysis Brief*, U.S. Energy Information Administration, U.S. Department of Energy, April 22, 2013, http://www.eia.gov/countries/country-data.cfm?fips=CH.

7. *Annual Report to Congress: Military and Security Developments Involving the People's Republic of China 2013*, U.S. Department of Defense (Washington, DC, 2013), 80, http://www.defense.gov/pubs/2013_China_Report_FINAL.pdf.

8. *China Country Analysis Brief*, Energy Information Administration, U.S. Department of Energy.

9. Edward Wong, "Air Pollution Linked to 1.2 Million Premature Deaths in China," *New York Times*, April 1, 2013, http://www.nytimes.com/2013/04/02/world/asia/air-pollution-linked-to-1–2-million-deaths-in-china.html?_r=0.

10. *Annual Report to Congress: Military and Security Developments Involving the People's Republic of China 2011*, U.S. Department of Defense (Washington, DC, 2011), 17, http://www.defense.gov/pubs/pdfs/2011_CMPR_Final.pdf.

11. Ibid., 16.

12. Ibid., 10.

13. Aaron L. Friedberg, *A Contest for Supremacy: China, America, and the Struggle for Mastery in Asia* (New York: W. W. Norton, 2011), 160.

14. *Annual Report to Congress: Military and Security Developments Involving the People's Republic of China 2011*, 15.

15. David E. Sanger, David Barboza, and Nicole Perlroth, "Chinese Army Unit Is Seen Tied to Hacking Against U.S.," *New York Times*, February 18, 2013, http://www.nytimes.com/2013/02/19/technology/chinas-army-is-seen-as-tied-to-hacking-against-us.html?_r=1&.

16. Edward N. Luttwak, *The Rise of China vs. the Logic of Strategy* (Cambridge, MA: Belknap Press of Harvard University Press, 2012).

17. See Edward Luttwak's presentation at the Center for Strategic and International Studies on February 23, 2013, http://csis.org/event/rise-china-vs-logic-strategy.

18. Henry Kissinger, *On China* (New York: Penguin Press, 2011), chapter 1.

19. *Annual Report to Congress: Military and Security Developments Involving the People's Republic of China 2011*, 15.

20. Ronald O'Rourke, "China Naval Modernization: Implications for U.S. Navy Capabilities—Background and Issues for Congress," *Congressional Research Service* (October 17, 2012), 17, http://www.fas.org/sgp/crs/row/RL33153.pdf.

21. Sheila A. Smith, "Japan, China, and the Tide of Nationalism," *Council on Foreign Relations*, September 19, 2012, http://www.cfr.org/asia/japan-china-tide-nationalism/p29080?cid=nlc-public-the_world_this_week-link13–2012 0921.

22. Kiyoshi Takenaka and Koh Gui Qing, "Japan PM Urges Chinese Restraint after Radar Lock-On," Reuters, February 6, 2013, http://www.reuters.com/article/2013/02/06/us-china-japan-idUSBRE9150ED20130206.

23. "Defense of Japan 2013," Japan Ministry of Defense, fig. III-1–1-2, http://www.mod.go.jp/e/publ/w_paper/2013.html.

24. Jane Perlez, "Calls Grow in China to Press Claim for Okinawa," *New York Times*, June 13, 2013, http://www.nytimes.com/2013/06/14/world/asia/sentiment-builds-in-china-to-press-claim-for-okinawa.html?_r=1&.

25. Jane Perlez and Martin Fackler, "China Patrols Air Zone over Disputed Islands," *New York Times*, November 28, 2013, http://www.nytimes.com/2013/11/29/world/asia/japan-south-korea-fly-military-planes-in-zone-set-by-china.html.

26. Alastair Gale and Min-Jeong Lee, "South Korea Expands Air-Defense Zone," *Wall Street Journal*, December 8, 2013, http://online.wsj.com/news/articles/SB10001424052702303722104579245253671874542.

27. *Annual Report to Congress: Military and Security Developments Involving the People's Republic of China 2013*, 21.

28. Sheila A. Smith, "Japan, China, and the Tide of Nationalism."

29. *Annual Report to Congress: Military and Security Developments Involving the People's Republic of China 2012*, U.S. Department of Defense, May 2012, 37, http://www.defense.gov/pubs/pdfs/2012_CMPR_Final.pdf.

30. Randy Fabi and Chen Aizhu, "Analysis: China Unveils Oil Offensive in South China Sea Squabble," Reuters, August 1, 2012, http://www.reuters.com/article/2012/08/01/us-southchinasea-china-idUSBRE8701LM20120801. See also "South China Sea," U.S. Energy Information Administration, http://www.eia.gov/countries/regions-topics.cfm?fips=SCS.

31. *Annual Report to Congress: Military and Security Developments Involving the People's Republic of China 2013*, 39.

32. Ann Scott Tyson, "Navy Sends Destroyer to Protect Surveillance Ship after Incident in South China Sea," *Washington Post*, March 13, 2009, http://www.washingtonpost.com/wp-dyn/content/article/2009/03/12/AR2009031203264.html.

33. Jane Perlez, "American and Chinese Navy Ships Nearly Collided in South China Sea," *New York Times*, December 14, 2013, http://www.nytimes.com/2013/12/15/world/asia/chinese-and-american-ships-nearly-collide-in-south-china-sea.html?_r=1&.

34. James R. Holmes and Toshi Yoshihara, "Hardly the First Time," U.S. Naval Institute *Proceedings*, April 2013, 25, http://www.usni.org/magazines/proceedings/2013–04/hardly-first-time.

35. "About Us," U.S.-China Economic and Security Review Commission, http://www.uscc.gov/about.

36. *Annual Report to Congress: Military and Security Developments Involving the People's Republic of China 2011*, cover page.

37. U.S. Government, *National Security Strategy* (Washington, DC, 2010), 17, http://www.whitehouse.gov/sites/default/files/rss_viewer/national_security_strategy.pdf.

38. Ibid., 35.

39. See the Penn World Table for international comparisons of real per capita income growth since 1950. Alan Heston, Robert Summers, and Bettina Aten, *Penn World Table Version 7.1*, Center for International Comparisons of Production, Income and Prices at the University of Pennsylvania, July 2012, https://pwt.sas.upenn.edu/php_site/pwt71/pwt71_form.php.

40. Hillary Clinton, "America's Pacific Century," *Foreign Policy*, November 2011, http://www.foreignpolicy.com/articles/2011/10/11/americas_pacific_century.

41. Bonnie S. Glaser, "Armed Clash in the South China Sea: Contingency Planning Memorandum #14," Council on Foreign Relations, April 2012, http://www.cfr.org/east-asia/armed-clash-south-china-sea/p27883.

42. *Annual Report to Congress: Military and Security Developments Involving the People's Republic of China 2013*, 22.

43. U.S. Department of Defense, *A Cooperative Strategy for 21st Century Seapower*, October 2007, http://www.navy.mil/maritime/Maritimestrategy.pdf.

44. U.S. Department of State, *Treaties in Force: A List of Treaties and Other International Agreements of the United States in Force on January 1, 2011*, http://www.state.gov/documents/organization/169274.pdf.

45. Ibid., 248.

46. "Joint Press Briefing with Secretary Panetta and Vietnamese Minister of Defense Gen. Phung Quang Thanh from Hanoi, Vietnam," news transcript, U.S. Department of Defense, June 4, 2012, http://www.defense.gov/transcripts/transcript.aspx?transcriptid=5052.

47. Mark E. Manyin, "Senkaku (Diaoyu/Diaoyutai) Islands Dispute: U.S. Treaty Obligations," Congressional Research Service, September 25, 2012, 5, http://www.fas.org/sgp/crs/row/R42761.pdf.

48. "The United States in the Trans-Pacific Partnership," Office of the United States Trade Representative Fact Sheet, November 2011, http://www.ustr.gov/about-us/press-office/fact-sheets/2011/november/united-states-trans-pacific-partnership. Calculated as a percentage of U.S. 2012 current-dollar gross domestic product of $15.684 trillion. See "Gross Domestic Product: First Quarter 2013 (Advanced Estimate)," U.S. Department of Commerce, Bureau of Economic Analysis, April 26, 2012, table 3, http://www.bea.gov/newsreleases/national/gdp/2013/txt/gdp1q13_adv.txt.

49. "The United States in the Trans-Pacific Partnership," Office of the United States Trade Representative Fact Sheet.

50. "Employment Situation Summary Table A. Household Data, Seasonally Adjusted," U.S. Department of Labor, May 3, 2013, http://www.bls.gov/news.release/empsit.a.htm.

51. "The United States in the Trans-Pacific Partnership," Office of the United States Trade Representative Fact Sheet.

52. See Richard Neustadt and Ernest R. May, *Thinking in Time: The Uses of History for Decision Makers* (New York: Macmillan USA, 1986).

53. See the introduction, notes 1–4.

54. Robert Haddick, "Doomed to Repeat It? To Understand the Rise of China, Study the Kaiser," *The American*, July/August 2008, http://www.american.com/archive/2008/july-august-magazine-contents/doomed-to-repeat-it/?searchterm=Haddick.

55. David C. Gompert, *Sea Power and American Interests in the Western Pacific* (Santa Monica, CA: RAND, 2013), 44–53, http://www.rand.org/pubs/research_reports/RR151.html#abstract.

56. See Toshi Yoshihara and James R. Holmes, *Red Star over the Pacific: China's Rise and the Challenge to U.S. Maritime Strategy* (Annapolis, MD: Naval Institute Press, 2010), chapter 2.

57. John J. Mearsheimer, "China's Unpeaceful Rise," *Current History* (April 2006): 160. See also John J. Mearsheimer, *The Tragedy of Great Power Politics* (New York: W. W. Norton, 2001), 401–2.

58. G. John Ikenberry, "The Rise of China and the Future of the West," *Foreign Affairs*, January/February 2008, 23–37.

59. Thomas Fingar, "China's Vision of World Order," *Strategic Asia 2012–13: China's Military Challenge*, Ashley J. Tellis and Travis Tanner, editors (Washington, DC: The National Bureau of Asian Research, 2012), 343–76.

60. Ruchir Sharma, "China Has Its Own Debt Bomb," *Wall Street Journal*, February 25, 2013, http://online.wsj.com/article/SB10001424127887324338604578325962705788582.html.

61. Jacqueline Newmyer Deal, "China's Approach to Strategy and Long-Term Competition," *Competitive Strategies for the 21st Century*, Thomas G. Mahnken, editor (Stanford, CA: Stanford Security Studies, 2012), 148–50.

62. See Edward Luttwak's presentation at the Center for Strategic and International Studies on February 23, 2013, http://csis.org/event/rise-china-vs-logic-strategy.

63. *Annual Report to Congress: Military and Security Developments Involving the People's Republic of China 2011*, 14.

64. Jacqueline Newmyer Deal, "China's Nationalist Heritage," *National Interest*, Jan–Feb 2013, http://nationalinterest.org/article/chinas-nationalist-heritage-7885. Newmyer Deal finds China's current form of nationalism both displays the elite's insecurities and is a disturbing zero-sum view of China's interactions with outside actors.

65. Martin Patience, "What Does Xi Jinping's China Dream Mean?" BBC, June 5, 2013, http://www.bbc.co.uk/news/world-asia-china-22726375.

66. Edward Luttwak's presentation at the Center for Strategic and International Studies.

67. *Annual Report to Congress: Military and Security Developments Involving the People's Republic of China 2013*, 80.

68. For more on these cases see *Annual Report to Congress: Military and Security Developments Involving the People's Republic of China 2011*, 15; M. Taylor Fravel, "Regime Insecurity and International Cooperation: Explaining China's Compromises in Territorial Disputes," *International Security* 30, no. 2 (Fall 2005): 46–47, http://www.mitpressjournals.org/doi/pdf/10.1162/016228805775124534.

69. Friedberg, *A Contest for Supremacy*, 127–30.

70. Gordon S. Barrass, "U.S. Competitive Strategy during the Cold War," *Competitive Strategies for the 21st Century,* Thomas G. Mahnken, editor (Stanford: Stanford Security Studies, 2012), 71–89.

Chapter 2. It Matters Who Runs the Pacific

1. See for example, Barry R. Posen, "Pull Back: The Case for a Less Activist Foreign Policy," *Foreign Affairs,* January/February 2013, http://www.foreignaffairs .com/articles/138466/barry-r-posen/pull-back?page=show; Christopher Layne, *The Peace of Illusions: American Grand Strategy from 1940 to the Present* (Ithaca, NY: Cornell University Press, 2007); and Justin Logan, "China, America, and the Pivot to Asia," CATO Institute Policy Analysis No. 717, January 8, 2013, http://www.cato.org/publications/policy-analysis/china-ameri ca-pivot-asia.

2. National Intelligence Council, *Global Trends 2030: Alternative Worlds* (Washington, DC: Office of Director of National Intelligence, 2012), http:// www.dni.gov/files/documents/GlobalTrends_2030.pdf.

3. Ibid., cover letter.

4. Ibid., 76–78.

5. I borrow the term "Hobbesian" from Daniel Twining, a senior fellow for Asia at the German Marshall Fund of the United States and a contributor to the *Global Trends 2030* report. See "Global Trends 2030: Pathways for Asia's Strategic Future," *Foreign Policy.com Shadow Government* (blog), December 10, 2012, http://shadow.foreignpolicy.com/posts/2012/12/10/global _trends_2030_pathways_for_asia_s_strategic_future.

6. See chapter 1, notes 64–66.

7. John Garnaut, "Xi's War Drums," *Foreign Policy* (May/June 2013), 4, http:// www.foreignpolicy.com/articles/2013/04/29/xis_war_drums?page=0,3.

8. See chapter 4, note 2, where this incident is discussed more fully.

9. Henry Kissinger, *On China* (New York: Penguin Press, 2011), chapter 1.

10. For more, see John Lee, "'Asia Century' Is Overhyped—U.S. Still Trumps China," Hudson Institute, October 11, 2011, http://www.hudson.org/index .cfm?fuseaction=publication_details&id=8411.

11. Jay Solomon and Miho Inada, "Japan's Nuclear Plan Unsettles U.S.," *Wall Street Journal,* May 2, 2013, http://online.wsj.com/article/SB1000142412788 7324582004578456943867189804.html.

12. Ibid.

13. Ibid.

14. "ISAS History," Japan Aerospace Exploration Agency, http://www.jaxa.jp/ about/history/isas/index_e.html.

15. "Overview of the KOUNOTORI (HTV)," Japan Aerospace Exploration Agency, http://www.jaxa.jp/countdown/h2bf3/overview/htv_e.html.

16. "Space Transportation Systems," Japan Aerospace Exploration Agency, http:// www.jaxa.jp/projects/rockets/index_e.html.

17. Toby Dalton and Yoon Ho Jin, "Reading into South Korea's Nuclear Debate," Carnegie Endowment for International Peace, March 18, 2013, http:// carnegieendowment.org/2013/03/18/reading-into-south-korea-s-nuclear-debate/frdc.

18. Jay Solomon, "Seoul Seeks Ability to Make Nuclear Fuel," *Wall Street Journal,* April 3, 2013, http://online.wsj.com/article/SB10001424127887324883604578399053942895628.html?mod=ITP_pageone_0.

19. Choe Sang-Hun, "South Korea Shows Military Muscle in Sparring with North," *New York Times,* February 14, 2013, http://www.nytimes.com/2013/02/15/world/asia/south-korea-shows-military-muscle.html?_r=1&.

20. "Secret Cooperation: Israel Deploys Nuclear Weapons on German-Built Submarines," *Der Spiegel,* June 3, 2012, http://www.spiegel.de/international/world/israel-deploys-nuclear-weapons-on-german-submarines-a-836671.html.

21. "Arms Control and Proliferation Profile: India," Arms Control Association, August 2012, http://www.armscontrol.org/factsheets/indiaprofile.

22. Heather Timmons and Jim Yardley, "Signs of an Asian Arms Buildup in India's Missile Test," *New York Times,* April 19, 2012, http://www.nytimes.com/2012/04/20/world/asia/india-says-it-successfully-tests-nuclear-capable-missile.html?pagewanted=all&_r=0; Jatindra Dash, "India Tests Nuclear Capable Missile with Range as Far as Beijing," Reuters, September 15, 2013, accessed September 16, 2013, http://www.reuters.com/article/2013/09/15/us-india-missile-idUSBRE98E03L20130915.

23. Dash, "India Tests Nuclear Capable Missile."

24. "Arms Control and Proliferation Profile: India," Arms Control Association.

25. Frank von Hippel, "Plutonium, Proliferation and Radioactive-Waste Politics in East Asia," Nonproliferation Policy Education Center, January 3, 2011, http://www.npolicy.org/article.php?aid=44&rt=~2~6~&key=proliferation%20japan&sec=article&author=.

26. Wendell Minnick, "Taiwan Working on New 'Cloud Peak' Missile," *Defense News,* January 18, 2013, http://www.defensenews.com/article/20130118/DEFREG03/301180021/-1/7daysarchives/Taiwan-Working-New-8216-Cloud-Peak-8217-Missile.

27. Christopher Layne, *The Peace of Illusions: American Grand Strategy from 1940 to the Present* (Ithaca, NY: Cornell University Press, 2007), 160.

28. Ibid.

29. Ibid., 178.

30. Ibid.

31. Hugh White, *The China Choice: Why America Should Share Power* (Collingswood, Australia: Black, 2012).

32. Hugh White, "The China Choice: A Bold Vision for U.S-China Relations," *The Diplomat,* August 17, 2012, http://thediplomat.com/2012/08/17/the-china-choice-a-bold-vision-for-u-s-china-relations/.

33. *Global Trends 2030: Alternative Worlds,* 34–36.

34. U.S. Energy Information Administration, "International Energy Outlook 2013," July 25, 2013, tables A5 and G1, http://www.eia.gov/oiaf/aeo/tablebrowser/#release=IEO2013&subject=0-IEO2013&table=38-IEO2013&region=0-0&cases=Reference-d041117.

35. Ibid.

36. U.S. Energy Information Administration, "Russia Country Report," September 18, 2012, http://www.eia.gov/countries/cab.cfm?fips=RS.

37. U.S. secretary of defense Chuck Hagel, "Speech to International Institute for Strategic Studies (Shangri-La Dialogue)," U.S. Department of Defense, Office

of the Assistant Secretary of Defense (Public Affairs), June 1, 2013, http://www. defense.gov/speeches/speech.aspx?speechid=1785.
38. See the introduction, note 6.

Chapter 3. America's Archaic Military Machine in the Pacific
1. Stacie L. Pettyjohn, *U.S. Global Defense Posture, 1783–2011* (Santa Monica, CA: RAND Corporation, 2012), 50–54, http://www.rand.org/pubs/mono graphs/MG1244.html.
2. U.S. Department of State, Office of the Historian, *The Tehran Conference, 1943*, http://history.state.gov/milestones/1937–1945/TehranConf.
3. Pettyjohn, *U.S. Global Defense Posture, 1783–2011,* 54.
4. Ibid., 51.
5. Ibid., 51–52.
6. Ibid., 52.
7. Ibid., 52–53.
8. Ibid.
9. Ibid., 62–63.
10. Ibid., 64.
11. Ibid., 75.
12. Ibid., see table 9.1, 67–69.
13. Ibid., 72.
14. Ibid., 51–52.
15. John B. Hattendorf, *The Evolution of the U.S. Navy's Maritime Strategy, 1977–1986* (Newport, RI: Naval War College Press, 2004), 17–20.
16. Ibid., 21.
17. Robert Haddick, "The New Pacific Theater," *Foreign Policy,* September 16, 2011, http://www.foreignpolicy.com/articles/2011/09/16/this_week_at_war_ the_new_pacific_theater.
18. Robert Haddick, "NIMBYs in the South China Sea," *Foreign Policy,* April 27, 2012, http://www.foreignpolicy.com/articles/2012/04/27/this_week_at_ war_nimbys_in_the_south_china_sea.
19. Ashton Carter, "The U.S. Defense Rebalance to Asia," Office of the Assistant Secretary of Defense (Public Affairs), April 8, 2013, http://www.defense.gov/ speeches/speech.aspx?speechid=1765.
20. Thomas P. Ehrhard, PhD, and Robert O. Work, *Range, Persistence, Stealth, and Networking: The Case for a Carrier-Based Unmanned Combat Air System* (Washington, DC: Center for Strategic and Budgetary Assessments, 2008), chapter 5, http://www.csbaonline.org/publications/2008/06/carrier-based-unmanned-combat-air-system/.
21. For historical U.S. Air Force aircraft inventories, see James C. Ruehrmund Jr. and Christopher J. Bowie, *Arsenal of Airpower: USAF Aircraft Inventory 1950–2009* (Arlington, VA: Air Force Association, Mitchell Institute Press, 2010), appendix B, http://www.afa.org/mitchell/reports/MS_TAI_1110.pdf.
22. U.S. Department of Defense, *Annual Aviation Inventory and Funding Plan: Fiscal Years (FY) 2013–2042*, http://timemilitary.files.wordpress.com/2012/ 04/30yearaviation2.pdf.

23. John A. Warden III, *The Air Campaign: Planning for Combat* (Washington, DC: National Defense University Press, 1988), chapter 1, http://www.au.af .mil/au/awc/awcgate/warden/wrdchp01.htm.

24. Ibid., 1.

25. See Dan Lamothe, "Bastion Attack Kills Squadron CO, Sergeant," *Marine Corps Times,* March 22, 2013, http://www.marinecorpstimes.com/article/20120917/ NEWS/209170313/Bastion-attack-kills-squadron-CO-sergeant.

26. Maj. Gen. Edward Bolton, deputy assistant secretary of the Air Force for Budget, "Air Force News Briefing on the FY 2014 Defense Budget Proposal from the Pentagon," U.S. Department of Defense, Office of the Assistant Secretary of Defense (Public Affairs), April 10, 2013, http://www.defense.gov/ transcripts/transcript.aspx?transcriptid=5218.

27. Michael A. Miller, "U.S. Air Force Bomber Sustainment and Modernization: Background and Issues for Congress," Congressional Research Service (April 23, 2013), 42, http://www.fas.org/sgp/crs/weapons/R43049.pdf.

28. "Air Force News Briefing on the FY 2014 Defense Budget Proposal from the Pentagon."

29. Ehrhard and Work, *Range, Persistence, Stealth, and Networking: The Case for a Carrier-Based Unmanned Combat Air System,* 35.

30. "Status of the Navy," U.S. Navy, http://www.navy.mil/navydata/nav_legacy .asp?id=146.

31. Edward J. Marolda, *Ready Seapower: A History of the U.S. Seventh Fleet* (Washington, DC: Department of the Navy, Naval History and Heritage Command, 2012), 23–26, http://www.history.navy.mil/pubs/ReadySeapower .pdf.

32. Ibid., 30.

33. Ibid., 59.

34. Ibid., 104–8.

35. Combat radius refers to the maximum range an aircraft can fly from its base or last aerial refueling point before it must either return to its base or to a refueling tanker aircraft.

36. Ehrhard and Work, *Range, Persistence, Stealth, and Networking: The Case for a Carrier-Based Unmanned Combat Air System,* 74–75.

37. Ibid., 86–89.

38. Rear Adm. Joseph Mulloy, deputy assistant secretary of the Navy for Budget, "Navy News Briefing on the FY 2014 Defense Budget Proposal from the Pentagon," U.S. Department of Defense, Office of the Assistant Secretary of Defense (Public Affairs), briefing slides 11–13, April 10, 2013, http://www .defense.gov/transcripts/transcript.aspx?transcriptid=5217.

39. David H. Buss, William F. Moran, and Thomas J. Moore, "Why America Still Needs Aircraft Carriers," *Foreign Policy,* April 26, 2013, http://www .foreignpolicy.com/articles/2013/04/26/why_america_still_needs_aircraft_ carriers.

40. See "F-35C Carrier Variant," Lockheed Martin F-35C Fact Sheet, http://www .lockheedmartin.com/us/products/f35/f-35c-carrier-variant.html; and "F/A-18 Hornet Strike Fighter," U.S. Navy Fact File, http://www.navy.mil/navydata/ fact_display.asp?cid=1100&tid=1200&ct=1.

41. Brandon Vinson, "X-47B Makes First Arrested Landing at Sea," U.S. Navy, July 10, 2013, http://www.navy.mil/submit/display.asp?story_id=75298.

42. "Unmanned Combat Air System Carrier Demonstrator (UCAS-D)," Northrop-Grumman Corporation, http://www.northropgrumman.com/Capabilities/X47 BUCAS/Documents/X-47B_Navy_UCAS_FactSheet.pdf.

43. See aircraft dimension data in notes 40 and 42.

44. Sam LaGrone, "Navy Doc Reveals UCLASS Minimum Ranges and Maximum Costs," *USNI News,* June 26, 2013, http://news.usni.org/2013/ 06/26/navy-docs-reveal-uclass-minimum-ranges-and-maximum-costs?utm_ source=rss&utm_medium=rss&utm_campaign=navy-docs-reveal-uclass-minimum-ranges-and-maximum-costs&utm_source=USNI+News&utm_ campaign=aa41817624-USNI_NEWS_WEEKLY&utm_m.

45. Sam LaGrone, "UCLASS by the Numbers," *USNI News,* June 26, 2013, http://news.usni.org/2013/06/26/uclass-by-the-numbers?utm_source=rss& utm_medium=rss&utm_campaign=uclass-by-the-numbers&utm_ source=USNI+News&utm_campaign=aa41817624-USNI_NEWS_ WEEKLY&utm_medium=email&utm_term=0_914494fc00-aa41817624– 228364209&mc_cid=aa418176.

46. LaGrone, "Navy Doc Reveals UCLASS Minimum Ranges and Maximum Costs."

47. Sam LaGrone, "Pentagon Altered UCLASS Requirements for Counterterrorism Mission," *USNI News,* August 29, 2013, http://news.usni.org/2013/ 08/29/pentagon-altered-uclass-requirements-for-counterterrorism-mission.

48. Dave Majumdar and Sam LaGrone, "Navy: UCLASS Will Be Stealthy and 'Tomcat Size,'" *USNI News,* December 23, 2013, http://news.usni .org/2013/12/23/navy-uclass-will-stealthy-tomcat-size.

49. "Tomahawk Cruise Missile," U.S. Navy Fact File, http://www.navy.mil/ navydata/fact_display.asp?cid=2200&tid=1300&ct=2.

50. See the U.S. Navy Fact Files for its submarines, http://www.navy.mil/navydata/ fact.asp.

51. Ashton Carter, "The U.S. Defense Rebalance to Asia."

52. Deputy Chief of Naval Operations (Integration of Capabilities and Resources) (N8), "Report to the Congress on the Annual Long-Range Plan for Construction of Naval Vessels for FY 2014," Office of the Chief of Naval Operations (May 2013), 5, http://projects.militarytimes.com/pdfs/USN-Plan-FY2014.pdf.

53. Bryan G. McGrath and Timothy A. Walton, "The Time for Lasers Is Now," U.S. Naval Institute *Proceedings,* April 2013, 64–69, http://www.usni.org/ magazines/proceedings/2013–04/time-lasers-now.

54. Phillip E. Pournelle, "The Rise of the Missile Carriers," U.S. Naval Institute *Proceedings,* May 2013, 30–34, http://www.usni.org/magazines/ proceedings/2013–05/rise-missile-carriers.

55. Thomas A. Keaney and Eliot A. Cohen, *Gulf War Air Power Survey Summary Report"* (1993), 65, http://www.afhso.af.mil/shared/media/document/AFD-100927–061.pdf.

56. Marolda, *Ready Seapower: A History of the U.S. Seventh Fleet,* 62.

57. Gordon S. Barrass, "U.S. Competitive Strategy during the Cold War," *Competitive Strategies for the 21st Century,* Thomas G. Mahnken, editor (Stanford, CA: Stanford Security Studies, 2012), 79–81, 83–85.

58. Bureau of Arms Control, Verification and Compliance, "Treaty between the United States of America and the Union of Soviet Socialist Republics on the Elimination of Their Intermediate-Range and Shorter-Range Missiles (INF Treaty)," U.S. Department of State, http://www.state.gov/t/avc/trty/102360.htm.

59. *Sustaining U.S. Global Leadership: Priorities for 21st Century Defense,* U.S. Department of Defense (January 5, 2012), 4–6, http://www.defense.gov/news/defense_strategic_guidance.pdf.

60. "F-22 Raptor," U.S. Air Force Fact Sheet, May 8, 2012, http://www.af.mil/information/factsheets/factsheet.asp?id=199.

61. "F-15E Strike Eagle," U.S. Air Force Fact Sheet, May 21, 2013, http://www.af.mil/information/factsheets/factsheet.asp?id=102; "General Dynamics F-111D-F," National Museum of the U.S. Air Force Fact Sheet, October 30, 2009, http://www.nationalmuseum.af.mil/factsheets/factsheet.asp?id=2322.

62. Robert Hicks, "7th BW Returns from Largest B-1 Deployment in Last Decade," U.S. Air Force, Dyess Air Force Base, 7th Bomb Wing Public Affairs, July 31, 2012, http://www.dyess.af.mil/news/story.asp?id=123312166.

63. Quadrennial Defense Review Report, Office of the Secretary of Defense (February 6, 2006), 29, http://www.defense.gov/qdr/report/report20060203.pdf.

64. Quadrennial Defense Review Report, Office of the Secretary of Defense (February 2010), 31, http://www.defense.gov/qdr/images/QDR_as_of_12Feb10_1000.pdf.

65. Ibid., 32.

66. "The China Syndrome," *The Economist,* June 9, 2012, http://www.economist.com/node/21556587.

67. I thank Frank Hoffman, a senior defense fellow at the U.S. National Defense University, for this observation.

Chapter 4. China's Strategy

1. Hillary Clinton, "Remarks at Press Availability," U.S. Department of State, July 23, 2010, http://www.state.gov/secretary/rm/2010/07/145095.htm.

2. Marvin C. Ott, "The Geopolitical Transformation of Southeast Asia," Foreign Policy Research Institute, February 2013, http://www.fpri.org/articles/2013/02/geopolitical-transformation-southeast-asia.

3. Prak Chan Thul and Stuart Grudgings, "SE Asia Meeting in Disarray over Sea Dispute with China," Reuters, July 13, 2012, http://www.reuters.com/article/2012/07/13/us-asean-summit-idUSBRE86C0BD20120713.

4. *Annual Report to Congress: Military and Security Developments Involving the People's Republic of China 2011,* Office of the Secretary of Defense (2011), 15, http://www.defense.gov/pubs/pdfs/2011_CMPR_Final.pdf.

5. "China Approves Military Garrison for Disputed Islands," *BBC News China,* July 22, 2012, http://www.bbc.co.uk/news/world-asia-china-18949941.

6. *Annual Report to Congress: Military and Security Developments Involving the People's Republic of China 2013,* Office of the Secretary of Defense (May 2013), 3–4, http://www.defense.gov/pubs/pdfs/2013_CMPR_Final.pdf.

7. "Filipino Fishermen Pay Price as China Ropes Off Disputed Scarborough Shoal," *South China Morning Post,* May 23, 2013, http://www.scmp.com/

news/asia/article/1243692/filipino-fishermen-pay-price-china-ropes-disputed-scarborough-shoal.

8. Ben Blanchard and Manuel Mogato, "Chinese Police Plan to Board Vessels in Disputed Seas," Reuters, November 29, 2012, http://www.reuters.com/article/2012/11/29/us-china-seas-idUSBRE8AS05E20121129.

9. Randy Fabi and Chen Aizhu, "Analysis: China Unveils Oil Offensive in South China Sea Squabble," Reuters, August 1, 2012, http://www.reuters.com/article/2012/08/01/us-southchinasea-china-idUSBRE8701LM20120801.

10. Ibid.

11. Zachary M. Hosford and Ely Ratner, "The Challenge of Chinese Revisionism: The Expanding Role of China's Non-Military Maritime Vessels," Center for a New American Security, February 1, 2013, http://www.cnas.org/files/doc uments/publications/CNAS_Bulletin_HosfordRatner_ChineseRevisionism.pdf.

12. "Defense of Japan 2013," Japan Ministry of Defense, fig. III–1–1-2, http://www.mod.go.jp/e/publ/w_paper/2013.html.

13. Toshi Yoshihara, "War by Other Means: China's Political Uses of Seapower," *The Diplomat* (September 26, 2012): 2, http://thediplomat.com/2012/09/26/war-by-other-means-chinas-political-uses-of-seapower/2/.

14. Toshi Yoshihara, "Japan's Competitive Strategies at Sea," *Competitive Strategies for the 21st Century,* Thomas G. Mahnken, editor (Stanford: Stanford Security Studies, 2012), chapter 13, 219–35.

15. Ann Scott Tyson, "Navy Sends Destroyer to Protect Surveillance Ship after Incident in South China Sea," *Washington Post,* March 13, 2009, http://www.washingtonpost.com/wp-dyn/content/article/2009/03/12/AR2009031203264.html.

16. Andrew S. Erickson and Adam P. Liff, "China's Military Development, beyond the Numbers," *The Diplomat* (March 12, 2013): 2, http://thediplomat.com/2013/03/12/chinas-military-development-beyond-the-numbers/.

17. *Military and Security Developments Involving the People's Republic of China 2013,* 45.

18. *Military and Security Developments Involving the People's Republic of China 2011,* 27–45.

19. Vice Adm. David J. Dorsett, Deputy CNO for Information Dominance, "Press Interview Transcript," *Defense Writers Group* (January 5, 2011): 4, http://www.airforce-magazine.com/DWG/Documents/2011/January%202011/010511dorsett.pdf.

20. Williamson Murray and MacGregor Knox, *The Dynamics of Military Revolution, 1300–2050,* MacGregor Knox and Williamson Murray, editors (Cambridge: Cambridge University Press, 2001), chapter 10, 181–82.

21. Erickson and Liff, "China's Military Development, beyond the Numbers," 1.

22. For the U.S. Defense Department's formal definitions of both "anti-access" and "area denial," see U.S. Department of Defense, *Joint Operational Access Concept, Version 1.0* (Arlington, VA: Department of Defense, 2011), 6, http://www.defense.gov/pubs/pdfs/JOAC_Jan%202012_Signed.pdf.

23. Andrew S. Erickson, "Are China's Near Seas 'Anti-Navy' Capabilities Aimed Directly at the United States?" *Information Dissemination,* June 14, 2012, http://www.informationdissemination.net/2012/06/are-chinas-near-seas-anti-navy.html.

24. Eric Stephen Gons, "Access Challenges and Implications for Airpower in the Western Pacific" (PhD dissertation, Pardee RAND Graduate School, 2011), 217, http://www.rand.org/pubs/rgs_dissertations/RGSD267.html.

25. *Annual Report to Congress: Military and Security Developments Involving the People's Republic of China 2010*, Office of the Secretary of Defense, 2010, 1–2, http://www.defense.gov/pubs/pdfs/2010_CMPR_Final.pdf.

26. For examples, see various projected missile and warships costs from "Defense Acquisition: Assessments of Selected Weapon Programs," United States Government Accountability Office (GAO-13-294SP) (Washington, DC, March 2013), http://www.gao.gov/products/GAO-13-294SP.

27. Ibid.

28. Chico Harlan, "With China's Rise, Japan Shifts to Right," *Washington Post,* September 20, 2012, http://www.washingtonpost.com/world/asia_pacific/with-chinas-rise-japan-shifts-to-the-right/2012/09/20/2d5db3fe-ffe9–11e1-b257-e1c2b3548a4a_story.html.

29. *Annual Report to Congress: Military and Security Developments Involving the People's Republic of China 2012*, Office of the Secretary of Defense (2012), 8, http://www.defense.gov/pubs/pdfs/2012_CMPR_Final.pdf.

30. *Annual Report to Congress: Military and Security Developments Involving the People's Republic of China 2011*, 27.

31. "China Confirms Leadership Change," *BBC News China,* November 15, 2012, http://www.bbc.co.uk/news/world-asia-china-20322288.

32. Gons, "Access Challenges and Implications for Airpower in the Western Pacific," 60–70.

33. *Military and Security Developments Involving the People's Republic of China 2012,* 29.

34. *2010 Report to Congress of the U.S.-China Economic and Security Review Commission,* November 2010, 89–90, http://www.uscc.gov/annual_report/2010/annual_report_full_10.pdf.

35. Christopher J. Bowie, "The Lessons of Salty Demo," *Air Force Magazine,* March 2009, http://www.airforce-magazine.com/MagazineArchive/Pages/2009/March%202009/0309salty.aspx.

36. *2010 Report to Congress of the U.S.-China Economic and Security Review Commission,* 89–90. See also Gons, "Access Challenges and Implications for Airpower in the Western Pacific," 63–65.

37. Wayne A. Ulman, "China's Military Aviation Forces," *Chinese Aerospace Power,* Andrew S. Erickson and Lyle J. Goldstein, editors (Annapolis: Naval Institute Press, 2011), 38.

38. Roger Cliff, John F. Fei, Jeff Hagen, Elizabeth Hague, Eric Heginbotham, and John Stillion, *Shaking the Heavens and Splitting the Earth: Chinese Air Force Employment Concepts in the 21st Century* (Santa Monica, CA: RAND, 2011), xxii, http://www.rand.org/pubs/monographs/MG915.html.

39. Andrew S. Erickson, "China's Modernization of Its Naval and Air Power Capabilities," *Strategic Asia 2012–2013: China's Military Challenge,* Ashley Tellis and Travis Tanner, editors (Washington, DC: The National Bureau of Asian Research, 2012), table A9, 114.

40. "Su-30MKK Multirole Fighter Aircraft," Sinodefense.com, http://www.sinodefence.com/airforce/fighter/su30.asp.

41. Gons, "Access Challenges and Implications for Airpower in the Western Pacific," 85.
42. "J-11 [Su-27 FLANKER] Su-27UBK / Su-30MKK/ Su-30MK2," Global Security.org, http://www.globalsecurity.org/military/world/china/j-11.htm.
43. 2012 Report to Congress of the U.S.-China Economic and Security Review Commission, November 2012, 129, http://www.uscc.gov/annual_report/2012/2012-Report-to-Congress.pdf.
44. "Military and Security Developments Involving the People's Republic of China 2012," 24, 39.
45. Jeff Hagen, "The U.S. Air Force and the Chinese Aerospace Challenge," *Chinese Aerospace Power,* 469–71.
46. Toshi Yoshihara and James R. Holmes, *Red Star over the Pacific: China's Rise and the Challenge to U.S. Maritime Strategy* (Annapolis: Naval Institute Press, 2010), chapter 4, 98–99. See also Vitaliy O. Pradun, "From Bottle Rockets to Lightning Bolts: China's Missile Revolution and PLA Strategy against U.S. Military Intervention," *Naval War College Review* 64, no. 2 (Spring 2011): 12–14, http://www.usnwc.edu/getattachment/23a01071–5dac-433a-8452–09c 542163ae8/From-Bottle-Rockets-to-Lightning-Bolts—China-s-Mi.
47. Pradun, "From Bottle Rockets to Lightning Bolts," 12–13.
48. Ibid., 22–23, 25. See also, *Defense Acquisition: Comprehensive Strategy Needed to Improve Ship Cruise Missile Defense,* United States General Accounting Office (GAO/NSIAD-00–149) (Washington, DC: July 2000), http://www .gao.gov/assets/230/229270.pdf. This report (with which the Navy agreed) concluded that the Navy's ship self-defense improvement plans in 2000 would provide only "low" capability against projected threats in 2012. Navy ship self-protection measures implemented since 2000 have matched those projected in the GAO report. But the magnitude of today's ASCM threat clearly exceeds that contemplated in the report (see 5, 13).
49. Dylan B. Ross and Jimmy A. Harmon, "New Navy Fighting Machine in the South China Sea" (Master's thesis, Naval Postgraduate School, Monterey, CA, 2012), 32, http://www.dtic.mil/cgi-bin/GetTRDoc?AD=ADA563777.
50. Ronald O'Rourke, "China Naval Modernization: Implications for U.S. Navy Capabilities—Background and Issues for Congress," Congressional Research Service, October 17, 2012, 11–17, http://www.fas.org/sgp/crs/row/RL33153 .pdf.
51. Owen R. Coté Jr., "Assessing the Undersea Balance between the United States and China," *Competitive Strategies for the 21st Century,* 184–86.
52. O'Rourke, "China Naval Modernization," 11–17.
53. Ibid.
54. Pradun, "From Bottle Rockets to Lightning Bolts," 14, 24. See also O'Rourke, "China Naval Modernization: Implications for U.S. Navy Capabilities," 17, and *Annual Report to Congress: Military and Security Developments Involving the People's Republic of China 2011.*
55. Pradun, "From Bottle Rockets to Lightning Bolts," 24–25.
56. Ibid., 12; Annual Report to Congress: Military and Security Developments Involving the People's Republic of China 2011, 42.

57. See also Paul S. Giarra, "A Chinese Antiship Ballistic Missile: Implications for the U.S. Navy," *Chinese Aerospace Power,* 359–74.

58. Pradun, "From Bottle Rockets to Lightning Bolts," 17.

59. Eric Hagt, "Integrating China's New Aerospace Power in the Maritime Realm," *Chinese Aerospace Power,* 390–91.

60. Ibid., 390–91.

61. Pradun, "From Bottle Rockets to Lightning Bolts," 17–18.

62. Hagt, "Integrating China's New Aerospace Power in the Maritime Realm," 391–92.

63. Ibid., 392–93.

64. Pradun, "From Bottle Rockets to Lightning Bolts," 17–18.

65. Garth Hekler, "Chinese Early-Warning Aircraft, Electronic Warfare, and Maritime C4ISR," *Chinese Aerospace Power,* 136–39.

66. James Holmes, "Red Tide," *Foreign Policy* (August 12, 2013): 2, http://www .foreignpolicy.com/articles/2013/08/12/red_tide_how_strong_is_the_chinese_ navy?page=0,1.

67. Ian M. Easton and L.C. Russell Hsiao, "The Chinese People's Liberation Army's Unmanned Aerial Vehicle Project: Organizational Capacities and Operational Capabilities," Project 2049 Institute, March 11, 2013, 11–14, http://project2049.net/documents/uav_easton_hsiao.pdf.

68. Richard D. Fisher Jr., "Maritime Employment of PLA Unmanned Aerial Vehicles," *Chinese Aerospace Power,* 120–23.

69. Giarra, "A Chinese Antiship Ballistic Missile: Implications for the U.S. Navy," 369–71.

70. Ibid., 370.

71. Recent Trends in Military Expenditure Data, 2012, Stockholm International Peace Research Institute, April 15, 2013, table 3.3, http://www.sipri.org/ research/armaments/milex/Top%2015%20table%202012.pdf.

72. For example, see "Infographic: China's Military," *US-China Today,* USC US-China Institute, University of Southern California, http://www.uschina .usc.edu/article@usct?infographic_chinas_military_17718.aspx.

73. Military and Security Developments Involving the People's Republic of China 2011, 27.

74. Robert Gates, "Remarks to the Navy League Sea-Air-Space Exposition," U.S. Department of Defense, May 3, 2010, http://www.defense.gov/speeches/ speech.aspx?speechid=1460.

75. Ibid.

Chapter 5. America Pivots to Asia, then Stumbles

1. See chapter 3, notes 64 and 65, and *Quadrennial Defense Review Report,* Office of the Secretary of Defense, February 2010, 31–32, http://www.defense .gov/qdr/images/QDR_as_of_12Feb10_1000.pdf.

2. U.S. Department of Defense, *Joint Operational Access Concept, Version 1.0* (Arlington, VA: Department of Defense, 2012), foreword, http://www.defense .gov/pubs/pdfs/JOAC_Jan%202012_Signed.pdf.

3. Jim Garamone, "Pentagon Office to Coordinate New Air-Sea Strategy," *Armed Forces Press Service,* November 10, 2011, http://www.defense.gov/ news/newsarticle.aspx?id=66042.

234 NOTES TO PAGES 103–13

4. Andrew F. Krepinevich, *Why AirSea Battle?* (Washington, DC: Center for Strategic and Budgetary Assessments, 2010), 8–9, http://www.csbaonline.org/publications/2010/02/why-airsea-battle/.

5. Barry D. Watts, *The Maturing Revolution in Military Affairs* (Washington, DC: Center for Strategic and Budgetary Assessments, 2011), 1–2, http://www.csbaonline.org/publications/2011/06/the-maturing-revolution-in-military-affairs/.

6. See note 2 above.

7. Joint Operational Access Concept, ii.

8. Ibid.

9. Ibid., 9.

10. Ibid., 17.

11. Ibid., 33–36.

12. Ibid., 36–38.

13. Jan van Tol, Mark Gunzinger, Andrew F. Krepinevich, and Jim Thomas, *AirSea Battle: A Point-of-Departure Operational Concept* (Washington, DC: Center for Strategic and Budgetary Assessments, 2010), http://www.csbaonline.org/publications/2010/05/airsea-battle-concept/.

14. *Quadrennial Defense Review Report* (2010), 32.

15. Gen. Norton A. Schwartz, USAF, and Adm. Jonathan W. Greenert, USN, "Air-Sea Battle: Promoting Stability in an Era of Uncertainty," *The American Interest*, February 20, 2012, http://www.the-american-interest.com/article.cfm?piece=1212.

16. *2012 Report to Congress of the U.S.-China Economic and Security Review Commission*, November 2012, 147–55, http://www.uscc.gov/annual_report/2012/2012-Report-to-Congress.pdf. For China's expanding space capabilities, see 130–31, and the 2011 report of the China Commission, http://www.uscc.gov/annual_report/2011/2011-Report-to-Congress.pdf.

17. Thomas A. Keaney and Eliot A. Cohen, *Gulf War Air Power Survey Summary Report*, 1993, 65, http://www.afhso.af.mil/shared/media/document/AFD-100927–061.pdf.

18. Mark Gunzinger, *Sustaining America's Strategic Advantage in Long-Range Strike* (Washington, DC: Center for Strategic and Budgetary Assessments, 2010), 56, http://www.csbaonline.org/publications/2010/09/americas-strategic-advantage-long-range-strike/; see chapter 3, notes 52 and 53.

19. Ashton Carter, "The U.S. Defense Rebalance to Asia," Office of the Assistant Secretary of Defense (Public Affairs), April 8, 2013, http://www.defense.gov/speeches/speech.aspx?speechid=1765.

20. See chapter 4, notes 26 and 27.

21. Eric Stephen Gons, "Access Challenges and Implications for Airpower in the Western Pacific" (PhD dissertation, Pardee RAND Graduate School, 2011) 67–70, http://www.rand.org/pubs/rgs_dissertations/RGSD267.html.

22. Christopher J. Bowie, "The Lessons of Salty Demo," *Air Force Magazine*, March 2009, http://www.airforce-magazinecom/MagazineArchive/Pages/2009/March%202009/0309salty.aspx.

23. Ibid.

24. Ronald O'Rourke, "Navy Shipboard Lasers for Surface, Air, and Missile Defense: Background and Issues for Congress," Congressional Research Service, June 27, 2013, 14, http://www.fas.org/sgp/crs/weapons/R41526.pdf.

25. David Gompert and Terrence Kelly, "Escalation Clause," *Foreign Policy,* August 2, 2013, http://www.foreignpolicy.com/articles/2013/08/02/escalation_cause_air_sea_battle_china?page=full&wp_login_redirect=0.

26. *Annual Report to Congress: Military and Security Developments Involving the People's Republic of China 2011,* Office of the Secretary of Defense, 2011, 25–26, http://www.defense.gov/pubs/pdfs/2011_CMPR_Final.pdf.

27. T. X. Hammes, *Offshore Control: A Proposed Strategy for an Unlikely Conflict,* National Defense University Strategic Forum, June 2012, http://www.ndu.edu/inss/docUploaded/SF%20278%20Hammes.pdf.

28. Ibid., 3–4 and 11–12.

29. U.S. Energy Information Administration, "World Oil Transit Chokepoints," updated August 22, 2012, http://www.eia.gov/countries/regions-topics.cfm?fips=WOTC&trk=p3.

30. United States Navy Fact File, http://www.navy.mil/navydata/fact.asp.

31. See chapter 1, notes 29 and 32.

32. Gabriel B. Collins and William S. Murray, "No Oil for the Lamps of China?" *Naval War College Review* 61, no. 2 (Spring 2008): 84–85, http://www.usnwc.edu/getattachment/22821a31-a443-4bc7-95a6-54527ad8924a/No-Oil-for-the-Lamps-of-China—Collins,-Gabriel-.aspx.

33. Ibid., 81.

Chapter 6. A Competitive Strategy for the Pacific

1. Richard Rumelt, *Good Strategy/Bad Strategy: The Difference and Why It Matters* (New York: Crown Business, 2011), 6.

2. Robert Haddick, "Why the New National Security Strategy Isn't Strategy," *Small Wars Journal* (blog), May 27, 2010, http://smallwarsjournal.com/blog/why-the-new-national-security-strategy-isnt-strategy. See also, Rumelt, *Good Strategy/Bad Strategy,* 33–37.

3. Henry Kissinger, *Diplomacy* (New York: Simon and Shuster, 1994), 201–6.

4. Bob Woodward, *Obama's Wars* (New York: Simon and Shuster, 2010), 278–83.

5. National Intelligence Council, *Global Trends 2030: Alternative Worlds* (Washington, DC: Office of Director of National Intelligence, 2012), http://www.dni.gov/files/documents/GlobalTrends_2030.pdf.

6. See chapter 5, notes 4 and 5.

7. Rumelt, *Good Strategy/Bad Strategy,* 32, 41–44.

8. Ibid., 32, 54–57.

9. "X" (George F. Kennan), "The Sources of Soviet Conduct," *Foreign Affairs,* July 1947, http://www.foreignaffairs.com/articles/23331/x/the-sources-of-soviet-conduct; *NSC 68: United States Objectives and Programs for National Security,* April 14, 1950, http://www.fas.org/irp/offdocs/nsc-hst/nsc-68.htm.

10. Kennan, "The Sources of Soviet Conduct."

11. *NSC 68,* Conclusions and Recommendations.

12. See chapter 1, notes 16 and 17.

13. For a thorough discussion of dissuasion as a strategy, see Andrew F. Krepinevich and Robert C. Martinage, *Dissuasion Strategy* (Washington, DC: Center for Strategic and Budgetary Assessments, 2008), http://www.csbaonline.org/publications/2008/05/dissuasion-strategy/.

14. The publication *Competitive Strategies for the 21st Century,* Thomas G. Mahnken, editor (Stanford, CA: Stanford Security Studies, 2012), along with research conducted at the U.S. Naval War College and several defense think tanks in the United States and Australia, are examples of the small network of analysts studying the competitive strategic environment in the Asia-Pacific region.

15. See for example Dan Blumenthal and Phillip Swagel, *An Awkward Embrace: The United States and China in the 21st Century* (Washington, DC: AEI Press, 2012).

16. Michael Pillsbury, "The Sixteen Fears: China's Strategic Psychology," *Survival: Global Politics and Strategy* 54, no. 5 (October–November 2012): 149–82, http://www.michaelpillsbury.net/articles/Michael-Pillsbury_The_Sixteen_Fears_Chinas_Strategic_Psychology_10–03–12.pdf.

17. Ibid., 162–65.

18. See Gordon S. Barrass, "U.S. Competitive Strategy during the Cold War," *Competitive Strategies for the 21st Century,* Thomas G. Mahnken, editor (Palo Alto: Stanford Security Studies, 2012), chapter 5, 71–89; and Gordon S. Barrass, *The Great Cold War—A Journey through the Hall of Mirrors* (Palo Alto, CA: Stanford University Press, 2009).

19. Barrass, *Competitive Strategies for the 21st Century,* 83–85.

20. Thomas Mahnken makes this explicit assertion in his conclusion to *Competitive Strategies for the 21st Century,* 301–3.

21. In the 1999 NATO air campaign against Serbia, attacks against Serbian infrastructure and assets personally valuable to regime leaders may have led to Serbian capitulation. See Benjamin S. Lambert, *NATO's Air War for Kosovo: A Strategic and Operational Assessment* (Santa Monica, CA: RAND, 2001), 68–72, http://www.rand.org/pubs/monograph_reports/MR1365.html.

Chapter 7. A New Approach to America's Pacific Partnerships

1. Adm. Jonathan Greenert, USN, "Sea Change: The Navy Pivots to Asia," *Foreign Policy* (November 14, 2012), 5, http://www.foreignpolicy.com/articles/2012/11/14/sea_change.

2. For a deeper discussion of these approaches, see Patrick M. Cronin, *Flashpoints: The Way Forward in the East and South China Seas,* Center for a New American Security, March 28, 2013, 6–7, http://www.cnas.org/files/documents/publications/CNAS_Bulletin_Cronin_TheWayForward.pdf.

3. Ibid.

4. Japanese cooperation with the Philippines on maritime security has already begun; see Martin Fackler, "To Counter China, Japan and Philippines Will Bolster Maritime Cooperation," *New York Times,* January 10, 2013, http://www.nytimes.com/2013/01/11/world/asia/japan-and-philippines-to-bolster-maritime-cooperation.html?_r=2&. See also, Nitin A. Gokhale, "India's Growing Military Diplomacy," *The Diplomat,* August 16, 2013, http://thediplomat.com/2013/08/16/indias-growing-military-diplomacy/.

5. For example, see this long multimedia essay from the *New York Times* about the standoff over Second Thomas Shoal in the South China Sea, which was very sympathetic to the Philippines: Jeff Himmelman, "A Game of Shark

and Minnow," *New York Times Magazine,* October 27, 2013, http://www
.nytimes.com/newsgraphics/2013/10/27/south-china-sea/.

6. Scott W. Harold and Lowell Schwartz, "A Russia-China Alliance Brewing?"
   The Diplomat, April 12, 2013, http://thediplomat.com/2013/04/12/a-russia-
   china-alliance-brewing/.

7. S. Amer Latif, *U.S.-India Military Engagement: Steady as They Go*
   (Washington, DC: Center for Strategic and International Studies, 2012), viii,
   http://csis.org/files/publication/121213_Latif_USIndiaMilEngage_Web.pdf.

8. Carl Thayer, "Vietnam Gradually Warms Up to US Military," *The Diplomat,*
   November 6, 2013, http://thediplomat.com/flashpoints-blog/2013/11/06/
   vietnam-gradually-warms-up-to-us-military/.

9. For more on this concept, see Thomas G. Mahnken, Thomas Donnelly, Dan
   Blumenthal, Gary J. Schmitt, Michael Mazza, and Andrew Shearer, *Asia in
   the Balance: Transforming U.S. Military Strategy in Asia* (Washington,
   DC: American Enterprise Institute, 2012), 19–20, http://www.aei.org/
   files/2012/05/31/-asia-in-the-balance-transforming-us-military-strategy-in-
   asia_134736206767.pdf.

10. Bradley Perrett, "Japan Boosts Its Submarine Fleet," *Aviation Week & Space
    Technology Ares* (blog), October 22, 2010, http://www.aviationweek.com/
    Blogs.aspx?plckBlogId=Blog:27ec4a53-dcc8–42d0-bd3a-01329aef79a7&plc
    kPostId=Blog:27ec4a53-dcc8–42d0-bd3a-01329aef79a7Post:f69cd6f7-b8ac-
    4630-a720-d5b4a1e35e25.

11. George Nishiyama and Toko Sekiguchi, "Korea Threat Gives Abe a Military
    Lift," *Wall Street Journal,* April 12, 2013, http://online.wsj.com/article/SB100
    01424127887324010704578418353717932798.html?mod=ITP_pageone_2.

12. Harry Kazianis, "Vietnam to Receive Advanced Russian Sub in 2013," *The
    Diplomat,* April 2, 2013, http://thediplomat.com/flashpoints-blog/2013/04/02/
    vietnam-to-recieve-advanced-russian-sub-in-2013/. See also, Sam LaGrone,
    "Vietnam Takes Delivery of First Kilo Attack Boat," *USNI News,* November 8,
    2013, http://news.usni.org/2013/11/08/vietnam-takes-delivery-first-kilo-attack-
    boat.

13. For one such example, see T. X. Hammes, "The Danes Have the Answer," U.S.
    Naval Institute *Proceedings,* April 2013, 12, http://www.usni.org/magazines/
    proceedings/2013–04/nobody-asked-me-danes-have-answer,   and   Eric
    Wertheim, "Combat Fleets," U.S. Naval Institute *Proceedings,* April 2013, 90,
    http://www.usni.org/magazines/proceedings/2013–04/combat-fleets.

14. *Defence White Paper 2013,* Australian Government Department of Defence,
    May 3, 2013, 82–83, http://www.defence.gov.au/whitepaper2013/docs/WP_
    2013_web.pdf.

15. *Annual Report to Congress: Military and Security Developments Involving
    the People's Republic of China 2011,* Office of the Secretary of Defense, 2011,
    26, http://www.defense.gov/pubs/pdfs/2011_CMPR_Final.pdf.

16. "USPACOM Strategy," United States Pacific Command website, http://www
    .pacom.mil/about-uspacom/2013-uspacom-strategy.shtml.   The   U.S.
    Department of Defense defines "security cooperation" as, "all activities
    undertaken by the Department of Defense (DoD) to encourage and enable
    international partners to work with the United States to achieve strategic
    objectives. It includes all DoD interactions with foreign defense and security

establishments, including all DoD-administered Security Assistance (SA) programs, that build defense and security relationships; promote specific U.S. security interests, including all international armaments cooperation activities and SA activities; develop allied and friendly military capabilities for self-defense and multinational operations; and provide U.S. forces with peacetime and contingency access to host nations." See Defense Security Cooperation Agency, http://www.dsca.osd.mil/samm/ESAMM/C01/1.htm. The U.S. Army defines security force assistance as "the unified action to generate, employ, and sustain local, host-nation, or regional security forces in support of a legitimate authority." See U.S. Army *Field Manual 3-07.1*, http://usacac.army.mil/cac2/Repository/FM3071.pdf.

17. Karen Parrish, "Chairman Visits Joint Special Operations Task Force," *Armed Forces Press Service*, June 4, 2012, http://www.defense.gov/news/newsarticle .aspx?id=116601.

18. Craig Whitlock, "U.S. Expands Counterterrorism Assistance in Cambodia in Spite of Human Rights Concerns," *Washington Post,* November 15, 2012, http://www.washingtonpost.com/world/national-security/us-expands-counterterrorism-assistance-in-cambodia-in-spite-of-human-rights-concerns/2012/11/15/f2df3de8–2e59–11e2-abff-7d780620a97a_story.html.

19. Robert Burns, "Postwar Corps Looks to Return to Its Roots," Associated Press, December 4, 2011, http://www.marinecorpstimes.com/article/20111204/NEWS/112040305/Postwar-Corps-looks-to-return-to-its-roots.

20. Lt. Gen. Robert B. Brown and Maj. Brennan F. Cook, "Help Others, Help Ourselves: A Better Strategy for Security Force Assistance in the Pacific," *Armed Forces Journal,* April 2013, http://www.armedforcesjournal.com/2013/04/13616901.

21. Ibid.

22. Jim Thomas and Christopher Dougherty, *Beyond the Ramparts: The Future of U.S. Special Operations Forces* (Washington, DC: Center for Strategic and Budgetary Assessments, 2013), 71, http://www.csbaonline.org/publications/2013/05/beyond-the-ramparts-the-future-of-u-s-special-operations-forces/.

23. Mark Kenny, "Gillard Scores Coup with China Agreement," *The Sydney Morning Herald,* April 10, 2013, http://www.smh.com.au/opinion/political-news/gillard-scores-coup-with-china-agreement-20130409–2hjin.html.

24. One should not underestimate the training value of multilateral humanitarian relief exercises. Even when they lack the practice of specific combat procedures, they are still an opportunity for partners to rehearse fleet operations, air control and coordination, land maneuver, and communications—all fundamental skills needed for any military operation.

25. For more on this, see David C. Gompert, *Sea Power and American Interests in the Western Pacific* (Santa Monica, CA: RAND, 2013), chapter 5, 155–80, http://www.rand.org/pubs/research_reports/RR151.html#abstract.

Chapter 8. The Future of Airpower in the Pacific

1. Eric Stephen Gons, "Access Challenges and Implications for Airpower in the Western Pacific" (PhD dissertation, Pardee RAND Graduate School, 2011), http://www.rand.org/pubs/rgs_dissertations/RGSD267.html.

2. Maj. Gen. Edward Bolton, deputy assistant secretary of the Air Force for budget, "Air Force News Briefing on the FY 2014 Defense Budget Proposal from the Pentagon," U.S. Department of Defense, Office of the Assistant Secretary of Defense (Public Affairs), April 10, 2013, http://www.defense.gov/transcripts/transcript.aspx?transcriptid=5218.

3. Julian E. Barnes, "Pentagon Toils to Build a Bomber on a Budget," *Wall Street Journal,* November 4, 2013, http://online.wsj.com/news/articles/SB10001424052702304384104579141982099354454.

4. Marcus Weisgerber, "Future USAF Acquisitions to Focus on Pacific," *Defense News,* July 16, 2012, http://www.defensenews.com/article/20120716/DEFREG02/307160003/Future-USAF-Acquisition-Focus-Pacific?odyssey=tab|topnews|text|FRONTPAGE. See also Michael A. Miller, "U.S. Air Force Bomber Sustainment and Modernization: Background and Issues for Congress," Congressional Research Service, April 23, 2013, 29, http://www.fas.org/sgp/crs/weapons/R43049.pdf.

5. Gons, "Access Challenges and Implications for Airpower in the Western Pacific," 79–81.

6. Robert Haddick, "Size Matters," *Foreign Policy,* July 12, 2012, http://www.foreignpolicy.com/articles/2012/07/12/this_week_at_war_size_matters?wp_login_redirect=0.

7. Robert Gates, "DoD News Briefing with Secretary Gates from the Pentagon," U.S. Department of Defense, Office of the Assistant Secretary of Defense (Public Affairs), April 6, 2009, http://www.defense.gov/transcripts/transcript.aspx?transcriptid=4396.

8. Mark Gunzinger, *Sustaining America's Strategic Advantage in Long-Range Strike* (Washington, DC: Center for Strategic and Budgetary Assessments, 2010), 53–54, http://www.defense.gov/transcripts/transcript.aspx?transcriptid=5218.

9. Damien McElroy, "Pentagon Redesigns Its 'Bunker Buster' Massive Ordnance Penetrator to Combat Iran," *The Telegraph,* May 3, 2013, http://www.telegraph.co.uk/news/worldnews/middleeast/iran/10035349/Pentagon-redesigns-its-bunker-buster-Massive-Ordnance-Penetrator-to-combat-Iran.html.

10. *Annual Report to Congress: Military and Security Developments Involving the People's Republic of China 2013,* Office of the Secretary of Defense, 2013, 31, http://www.defense.gov/pubs/2013_China_Report_FINAL.pdf. See also Gons, "Access Challenges and Implications for Airpower in the Western Pacific," 159–63.

11. Gons, "Access Challenges and Implications for Airpower in the Western Pacific," 100–102.

12. Ibid., 133–34.

13. Ibid., 139.

14. Ibid., 143–49.

15. John Reed, "Predator Drone 'Useless' in Most Wars, Top Air Force General Says," *Foreign Policy,* September 19, 2013, http://killerapps.foreignpolicy.com/posts/2013/09/19/predator_drones_useless_in_most_wars_top_air_force_general_says.

16. Jason Ukman, "RQ-170: A Primer on the 'Beast of Kandahar,'" *Washington Post,* December 8, 2011, http://www.washingtonpost.com/blogs/checkpoint-washington/post/rq-170-a-primer-on-the-beast-of-kandahar/2011/12/08/gIQA7rYjfO_blog.html.

17. Robert Haddick, "Baseless," *Foreign Policy,* May 11, 2012, http://www.foreignpolicy.com/articles/2012/05/11/baseless. In December 2013 reporters at *Aviation Week & Space Technology* revealed the previously secret RQ-180, a long-range stealthy unmanned reconnaissance prototype aircraft. See Amy Butler and Bill Sweetman, "EXCLUSIVE: Secret New UAS Shows Stealth, Efficiency Advances," *Aviation Week & Space Technology,* December 6, 2013, http://www.aviationweek.com/Article.aspx?id=/article-xml/awx_12_06_2013_p0–643783.xml.

18. Guy Norris and Amy Butler, "Northrop Fights for Global Hawk as Triton Flights Start," *Aviation Week and Space Technology,* May 27, 2013, http://www.aviationweek.com/Article.aspx?id=/article-xml/AW_05_27_2013_p22–581209.xml.

19. Jim Thomas and Chris Dougherty, *Beyond the Ramparts: The Future of U.S. Special Operations Forces* (Washington, DC: Center for Strategic and Budgetary Assessments, 2013), 99, http://www.csbaonline.org/publications/2013/05/beyond-the-ramparts-the-future-of-u-s-special-operations-forces/.

20. See note 3 above.

21. Adm. Jonathan Greenert, USN, "Payloads over Platforms: Charting a New Course," U.S. Naval Institute *Proceedings,* July 2012, http://www.usni.org/magazines/proceedings/2012–07/payloads-over-platforms-charting-new-course.

22. "Program Acquisition Cost by Weapon System," Office of the Under Secretary of Defense (Comptroller)/Chief Financial Officer (April 2013), 5-5, http://comptroller.defense.gov/defbudget/fy2014/FY2014_Weapons.pdf.

23. Miller, "U.S. Air Force Bomber Sustainment and Modernization: Background and Issues for Congress," 32.

24. "SLAM-ER Missile," U.S. Navy Fact File, February 20, 2009, http://www.navy.mil/navydata/fact_display.asp?cid=2200&tid=1100&ct=2.

25. Miller, "U.S. Air Force Bomber Sustainment and Modernization: Background and Issues for Congress," 32.

26. Graham Warwick, "Darpa Tests Jassm-Based Stealthy Anti-Ship Missile," *Aviation Week and Space Technology,* September 6, 2013, http://www.aviationweek.com/Article.aspx?id=/article-xml/awx_09_06_2013_p0–613665.xml.

27. *Annual Report to Congress: Military and Security Developments Involving the People's Republic of China 2013,* 81.

28. John Reed, "A C-5 Galaxy Air Launches an ICBM. What!?" *Defensetech,* February 17, 2012, http://defensetech.org/2012/02/17/video-a-c-5-galaxy-air-launches-an-icbm-what/.

29. Amy Butler, "MDA Goes Two for Two in First Operational Test Event," *Aviation Week and Space Technology,* September 10, 2013, http://www.aviationweek.com/Article.aspx?id=/article-xml/awx_09_10_2013_p0–614997.xml.

30. Jeff Hagen, "The U.S. Air Force and the Chinese Aerospace Challenge," *Chinese Aerospace Power,* Andrew S. Erickson and Lyle J. Goldstein, editors (Annapolis, MD: Naval Institute Press, 2011), 469–71. See also, Gons, "Access Challenges and Implications for Airpower in the Western Pacific," 154–83.

31. James R. FitzSimonds, "Cultural Barriers to Implementing a Competitive Strategy," *Competitive Strategies for the 21st Century,* Thomas G. Mahnken, editor (Stanford: Stanford Security Studies, 2012), 290–92.

32. Ibid., 291.

33. Ibid., 291–92.

34. "Low Cost Autonomous Attack System (LOCAAS) Miniature Munition Capability," Federation of American Scientists, November 29, 1999, http://www.fas.org/man/dod-101/sys/smart/locaas.htm.

35. In 2014 Aurora Flight Sciences plans to fly an unmanned aircraft prototype on a 120-hour demonstration mission. See Graham Warwick, "Aurora's Orion MALE UAV Aims for 120-hr. Flight," *Aviation Week and Space Technology,* September 17, 2013, http://www.aviationweek.com/Article.aspx?id=/article-xml/asd_09_17_2013_p01–01–617219.xml.

36. Todd Harrison, *The Future of MILSATCOM* (Washington, DC: Center for Strategic and Budgetary Assessments, 2013), 8–13, http://www.csbaonline.org/publications/2013/07/the-future-of-milsatcom/.

37. Robert M. Gates and James R. Clapper, *National Security Space Strategy: Unclassified Summary* (Washington, DC: Department of Defense and Office of the Director of National Intelligence, 2011), http://www.defense.gov/home/features/2011/0111_nsss/docs/NationalSecuritySpaceStrategyUnclassified Summary_Jan2011.pdf.

38. Ibid., 1.

39. See Robert Haddick, "Lost in Space," *Foreign Policy,* February 11, 2011, http://www.foreignpolicy.com/articles/2011/02/11/this_week_at_war_lost_in_space?page=0,0.

40. Kevin Pollpeter, "Controlling the Information Domain: Space, Cyber, and Electronic Warfare," *Strategic Asia 2012-2013: China's Military Challenge,* Ashley Tellis and Travis Tanner, editors (Washington, DC: National Bureau of Asian Research, 2012), 171–73.

41. United States Air Force Chief Scientist (AF/ST), *A Report on Technology Horizons: A Vision for Air Force Science and Technology during 2010–2030* (Washington, DC: United States Air Force, 2010), ix, http://www.defense innovationmarketplace.mil/resources/AF_TechnologyHorizons2010–2030.pdf. See also, "Extreme Miniaturization: Seven Devices, One Chip to Navigate Without GPS," DARPA, April 10, 2013, http://www.darpa.mil/NewsEvents/Releases/2013/04/10.aspx.

42. Dylan B. Ross and Jimmy A. Harmon, "New Navy Fighting Machine in the South China Sea" (Master's thesis, Naval Postgraduate School, Monterey, CA, 2012), 86–102, http://www.dtic.mil/cgi-bin/GetTRDoc?AD=ADA563777.

43. "Multi-Service Office to Advance Air-Sea Battle Concept," U.S. Department of Defense, Office of the Assistant Secretary of Defense (Public Affairs), November 9, 2011, http://www.defense.gov/releases/release.aspx?releaseid=14910.

44. Williamson Murray, "May 1940: Contingency and Fragility of the German RMA," *The Dynamics of Military Revolution, 1300–2050*, MacGregor Knox and Williamson Murray, editors (Cambridge: Cambridge University Press, 2001), 154–74.
45. Ibid., 157–59.

Chapter 9. The Struggle for Control of the Western Pacific

 1. U.S. Naval Institute and AFCEA WEST 2013 Conference, "Chinese Navy: Operational Challenge or Potential Partner?" January 31, 2013, http://www .usni.org/events/2013-west-conference-exposition, video: http://www.youtube .com/watch?v=nLrO1GI8ZIY&list=PLWX4R7nG6a8moZ0bIUtkBBIqaOkbr 85zb&index=9, 21:02.
 2. An essay written by a former U.S. Navy surface warfare officer explains how U.S. naval strike group commanders can employ deception and electronic support in an attempt to disrupt adversary reconnaissance and targeting efforts. Although possibly practicable in a single case where policymakers and commanders were willing to take high risk for a particular objective, by 2020 there seems little prospect of U.S. strike group commanders sustaining such deception and concealment against the PLA in the Near Seas. See Jonathan F. Solomon, "Maritime Deception and Concealment: Concepts for Defeating Wide-Area Oceanic Surveillance-Reconnaissance-Strike Networks," *Naval War College Review*, Autumn 2013, http://www.usnwc.edu/getattachment/e2f92747- f9f1–4987–8db4–7e99874214b2/Maritime-Deception-and-Concealment— Concepts-for-D.aspx.
 3. Ronald O'Rourke, "Navy Shipboard Lasers for Surface, Air, and Missile Defense: Background and Issues for Congress," Congressional Research Service, June 27, 2013, 14, http://www.fas.org/sgp/crs/weapons/R41526.pdf.
 4. Wayne P. Hughes Jr., *The New Navy Fighting Machine: A Study of the Connections between Contemporary Policy, Strategy, Sea Power, Naval Operations, and the Composition of the United States Fleet* (Monterey, CA: Naval Postgraduate School, 2009), 11, 48, https://docs.google.com/file/ d/0B4aOmucPTb-IYjY3OTRkODMtN2NjZS00MWFmLWFhOTUtMDc0Nj QzNGQxODY0/edit?pli=1.
 5. Phillip E. Pournelle, "The Rise of the Missile Carriers," U.S. Naval Institute *Proceedings*, May 2013, 32, http://www.usni.org/magazines/ proceedings/2013–05/rise-missile-carriers.
 6. Thomas Hamilton, "Comparing the Cost of Penetrating Bombers to Expendable Missiles over Thirty Years," RAND Corporation (WR-778-AF), 2011, http:// www.rand.org/pubs/working_papers/WR778.html.
 7. Pournelle, "The Rise of the Missile Carriers," 31–32.
 8. "Tomahawk Cruise Missile," United States Navy Fact File, April 23, 2010, http://www.navy.mil/navydata/fact_display.asp?cid=2200&tid=1300&ct=2.
 9. David C. Gompert, *Sea Power and American Interests in the Western Pacific* (Santa Monica, CA: RAND, 2013), 186–88, http://www.rand.org/pubs/ research_reports/RR151.html#abstract.
10. Ronald O'Rourke, "China Naval Modernization: Implications for U.S. Navy Capabilities—Background and Issues for Congress," Congressional Research

Service, October 17, 2012, 24–26, http://www.fas.org/sgp/crs/row/RL33153
.pdf.

11. Hughes, *The New Navy Fighting Machine*, 35.

12. Owen R. Coté Jr., "Assessing the Undersea Balance between the United States and China," *Competitive Strategies for the 21st Century*, Thomas G. Mahnken, editor (Stanford: Stanford Security Studies, 2012), 186–88.

13. Ibid., 184–85.

14. Ronald O'Rourke, "Navy Force Structure and Shipbuilding Plan: Background and Issues for Congress," Congressional Research Service, December 10, 2012, 9, http://www.fas.org/sgp/crs/weapons/RL32665.pdf.

15. O'Rourke, "China Naval Modernization," 41.

16. Thomas G. Mahnken, "Striking a Strategic Balance in Asia," U.S. Naval Institute *Proceedings*, May 2013, 28, http://www.usni.org/magazines/proceedings/2013–05/striking-strategic-balance-asia.

17. Coté Jr., "Assessing the Undersea Balance between the United States and China," *Competitive Strategies for the 21st Century*, 185–86.

18. Hughes, *The New Navy Fighting Machine*, 46–47.

19. Dave Majumdar, "Work and Roughead Talk Fleet Protection," *USNI News*, May 7, 2013, http://news.usni.org/2013/05/07/work-and-roughead-talk-fleet-protection#more-3110.

20. Hughes, *The New Navy Fighting Machine*, vii–viii.

21. Ibid., viii–ix.

22. Ibid., 5.

23. Ibid.

24. Robert C. Rubel, "Cede No Water: Strategy, Littorals, and Flotillas," U.S. Naval Institute *Proceedings*, September 2013, 41, http://www.usni.org/magazines/proceedings/2013–09/cede-no-water-strategy-littorals-and-flotillas.

25. Ibid., 43–45.

26. See chapter 4, notes 62, 68, and 69.

27. Vitaliy O. Pradun, "From Bottle Rockets to Lightning Bolts: China's Missile Revolution and PLA Strategy against U.S. Military Intervention," *Naval War College Review* 64, no. 2 (Spring 2011): 17, http://www.usnwc.edu/getattachment/23a01071–5dac-433a-8452–09c542163ae8/From-Bottle-Rockets-to-Lightning-Bolts—China-s-Mi.

28. Unit cost from *Defense Acquisitions: Assessment of Selected Weapon Programs*, Government Accountability Office (GAO-13–294SP), March 2013, 95, http://www.gao.gov/assets/660/653379.pdf.

29. Dan Reiter, *How Wars End* (Princeton, NJ: Princeton University Press, 2009), 20–21.

30. John A. Warden III, "Strategy and Airpower," *Air & Space Power Journal*, 25, no.1 (2011): 67–71, http://www.airpower.maxwell.af.mil/airchronicles/apj/2011/2011–1/2011_1_04_warden.pdf.

31. Ibid., 71.

32. GAO, *Defense Acquisitions: Assessment of Selected Weapon Programs*, 69; ibid., 65. The unit cost is $136.8 million; multiplied by 24 (two squadrons) equals $3.3 billion.

33. Ibid., 139.

34. Guy M. Snodgrass, "Naval Aviation's Transition Starts with Why," U.S. Naval Institute *Proceedings,* September 2013, 19, http://www.usni.org/magazines/proceedings/2013–09/naval-aviations-transition-starts-why.

35. Dave Kurtz, "Dawn of the Expeditionary Growler," U.S. Naval Institute *Proceedings,* September 2013, 24–25, http://www.usni.org/magazines/proceedings/2013–09/dawn-expeditionary-growler.

36. G. J. Flynn, *Marine Corps Operating Concepts: Assuring Littoral Access . . . Proven Crisis Response* (Quantico, VA: United States Marine Corps, June 2010), 1, http://www.dtic.mil/futurejointwarfare/strategic/usmc_oc.pdf.

37. Ibid., 1–2.

38. Ibid., 97–98.

39. Robert Gates, "Statement on Department Budget and Efficiencies," U.S. Department of Defense, Office of the Assistant Secretary of Defense (Public Affairs), January 6, 2011, http://www.defense.gov/speeches/speech.aspx?speech id=1527.

40. Paul T. Deutsch, "The EFV Is Dead: Now What?" *The Marine Corps Gazette,* December 2011, http://www.mca-marines.org/gazette/article/efv-dead.

41. Pradun, "From Bottle Rockets to Lightning Bolts," 14.

42. Robert O. Work and F. G. Hoffman, "Hitting the Beach in the 21st Century," U.S. Naval Institute *Proceedings,* November 2010, http://www.usni.org/magazines/proceedings/2010–11/hitting-beach-21st-century.

43. Sergei DeSilva-Ranasinghe, "The U.S. Marine Corps Surges to the Asia-Pacific," *The Diplomat,* December 11, 2012, http://thediplomat.com/2012/12/11/our-institutional-dna-the-u-s-marine-corps-surges-to-the-asia-pacific/.

44. Flynn, *Marine Corps Operating Concepts,* 3–4.

45. As an example, the U.S. Marine Corps is helping Japan to build an amphibious assault capacity. See Helene Cooper, "In Japan's Drill with the U.S., a Message for Beijing," *New York Times,* February 22, 2014, http://www.nytimes.com/2014/02/23/world/asia/in-japans-drill-with-the-us-a-message-for-beijing.html?_r=0.

46. *Sustaining U.S. Global Leadership: Priorities for 21st Century Defense,* U.S. Department of Defense (January 2012), 2, http://www.defense.gov/news/Defense_Strategic_Guidance.pdf.

47. "Senkakus a 'Core Interest,' Chinese Military Scholar Tells Japan," *Japan Times,* August 20, 2013, http://www.japantimes.co.jp/news/2013/08/20/national/senkakus-a-core-interest-chinese-military-scholar-tells-japan/#.Uh4 xmz_BwYR. See also "Department of Defense Press Briefing with Secretary Hagel and Gen. Chang from the Pentagon," U.S. Department of Defense, Office of the Assistant Secretary of Defense (Public Affairs), August 19, 2013, http://www.defense.gov/transcripts/transcript.aspx?transcriptid=5289.

48. Gompert, *Sea Power and American Interests in the Western Pacific,* 144–47.

49. Ibid., 148.

50. Edward S. Miller, *War Plan Orange: The U.S. Strategy to Defeat Japan, 1897–1945* (Annapolis, MD: Naval Institute Press, 1991), 10.

Chapter 10. A New American Strategy for the Asia-Pacific Region

1. The combined armaments production in 1943 of the Allied powers (United States, Soviet Union, and Great Britain) exceeded that of Germany and Japan by a ratio of 3.4 to 1. See Paul Kennedy, *The Rise and Fall of the Great Powers* (New York: Random House, 1987), 355, table 35.

2. That was the conclusion of Marshal Sergei Akhromeyev, chief of the Soviet General Staff at the end of the Cold War. See chapter 6, note 19.

3. Hugh White, "The China Choice: A Bold Vision for U.S.-China Relations," *The Diplomat* (August 17, 2012): 2, http://thediplomat.com/2012/08/17/the-china-choice-a-bold-vision-for-u-s-china-relations/.

4. Joseph Bosco, "Entrapment and Abandonment in Asia," *The National Interest*, July 8, 2013, http://nationalinterest.org/commentary/entrapment-abandonment-asia-8697.

5. "U.S. Public, Experts Differ on China Policies," Pew Research Global Attitudes Project, September 18, 2012, http://www.pewglobal.org/2012/09/18/u-s-public-experts-differ-on-china-policies/.

6. Andrew Kohut, "American International Engagement on the Rocks," Pew Research Global Attitudes Project, July 11, 2013, http://www.pewglobal.org/2013/07/11/american-international-engagement-on-the-rocks/.

7. "U.S. Public, Experts Differ on China Policies," Pew Research Global Attitudes Project, September 18, 2012.

8. Paul Johnson, *The Birth of the Modern: World Society 1815–1830* (New York: Harper Collins 1991), 9–11.

9. Gian Gentile, "Vietnam: Ending the Lost War," *Between War and Peace: How America Ends Its Wars,* Matthew Moten, editor (New York: Free Press, 2011), 263–64.

10. Rick Atkinson, *Crusade: The Untold Story of the Persian Gulf War* (New York: Houghton Mifflin, 1993), 349–53.

11. Graham Allison and Philip Zelikow, *Essence of Decision: Explaining the Cuban Missile Crisis* (New York: Addison-Wesley, 1999), 121–29.

12. "Defense of Japan 2013," Japan Ministry of Defense, pt. I, sec. 2, p. 4, http://www.mod.go.jp/e/publ/w_paper/2013.html.

13. Yuka Hayashi, "Japan Defense White Paper Raises Nationalist Tone on Defense, Calls for Stronger Ties with the U.S.," *Wall Street Journal,* July 9, 2013, http://online.wsj.com/article/SB10001424127887323823004578594703681295448.html#printMode.

14. "Defense of Japan 2013," pt. III, sec. 1, pp. 218–19.

15. Michael Fabey, "U.S. Asian Allies Raise Regional Stakes with Military Spending," *Aviation Week and Space Technology,* July 22, 2013, http://www.aviationweek.com/Article.aspx?id=/article-xml/AW_07_22_2013_p31-597837.xml.

16. Examples include Hugh White (see note 3, above); Christopher Layne, *The Peace of Illusions: American Grand Strategy from 1940 to the Present* (Ithaca, NY: Cornell University Press, 2007); and Barry R. Posen, "Pull Back: The Case for a Less Activist Foreign Policy," *Foreign Affairs,* January/February 2013, http://www.foreignaffairs.com/articles/138466/barry-r-posen/pull-back?page=show.

17. See for example the remarks of Gen. James Cartwright, USMC (Ret.), from chapter 3 note 66.

18. See for example, Norman Angell, *The Great Illusion* (reprint, New York: Cosimo, 2007), first published in 1909.

19. "X" (George F. Kennan), "The Sources of Soviet Conduct," *Foreign Affairs,* July 1947, http://www.foreignaffairs.com/articles/23331/x/the-sources-of-soviet-conduct.

20. Chris Buckley, "China Takes Aim at Western Ideas," *New York Times,* August 19, 2013, http://www.nytimes.com/2013/08/20/world/asia/chinas-new-leadership-takes-hard-line-in-secret-memo.html?_r=0.

21. See David Fromkin, *Europe's Last Summer: Who Started the Great War in 1914?* (New York: Alfred A. Knopf, 2004).

Selected Bibliography

Publications

Allison, Graham, and Philip Zelikow. *Essence of Decision: Explaining the Cuban Missile Crisis.* New York: Addison-Wesley, 1999.

Angell, Norman. *The Great Illusion.* New York: Cosimo, 2007. First published in 1909.

Arms Control Association. "Arms Control and Proliferation Profile: India," August 2012. http://www.armscontrol.org/factsheets/indiaprofile.

Atkinson, Rick. *Crusade: The Untold Story of the Persian Gulf War.* New York: Houghton Mifflin, 1993.

Australian Government Department of Defence. *Defence White Paper 2013.* http://www.defence.gov.au/whitepaper2013/docs/WP_2013_web.pdf.

Barrass, Gordon S. *The Great Cold War—A Journey through the Hall of Mirrors.* Palo Alto, CA: Stanford University Press, 2009.

———. "U.S. Competitive Strategy during the Cold War." *Competitive Strategies for the 21st Century,* edited by Thomas G. Mahnken, 71–89. Stanford, CA: Stanford Security Studies, 2012.

Blumenthal, Dan, and Phillip Swagel. *An Awkward Embrace: The United States and China in the 21st Century.* Washington, DC: AEI Press, 2012.

Bosco, Joseph. "Entrapment and Abandonment in Asia." *The National Interest,* July 8, 2013. http://nationalinterest.org/commentary/entrapment-abandon ment-asia-8697.

Bowie, Christopher J. "The Lessons of Salty Demo." *Air Force Magazine,* March 2009. http://www.airforce-magazine.com/MagazineArchive/Pages/2009/March %202009/0309salty.aspx.

Brown, Robert B., and Brennan F. Cook. "Help Others, Help Ourselves: A Better Strategy for Security Force Assistance in the Pacific." *Armed Forces Journal,* April 2013. http://www.armedforcesjournal.com/2013/04/13616901.

Buss, David H., William F. Moran, and Thomas J. Moore. "Why America Still Needs Aircraft Carriers." *Foreign Policy,* April 26, 2013. http://www.foreign policy.com/articles/2013/04/26/why_america_still_needs_aircraft_carriers.

Butler, Amy. "MDA Goes Two for Two in First Operational Test Event." *Aviation Week and Space Technology*, September 10, 2013. http://www.aviationweek .com/Article.aspx?id=/article-xml/awx_09_10_2013_p0-614997.xml.

Butler, Amy, and Bill Sweetman. "EXCLUSIVE: Secret New UAS Shows Stealth, Efficiency Advances." *Aviation Week & Space Technology*, December 6, 2013. http://www.aviationweek.com/Article.aspx?id=/article-xml/awx_12_06 _2013_p0-643783.xml.

Campbell, Kurt. "Threats to Peace Are Lurking in the East China Sea." *Financial Times*, June 25, 2013. http://www.ft.com/intl/cms/s/0/b924cc56-dda1-11e2-a756-00144feab7de.html#axzz2ZtGart72.

Carter, Ashton. "The U.S. Defense Rebalance to Asia." Office of the Assistant Secretary of Defense (Public Affairs), April 8, 2013. http://www.defense.gov/ speeches/speech.aspx?speechid=1765.

Cliff, Roger, John F. Fei, Jeff Hagen, Elizabeth Hague, Eric Heginbotham, and John Stillion. *Shaking the Heavens and Splitting the Earth: Chinese Air Force Employment Concepts in the 21st Century*. Santa Monica, CA: RAND Corporation, 2011.

Clinton, Hillary. "America's Pacific Century." *Foreign Policy*, November 2011. http://www.foreignpolicy.com/articles/2011/10/11/americas_pacific_century.

———. "Remarks at Press Availability." U.S. Department of State, July 23, 2010. http://www.state.gov/secretary/rm/2010/07/145095.htm.

Collins, Gabriel B., and William S. Murray. "No Oil for the Lamps of China?" *Naval War College Review* 61, no. 2 (2008): 79–95.

Coté, Owen R., Jr. "Assessing the Undersea Balance between the United States and China." *Competitive Strategies for the 21st Century*, edited by Thomas G. Mahnken, 184–205. Stanford, CA: Stanford Security Studies, 2012.

Cronin, Patrick M. *Flashpoints: The Way Forward in the East and South China Seas*. Center for a New American Security, March 28, 2013. http://www.cnas .org/files/documents/publications/CNAS_Bulletin_Cronin_TheWayForward .pdf.

Dalton, Toby, and Yoon Ho Jin. "Reading into South Korea's Nuclear Debate." Carnegie Endowment for International Peace, March 18, 2013. http:// carnegieendowment.org/2013/03/18/reading-into-south-korea-s-nuclear-debate/frdc.

Defense Advanced Research Projects Agency. "Extreme Miniaturization: Seven Devices, One Chip to Navigate Without GPS." DARPA, April 10, 2013. http:// www.darpa.mil/NewsEvents/Releases/2013/04/10.aspx.

Defense Security Cooperation Agency. "Security Cooperation." http://www.dsca .osd.mil/samm/ESAMM/C01/1.htm.

Deputy Chief of Naval Operations (Integration of Capabilities and Resources)(N8). *Report to the Congress on the Annual Long-Range Plan for Construction of Naval Vessels for FY 2014*. Office of the Chief of Naval Operations, May 2013. http://projects.militarytimes.com/pdfs/USN-Plan-FY2014.pdf.

DeSilva-Ranasinghe, Sergei. "The U.S. Marine Corps Surges to the Asia-Pacific." *The Diplomat*, December 11, 2012. http://thediplomat.com/2012/12/11/our-institutional-dna-the-u-s-marine-corps-surges-to-the-asia-pacific/.

Deutsch, Paul T. "The EFV Is Dead: Now What?" *The Marine Corps Gazette,* 2013. http://www.mca-marines.org/gazette/article/efv-dead.

Dorsett, David J., Deputy CNO for Information Dominance. "Press Interview Transcript." *Defense Writers Group,* January 5, 2011. http://www.airforce-magazine.com/DWG/Documents/2011/January%202011/010511dorsett.pdf.

Easton, Ian M., and L. C. Russell Hsiao. "The Chinese People's Liberation Army's Unmanned Aerial Vehicle Project: Organizational Capacities and Operational Capabilities." *Project 2049 Institute,* March 11, 2013. http://project2049.net/documents/uav_easton_hsiao.pdf.

Ehrhard, Thomas P., PhD, and Robert O. Work. *Range, Persistence, Stealth, and Networking: The Case for a Carrier-Based Unmanned Combat Air System.* Washington, DC: Center for Strategic and Budgetary Assessments, 2008.

Erickson, Andrew S. "Are China's Near Seas 'Anti-Navy' Capabilities Aimed Directly at the United States?" *Information Dissemination,* June 14, 2012. http://www.informationdissemination.net/2012/06/are-chinas-near-seas-anti-navy.html.

———. "China's Modernization of Its Naval and Air Power Capabilities." *Strategic Asia 2012–2013: China's Military Challenge,* edited by Ashley Tellis and Travis Tanner, 61–126. Washington, DC: The National Bureau of Asian Research, 2012.

Erickson, Andrew S., and Adam P. Liff. "China's Military Development, beyond the Numbers." *The Diplomat,* March 12, 2013. http://thediplomat.com/2013/03/12/chinas-military-development-beyond-the-numbers/.

Fabey, Michael. "U.S. Asian Allies Raise Regional Stakes with Military Spending." *Aviation Week and Space Technology,* July 22, 2013. http://www.aviationweek.com/Article.aspx?id=/article-xml/AW_07_22_2013_p31-597837.xml.

Federation of American Scientists. "Low Cost Autonomous Attack System (LOCAAS) Miniature Munition Capability." November 29, 1999. http://www.fas.org/man/dod-101/sys/smart/locaas.htm.

Fingar, Thomas. "China's Vision of World Order." *Strategic Asia 2012–13: China's Military Challenge,* edited by Ashley J. Tellis and Travis Tanner, 343–76. Washington DC: The National Bureau of Asian Research, 2012.

Fisher, Richard D., Jr. "Maritime Employment of PLA Unmanned Aerial Vehicles." *Chinese Aerospace Power,* edited by Andrew S. Erickson and Lyle J. Goldstein, 108–29. Annapolis, MD: Naval Institute Press, 2011.

FitzSimonds, James R. "Cultural Barriers to Implementing a Competitive Strategy." *Competitive Strategies for the 21st Century,* edited by Thomas G. Mahnken, 289–300. Stanford, CA: Stanford Security Studies, 2012.

Flynn, G. J. *Marine Corps Operating Concepts: Assuring Littoral Access . . . Proven Crisis Response.* Quantico, VA: United States Marine Corps, 2010.

Fravel, M. Taylor. "Regime Insecurity and International Cooperation: Explaining China's Compromises in Territorial Disputes." *International Security* 30, no. 2 (2005): 46–83.

Friedberg, Aaron L. *A Contest for Supremacy: China, America, and the Struggle for Mastery in Asia.* New York: W. W. Norton, 2011.

Fromkin, David. *Europe's Last Summer: Who Started the Great War in 1914?* New York: Alfred A. Knopf, 2004.

Garamone, Jim. "Pentagon Office to Coordinate New Air-Sea Strategy." Armed Forces Press Service, November 10, 2011. http://www.defense.gov/news/news article.aspx?id=66042.

Garnaut, John. "Xi's War Drums." *Foreign Policy,* May/June 2013. http://www .foreignpolicy.com/articles/2013/04/29/xis_war_drums?page=0,3.

Gates, Robert. "DoD News Briefing with Secretary Gates from the Pentagon." U.S. Department of Defense, Office of the Assistant Secretary of Defense (Public Affairs), April 6, 2009. http://www.defense.gov/transcripts/transcript .aspx?transcriptid=4396.

———. "Remarks to the Navy League Sea-Air-Space Exposition." U.S. Department of Defense, May 3, 2010. http://www.defense.gov/speeches/speech.aspx?speech id=1460.

———. "Statement on Department Budget and Efficiencies." U.S. Department of Defense, Office of the Assistant Secretary of Defense (Public Affairs), January 6, 2011. http://www.defense.gov/speeches/speech.aspx?speechid=1527.

Gates, Robert M., and James R. Clapper. *National Security Space Strategy: Unclassified Summary.* Washington, DC: Department of Defense and Office of the Director of National Intelligence, 2011.

Gentile, Gian. "Vietnam: Ending the Lost War." *Between War and Peace: How America Ends Its Wars,* edited by Matthew Moten, 259–80. New York: Free Press, 2011.

Giarra, Paul S. "A Chinese Antiship Ballistic Missile: Implications for the U.S. Navy." *Chinese Aerospace Power,* edited by Andrew S. Erickson and Lyle J. Goldstein, 359–74. Annapolis, MD: Naval Institute Press, 2011.

Glaser, Bonnie S. "Armed Clash in the South China Sea: Contingency Planning Memorandum #14." *Council on Foreign Relations,* April 2012. http://www .cfr.org/east-asia/armed-clash-south-china-sea/p27883.

GlobalSecurity.org. "J-11 [Su-27 FLANKER] Su-27UBK / Su-30MKK/ Su-30MK2." http://www.globalsecurity.org/military/world/china/j-11.htm.

Gokhale, Nitin A. "India's Growing Military Diplomacy." *The Diplomat,* August 16, 2013. http://thediplomat.com/2013/08/16/indias-growing-military-diplo macy/.

Gompert, David C. *Sea Power and American Interests in the Western Pacific.* Santa Monica, CA: RAND Corporation, 2013.

Gompert, David, and Terrence Kelly. "Escalation Clause." *Foreign Policy,* August 2, 2013. http://www.foreignpolicy.com/articles/2013/08/02/escalation_cause_ air_sea_battle_china?page=full&wp_login_redirect=0.

Gons, Eric Stephen. "Access Challenges and Implications for Airpower in the Western Pacific." PhD diss., Pardee RAND Graduate School, 2011.

Greenert, Jonathan. "Payloads over Platforms: Charting a New Course." U.S. Naval Institute *Proceedings,* July 2012. http://www.usni.org/magazines/ proceedings/2012–07/payloads-over-platforms-charting-new-course.

———. "Sea Change: The Navy Pivots to Asia." *Foreign Policy,* November 14, 2012. http://www.foreignpolicy.com/articles/2012/11/14/sea_change.

Gunzinger, Mark. *Sustaining America's Strategic Advantage in Long-Range Strike.* Washington, DC: Center for Strategic and Budgetary Assessments, 2010.

Haddick, Robert. "Baseless." *Foreign Policy,* May 11, 2012. http://www.foreign policy.com/articles/2012/05/11/baseless.

———. "Doomed to Repeat It? To Understand the Rise of China, Study the Kaiser." *The American,* July/August 2008. http://www.american.com/archive /2008/july-august-magazine-contents/doomed-to-repeat-it/?search term=Haddick.

———. "Lost in Space." *Foreign Policy,* February 11, 2011. http://www.foreign policy.com/articles/2011/02/11/this_week_at_war_lost_in_space?page=0,0.

———. "The New Pacific Theater." *Foreign Policy,* September 16, 2011. http:// www.foreignpolicy.com/articles/2011/09/16/this_week_at_war_the_new_ pacific_theater.

———. "NIMBYs in the South China Sea." *Foreign Policy,* April 27, 2012. http:// www.foreignpolicy.com/articles/2012/04/27/this_week_at_war_nimbys_in_ the_south_china_sea.

———. "Size Matters." *Foreign Policy,* July 12, 2012. http://www.foreignpolicy .com/articles/2012/07/12/this_week_at_war_size_matters?wp_login_ redirect=0.

———. "Why the New National Security Strategy Isn't Strategy." *Small Wars Journal* (blog), May 27, 2010. http://smallwarsjournal.com/blog/why-the-new-national-security-strategy-isnt-strategy.

Hagen, Jeff. "The U.S. Air Force and the Chinese Aerospace Challenge." *Chinese Aerospace Power,* edited by Andrew S. Erickson and Lyle J. Goldstein, 466–76. Annapolis, MD: Naval Institute Press, 2011.

Hagt, Eric. "Integrating China's New Aerospace Power in the Maritime Realm." *Chinese Aerospace Power,* edited by Andrew S. Erickson and Lyle J. Goldstein, 377–406. Annapolis, MD: Naval Institute Press, 2011.

Hamilton, Thomas. "Comparing the Cost of Penetrating Bombers to Expendable Missiles over Thirty Years." Santa Monica, CA: RAND Corporation, 2011. http://www.rand.org/pubs/working_papers/WR778.html.

Hammes, T. X. "The Danes Have the Answer." U.S. Naval Institute *Proceedings,* April 2013. http://www.usni.org/magazines/proceedings/2013–04/nobody-ask ed-me-danes-have-answer.

———. *Offshore Control: A Proposed Strategy for an Unlikely Conflict.* National Defense University Strategic Forum, June 2012. http://www.ndu.edu/ inss/docUploaded/SF%20278%20Hammes.pdf.

Harold, Scott W., and Lowell Schwartz. "A Russia-China Alliance Brewing?" *The Diplomat,* April 12, 2013. http://thediplomat.com/2013/04/12/a-russia-china-alliance-brewing/.

Harrison, Todd. *The Future of MILSATCOM.* Washington, DC: Center for Strategic and Budgetary Assessments, 2013.

Hattendorf, John B. *The Evolution of the U.S. Navy's Maritime Strategy, 1977–1986.* Newport, RI: Naval War College Press, 2004.

Hekler, Garth. "Chinese Early-Warning Aircraft, Electronic Warfare, and Maritime C4ISR." *Chinese Aerospace Power,* edited by Andrew S. Erickson and Lyle J. Goldstein, 130–50. Annapolis, MD: Naval Institute Press, 2011.

Heston, Alan, Robert Summers, and Bettina Aten. *Penn World Table Version 7.1.* Center for International Comparisons of Production, Income and Prices at the University of Pennsylvania, July 2012. https://pwt.sas.upenn.edu/php_site/ pwt71/pwt71_form.php.

Hicks, Robert. "7th BW Returns from Largest B-1 Deployment in Last Decade." U.S. Air Force, Dyess Air Force Base, 7th Bomb Wing Public Affairs, July 31, 2012. http://www.dyess.af.mil/news/story.asp?id=123312166.

Holmes, James R. "Red Tide." *Foreign Policy*, August 12, 2013. http://www .foreignpolicy.com/articles/2013/08/12/red_tide_how_strong_is_the_chinese_ navy?page=0,1.

Holmes, James R., and Toshi Yoshihara. "Hardly the First Time." U.S. Naval Institute *Proceedings*, April 2013. http://www.usni.org/magazines/proceedings/ 2013–04/hardly-first-time.

Hosford, Zachary M., and Ely Ratner. "The Challenge of Chinese Revisionism: The Expanding Role of China's Non-Military Maritime Vessels." Center for a New American Security, February 1, 2013. http://www.cnas.org/files/ documents/publications/CNAS_Bulletin_HosfordRatner_ChineseRevisionism .pdf.

Hughes, Wayne P., Jr. *The New Navy Fighting Machine: A Study of the Connections between Contemporary Policy, Strategy, Sea Power, Naval Operations, and the Composition of the United States Fleet.* Monterey, CA: Naval Postgraduate School, 2009.

Ikenberry, G. John. "The Rise of China and the Future of the West." *Foreign Affairs* 87, no. 1 (2008): 23–37.

International Monetary Fund. *People's Republic of China: 2012 Article IV Consultation Report.* IMF Country Report No. 12/195. Washington, DC: July 2012. http://www.imf.org/external/pubs/ft/scr/2012/cr12195.pdf.

Japan Aerospace Exploration Agency. *ISAS History.* http://www.jaxa.jp/about/ history/isas/index_e.html.

———. "Overview of the KOUNOTORI (HTV)." http://www.jaxa.jp/countdown/ h2bf3/overview/htv_e.html.

———. "Space Transportation Systems." http://www.jaxa.jp/projects/rockets/ind ex_e.html.

Japan Ministry of Defense. "Defense of Japan 2013." http://www.mod.go.jp/e/publ/ w_paper/2013.html.

Johnson, Paul. *The Birth of the Modern: World Society 1815–1830.* New York: Harper Collins, 1991.

Kazianis, Harry. "Vietnam to Receive Advanced Russian Sub in 2013." *The Diplomat*, April 2, 2013. http://thediplomat.com/flashpoints-blog/2013/04/02/ vietnam-to-recieve-advanced-russian-sub-in-2013/.

Keaney, Thomas A., and Eliot A. Cohen. *Gulf War Air Power Survey Summary Report.* Washington, DC: U.S. Air Force, 1993.

Kennedy, Paul. *The Rise and Fall of the Great Powers.* New York: Random House, 1987.

Kissinger, Henry. *Diplomacy.* New York: Simon and Shuster, 1994.

———. *On China.* New York: Penguin Press, 2011.

Knox, MacGregor, and Williamson Murray. *The Dynamics of Military Revolution, 1300–2050*, edited by MacGregor Knox and Williamson Murray, 175–94. Cambridge: Cambridge University Press, 2001.

Kohut, Andrew. "American International Engagement on the Rocks." Pew Research Global Attitudes Project, July 11, 2013. http://www.pewglobal.org/ 2013/07/11/american-international-engagement-on-the-rocks/.

Krepinevich, Andrew F. *Why AirSea Battle?* Washington, DC: Center for Strategic and Budgetary Assessments, 2010.

Krepinevich, Andrew F., and Robert C. Martinage. *Dissuasion Strategy.* Washington, DC: Center for Strategic and Budgetary Assessments, 2008.

Kurtz, Dave. "Dawn of the Expeditionary Growler." U.S. Naval Institute *Proceedings,* September 2013. http://www.usni.org/magazines/proceedings/2013–09/dawn-expeditionary-growler.

LaGrone, Sam. "Navy Doc Reveals UCLASS Minimum Ranges and Maximum Costs." *USNI News,* June 26, 2013. http://news.usni.org/2013/06/26/navy-docs-reveal-uclass-minimum-ranges-and-maximum-costs?utm_source=rss&utm_medium=rss&utm_campaign=navy-docs-reveal-uclass-minimum-ranges-and-maximum-costs&utm_source=USNI+News&utm_campaign=aa41817624-USNI_NEWS_WEEKLY&utm_m.

———. "Pentagon Altered UCLASS Requirements for Counterterrorism Mission." *USNI News,* August 29, 2013. http://news.usni.org/2013/08/29/pentagon-altered-uclass-requirements-for-counterterrorism-mission.

———. "UCLASS by the Numbers." *USNI News,* June 26, 2013. http://news.usni.org/2013/06/26/uclass-by-the-numbers?utm_source=rss&utm_medium=rss&utm_campaign=uclass-by-the-numbers&utm_source=USNI+News&utm_campaign=aa41817624-USNI_NEWS_WEEKLY&utm_medium=email&utm_term=0_914494fc00-aa41817624–228364209&mc_cid=aa418176.

———. "Vietnam Takes Delivery of First Kilo Attack Boat." *USNI News,* November 8, 2013. http://news.usni.org/2013/11/08/vietnam-takes-delivery-first-kilo-attack-boat.

Lambert, Benjamin S. *NATO's Air War for Kosovo: A Strategic and Operational Assessment.* Santa Monica, CA: RAND Corporation, 2001.

Latif, S. Amer. *U.S.-India Military Engagement: Steady as They Go.* Washington, DC: Center for Strategic and International Studies, 2012.

Layne, Christopher. *The Peace of Illusions: American Grand Strategy from 1940 to the Present.* Ithaca, NY: Cornell University Press, 2007.

Lee, John. "'Asia Century' Is Overhyped—U.S. Still Trumps China." Hudson Institute, October 11, 2011. http://www.hudson.org/index.cfm?fuseaction=publication_details&id=8411.

Lockheed Martin Corporation. "F-35C Carrier Variant." http://www.lockheedmartin.com/us/products/f35/f-35c-carrier-variant.html

Logan, Justin. "China, America, and the Pivot to Asia." CATO Institute Policy Analysis No. 71, January 8, 2013. http://www.cato.org/publications/policy-analysis/china-america-pivot-asia.

Luttwak, Edward N. *The Rise of China vs. the Logic of Strategy.* Cambridge, MA: Belknap Press of Harvard University Press, 2012.

Mahnken, Thomas G. "Striking a Strategic Balance in Asia." U.S. Naval Institute *Proceedings,* May 2013. http://www.usni.org/magazines/proceedings/2013–05/striking-strategic-balance-asia.

Mahnken, Thomas G., Thomas Donnelly, Dan Blumenthal, Gary J. Schmitt, Michael Maza, Andrew Sheare. *Asia in the Balance: Transforming U.S. Military Strategy in Asia.* Washington, DC: American Enterprise Institute, 2012.

Majumdar, Dave. "Work and Roughead Talk Fleet Protection." *USNI News,* May 7, 2013. http://news.usni.org/2013/05/07/work-and-roughead-talk-fleet-protection#more-3110.

Majumdar, Dave, and Sam LaGrone. "Navy: UCLASS Will Be Stealthy and 'Tomcat Size.'" *USNI News,* December 23, 2013. http://news.usni.org/2013/12/23/navy-uclass-will-stealthy-tomcat-size.

Manyin, Mark E. "Senkaku (Diaoyu/Diaoyutai) Islands Dispute: U.S. Treaty Obligations." Congressional Research Service, September 25, 2012. http://www.fas.org/sgp/crs/row/R42761.pdf.

Marolda, Edward J. *Ready Seapower: A History of the U.S. Seventh Fleet.* Washington DC: Department of the Navy, Naval History and Heritage Command, 2012.

McGrath, Bryan G., and Timothy A. Walton. "The Time for Lasers Is Now." U.S. Naval Institute *Proceedings,* April 2013. http://www.usni.org/magazines/proceedings/2013–04/time-lasers-now.

Mearsheimer, John J. "China's Unpeaceful Rise." *Current History* (April 2006): 160–62.

———. *The Tragedy of Great Power Politics.* New York: W. W. Norton, 2001.

Miller, Edward S. *War Plan Orange: The U.S. Strategy to Defeat Japan, 1897–1945.* Annapolis, MD: Naval Institute Press, 1991.

Miller, Michael A. "U.S. Air Force Bomber Sustainment and Modernization: Background and Issues for Congress." Congressional Research Service, April 23, 2013. http://www.fas.org/sgp/crs/weapons/R43049.pdf.

Minnick, Wendell. "Taiwan Working on New 'Cloud Peak' Missile." *Defense News,* January 18, 2013. http://www.defensenews.com/article/20130118/DEFREG03/301180021/-1/7daysarchives/Taiwan-Working-New-8216-Cloud-Peak-8217-Missile.

National Intelligence Council. *Global Trends 2030: Alternative Worlds.* Washington, DC: Office of the Director of National Intelligence, 2012.

National Museum of the U.S. Air Force. "General Dynamics F-111D-F." National Museum of the U.S. Air Force Fact Sheet, October 30, 2009. http://www.nationalmuseum.af.mil/factsheets/factsheet.asp?id=2322.

Neustadt, Richard, and Ernest R. May. *Thinking in Time: The Uses of History for Decision Makers.* New York: Macmillan USA, 1986.

Newmyer Deal, Jacqueline. "China's Approach to Strategy and Long-Term Competition." *Competitive Strategies for the 21st Century,* edited by Thomas G. Mahnken, 147–67. Stanford, CA: Stanford Security Studies, 2012.

———. "China's Nationalist Heritage." *National Interest,* Jan–Feb 2013. http://nationalinterest.org/article/chinas-nationalist-heritage-7885.

Norris, Guy, and Amy Butler. "Northrop Fights for Global Hawk as Triton Flights Start." *Aviation Week and Space Technology,* May 27, 2013. http://www.aviationweek.com/Article.aspx?id=/article-xml/AW_05_27_2013_p22–581209.xml.

Northrop-Grumman Corporation. "Unmanned Combat Air System Carrier Demonstrator (UCAS-D)." 2013. http://www.northropgrumman.com/Capabilities/X47BUCAS/Documents/X-47B_Navy_UCAS_FactSheet.pdf.

Office of the United States Trade Representative. "The United States in the Trans-Pacific Partnership." November 2011. http://www.ustr.gov/about-us/press-office/fact-sheets/2011/november/united-states-trans-pacific-partnership.

O'Rourke, Ronald. "China Naval Modernization: Implications for U.S. Navy Capabilities—Background and Issues for Congress." Congressional Research Service, October 17, 2012. http://www.fas.org/sgp/crs/row/RL33153.pdf.

———. "Navy Force Structure and Shipbuilding Plan: Background and Issues for Congress." Congressional Research Service, December 10, 2012. http://www.fas.org/sgp/crs/weapons/RL32665.pdf.

———. "Navy Shipboard Lasers for Surface, Air, and Missile Defense: Background and Issues for Congress." Congressional Research Service, June 27, 2013. http://www.fas.org/sgp/crs/weapons/R41526.pdf.

Ott, Marvin C. "The Geopolitical Transformation of Southeast Asia." Foreign Policy Research Institute, February 2013. http://www.fpri.org/articles/2013/02/geopolitical-transformation-southeast-asia.

Parrish, Karen. "Chairman Visits Joint Special Operations Task Force." Armed Forces Press Service, June 4, 2012. http://www.defense.gov/news/newsarticle.aspx?id=116601.

Perrett, Bradley. "Japan Boosts Its Submarine Fleet." *Aviation Week & Space Technology Ares* (blog), October 22, 2010. http://www.aviationweek.com/Blogs.aspx?plckBlogId=Blog:27ec4a53-dcc8–42d0-bd3a-01329aef79a7&plckPostId=Blog:27ec4a53-dcc8–42d0-bd3a-01329aef79a7Post:f69cd6f7-b8ac-4630-a720-d5b4a1e35e25.

Pettyjohn, Stacie L. *U.S. Global Defense Posture, 1783–2011.* Santa Monica, CA: RAND Corporation, 2012.

Pew Research Global Attitudes Project. "U.S. Public, Experts Differ on China Policies." September 18, 2012. http://www.pewglobal.org/2012/09/18/u-s-public-experts-differ-on-china-policies/.

Pillsbury, Michael. "The Sixteen Fears: China's Strategic Psychology." *Survival: Global Politics and Strategy* 54, no. 5 (2012): 149–82.

Pollpeter, Kevin. "Controlling the Information Domain: Space, Cyber, and Electronic Warfare." *Strategic Asia 2012–2013: China's Military Challenge*, edited by Ashley Tellis and Travis Tanner, 163–96. Washington, DC: National Bureau of Asian Research, 2012.

Posen, Barry R. "Pull Back: The Case for a Less Activist Foreign Policy." *Foreign Affairs*, January/February 2013. http://www.foreignaffairs.com/articles/138466/barry-r-posen/pull-back?page=show.

Pournelle, Phillip E. "The Rise of the Missile Carriers." U.S. Naval Institute Proceedings, May 2013. http://www.usni.org/magazines/proceedings/2013–05/rise-missile-carriers.

Pradun, Vitaliy O. "From Bottle Rockets to Lightning Bolts: China's Missile Revolution and PLA Strategy against U.S. Military Intervention." *Naval War College Review* 64, no. 2 (2011): 7–39.

Reed, John. "Predator Drone 'Useless' in Most Wars, Top Air Force General Says." *Foreign Policy*, September 19, 2013. http://killerapps.foreignpolicy.com/posts/2013/09/19/predator_drones_useless_in_most_wars_top_air_force_general_says.

———. "A C-5 Galaxy Air Launches an ICBM. What!?" *Defensetech*, February 17, 2012. http://defensetech.org/2012/02/17/video-a-c-5-galaxy-air-launches-an-icbm-what/.

Reiter, Dan. *How Wars End.* Princeton, NJ: Princeton University Press, 2009.

Ross, Dylan B., and Jimmy A. Harmon. "New Navy Fighting Machine in the South China Sea." Master's thesis, Naval Postgraduate School, Monterey, CA, 2012.

Rubel, Robert C. "Cede No Water: Strategy, Littorals, and Flotillas." U.S. Naval Institute *Proceedings*, September 2013. http://www.usni.org/magazines/proceedings/2013–09/cede-no-water-strategy-littorals-and-flotillas.

Rudd, Kevin. "A Maritime Balkans of the 21st Century?" *Foreign Policy*, January 30, 2013. http://www.foreignpolicy.com/articles/2013/01/30/a_maritime_balkans_of_the_21st_century_east_asia?wp_login_redirect=0.

Ruehrmund, James C., Jr. and Christopher J. Bowie. *Arsenal of Airpower: USAF Aircraft Inventory 1950–2009*. Arlington, VA: Air Force Association, Mitchell Institute Press, 2010.

Rumelt, Richard. *Good Strategy/Bad Strategy: The Difference and Why It Matters.* New York: Crown Business, 2011.

Schwartz, Norton A., and Jonathan W. Greenert. "Air-Sea Battle: Promoting Stability in an Era of Uncertainty." *The American Interest*, February 20, 2012. http://www.the-american-interest.com/article.cfm?piece=1212.

Sinodefense.com. "Su-30MKK Multirole Fighter Aircraft." http://www.sinodefence .com/airforce/fighter/su30.asp.

Smith, Sheila A. "Japan, China, and the Tide of Nationalism." *Council on Foreign Relations*, September 19, 2012. http://www.cfr.org/asia/japan-china-tide-nationalism/p29080?cid=nlc-public-the_world_this_week-link13–20120921.

Snodgrass, Guy M. "Naval Aviation's Transition Starts with Why." U.S. Naval Institute *Proceedings*, September 2013. http://www.usni.org/magazines/proceedings/2013–09/naval-aviations-transition-starts-why.

Solomon, Jonathan F. "Maritime Deception and Concealment: Concepts for Defeating Wide-Area Oceanic Surveillance-Reconnaissance-Strike Networks." *Naval War College Review* 66, no. 4 (2013): 87–116.

Stockholm International Peace Research Institute. *Recent Trends in Military Expenditure Data, 2012.* April 15, 2013. http://www.sipri.org/research/armaments/milex/Top%2015%20table%202012.pdf.

Thayer, Carl. "Vietnam Gradually Warms Up to US Military." *The Diplomat*, November 6, 2013. http://thediplomat.com/flashpoints-blog/2013/11/06/vietnam-gradually-warms-up-to-us-military/.

Thomas, Jim, and Christopher Dougherty. *Beyond the Ramparts: The Future of U.S. Special Operations Forces.* Washington, DC: Center for Strategic and Budgetary Assessments, 2013.

Twining, Daniel. "Global Trends 2030: Pathways for Asia's Strategic Future." *Foreign Policy.com Shadow Government* (blog), December 10, 2012. http://shadow.foreignpolicy.com/posts/2012/12/10/global_trends_2030_pathways_for_asia_s_strategic_future.

Ulman, Wayne A. "China's Military Aviation Forces." *Chinese Aerospace Power*, edited by Andrew S. Erickson and Lyle J. Goldstein, 34–49, Annapolis, MD: Naval Institute Press, 2011.

University of Southern California. USC US-China Institute. "Infographic: China's Military." http://www.uschina.usc.edu/article@usct?infographic_chinas_military_17718.aspx.

U.S. Air Force. *F-15E Strike Eagle.* U.S. Air Force Fact Sheet, 2013. http://www.af.mil/information/factsheets/factsheet.asp?id=102.

———. *F-22 Raptor.* U.S. Air Force Fact Sheet, 2012. http://www.af.mil/information/factsheets/factsheet.asp?id=199.

———. *A Report on Technology Horizons: A Vision for Air Force Science and Technology during 2010–2030.* Washington, DC: United States Air Force, 2011.

U.S. Army. *Field Manual 3-07.1.* U.S. Army Combined Arms Center, 2013. http://usacac.army.mil/cac2/Repository/FM3071.pdf.

U.S. Central Intelligence Agency. *The World Factbook: China,* Economy tab. https://www.cia.gov/library/publications/the-world-factbook/geos/ch.html.

U.S.-China Economic and Security Review Commission. *2010 Report to Congress of the U.S.-China Economic and Security Review Commission.* November 2010. http://www.uscc.gov/annual_report/2010/annual_report_full_10.pdf.

———. *2011 Report to Congress of the U.S.-China Economic and Security Review Commission.* November 2011. http://www.uscc.gov/annual_report/2011/2011-Report-to-Congress.pdf.

———. *2012 Report to Congress of the U.S.-China Economic and Security Review Commission.* November 2012. http://www.uscc.gov/annual_report/2012/2012-Report-to-Congress.pdf.

U.S. Department of Commerce, Bureau of Economic Analysis. *Gross Domestic Product: First Quarter 2013 (Advanced Estimate).* April 26, 2013. http://www.bea.gov/newsreleases/national/gdp/2013/txt/gdp1q13_adv.txt.

U.S. Department of Defense. *Air Force News Briefing on the FY 2014 Defense Budget Proposal from the Pentagon,* by Maj. Gen. Edward Bolton. April 10, 2013. http://www.defense.gov/transcripts/transcript.aspx?transcriptid=5218.

———. *Annual Aviation Inventory and Funding Plan: Fiscal Years (FY) 2013–2042.* http://timemilitary.files.wordpress.com/2012/04/30yearaviation2.pdf.

———. *Annual Report to Congress: Military and Security Developments Involving the People's Republic of China 2010.* http://www.defense.gov/pubs/pdfs/2010_CMPR_Final.pdf.

———. *Annual Report to Congress: Military and Security Developments Involving the People's Republic of China 2011.* http://www.defense.gov/pubs/pdfs/2011_CMPR_Final.pdf.

———. *Annual Report to Congress: Military and Security Developments Involving the People's Republic of China 2012.* http://www.defense.gov/pubs/pdfs/2012_CMPR_Final.pdf.

———. *Annual Report to Congress: Military and Security Developments Involving the People's Republic of China 2013.* http://www.defense.gov/pubs/2013_China_Report_FINAL.pdf.

———. *A Cooperative Strategy for 21st Century Seapower.* October 2007. http://www.navy.mil/maritime/Maritimestrategy.pdf.

———. Department of Defense Press Briefing with Secretary Hagel and Gen. Chang from the Pentagon. August 19, 2013. http://www.defense.gov/transcripts/transcript.aspx?transcriptid=5289.

———. *Joint Operational Access Concept, Version 1.0,* 2012. http://www.defense.gov/pubs/pdfs/JOAC_Jan%202012_Signed.pdf.

———. *Joint Press Briefing with Secretary Panetta and Vietnamese Minister of Defense Gen. Phung Quang Thanh from Hanoi, Vietnam.* June 4, 2012. http://www.defense.gov/transcripts/transcript.aspx?transcriptid=5052.

———. Multi-Service Office to Advance Air-Sea Battle Concept. November 9, 2011. http://www.defense.gov/releases/release.aspx?releaseid=14910.

———. *Navy News Briefing on the FY 2014 Defense Budget Proposal from the Pentagon,* by Rear Adm. Joseph Mulloy. April 10, 2013. http://www.defense.gov/transcripts/transcript.aspx?transcriptid=5217.

———. *Program Acquisition Cost by Weapon System.* Office of the Under Secretary of Defense (Comptroller)/Chief Financial Officer, April 2013. http://comptroller.defense.gov/defbudget/fy2014/FY2014_Weapons.pdf.

———. *Quadrennial Defense Review Report,* 2006. http://www.defense.gov/qdr/report/report20060203.pdf.

———. *Quadrennial Defense Review Report,* 2010. http://www.defense.gov/qdr/images/QDR_as_of_12Feb10_1000.pdf.

———. *Speech to International Institute for Strategic Studies (Shangri-La Dialogue),* delivered by Secretary of Defense Chuck Hagel. June 1, 2013. http://www.defense.gov/speeches/speech.aspx?speechid=1785.

———. *Sustaining U.S. Global Leadership: Priorities for 21st Century Defense.* January 2012. http://www.defense.gov/news/defense_strategic_guidance.pdf.

U.S. Department of Energy, U.S. Energy Information Administration. *China Country Analysis Brief.* April 22, 2013. http://www.eia.gov/countries/country-data.cfm?fips=CH.

———. *International Energy Outlook 2013,* tables A5 and G1. July 25, 2013. http://www.eia.gov/oiaf/aeo/tablebrowser/#release=IEO2013&subject=0-IEO2013&table=38-IEO2013&region=0-0&cases=Reference-d041117.

———. *Russia Country Report.* September 18, 2012. http://www.eia.gov/countries/cab.cfm?fips=RS.

———. *South China Sea.* February 24, 2013. http://www.eia.gov/countries/regions-topics.cfm?fips=SCS.

———. *World Oil Transit Chokepoints.* August 22, 2012. http://www.eia.gov/countries/regions-topics.cfm?fips=WOTC&trk=p3.

U.S. Department of Labor. *Employment Situation Summary Table A. Household Data, Seasonally Adjusted.* May 3, 2013. http://www.bls.gov/news.release/empsit.a.htm.

U.S. Department of State. *The Tehran Conference, 1943.* http://history.state.gov/milestones/1937–1945/TehranConf.

———. *Treaties in Force: A List of Treaties and Other International Agreements of the United States in Force on January 1, 2011.* http://www.state.gov/documents/organization/169274.pdf.

———. *Treaty between the United States of America and the Union of Soviet Socialist Republics on the Elimination of Their Intermediate-Range and Shorter-Range Missiles (INF Treaty).* http://www.state.gov/t/avc/trty/102360.htm.

U.S. Government. *National Security Strategy.* Washington, DC, 2010. http://www.whitehouse.gov/sites/default/files/rss_viewer/national_security_strategy.pdf.

———. *NSC 68: United States Objectives and Programs for National Security.* April 14, 1950. http://www.fas.org/irp/offdocs/nsc-hst/nsc-68.htm.

U.S. Government Accountability Office. *Defense Acquisition: Assessments of Selected Weapon Programs* (GAO-13–294SP). Washington, DC: March 2013. http://www.gao.gov/assets/660/653379.pdf.

———. *Defense Acquisition: Comprehensive Strategy Needed to Improve Ship Cruise Missile Defense* (GAO/NSIAD-00–149). Washington, DC: July 2000. http://www.gao.gov/assets/230/229270.pdf.

U.S. Naval Institute. "Chinese Navy: Operational Challenge or Potential Partner?" U.S. Naval Institute and AFCEA WEST 2013 Conference, January 31, 2013. http:// www.usni.org/events/2013-west-conference-exposition, video: http://www .youtube.com/watch?v=nLrO1GI8ZIY&list=PLWX4R7nG6a8moZ0bIUtkBB IqaOkbr85zb&index=9, 21:02.

U.S. Navy. *F/A-18 Hornet Strike Fighter*. 2013. http://www.navy.mil/navydata/ fact_display.asp?cid=1100&tid=1200&ct=1.

———. *SLAM-ER Missile Fact File*. 2009. http://www.navy.mil/navydata/fact_ display.asp?cid=2200&tid=1100&ct=2.

———. *Tomahawk Cruise Missile*. 2010. http://www.navy.mil/navydata/fact_ display.asp?cid=2200&tid=1300&ct=2.

U.S. Pacific Command. "USPACOM Strategy," http://www.pacom.mil/about-uspacom/2013-uspacom-strategy.shtml.

van Tol, Jan, Mark Gunzinger, Andrew F. Krepinevich, and Jim Thomas. *AirSea Battle: A Point-of-Departure Operational Concept*. Washington, DC: Center for Strategic and Budgetary Assessments, 2010.

Vinson, Brandon. "X-47B Makes First Arrested Landing at Sea" U.S. Navy. July 10, 2013. http://www.navy.mil/submit/display.asp?story_id=75298.

von Hippel, Frank. "Plutonium, Proliferation and Radioactive-Waste Politics in East Asia." Nonproliferation Policy Education Center, January 3, 2011. http:// www.npolicy.org/article.php?aid=44&rt=~2~6~&key=proliferation%20 japan&sec=article&author=.

Warden, John A., III. *The Air Campaign: Planning for Combat*. Washington DC: National Defense University Press, 1988.

———. "Strategy and Airpower." *Air & Space Power Journal* 25, no. 1 (2011): 64–77.

Warwick, Graham. "Aurora's Orion MALE UAV Aims for 120-hr. Flight." *Aviation Week and Space Technology,* September 17, 2013. http://www .aviationweek.com/Article.aspx?id=/article-xml/asd_09_17_2013_p01–01– 617219.xml.

———. "Darpa Tests Jassm-Based Stealthy Anti-Ship Missile." *Aviation Week and Space Technology,* September 6, 2013. http://www.aviationweek.com/Article. aspx?id=/article-xml/awx_09_06_2013_p0–613665.xml.

Watts, Barry D. *The Maturing Revolution in Military Affairs*. Washington, DC: Center for Strategic and Budgetary Assessments, 2011.

Weisgerber, Marcus. "Future USAF Acquisitions to Focus on Pacific." *Defense News,* July 16, 2012. http://www.defensenews.com/article/20120716/DEF REG02/307160003/Future-USAF-Acquisition-Focus-Pacific?odyssey=tab|topn ews|text|FRONTPAGE.

Wertheim, Eric. "Combat Fleets." U.S. Naval Institute *Proceedings,* April 2013, 90. http://www.usni.org/magazines/proceedings/2013–04/combat-fleets.

White, Hugh. "The China Choice: A Bold Vision for U.S-China Relations." *The Diplomat,* August 17, 2012. http://thediplomat.com/2012/08/17/the-china-choice-a-bold-vision-for-u-s-china-relations/.

———. *The China Choice: Why America Should Share Power.* Collingswood, Australia: Black, Inc. 2012.

Woodward, Bob. *Obama's Wars.* New York: Simon and Schuster, 2010.

Work, Robert O., and F. G. Hoffman. "Hitting the Beach in the 21st Century." U.S. Naval Institute *Proceedings,* November 2010. http://www.usni.org/magazines/proceedings/2010–11/hitting-beach-21st-century.

"X" (George F. Kennan). "The Sources of Soviet Conduct." *Foreign Affairs,* July 1947. http://www.foreignaffairs.com/articles/23331/x/the-sources-of-soviet-conduct.

Yoshihara, Toshi. "Japan's Competitive Strategies at Sea." *Competitive Strategies for the 21st Century,* edited by Thomas G. Mahnken, 219–35. Stanford, CA: Stanford Security Studies, 2012.

———. "War by Other Means: China's Political Uses of Seapower." *The Diplomat,* September 26, 2012. http://thediplomat.com/2012/09/26/war-by-other-means-chinas-political-uses-of-seapower/2/.

Yoshihara, Toshi, and James R. Holmes. *Red Star over the Pacific: China's Rise and the Challenge to U.S. Maritime Strategy.* Annapolis, MD: Naval Institute Press, 2010.

Newspapers and News Services

Associated Press
Der Spiegel
The Economist
Financial Times
Japan Times
Marine Corps Times
New York Times
Reuters
South China Morning Post
The Sydney Morning Herald
The Telegraph
Wall Street Journal
Washington Post

Index

access denial: active defense/
counterintervention doctrine and
land-based missile strategy, 83–85;
active defense/counterintervention
doctrine, US response to, 101–20;
anti-access and area denial
challenges, concerns about, 75, 83–
85, 100; anti-access and area denial
challenges, response to, 101–20;
capabilities for allies and partners
of US, development of, 145–47,
151; WWII operations, 102, 108
aerospace: Chinese aerospace power,
growth of, 29, 176–77; Japanese
expertise and capacity, 42;
military challenges in region,
150; space-based surveillance and
communication networks, 109,
175–77, 216
Afghanistan: air base in, attack on, 62;
aircraft carrier role in operations
in, 65; bombing operations in, 74;
insurgency risks in, 125; nonstate
actors and operations in, 144–45;
public opinion of strategy in, 124;
security force in, limitations of,
126; short travel distances for
forces, 60; Soviet invasion of,
20; US basing operations in, 61;
US relations with Central Asia
countries and, 143

air bases, US: American way of war
and use of, 53; attacks on, 62; base
hardening and air defense systems,
110–12; China fighter aircraft
and vulnerability of, 91; China
missile program and vulnerability
of, 88–90, 100; expeditionary
air bases, 112; land-based basing
arrangements, 61–63, 161–62;
large bases, concentration of
operations at, 62–63, 73; post–
WWII study and plans, 53–55, 60;
tactical utility of, 190
air defense identification zone (ADIZ),
16–17
Air Force, U.S.: air superiority doctrine,
164–66, 167, 178–79; airpower
and air superiority, 61–62, 73–74;
basing strategy for, 61–63, 73;
bomber aircraft, 61, 63, 74, 92,
100, 110, 160, 162–64, 165–66,
167, 194; command and logistics
system to support, 62; culture of
and capabilities of, 61–63, 72–74;
duplication of capabilities by Navy,
193; fighter aircraft, 61, 62–63,
73–74; fighter-to-bomber ratio, 61;
long-range airpower, 61, 92, 100,
114, 160–69, 194, 210; security
cooperation and security assistance
programs, 149–51; short-range

plausibility of, 27–29, 33; conflict between US and, prevention of, 29; dissuasive and cost-imposing courses of action against, 133–34, 135–38, 158–59, 174, 192, 208–10, 213; external security requirements, 30–31, 132; income of citizens in, 10, 132; intentions of leadership as basis for US foreign policy development, 8; internal development and challenges, 29–30; internal instability, 132, 133–34; invasions of, fear of, 135; invasions of, history of, 15, 28; leadership decisions, incentives for favorable actions, 133–34, 135–38, 174–75, 192, 213; leadership role in command and control of military, 132; national security concerns of, 157; nationalism in, 30, 86, 132, 223n64; Near Seas claims and salami slicing, 77, 78–81, 100, 135, 140–43, 154–55, 180–82; political fragility and stability in, 86–87; political liberalization in, 38; power status following WWII, 7; protection of interest of, 2; protests in, 29; public opinion about threat from, 204–5; reforms and transformation under Deng, 7–8, 9–10, 75; relationship between Australia and, 153; relationship between Russia and, 143–44; relationship between US and, 9, 30, 132, 134, 143–44, 205–6, 211; reunification of, 14; rise in power of, xi, 2, 4, 38; rise in power of and global interests of, 19–20; rise in power of and regional security, 51, 75–76, 83, 131, 153–54, 212; rise in power of, historical analogies to, 25–27; rise in power of, US accommodation of, 5, 46–48; sea battles between Japan and, 15; security structure in, 87; smile diplomacy of, 75; "sphere of influence" negotiation and regional security, 47–48, 49;

strategic behavior and national security strategy, 12–14; tension between Japan and, 1, 16–18, 24, 33, 78, 80–81, 86, 155, 180–82, 207; territorial claims by, 1, 2, 3, 14–18, 28–29, 31, 33, 77; territorial claims by, US response to, 3; "Three Warfares" doctrine, 148; weaknesses and vulnerabilities of, 133, 134–38, 158–59. *See also* economy of China
The China Choice (White), 46–48
Chinese Communist Party (CCP): challenges faced by, 87; national security strategy of, 12–14; prestige of, 14, 19; relationship between PLA and, 13, 38; reunification of China and prestige of, 14; Soviet support for, 20; success of leadership of, 13
Civil War, US, 128–29
Clinton, Hillary, 23, 24, 78–79, 155
Clinton administration and Bill Clinton, 8, 21, 82
coal and electricity production, 12
Cold War: basing strategy for, 55–57; costs of, 203, 245n2; deterrence and prevention of nuclear war, 130; military competition during, 5, 98, 136; military culture and capabilities of US, 59–60; national security challenges during, xi; Salty Demo exercise, 88, 90, 111–12; sea-based nuclear deterrent, importance of, 15; Soviet–US relations during, 9; US policy, 129
containment strategy, 159, 213
cross-domain synergy, 104, 106, 108

Dempsey, Martin, 101, 103, 106–7
Deng Xiaoping, 7–8, 9–10, 12, 75
drones and unmanned aircraft, 166, 240n17

East Asia: balance of power in and stability, 4; balance of power in and tensions in, 1–4; clash between Chinese and US interests in, 7–9,

About the Author

Robert Haddick is a military analyst with three decades of experience researching security trends in Asia. Currently he is based in Washington, D.C., as a research contractor for U.S. Special Operations Command. A former U.S. Marine Corps officer with service in East Asia and Africa, he has also been a columnist for *Foreign Policy Magazine,* the managing editor of *Small Wars Journal*, and a consultant to U.S. Central Command, the U.S. State Department, and the National Intelligence Council.

The Naval Institute Press is the book-publishing arm of the U.S. Naval Institute, a private, nonprofit, membership society for sea service professionals and others who share an interest in naval and maritime affairs. Established in 1873 at the U.S. Naval Academy in Annapolis, Maryland, where its offices remain today, the Naval Institute has members worldwide.

Members of the Naval Institute support the education programs of the society and receive the influential monthly magazine *Proceedings* or the colorful bimonthly magazine *Naval History* and discounts on fine nautical prints and on ship and aircraft photos. They also have access to the transcripts of the Institute's Oral History Program and get discounted admission to any of the Institute-sponsored seminars offered around the country.

The Naval Institute's book-publishing program, begun in 1898 with basic guides to naval practices, has broadened its scope to include books of more general interest. Now the Naval Institute Press publishes about seventy titles each year, ranging from how-to books on boating and navigation to battle histories, biographies, ship and aircraft guides, and novels. Institute members receive significant discounts on the Press's more than eight hundred books in print.

Full-time students are eligible for special half-price membership rates. Life memberships are also available.

For a free catalog describing Naval Institute Press books currently available, and for further information about joining the U.S. Naval Institute, please write to:

Member Services
U.S. Naval Institute
291 Wood Road
Annapolis, MD 21402-5034
Telephone: (800) 233-8764
Fax: (410) 571-1703
Web address: www.usni.org